Introduction to Artificial Intelligence

RAJENDRA AKERKAR
Professor
Computer and Information Science
American University of Armenia, Armenia

PHI Learning Private Limited
New Delhi-110001
2012

₹ 275.00

INTRODUCTION TO ARTIFICIAL INTELLIGENCE
Rajendra Akerkar

ISBN-978-81-203-2864-8

Sixth Printing ... ... September, 2012

Published by Asoke K. Ghosh, PHI Learning Private Limited, M-97, Connaught Circus, New Delhi-110001 and Printed by Mudrak, 30-A, Patparganj, Delhi-110091.

To

my wife Rupali

for supporting me all along in pursuit of my goals

Contents

Preface

Artificial intelligence (AI) is a blend of three academic disciplines: psychology (cognitive modeling), philosophy (philosophy of mind), and computer science—with further strands from linguistics, mathematics, and logic. For many purposes these disciplines belong together but joining them is not an easy task. Psychology and philosophy split in the late nineteenth century; computer science grew up as a branch of mathematics. But the aim of AI is broad: to get below the surface of human behaviour; to discover the processes, systems, and principles that make intelligent behaviour possible. Computers are needed as tools for modeling these mental states and processes.

There are many practical applications of AI which include the design of computer systems that can perceive, learn, solve problems, make plans, and converse in natural language. Such systems are already in commercial use for medical diagnosis, identifying ships from satellite pictures, mineral prospecting, language translation, and science training.

The theoretical aims include attempting to understand how the mind works by investigating the problem of designing machines that have abilities previously possessed only by human beings. This work can only be done successfully if combined with other disciplines that involve a study of the human mind. For example, psychology provides information about human perception, memory, and learning skills. Linguistics illuminates the structures and functions of human languages. Philosophy seeks to clarify our understanding of what it is to be human, typically by examining the concepts we use in explanations of the world, of our own actions, and of the behaviour of others.

The book does not require much formal mathematics, but does require some mathematical maturity. Much of the material can, in theory, be read and understood with no more background than high school mathematics. In practice, however, readers need more than this or they will be besieged by the need to think mathematically.

This book is an outgrowth of my accumulated experience of teaching the subject as well as conducting various research activities in this field. I have class tested the material of this book at the MCA level in Chh. Shahu Central Institute of Business Education & Research, as well as in M.S. programmes in various European institutions.

This comprehensive text is primarily designed for the postgraduate students of computer science, computer engineering, computer application, and information technology. The book will also serve as a useful text for students of B.E. and B.Tech., offering courses in artificial intelligence or expert (knowledge-based) systems. The book covers almost all essential components of artificial intelligence or knowledge-based systems syllabus of Universities in India. Many courses are possible, depending on the time available, the capabilities of the students, and the interests of the instructor. The part of this text can also be used for a second course in AI for students interested in AI research.

To the possible extent, each chapter has been kept independent and stand-alone and has been organized as follows. Chapter 1 contains a brief introduction to artificial intelligence including application areas, history, future, and programming. The rest of the text discusses knowledge representation schemes, advance concepts and real world applications. Chapter 2 focuses on symbolic logic. This includes the predicate calculus language to describe the essential features of a problem domain. Chapters 3 to 5 discuss knowledge acquisition, representation schemes, reasoning, and uncertainty issues. Here, we discuss semantic networks and extend this model to include conceptual dependency theory, frames, and scripts. Further we present models for reasoning with uncertainty as well as the use of unreliable information. We discuss Bayesian models, belief networks, and Dempster-Shafer. Chapter 4 also focuses at well-known knowledge representation and reasoning systems. Chapter 6 presents problem solving technique called searching. Chapter 7 concentrates on AI technologies such as computer vision, natural language processing and speech recognition. Besides, Chapters 8 to 11 present expert systems, neural networks, constraint programming and case-based reasoning. Finally, Chapter 12 gives a glance at real world applications of artificial intelligence. There are appendices on Projects, PROLOG, and LISP programming and glossary of AI terms at the end of the book. It is possible to treat topics selectively to plan one or two—semester course on artificial intelligence or on knowledge-based systems.

Many organizations have extended their facilities to me during the preparation of the book. They are Technomathematics Research Foundation, American University, and Chh. Shahu Central Institute of Business Education & Research. My doctoral students—D. Rajesh Duthie, Manish Joshi, and Pallavi Jamsandekar helped me during the preparation of the manuscript.

There are number of individuals whose grateful help I would like to acknowledge. Professor Barry Levine offered me assignment in American University. Much of the book was completed during this assignment. I remain grateful to Professor Ion Olimpiu Stamatescu (FEST, Heidelberg, Germany),Professor Henry Hexmoor (University of Arkansas, Fayetteville, USA), Professor K.V. Dinesha (IIIT, Bangalore) for constant encouragement and support for my professional development. I would like to thank the Prentice-Hall of India for agreeing to publish this book and Mr. Srinivas Chaubey's personal interest in the book has helped me to complete the manuscript. Last but not the least, I owe much to my family.

I hope the reader will enjoy reading this book.

Rajendra Akerkar

CHAPTER 1

Overview of Artificial Intelligence

1.1 INTRODUCTION

Early computers dealt with numerical computations. Current computers are involved in reasoning with knowledge in addition to numerical computations. With artificial intelligence (AI) the role of computers changes from something useful to something essential.

The aim of artificial intelligence (AI) is in some way to try to make computers perform tasks that humans tend to be good at. In a sense it is an investigation into the attempt to make computers behave in a smarter manner. The actual name Artificial Intelligence was coined by John McCarthy in the 60s—he was the designer of the language LISP.

Artificial intelligence fills the gap between the scientists of human behaviour and the computer scientists. One thing we know about computers is that given a set of rules written in the programming language of the computer the rules will always be obeyed exactly. So, human scientists can test their theories about human behaviour by converting their rules to computer programs and seeing if the behaviour of the computer in executing these programs is like the natural behaviour of a human being, or at least that small subset of human behaviour they are studying. Computer scientists can look at modeling human behaviour as a challenge to their programming abilities: if a person can do something, can we write a computer program which does the same thing?

John McCarthy in the 60s

The name 'Artificial Intelligence' is rather an emotive one, though it has become established now and is unlikely to be changed. It may be interesting to debate whether human beings are just very complex 'meat machines' or whether it would be theoretically possible to create a real 'artificial intelligence', that is a computer program which really does behave as a full human being, but studying AI does not involve commiting oneself to such beliefs. In fact, one thing that AI has quite firmly established is that human beings are more complex than some rather naïve analyses have suggested. Predictions that human-like AI are soon to be built are often just media sensationalism, and have so far proved wrong.

It is often said that though the space programme which led to the landing on the moon did not in itself lead to a useful end, it spun off much in the way of useful technological development. This appears to be the case with AI: the real benefits in research in the field come in the spin-offs which advance computer science in general. In particular, AI researchers have often faced particularly difficult programming problems, so many of the concepts in programming language design and programming methodology which are now general in computer science have their origin in AI programming.

1.1.1 Definition

Many human mental activities like writing programs, understanding language, engaging in common-sense reasoning or even driving an automobile are said to demand intelligence. Over the past few decades, computers have been built to perform such tasks. Specifically, there are systems that can generate computer code automatically, perform symbolic differentiation and integration, understand text to a certain extent, etc. We can say that such systems possess some degree of artificial intelligence.

With this introduction, one can define AI in many ways. Some of them are:

- AI is the study of how to make computers do things at which, people are better at the moment.
- AI is that branch of computer science dealing with symbolic, non-algorithmic methods of problem solving.
- AI is that part of computer science concerned with designing intelligent computer systems that exhibit the characteristics used to associate with intelligence in human behaviour.

AI is a mindset, a way of looking at and solving problems from a particular point of view. The concepts, methods, and techniques discussed in this book have been developed as a consequence of approaching problems from the relatively heuristic point of view that distinguishes the field of artificial intelligence from other computer science and system engineering disciplines.

AI problems span a very broad spectrum. They appear to have very little in common except that they are difficult. AI techniques are designed to manipulate symbols as well as numerical information, and a wide range of them have been developed by AI researchers (The Artificial Intelligentsia). This book will introduce a range of these techniques.

1.1.2 Why AI?

Computers have outperformed people in the many tasks. A sample of these tasks is as follows:

1. ***Numerical computations.*** Computers are definitely faster and more accurate than humans when it comes to numerical computations. For example, a computer can multiply 189254 and 82909743 and give the result almost instantaneously whereas it would take a couple of minutes for an average human being to do the same multiplication. Also, in the latter case the chances of errors are more.
2. ***Information storage.*** Computers can store very huge amounts of information. The volume being limited only by the availability of information. This is contrast to the human beings wherein it seems that only a certain amount of knowledge can be stored.
3. ***Repetitive operations.*** It goes without saying that human beings get bored and commit mistakes as fatigue sets in while performing repetitive tasks. On the other hand, computers are specifically built to do such tasks. This is because they neither complain nor get fatigued or bored while doing the same tasks over and over again.

The list above denotes tasks that are 'mechanical' or 'mindless'. Performing 'intelligent' tasks, humans are better than computers. Before proceeding further, let us try to understand as to what intelligence means.

Intelligence is very loosely defined term and there is no single exact definition in that direction. What seems intelligent to one person may not be so for another person but the following characteristics are of essential abilities for possessing intelligence.

- To respond to situations very flexibly.
- To make sense of ambiguous or erroneous messages.
- To assign relative importance to elements for a situation.
- To find similarities even though the situations might be different.
- To draw distinctions between situations even though there may be many similarities between them.

Assuming that intelligence could be defined, as above, following is a list of tasks that demand intelligence.

- Speech generation and understanding.
- Pattern recognition.
- Motion in a dynamic obstacle filled space.
- Mathematical theorem proving.
- Reasoning.

Now we have made an attempt at understanding as to what AI is and why we need AI, let us look at the progress of AI from the time of its inception till now. In other words, let us look at the history of AI, in order to get a better understanding of where we are; it is often helpful to examine where we have been.

One of the results of early AI work was the realization that the tasks which are difficult problems for human intelligence may be easy for artificial intelligence, and vice versa. We regard a human being who can perform tasks of mental arithmetic quickly as intelligent, whereas we are now familiar with calculators which can do arithmetic quickly. It is fairly easy to write computer programs to solve the sort of puzzles that make up IQ tests. But it is extremely difficult to write programs that can do things human beings can do naturally, even those we would regard as of well below average intelligence. For example, writing computer programs to understand simple sentences in human languages, or to interpret simple pictures, is a difficult task which has not been fully solved yet.

The reason comes down to the fact that computers are essentially machines for obeying rules speedily and accurately. Human beings work by intuition in a way that psychologists still do not fully understand. We find that if we are asked to consciously memorize more than a small number of items or rules we cannot do so, but we can when solving problems which cannot be broken down into simple rules bring to mind all sorts of information from our lifetime's experience which may be of assistance.

As an example, let us consider the analysis of two simple pieces of English:

"I stood on the table to paint the window. It broke and I fell through onto the flowerbed below."
"I stood on the table to paint the window. It broke and I fell through onto the carpet below."

This is a simple example of one of the ways in which human language is ambiguous —when we use pronouns such as "it" we do not always know which object is meant by them. In both cases "it" could be the table or the window. If the sentences were the part of a larger paragraph "it" could refer to something else first mentioned in an earlier sentence; if the second sentence in the example were, say, "I should not have done it, as I damaged the table", "it" refers to the action of the first sentence rather than to some specific object (the old song "If I said you had a beautiful body, would you hold it against me?" makes deliberate use of this ambiguity!).

However, in the first example we will naturally assume that "it" means the window and in the second "it" means the table. The reason for this is that we know that flowerbeds are more likely to be the other side of windows from tables, and carpets more likely to be below tables. From this it can be seen that analysis of natural language sentences requires common sense knowledge of the world. If we write a computer program to interpret natural language statements and store the information required, as sets of statements in logic, it will be a difficult task to ensure that it always interpret "it" to mean the thing that a human would naturally interpret it to mean. In fact it will be almost impossible to devise rules to cover every possible situation.

1.1.3 Difference between Symbolic and Non-symbolic Representation

To construct intelligent systems it is necessary to employ internal representations of a symbolic nature, with cognitive activity corresponding to computational manipulation of these symbolic representations. The *symbolic representations* (Figure 1.1) refer to the external world.

Advantages of symbolic representation are:

- The system builder can read what the system knows.

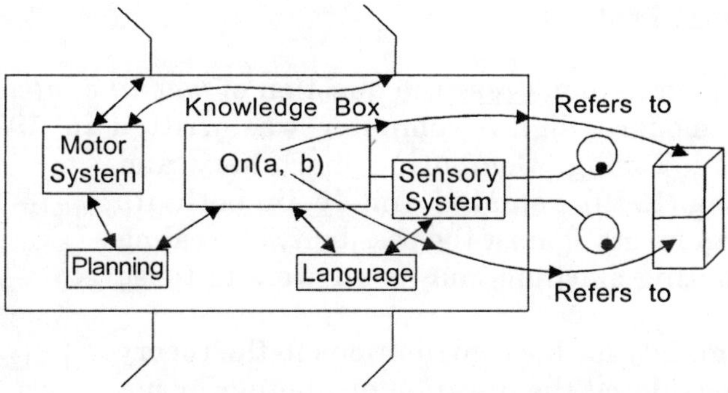

Knowledge Box
Refers to
Motor System
On(a, b)
Sensory System
Planning
Language
Refers to

Figure 1.1 Symbolic representation.

- Knowledge is represented by sentences in a formal language.
- It is possible to read the representation and understand the meaning of the knowledge.

Whereas, knowledge is represented by weights on connections in a network (Figure 1.2).

Non-symbolic representation can deal with combinations of attributes such as an image, and they are noise tolerant.

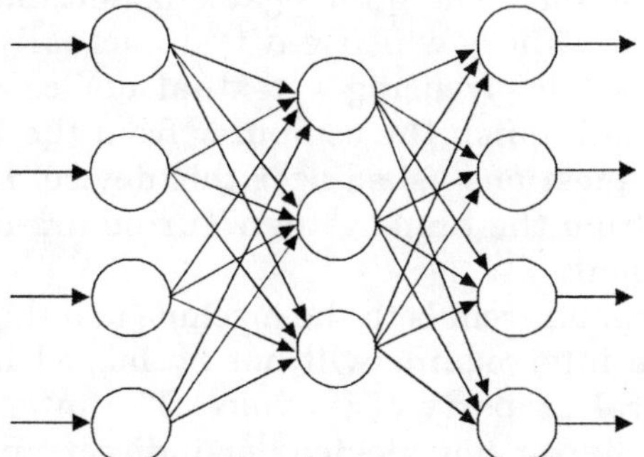

Figure 1.2 Non-symbolic representation.

1.2 HISTORY OF AI

While knowledge of the history of AI is not essential to understand the subject, it however presents a context by which we can interpret current developments and appreciate the progress that AI has made till date.

The players who demonstrated the capabilities and techniques of AI systems (often under different names) were Alan Turing, Warren McCulloch, Claude Shannon, Norbert Wiener, John McCarthy, Marvin Minsky, Newell, Simon, Arthur Samuel, etc. to name a few.

1.2.1 The Turing Test

One of the earliest papers to address the question of *machine intelligence* specifically in relation to the modern digital computer was written in 1950 by the British mathematician Alan Turing. Computing machinery and intelligence (Turing 1950) remains timely in both its assessment of the arguments against the possibility of creating an intelligent computing machine and its answers to those arguments.

Alan Turing,
One of the founders of Computer Science

Turing, known mainly for his contributions to the theory of computability, considered the question of whether or not a machine could actually be made to think. Noting that the fundamental ambiguities in the question itself (what is thinking? what is a machine?) precluded any rational answer, he proposed that the question of intelligence be replaced by a more clearly defined empirical test.

The *Turing test* measures the performance of an allegedly intelligent machine against that of a human being, arguably the best and only standard for intelligent behaviour. The test, which Turing called the "imitation game", places the machine and a human counterpart in rooms apart from a second human being, referred to as the "interrogator". The interrogator is not able to see or speak directly to either of them, does not know which entity is actually the machine, and may communicate with them solely by using a textual device such as a terminal. The interrogator is asked to distinguish the computer from the human being only on the basis of their answers to questions asked over this device. If the interrogator cannot distinguish the machine from the human, then Turing argues that the machine may be assumed to be intelligent.

By isolating the interrogator from both the machine and the other human participant, the test ensures that the interrogator will not be biased by the appearance of the machine or any mechanical property of its voice. The interrogator is free, however, to ask any questions, no matter how devious or indirect, in an effort to uncover the computer's identity. For example, the interrogator may ask both subjects to perform a rather complex arithmetic calculation, assuming that the computer will be more likely to get it correct than the human; to counter this strategy, the computer will need to know when it should fail to get a correct answer to such problems in order to seem like a human. To discover the human's identity on the basis of emotional nature, the interrogator may ask both subjects to respond to a poem or work of art; this strategy will require that the computer have knowledge concerning the emotional make up of human beings.

The important features of this test are:

(a) It gives us an objective notion of intelligence, i.e. the behaviour of a known intelligent being in response to a particular set of questions. This provides a standard for determining intelligence that avoids the inevitable debates over its "true" nature.

(b) It prevents us from being sidetracked by such confusing and currently unanswerable questions as whether or not the computer uses the appropriate internal processes or whether or not the machine is actually conscious of its actions.
(c) It eliminates any bias in favour of living organisms by forcing the interrogator to focus solely on the content of the answers to questions.

Because of these advantages, the Turing test provides a basis for many of the schemes actually used to evaluate modern AI programs. A program that has potentially achieved intelligence in some area of expertise may be evaluated by comparing its performance on a given set of problems to that of a human expert. This evaluation technique is just a variation of the Turing test: a group of humans are asked to blindly compare the performance of a computer and a human being on a particular set of problems. As we will see, this methodology has become an essential tool in both the development and verification of modern expert systems.

The Turing test, in spite of its intuitive appeal, is vulnerable to a number of justifiable criticisms. One of the most important of these is aimed at its bias toward purely symbolic problem-solving tasks. It does not test abilities requiring perceptual skill or manual dexterity, even though these are important components of human intelligence. Conversely, it is sometimes suggested that the Turing test needlessly constrains machine intelligence to fit a human mould. Perhaps machine intelligence is simply different from human intelligence and trying to evaluate it in human terms is a fundamental mistake. Do we really wish a machine would do mathematics as slowly and inaccurately as a human? Shouldn't an intelligent machine capitalize on its own assets, such as a large, fast, reliable memory, rather than trying to emulate human cognition? In fact, a number of modern AI practitioners (e.g. Ford and Hayes, 1995) see responding to the full challenge of Turing test as a mistake and a major distraction to the more important work at hand: developing general theories to explain the mechanisms of intelligence in humans and machines, and applying those theories to the development of tools to solve specific, practical problems. Although we agree with the Ford and Hayes concerns in the large, we still see Turing test as an important component in the verification and validation of modern AI software.

Turing also addressed the very feasibility of constructing an intelligent program on a digital computer. By thinking in terms of a specific model of computation (an electronic discrete state computing machine), he made some well-founded conjectures concerning the storage capacity, program complexity, and basic design philosophy required for such a system. Finally, he addressed a number of moral, philosophical, and scientific objections to the possibility of constructing such a program in terms of an actual technology. The reader is referred to Turing's article for a perceptive and still relevant summary of the debate over the possibility of intelligent machines.

There is also often a two way interaction—by observing how humans perform a particular task it may be possible to imitate this by means of a program and from the program (especially a learning program) it may be possible to improve the human performance. A good illustration of this is the DENDRAL system for recognizing chemical structures from mass spectrograms—rules were derived which were not known by the experts. It should be pointed out that DENDRAL is a very successful program and is in fact the world expert on such analysis. Now what does it mean for a machine to be intelligent? Turing thought about this problem in the 50s and came up with the following test.

A human interrogator can ask questions, via say a VDU, to a machine in one room and a human in another. If he is unable to decide from the answers received which is connected to the machine then Turing would say that it should be deemed intelligent. A very early attempt to try to build a program which would pass the Turing test was the ELIZA program of Weizenbaum—MIT 1966. This is supposed to mimic a conversation with a psychologist. When one first sees it, it does seem quite effective but once one has played with it for a little time it is quite easy to trick it and in fact infer how it works. We shall see an implementation of ELIZA later.

Clearly in order to pass the Turing test the system must understand natural language. This is an extremely difficult task to say the least! For humans make all sorts of assumptions and inferences in order to make sense of sentences and utterances. It is generally believed that to really handle natural language in a manner comparable to humans then a system must incorporate common sense reasoning and have access to the kind of general knowledge a human would expect to know.

One attempt to provide this background knowledge is the CYC project of Lenat. He is building an enormous system at MCC Texas which is trying to capture the full breadth of human knowledge. A company, CYCORP has now been set up to market the technology. The team examines text from encyclopedias; newspapers, etc. and code this information (making use of what the writer assumed the reader knew of the world) into the database. There are currently several million entries in the knowledge base.

1.2.2 The Chinese Room

The philosopher, Searle uses the 'experiment' of the *Chinese Room* to demonstrate that the machine does not understand.

The Chinese Room is a thought experiment in which we are asked to imagine a room containing a complete set of instructions for manipulating and combining Chinese characters. These instructions are written in English and can be implemented by a group of people who can follow the instructions, matching the characters on the basis of appearance. Suppose a story is passed into the hatch followed by a series of questions about the story, also in Chinese. By referring to their rules the people in the room are able to produce a third set of Chinese characters, representing the answers.

Searle showed that in principle, if not in practice, people can behave as if they are fluent in a foreign language while, in reality, not being able to understand a word of it.

1.3 APPLICATIONS OF AI

1.3.1 Natural Language Processing

When humans communicate with each other they employ, almost effortlessly, very complex and yet still little understood processes. It has been very difficult to build computers which can generate and understand even fragments of natural language like English. This is because, language has developed as an effective communication medium between intelligent beings. It is seen as transmitting a bit of 'mental structure' from one brain to another under circumstances in which each brain possesses large, highly similar mental structures that serve as a common context. This similarity in contexts helps in generating and understanding highly condensed messages. Thus natural language understanding is a highly complex problem of encoding and decoding.

One of the long-standing goals of artificial intelligence is the creation of programs that are capable of understanding and generating human language. Not only does the ability to use and understand natural language seem to be a fundamental aspect of human intelligence, but also its successful automation would have an incredible impact on the usability and effectiveness of computers themselves. Much effort has been put into writing programs that understand natural language. Although these programs have achieved success within restricted contexts, systems that can use natural language with the flexibility and generality that characterize human speech are beyond current methodologies.

Understanding natural language involves much more than parsing sentences into their individual parts of speech and looking those words up in a dictionary. Real understanding depends on extensive background knowledge about the domain of discourse and the idioms used in that domain as well as an ability to apply general contextual knowledge to resolve the omissions and ambiguities that are a normal part of human speech.

Therefore, in order to build computer systems which can understand natural language, both the contextual knowledge and the process for making effective inferences is required. This is a very important domain, which still fascinates a number of researchers.

1.3.2 Intelligent Retrieval from Databases

Database systems are large bodies of facts about some subjects, which are used to answer users' queries about that subject. For example, consider a player database. For each player listed in the database, there could be entities representing his age, height, weight, number of caps, total earnings, etc. With these facts stored in an orderly from, one can obtain answers to queries like "List all players who are over 6 feet tall." or "What is the average yearly salary of player X?", etc. The design of database systems is a very active field in the area of computer science even today. From the point of view of AI, the field becomes even more interesting if the answers require deductive reasoning with the facts in the database.

There are numerous problems that confront an individual trying to build such an intelligent retrieval system. First, the problem of understanding queries stated in a natural language like English. Second, assuming that the system has fully understood the query, how should it deduce the answer from the facts in the database? Third, for the given facts there are some queries which require common knowledge. For example, if player P is the captain of a side, then the system should be in a position to know that P leads the team always on the field and he is a part of the core group which has chosen the team. Such facts may not be explicitly stated during the development of the database.

1.3.3 Expert Systems

Expert systems are automatic consulting systems. They provide expert conclusions about specialized areas. Expert systems have been built that can diagnose faults in military systems like aircrafts, radars, etc., taxonomically classify members of a particular species, advice on possible chemical structures, evaluate potential ore deposits, diagnose diseases, etc.

There are two key components in the design of every expert system. One is the representation of knowledge and the other is the usage of this knowledge while drawing conclusions. Representation of knowledge is difficult because the expert knowledge can be imprecise and/or uncertain. Mostly the knowledge is represented as a large set of simple rules. Knowledge is also represented in structures called *frames and scripts*. Conclusions are generally obtained by the technique of *rule-based deduction*. Other forms of deduction like probabilistic deduction are also seriously being looked into in the recent years.

One of the earliest systems to exploit domain-specific knowledge in problem solving was DENDRAL, developed at Stanford in the late 1960s. DENDRAL was designed to infer the structure of organic molecules from their chemical formulas and mass spectrographic information about the chemical bonds present in the molecules. Because organic molecules tend to be very large, the number of possible structures for these molecules tends to be huge. DENDRAL addresses the problem of this large search space by applying the heuristic knowledge of expert chemists to the structure elucidation problem. DENDRAL's methods proved remarkably effective, routinely finding the correct structure out of millions of possibilities after only a few trials. The approach has proved so successful that descendants of the system are used in chemical and pharmaceutical laboratories throughout the world.

Whereas DENDRAL was one of the first programs to effectively use domain-specific knowledge to achieve expert level problem-solving performance, MYCIN established the methodology of contemporary expert systems. MYCIN uses expert medical knowledge to diagnose and prescribe treatment for spinal meningitis and bacterial infections of the blood.

MYCIN, developed at Stanford in the mid-1970s, was one of the first programs to address the problems of reasoning with uncertain or incomplete information. MYCIN provided clear and logical explanations of its reasoning, used a control structure appropriate to the specific problem domain, and identified criteria to reliably evaluate its performance.

1.3.4 Theorem Proving

Proving (or disproving) mathematical theorems are an intensive intellectual task. This is because it requires deductions from hypotheses and also involves judgement. This judgement is based on a large amount of specialized knowledge and to guess accurately as to which previously proven theorem would help in the present proof. This helps to break the main problem into subproblems to work on independently. Several automatic theorem-proving programs have been developed which possess this ability to a limited extent. The formalization of deductive techniques using the language of predicate logic helps in understanding the components of reasoning more clearly. Many informal tasks like medical diagnosis can be formalized to theorem-proving problems.

Most of the appeal of automated theorem proving lies in the rigour and generality of logic. Because it is a formal system, logic lends itself to automation. A wide variety of problems can be attacked by representing the problem description and relevant background information as logical axioms and treating problem instances as theorems to be proved. The reason for the continued interest in automatic theorem provers is the realization that such a system does not have to be capable of independently solving extremely complex problems without human assistance. Many modern theorem provers function as intelligent assistants, letting humans perform the more demanding tasks of decomposing a large problem into subproblems and devising heuristics for searching the space of possible proofs. The theorem prover then performs the simpler but still demanding task of proving lemmas, verifying smaller conjectures, and completing the formal aspects of a proof outlined by its human associate. Hence theorem proving is an important subfield of AI.

1.3.5 Robotics

Humans are able to successfully navigate through their environment and to manipulate things like light switches, toy blocks, etc. These tasks, though performed unconsciously by humans, involve a great deal of complexity. When we try to program machines to perform the same tasks, we see that this requires many of the capabilities used in solving more intellectually demanding problems.

Planning is an important aspect of the effort to design robots that perform their task with some degree of flexibility and responsiveness to the outside world. Briefly, planning assumes a robot that is capable of performing certain atomic actions. It attempts to find a sequence of those actions that will accomplish some higher-level task, such as moving across an obstacle-filled room.

Planning is a difficult problem for a number of reasons, not the least of which is the size of the space of possible sequences of moves. Even an extremely simple robot is capable of generating a vast number of potential move sequences. Imagine, for example, a robot that can move forward, backward, right, or left, and consider how many different ways that robot can possibly move around a room. Assume also that there are obstacles in the room and that the robot must select a path that moves around them in some efficient fashion. Writing a program that can intelligently discover the best path under these circumstances, without being overwhelmed by the huge number of possibilities, requires sophisticated techniques for representing spatial knowledge and controlling search through possible environments.

Research in robotics has helped to develop many AI techniques for modelling states of the world and transformation from one state to another have been found.

1.3.6 Combinatorial and Scheduling Problems

One class of problems is concerned with specifying optimal scheduled. A classical example is the *Travelling Salesperson Problem*, where the problem is to find a minimum distance tour, starting at one of the several cities, visiting other cities only once and then returning back to the starting city. The problem generalizes to finding a minimum cost path over the edges of a graph containing n nodes such that each of the n nodes is visited not more than once. In such problems the domain of possible combinations or sequences from which to choose an answer is very large. Brute force attempts to generate solution very often leads to *combinatorial explosion* of possibilities that exhaust the resources of even large computers. Such problems are called as NP-complete problems by the computational.

AI researchers have worked on methods for solving various types of combinatorial problems. The key to solving such problems is the knowledge about the problem domain. Methods developed to solve combinatorial problems have proven to be helpful in solving other less combinatorial severe problems.

1.3.7 Perception Problems

Attempts have been made for computers to *see* (by fitting them with television inputs) and *hear* (by fitting microphone inputs). These have achieved only limited success since useful processing of complex input data requires understanding, and understanding in turn requires a large amount of knowledge about the things that have to perceived.

In AI, the process of perception is studied as a set of operations. A visual scene may be encoded by sensors and represented as matrix of intensity values. These are processed by detectors that search for primitive picture components like line segments, simple curves, corners, etc. These in turn are processed to infer information regarding the objects in the scene. The ultimate aim is to represent the scene by a suitable model. This model may be a high level description of the scene like *A hill with a tree on top*.

The point of the whole perception problem is to provide a condensed version of the input from the unmanageably large amount of raw input data. The main difficulty though, in perception problems is the enormous amount of candidate descriptions of a scene. One solution for this is the strategy of making hypotheses of each description and then to test them to come to a goal. For this hypotheses formation, a large amount of knowledge about the expected scenes is required.

1.3.8 Neural Architectures

Neural architectures are appealing as mechanisms for implementing intelligence for a number of reasons. Traditional AI programs tend to be brittle and overly sensitive to noise rather than degrading gracefully, such programs tend to either be right or fail completely. Human intelligence is much more flexible; we are good at interpreting noisy input, such as recognizing a face in a darkened room from an odd angle or following a single conversation in a noisy party. Even where a human may not be able to solve some problem, we generally can make a reasonable guess as to its solution. Neural architectures, because they capture knowledge in a large number of fine-grained units, seem to have more potential for partially matching noisy and incomplete data. Neural architectures are also more robust because knowledge is distributed somewhat uniformly around the network.

Neural architectures also provide a natural model for parallelism, because each neuron is an independent unit. Hillis (1985) has commented on the fact that humans get faster at a task as they acquire more knowledge, while computers tend to slow down. This slowdown is due to the cost of sequentially searching a knowledge base; a massively parallel architecture like the human brain would not suffer from this problem.

1.3.9 Game Playing

Much of the early research in state space search was done using common board games such as checkers, chess, and the 15-puzzle. In addition to their inherent intellectual appeal, board games have certain properties that made them ideal subjects for this early work. Most games are played using a well-defined set of rules: this makes it easy to generate the search space and frees the researcher from many of the ambiguities and complexities inherent in less structured problems. The board configurations used in playing these games are easily represented on a computer, requiring none of the complex formalisms needed to capture the semantic subtleties of more complex problem domains. Games can generate extremely large search spaces. These are large and complex enough to require powerful techniques for determining what alternatives to explore in the problem space. These techniques are called *heuristics* and constitute a major area of AI research. Much of what we commonly call intelligence seems to reside in the heuristics used by humans to solve problems.

1.4 OBJECTIVES OF AI

The main objectives of AI research are:

- *Understand human cognition*, i.e. how do humans solve problems? Try to obtain deep knowledge of human memory, problem-solving abilities, learning, decision making, etc.
- *Cost-effective automation* replace humans in intelligent tasks. Have programs which perform as well as humans currently doing the job?

- *Cost-effective intelligent amplification* builds systems to help humans think better, faster, deeper ... For example system to help GP diagnose disease.
- *Superhuman intelligence* build programs to exceed human intelligence.
- *General problem solving* solves broad range of problems. Systems with breadth of mind.
- *Coherent discourse* communicates with people using natural language. Carries out an intelligent dialogue. (c.f. Turing test).
- *Autonomy* has intelligent systems acting on own initiative. Must react to the real world.
- *Learning* (induction) the system should be able to gather own data and how. Generalize, hypothesize, apply/learn heuristics; reason by analogy.
- *Store information* and know how to retrieve it.

1.5 ARTIFICIAL INTELLIGENCE PROGRAMMING

The conventional software engineering approach to programming emphasizes starting with requirements, developing formal specifications, breaking the problem into parts and coding at a late stage in the development. Programming artificial intelligence systems, however, does not fit so easily into conventional software engineering models. By their very nature, AI problems cannot be formally specified. The correctness of an AI system is measured not by its performing according to some formal specification, but by its closeness to human performance. This leads to an approach to programming described as 'exploratory' or 'prototyping'. This means that programs are developed in a less formal way than with conventional software engineering, but may be regarded as experimental prototypes rather than semi-completed products. An AI program may be tested against a range of human examples, and if necessary modified so that it performs as a human on those examples. Some modifications may prove successful in improving performance (as measured by closeness to human performance) over a variety of examples. Others may prove to be useful only in one or two examples, and to degrade performance in others, and so be abandoned. However, as modifications accumulate, a program structure may become complex as modifications interact with other modifications. Eventually, the point may be reached where the program is abandoned but those lessons learnt from building it are kept and used to build a cleaner program. This process may go through several cycles, each cycle building a better prototype. This has been described as the Run-Understand-Debug-Edit (RUDE) approach to programming. If we define AI as those aspects of programming which of necessity are programmed using a RUDE method rather than a more formal software engineering approach, then chess playing, for example, which previously we suggested was only doubtful part of AI, can be seen as firm part of AI. We may now be able to write programs which can beat all but the most exceptional human chess players. But we cannot write a formal specification which defines the best next move to make from any given position. Improving our basic chess playing model involves adding variations to the underlying search procedure which are tested in an experimental way by running a complete program against human chess players. It might be noted that the software engineering process of producing a program from formal specifications is itself an AI problem, otherwise we would not have to employ human programmers to do it, and we could do it automatically. 'Automatic programming' is itself a branch of AI. Note that this is a term which has changed its meaning as time has passed. When human programmers wrote in machine code, the *compilers* which translated from the first *high-level languages*, such as FORTRAN, into *machine code*, were described as 'automatic programming' systems. Nowadays we reserve the term for those systems which produce executable programs from non-executable specifications. Those specifications may be in logic or some other formal specification language, but another branch of automatic programming "synthesis from examples" produces programs from an informal specification consisting of examples of inputs and the expected outputs for these inputs.

AI programming has often made use of declarative languages which attempt to be closer to a human way of reasoning about problems than conventional programming languages. The exploratory nature of AI programming means that it is essential that AI programs retain their understandability and do not get bogged down in the details required to manipulate conventional computer store. Much early work in AI was done in the language LISP, a forerunner to the functional language Miranda. The argument for using LISP was that the use of lists for storing data and the emphasis on symbol manipulation was more appropriate for AI work than the arrays and numerical data of scientific/engineering (principally FORTRAN) and data processing (principally Cobol) languages then in use.

PROLOG, now the preferred language for many AI programmers, has the list processing and symbolic manipulation qualities of LISP. The ideal of the developers of PROLOG was that it would be simply machine-executable logic, which would mean that a PROLOG program would be its own specification.

Thus an AI program developed in an exploratory way would still be fully specified. The equation ALGORITHM = LOGIC + CONTROL was suggested, suggesting that the programmer needs simply specify logic relationships between the data and the control which would be a separate aspect, managed by the computer, which manipulated the data according to the rules expressed in the logic. It was suggested that imperative languages are confusing because they mix up the logic aspects of programming with the control aspects.

One important aspect of the separation of logic and control that has an important place in AI programming is the distinction between language and meta-language. Conventional programming makes a separation between the data of the program and the program itself written in a language for manipulating that data. AI programming often makes a three fold separation into data, rules for manipulating the data, and rules for saying how the rules to manipulate the data are to be used. A meta-program is the top-level set of rules; a program which treats a program as data.

1.6 CRITICISM OF AI

A legitimate criticism of AI is that it is concentrating on micro-worlds and it is not really looking at intelligence in the sense of modelling human behaviour—it is simply about solving tricky problems. The problem is perhaps more with the name 'Artificial

Intelligence'. We can surely regard it as legitimate and useful to look into the ways of writing computer programs which can solve tricky problems, whether or not those computer programs can be considered building blocks towards a larger goal of building 'artificial human beings'.

However, following from these criticisms there has been a growing trend in AI work to try and capture some aspects of 'common sense' reasoning. For instance, standard predicate logic can be criticized for not being able to capture the fact that we often make default assumptions. We know, for example, that if we have the facts $p(x) \rightarrow q(x)$ where x is a variable, and p(a) where a is a constant we can conclude q(a). As a typical example, suppose we say 'all Computer Science students take Logic' we can express that by CompSci(X) → Logic(X), then if we have the fact 'Gopal is a Computer Science student', expressed by CompSci(Gopal), we can conclude Logic(Gopal), i.e. "Gopal takes Logic". It is, though, a well-known fallacy that one can conclude p(a) from q(a) and $p(x) \rightarrow q(x)$. If we have the fact that "Rajesh takes Logic" or Logic(Rajesh), we can't conclude CompSci(Rajesh) meaning "Rajesh is a Computer Science student", because it may be the case that Maths students take Logic as well, expressed by the fact Maths(X) → Logic(X).

People often make this false step in an argument though, and we cannot always just dismiss them as illogical. It may be the case that all Computer Science students take Logic, but there are one or two students from other departments who also take Logic. It would therefore be a reasonable common sense conclusion if we have the fact "Rajesh takes Logic" to say that Rajesh is a Computer Science student unless we have some reason to conclude he is not. Ordinary predicate logic cannot make this sort of jump, but there has been research on variations of logic that can. In this case there is an element of probability involved: the assumption is a reasonable common sense one under the conditions given above, but it would not be reasonable if we also knew that Computer Science students formed only a small fraction of those taking Logic.

Associated to the idea of micro-worlds is the "closed world assumption", that is the assumption that the data we have represented all that can be known. This enables us to assume that if we cannot prove something true it must be false. This may be reasonable in a micro-world, but is less so when we are reasoning about the real world. For example, if the only rules we have about who takes logic are CompSci(X) → Logic(X) and Maths(X) → Logic(X), we can conclude if we don't have the fact CompSci(Ravi) or Maths(Ravi) that Logic(Ravi) is false (i.e. Ravi does not take Logic).

This conclusion will always be correct under the closed world assumption, but the real world is not closed, and in practice there may be reasons that we do not know about a student to take Logic other than he or she is a Mathematics or a Computer Science student. Of course, we can still make the assumption that Ravi does not take Logic, but like the above case it is only an assumption we hold until we obtain further knowledge.

1.7 FUTURE OF AI

Artificial intelligence will be broaden in the next decades in many respects. From the various perspectives for the future, a particular one is of importance for the interaction with many other disciplines. The concerned disciplines are those where humans play an active role with their actions and decisions. To be more precise, we mean complex actions where actions performed by humans and machines alternate. Such situations occur frequently when the capability of machines are not strong enough to carry out the whole action but can do parts of it and when planning and execution of actions are interleaved.

This is in contrast to most activities in AI in the past decades which have been performed mainly from a logical point of view. The systems had a black box character and logical reasoning was the main concern. This had in fact impressing success stories to present. In practical applications knowledge-based systems have been developed, e.g. for diagnosis (both in medical as well as in technical domains), configuration and design, and for action planning.

It was soon realized that logic, as the only view, was clearly insufficient. Therefore logic was complemented by various forms of uncertainty reasoning, e.g. certainty factors, Bayesian nets, evidences, fuzzy sets, similarity reasoning, etc. An observation is that these attempts had mostly some precise mathematical assumptions which had to be fulfilled. All these approaches had again remarkable successes, realized either in stand alone systems or as parts of more general knowledge based systems.

It was also clear that classical AI-systems were not able to deal with the phenomena arising in the context of 'common sense' in a satisfactory way.

About twenty years ago, the overwhelming opinion was that this was due to the fact that common sense knowledge was very complex: Humans needed many years of education in order to master the everyday world. From this view it was only a simple step to start the CYC-project (D. Lenat in Austin, Texas) with the aim to collect and structure about 100 million knowledge units (the number can be justified by assuming that a human learns 10.000 knowledge units per day for thirty years).

The results have shown that the approach was not successful in the overall (although it had many merits). One of the reasons for the negative results was that very large sets of knowledge units, and their interactions are too difficult to control.

D. Lenat,
a man behind the CYC-project.

In the past years an idea was extended which was in principle not so new but which did not get a systematic attention. The intended approach was to split the work between humans who have creative ideas, have common sense and can provide background ideas on the one side and machines which can do stupid but time resuming search, can handle large databases and can perform extensive computations on the other side. This was leading to the idea of an *assistant system.* In the past assistant systems were mostly ad hoc solutions to supplement knowledge based systems if they were not able to achieve the desired results. The role of humans was mainly to help when the machine was unable to solve the problem.

A systematic approach would require a rigorous investigation of the following problem types:

(i) A characterization of what humans can do better than machines and vice versa.
(ii) A deduction of a work plan which in principle splits the labour between human and software agents.
(iii) A description of the principles as well as of the technical aspects in the communications between such different agents.
(iv) An integration of common sense reasoning and use of informal concepts with logical thinking and computer computations. This leads to research about semi-formal systems.

In a nutshell two worlds are here confronting each other: formalisms versus informal concepts, logical truth versus approximate reasoning, deduction versus induction and learning. In contrast to the ideas of the CYC-project one tries here to master the complexity of the world by admitting inexactness. This is the way humans proceed and assistant systems should incorporate these abilities. In the man-machine cooperation humans are clearly the dominating partners. They make the ultimate decisions and they have the responsibility for the consequences. One way to describe the subordinate character of the machines is to view them as servants who support the humans by providing the necessary knowledge in a usable form at the right time. The organizational structure for this is known as knowledge management which is of increasing importance.

The next problem which immediately arises is to control the inexactness because arbitrary errors cannot be admitted. This means to have safe boundaries and the analogue of numerical error handling in symbolic reasoning. There are presently several areas dealing with such topics where the most prominent are similarity based reasoning and fuzzy reasoning.

For the future development of AI in the context of these considerations the most important steps are not to extend the scope of the traditional AI-techniques but rather to open the view for reasoning which is done by humans. This is a stepwise approach which incorporates humans in the form of assistant systems but at the same allows the machine to deal with typical human ways of thinking with informal concepts. This will certainly be of great benefit for many applications, e.g. electronic commerce, medicine, education, etc. Here we need a progress both in the foundations and the applied systems.

The future main directions of research and development in AI can be bundled up in three terms:

- Information creation
- Autonomy
- Situatedness.

1.7.1 Information Creation

The huge amount of data collected in existing databases is of very limited use if only the usual retrieval mechanisms are applied. Asking the right questions and connecting the data in a way that fits to the questions may yield relevant information. A whole arsenal of methods is now at hand to do this, e.g. data warehouses, classical statistical methods, neural networks, and machine learning algorithms. Recently developed methods can even cope with mass data in an efficient way. AI has made a substantial contribution to this technology which is commercially used in recent years and is usually called *data mining*, for non-formatted data also *text mining*, *web mining*, or *image mining*.

The information produced in this way is not created from the empty space, rather it is implicitly contained in the data, it is in some sense a condensation of the data. It is this aspect that makes or should make data mining an interesting field for AI researchers, besides the methods. Often machine learning is regarded as a paradigm for human learning. This view is certainly not wrong but too restricted. From cognitive science we learn that in human learning also statistics plays some role, so we can assume that learning is a complex process where different methods interact. This is very well reflected by the mixture of methods in data mining.

However, at present the different methods are used separately, they are not really tied together and used within a single information creation process. It is a research task of the future to solve this problem. A solution would not only improve the efficiency of existing data mining technology but has also a cognitive aspect. We can follow the hypothesis that humans gain knowledge from experience, the so called expert knowledge, by abstracting from large sets of examples that they see during their life. The abstraction process runs in part consciously and in part unconsciously and is guided by background knowledge and specialized knowledge of some subject. This process may be simulated by improved data mining techniques and thus expert knowledge may be automatically produced from data.

1.7.2 Autonomy

In computer science, distributed systems have been developed since a number of years and have proved to be a powerful means for increasing efficiency of problem solving but also to open new application domains for computer technology. The contribution of AI to the field of distributed systems was not only to develop new algorithms for such systems but to equip the components of distributed systems with some degree of autonomy.

Up to now, computer systems were mostly viewed as computing machines and storages of mass data and used for decision support. Humans hesitated to accept decisions made by computer systems. However, in some technical domains computers already control big installations, which include decision making in some sense although humans still act as supervisors. Thus computer systems have already started to become autonomous. But this is just the beginning of a long process.

In multi-agent systems, which are the contribution of AI to distributedness, autonomy is a key issue. A component of a system can be viewed or modelled as an agent only if it has some degree of autonomy, otherwise it is regarded as a passive component. Autonomy can be characterized by a number of features. First of all, it means the capability of choosing some action from a set of possible actions in a certain situation, including the decision between staying inactive or becoming active when it is required. This ability is called *proactivity*. Another important feature is the ability of maintaining goals. It is not only required that an agent can have goals that guide its planning and activity, but also that it can change them, drop them, or adopt new ones. A third feature is the ability of active communication and cooperation. The word "active" is important here because the exchange of messages in the sense of functional calls between passive components usually is also called communication, but that is not meant here. Communication and cooperation between agents is also a proactive behaviour, an agent can start communication or look for cooperation with others whenever it believes it is necessary.

The property of autonomy creates a new relationship between agents—whether they are realized as robots or as software systems, and humans that has the quality of partnership. Autonomous agents can no longer be regarded as mere machines that are started when needed, do their job, and are stopped. One may view them as servants, but servants have their own will and complex cognitive abilities, and these must be conceded to the agents as well. We must expect to live in a much more complex society in the future than we do today together with agents as some kind of 'living' entities. They will be present in our everyday life, e.g. as personal assistants in our wearable computer system, as drivers of our car, or as caretakers of our household. AI researchers should together with sociologists deal with the problems that may be caused by this perspective.

1.7.3 Situatedness

In a general sense, all computer systems are situated, but traditional systems exist in very restricted well-defined situations completely determined by humans. Situatedness only became an important topic of research with the advent of agents in multi-agent systems and of adaptable mobile robots. Obviously, situatedness is closely related to the issue of autonomy. Only autonomous systems must locate and orientate themselves and act in situations. Situation here means a set of influences from the environment that are at least partly unforeseeable but of great importance for the system, so that it has to react in an appropriate way.

A situated system has to solve two main problems, namely how to sense the situation and how to choose an appropriate reaction. Sensing a situation may be a simple task for a mere software agent in a well-defined environment. However, if we think of agents acting in, e.g. the Internet, things become much more complicated because this environment is highly unstructured and dynamic. Even more complex is sensing with robots. Here, first physical signals are to be transformed into data, a task they may delegate to physicists and electrical engineers. But in the next step, the signals from different sources must be put together to yield a description of the situation that enables the situated system to react appropriately.

This task is called *sensor fusion* and this is where AI methods come in. From cognitive science we learn that understanding a situation is a very complex process that requires a lot of background knowledge and a lot of nervous activity. The brain constructs the situation from the different inputs. We still know little about this process and for obvious reasons it is hard to reconstruct it. Simulations by means of AI methods may help to get insight into it. If simulation is possible, it can also be used by artificial situated systems to build up the description of a situation for their own purposes.

For situated systems the main purpose of constructing situation descriptions is to use them for their own activities. The basic tasks of self-localization and orientation and the derived task of acting can be done only on the basis of situation descriptions. This means, on the other hand, that the construction of a situation description is always aimed to support the situated system in fulfilling its tasks; it is not an end in itself. Criteria like completeness or consistency do not have priority; rather a description satisfies the needs of the situated system if it helps to choose the appropriate actions. Some kind of situated knowledge bases are required consisting of broad background knowledge and chunks of relevant knowledge that need not be consistent with each other nor with the background knowledge. The knowledge in these chunks may even be represented in different forms and different granularities. Methods for selecting the right knowledge chunk, for combining them, and for transforming the knowledge from one form to another have to be developed.

Obviously, situated systems must have planning capabilities for choosing sequences of actions. They also must have learning capabilities because, as mentioned above, the influences that constitute a situation are partly unforeseeable. However, new situations differ not completely from each other, rather in all reasonable environments there are similarities between them, such that learning, i.e. detecting and classifiying similar cases, makes sense. Learning can improve the behaviour of a situated system.

To summarize: information creation, autonomy, and situatedness can be regarded as focuses for the AI research and development in the future. In order to come up to these challenges, a lot of single methods have to be integrated into greater systems. So the general direction of AI research and development can be characterized by the development of complex systems that integrate different methods and fulfil the three requirements.

EXERCISES

1. Create and justify your own definition of artificial intelligence.
2. Describe the Turing test. If the Turing test is passed, does this show that computers exhibit intelligence? State your reasons.
3. What advances do you think need to be made in order for the Turing test to be passed?
4. Criticize Turing's criteria for computer software being "intelligent".
5. Although computing is a relatively new discipline, philosophers and mathematicians have been thinking about the issues involved in automating problem solving for thousands of years. What is your opinion of the relevance of these philosophical issues to the design of a device for intelligent problem solving? Justify your answer.
6. What do the following tasks have in common?
   - Design a program to identify and delete junk e-mail.
   - Design a robot to deliver packages in an office.
   - Design a spacecraft to gather information about Saturn.

7. When you think of AI what sort of challenges come to mind?
8. Come up with a working definition for what it means for an agent to know something.
9. List and discuss two potentially negative effects on society of the development of artificial intelligence techniques.
10. The syntax used to represent a computer program is pretty straightforward, but what is the semantics of a computer program? What is the syntax of representations stored in the human brain?
11. Provide a working definition for the notion of "symbol" that might apply to representing useful information about the world in human brains.
12. Discuss whether or not you think it is possible for a computer to understand and use a natural (human) language.
13. Compare and contrast numeric and symbolic processing techniques.
14. What are the major factors that can help push AI from the lab to the real word?
15. Explain why AI is beneficial even though computers cannot really think.

CHAPTER 2

Symbolic Logic

2.1 INTRODUCTION

The ability to make logical deductions is an integral part of human intelligence. The awareness of this fact increased the interest in mechanical theorem proving. Parallel to the progress in improving theorem proving techniques, was the progress in applying these techniques in artificial intelligence (AI). These were applied to deductive question answering and later to problem solving, program synthesis, program analysis, and many others. When we talk of mechanical theorem proving, we are concerned with "logic". Especially when it is concerned with (AI), it is "symbolic logic". There are many points of view from which we can study symbolic logic. Traditionally, it has been studied from philosophical and mathematical orientations. Here, we are interested in the applications of symbolic logic to solving intellectually difficult problems. That is, we want to use symbolic logic to represent problems and obtain their solutions. Let us see how symbolic logic can be used to represent problems. Let us consider simple examples.

EXAMPLE 1. Assume that we have the following facts:

F(1) : If it is hot and humid, then it will rain.
F(2) : If it is humid, then it is hot.
F(3) : It is humid now.

The question is: Will it rain?

The above facts are given in English. We shall use symbols to represent them. Let P, Q, and R represent "It is hot", "It is humid", and "It will rain", respectively. We also need some logical symbols. In this case, we shall use "$\wedge$" to represent "and" and "$\rightarrow$" to represent "imply". Then the above three facts are represented as:

F(1) : $P \wedge Q \rightarrow R$
F(2) : $Q \rightarrow P$
F(3) : Q

Thus we have translated English sentences into logical formulas. We shall see later that whenever F(1), F(2), and F(3) are *true*, the formula

F(4) : R

is *true*.

Therefore, we say that F(4) logically follows from F(1), F(2), and F(3). That is, "it will rain".

EXAMPLE 2. We have the following facts:

F(1) : Confucius is a man.
F(2) : Every man is mortal.

What can we conclude?

To represent F(1) and F(2), we need a new concept, called a *predicate*. We may let P(x) and Q(x) represent "x is a man" and "x is mortal", respectively. We also use (Vx) to represent "for all x". Then the above facts are represented by:

F(1) : P(Confucius)
F(2) : (Vx) (P(x) → Q11(x))

It will be seen later that from F(1) and F(2), we can logically deduce

F(3) : Q(Confucius)

which means that Confucius is mortal.

In the above two examples, we essentially had to prove that a formula "logically follows from" other formulas. We shall call a statement that a formula logically follows from formulas, a *theorem*. A demonstration that a theorem is true, that is that a formula logically follows from other formulas, well be called a *proof* of the *theorem*. The "problem of mechanical theorem proving" is to consider mechanical methods for finding proofs of theorems.

2.2 LOGIC

There are various views about the definition of "logic". But in our context, "Logic is the Art of Correct Reasoning".

Why "Correct"?

There are two main issues with reasoning. Suppose we are given a set of statements. The issues are:

(a) Can we get all the correct facts through reasoning (also known as *inferencing*), over the given set of statements? This issue refers to the completeness of reasoning.
(b) Will we derive a *wrong* fact through reasoning? This issue refers to the *soundness* of reasoning.

Hence when our reasoning possesses the above two properties over the given set of statements (also known as the *domain of knowledge*), we call the reasoning to be *correct*. This art of correct reasoning is "logic".

But here we are talking about "symbolic logic". The purpose of this symbolic logic is to symbolize reasoning encountered not only in mathematics but also in daily life.

In this particular section we are dealing with the simplest of the symbolic logic, namely *propositional logic*.

What do we understand by "propositional logic"?

We have said that the purpose of symbolic logic is to symbolize reasoning. In propositional logic, this symbolization is done by using *declarative statements* that can be either true or false, but not both. Hence, propositional logic refers to the style of reasoning which reasons over a given set of declarative statements. Any such declarative statement is known as a *proposition*. So, now we have, broadly, two major points to look at. Just as the name of the topic goes, i.e. propositional logic, the first point is to study the issues concerning propositions, and the second is concerning logic. Let us start with propositions.

2.3 PROPOSITIONS

2.3.1 Statement

In propositional logic, we are interested in declarative sentences that can be either true or false, but not both. Any such declarative sentence is called a proposition or statement.

Definition 1: *A "proposition" is a declarative sentence that is either true or false, but, not both.*

Examples of propositions are: "Sky is blue", "sugar is a hydrocarbon", "Ramesh has a Ph.D. degree". The true or false assigned to a proposition is called the "truth value" of the proposition. Customarily, we represent true by T and false by F. Furthermore, we shall use an uppercase symbol or a string of uppercase symbols to denote a proposition. For instance, we may denote the propositions above as follows:

P = Sky is blue.
Q = Sugar is a hydrocarbon.
R = Ramesh has a Ph.D. degree.

Definition 2: *The symbols, such as P, Q, and R, that are used to denote propositions are called 'atomic formulas' or 'atoms'.*

From propositions, we can build "compound propositions" by using "logical connectives". Examples of compound propositions are: "Snow is white and the sky is clear" and "If Gopal is not at home then Gita is at home." The logical connectives in the above two compound propositions are "and" and "if ... then". In propositional logic, we shall use 5 logical connectives:

$\sim$ (not),
$\wedge$ (and),
$\vee$ (or),
$\rightarrow$ (if ... then), and
$\leftrightarrow$ (if and only if).

These five logical connectives can be used to build compound propositions form propositions. More generally, they can be used to construct more complicated compound propositions from compound propositions by applying them repeatedly. Let us consider an example where we represent,

"Humidity is high" by P,
"Temperature is high" by Q', and
"One feels comfortable" by C.

Then the sentence "If the humidity is high and the temperature is high, then one does not feel comfortable" may be represented by:

$((P \wedge Q) \rightarrow (\sim C))$.

Therefore, we see that a compound proposition can express a rather complicated idea. In propositional logic, an expression that represents a proposition, such as P, or a compound proposition, such as $((P \wedge Q) \rightarrow \sim C))$, is called a *well-formed formula*.

Definition 3: *'Well-formed' or 'formulas' for short, in propositional logic are defined recursively as follows:*

1. An *atom* is a formula
2. If G is a formula then $(- G)$ is a formula.
3. If G and H are formulas, then
   $(G \wedge H)$,
   $(G \vee H)$,
   $(G \rightarrow H)$, and
   $(G \leftrightarrow H)$ are formulas.
4. All formulas are generated applying the above rules.

Let G and H be two formulas. Then the truth values of the formulas generated using logical connectives over G and H are related to the truth values of G and H in the following way.

1. $\sim$G is *true* when G is *false*, and is *false* when G is *true*. G is called the *negation* of G.
2. $(G \wedge H)$ is *true* if G and H are both true; otherwise, $(G \wedge H)$ is *false*. $(G \wedge H)$ is called the *conjunction* of G and H.
3. $(G \vee H)$ is *true* if at least one of G and H is *true*; otherwise, $(G \vee H)$ is *false*. $(G \vee H)$ is called the *disjunction* of G and H.
4. $(G \rightarrow H)$ is *false* if G is true and H is *false*; otherwise, $(G \rightarrow H)$ is *true*. $(G \rightarrow H)$ is read as "If G, then H", or "G implies H".
5. $(G \leftrightarrow H)$ is *true* whenever G and H have the same truth values; otherwise, $(G \leftrightarrow H)$ is *false*.

The above relations can be represented conveniently as shown in Table 2.1.

Table 2.1

G	H	G	$(G \wedge H)$	$(G \vee H)$	$(G \rightarrow H)$	$(G \leftrightarrow H)$
T	T	F	T	T	T	T
T	F	F	F	T	F	F
F	T	T	F	T	T	F
F	F	T	F	F	T	T

2.3.2 Interpretations of Formulas

Suppose that P and Q are two atoms and that the truth values of P and Q are T and F, respectively. Then according to the second row of the above table with P and Q substituted for G and H, respectively, we find that the truth values of (~P), $(P \wedge Q)$, $(P \vee Q) < (P \rightarrow Q)$, and $(P \leftrightarrow Q)$ are F, F, T, F, F, respectively. Similarly, the truth values of any formula can be evaluated in terms of truth values of atoms.

EXAMPLE 3. Consider the formula:

$$G = (P \sim Q) \rightarrow (R \leftrightarrow (S))$$

The atoms in this formula are P, Q, R, and S. Suppose the truth values of P, Q, R, and S are T, F, T, and T, respectively. Then $(P \wedge Q)$ is F since Q is false; (~ S) is F since S is T; $(R \leftrightarrow (\sim S))$ is F since R is T and (~ S) is F; and $(P \wedge Q) \rightarrow (R \leftrightarrow (\sim S))$ is T since $(P \wedge Q)$ is F and $(R \leftrightarrow (\sim S))$ is F. Hence, the formula G is T if P, Q, R, and S are assigned T, F, T, T respectively, will be called as the *interpretation* of the formula G. Since each one of P, Q, R, and S can be assigned either T or F, there are = 16 interpretations of the formula G. A table that displays the truth values of a formula G for all possible assignments of truth values to atoms occurring in G is called a truth table of G.

Definition 4: *Given a propositional formula G, let A1, A2, ..., An be the atoms occurring in the formula G. Then an "interpretation" of G is an assgnment of truth values to A1, A2, ..., An in which every Ai is assigned either T or F, but not both.*

Definition 5: *A formula G is said to be "true under (or in) an interpretation" if and only if G is evaluated to T in the interpretation; otherwise, G is said to be "false under the interpretation".*

If there are n distinct atoms in a formula, then there will be 2 to the power of n distinct interpretations for the formula. Sometimes, if AI, ..., An are all atoms occurring in a formula, it may be more convenient to represent an interpretation by a set m1 ... mn, where mi is either Ai or ~Ai. For example. the set P, ~Q, ~R, S represents an interpretation in which P, Q, R, and S are, respectively, assigned T, F, F, and T. That is, if an atom A is in a set that represents an interpretation, then A is assigned T; while if the negation of the atom A is in the set, then A is assigned F

2.3.3 Validity and Inconsistency of Formulas

Let us consider the formula:

$$G = ((P \rightarrow Q)\ P) \rightarrow Q$$

The atoms in the formula are P and Q. Hence, the formula G has sqr(2) = 4 interpretations. The truth values of G under all its four interpretations are given in Table 2.2.

Table 2.2

P	Q	$(P \rightarrow Q)$	$(P \rightarrow Q)P$	$((P \rightarrow Q)) \rightarrow Q$
T	T	T	T	T
T	F	F	F	T
F	T	T	F	T
F	F	T	F	T

We see that the formula G is true under all its interpretations. This formula will be called a *valid formula* or a *tautology*.

Now consider the formula:

$$G = (P \rightarrow Q) \wedge (P \rightarrow \sim Q)$$

The truth table for G is as given in Table 2.3.

P	Q	$\sim Q$	$(P \rightarrow Q)$	$(P \wedge \sim Q)$	$(P \rightarrow Q)\ (P \wedge \sim Q)$
T	T	F	T	F	F
T	F	T	F	T	F
F	T	F	T	F	F
F	F	T	T	F	F

We see that G is FALSE under all its interpretations. This formula will be called an *inconsistent formula* or a *contradiction*.

Definition 1: *A formula is said to be 'valid' if and only if it is true under all its interpretations. A formula is said to be 'invalid' if and only if it is not valid.*

Definition 2: *A formula is said to be 'inconsistent' (or 'unsatisfiable' if and only if it is false under all its interpretations. A formula is said in the 'consistent' (or 'satisfiable') if and only if it is not 'inconsistent'. Hence*

1. A formula is valid iff its negation is inconsistent.
2. A formula is inconsistent iff its negation is valid.
3. A formula is invalid iff it is false under at least one interpretation.

4. A formula is consistent iff it is true under at least one interpretation.
5. If a formula is valid, then it is consistent, but not vice versa.
6. If a formula is inconsistent, then it is invalid, but not vice versa.

2.4 NORMAL FORMS IN PROPOSITIONAL LOGIC

When we are dealing with formulas we are concerned with representations of these formulas. So, by common sense one can say that it would be easier to infer over a set of propositions if all of them are represented similarly or in other words, if all of them belong to the same form. Thus, it is necessary to transform a formula from one form to another, especially to a *'normal form'*, i.e. it is necessary to transform the given set of formulas to a common standard form. This is accomplished by replacing a formula in the given form by a formula equivalent to it and repeating this process until the desired form is obtained.

Definition 1: *Two formulas F and G are said to be equivalent (or F is equivalent to G) denoted as F = G, if and only if truth values of F and G are the same under every interpretation of F and G.*

Definition 2: *A 'literal' is an atom or negation of an atom.*

In propositional logic we use either one of two kinds of representations or forms of formulas. They are as follows.

Definition 3: *A formula F is said to be in 'Conjunctive Normal Form' if and only if f has the form : $F = F1 \wedge \ldots \wedge Fn$, $n > = 1$, where each F1, ..., Fn is a disjunction of literals. When we say that F1 is a disjunction of literals, it means that F1 is of the form $F1 = A1 \vee A2 \vee \ldots \vee An$, where A1, ..., An are literals.*

Definition 4: *A formula F is said to be in 'Disjuntive Normal Form' if and only if f has the form: $F = F1 \vee \ldots \vee fn$, $n > = l$, where ench F1 ... Fn is a conjuntion of literals. When we say that F1 is a conjuntion of literals, it means that f1 is of the form $F1 = A1 \wedge A2 \wedge \ldots \wedge An$, where A1 ... An literals.*

In order to to carry out the transformation of formulas to a desired form, we need an adequate supply of equivalent formulas. Let '$' denote the formula that is always *true*, and "#" denote the formula that is always *false*. Given below are some useful pairs of equivalent formulas, also called as *laws*. Here F, G, and H are all formulas.

1. $F \leftrightarrow G = (F \rightarrow G)\ (G \rightarrow F)$
2. $F \rightarrow G = F \vee G$

   Commutative Laws:
3. (a) $F \vee G = G \vee F$, (b) $F \wedge G \wedge F$

   Associative Laws:
4. (a) $(F \vee G) \vee H = F \vee (G \vee H)$; (b) $(F \wedge G) \wedge H = F \wedge (G \wedge H)$

   Distributive Laws:
5. (a) $F \vee (G \wedge H) = (F \vee G) \wedge (F \vee H)$; (b) $F \wedge (G \vee H) = (F \wedge G) \vee (F \wedge H)$

D'Morgan's Laws:
6. (a) $\sim(F \vee G) = \sim F \wedge \sim G$; (b) $\sim(F \wedge G) = \sim F \vee \sim G$
Other Laws:
7. (a) $F \vee \# = F$; (b) $F \wedge \$ = F$
8. (a) $F \vee \$ = \$$; (b) $F \wedge \# = \#$
9. (a) $F \vee \sim F = \$$; (b) $F \wedge \sim F = \#$
10. $\sim(\sim F) = F$

2.5 LOGICAL CONSEQUENCES

In mathematics as well as in daily life, we often have to decide whether one statement follows from some other statements. This leads to the concept of *logical consequence.*

Definition: *Given formulas F1, F2, ..., Fn and a formula G, G is said to be a "logical consequence" of F1, F2, ..., Fn (or G "logically follows from" F1, f2, ..., Fn) if and only if for any interpretation I in which F1 ∧ F2 ∧ ... ∧ Fn is True, G is also True. F1, F2, ..., Fn are called "axoims" (or "postulates", "premises") of G.*

Theorem 1 (Deduction Theorem): *Given formulas F1, f2, ..., Fn and a formula G, G is said to be a "logical consequence" of F1, F2, ..., Fn, if and only if the formula ((F1 ∧ F2 ∧ ... ∧ Fn) → G) is valid.*

Proof: Suppose G is a logical consequence of F1, F2, ..., Fn. Let I be an arbitrary interpretation. If Fl, F2, ..., Fn are *true* in I, then by the definition of logical consequence, G is *true* in I. Hence the formula ((F1 ∧ F2 ∧ ... ∧ Fn) → G) is *true* in I. On the other hand, if F1, F2, ..., Fn are *false* in I, then ((F1 — F2 ∧ ... ∧ Fn) → G) is *true* under any interpretation. That is ((F1 ∧ F2 ∧ ... ∧ Fn) → G) is a vaild formula.

Suppose ((F1 ∧ F2 ∧ ... ∧ Fn) → G) is valid formula. For any interpretation I, if F1 ∧ F2 ∧ ... ∧ Fn is *true* in I, G must be *true* in I. Therefore, G is a logical consequence of F1 ∧ F2 ∧ ... Fn.

Theorem 2: *Given formulas F1, F2, ..., Fn and a formula G. G is said to be a "logical consequence" of F1, F2, ..., Fn, if and only if the formula (F1 ∧ F2 ∧ ... ∧ Fn ~G) is inconsistent.*

Proof: By Theorem 1, G is "logical consequence" of F1, F2, ..., Fn if and only if the formula ((F1 ∧ F2 ∧ ... ∧ Fn) → G) is valid. Hence G is a logical consequence of F1, F2, ..., Fn if and only if the negation of the formula ((F1 ∧ F2 ∧ ... ∧ Fn) → Fn) → G) is inconsistent. Since

$$\begin{aligned}\sim((F1 \wedge F2 \wedge \ldots \wedge Fn) \rightarrow G) &= (\sim(F1 \wedge F2 \wedge \ldots \wedge Fn) \vee G)\\ &= (\sim((F1 \wedge F2 \wedge \ldots \wedge Fn)) \wedge \sim G)\\ &= (F1 \wedge F2 \wedge \ldots \wedge Fn) \wedge \sim G\\ &= F1 \wedge F2 \wedge \ldots \wedge Fn \wedge \sim G\end{aligned}$$

we conclude that Theorem 2 is *true.*

Theorems 1 and 2 are very important. They show that proving that a particular formula is a logical consequence of a finite set of formulas is equivalent to proving that a certain related formula is valid or inconsistent. If G is logical consequence of F1 ∧ F2 ∧ ... ∧ Fn, the formula ((F1 ∧ F2 ∧ ... ∧ Fn) → G) is called a theorem, and G is called the conclusion of the theorem.

The above method of proving is known as the natural deduction method. Another method is the resolution principle as discussed below.

2.6 RESOLUTION PRINCIPLE

For any two clauses C1 and C2, if there is a literal L1 in C1 that is complimentary to a literal L2 in C2, then delete L1 and L2 from C1 and C2, respectively, and construct the disjunction of remaining clauses. The constructed clause is a resolvent of C1 and C2.

EXAMPLE 4. Consider the following clauses:

C1 : P ∨ R
C2 : ¬P ∨ Q

Clause C1 has a literal P which is complimentary to P in C2. Therefore by deleting P and P from C1 and C2. Respectively, and constructing the disjunction of the remaining clauses R and Q, we obtain a resolvant R ∨ Q.

2.7 PREDICATE CALCULUS

Predicate calculus or *First order predicate logic* (FOPL) is one of the oldest and most important knowledge representation schemes used in artificial intelligence. We can say that predicate logic is a high level human-oriented language for describing problems and problem-solving methods. It was developed by logicians as a means for formal reasoning, primarily in the areas of Mathematics. A familiarity to FOPL is important to the student of AI for several reasons.

- It offers the only formal approach to reasoning that has a sound theoretical foundation.
- Structure of predicate logic is flexible enough to permit the accurate representation of natural language statements reasonably well.
- Predicate logic is widely accepted by the workers in AI field as one of the most uselful representation methods.

Logic is a formal method of reasoning. Many concepts which can be verbalized can be translated into symbolic representations which closely approximate the meaning of these concepts and these symbolic structures can be manipulated in programs to deduce various facts to carry out a form of automatic reasoning.

2.7.1 Syntax of Predicate Logic

Basic ingredient of the predicate logic are the following:

1. ***Connectives***

   ~ or ¬ represents negation
   & or ∧ represents conjunction or AND
   | or ∨ represents disjunction or OR
   → represents implicatin (If ... then).
   ↔ represents equivalence or if and only if (iff)

2. ***Quantifiers***

   ∃ Existential quantifier (There exists)
   ∀ Universal quantifier (For all values)

3. ***Constants***

   Fixed value terms, belong to a given domain. Usually denoted by letters near the beginning of the English alphabet and numbers, e.g. a, b, D, 10, 2.5, ...

4. ***Variables***

   Terms that can assume different values over a given dumain. They are usually denote by word and letters near the end of the English alphabet, e.g., x, y, z, ...

5. ***Auxiliary symbols***

   ), (and some places [ ], { } are used for punctuation.

6. ***Functions***

   Function symbols defined over a domain (say *D*) map *n* elements ($n > 0$) to a single element of the domain. Here *n* is called the *rank* or *ary* or *degree* of the function. Letters f, g, h and words such as age_of ( ), cause_of ( ) represents functions.

   An *n*-ary function is written as $f(t_1, t_2, ..., t_n)$, where *t* are terms defined over some domain. A 0-ary function is a constant.

   Term: Constant variables and functions are referred as *terms*.

7. ***Predicates***

   Predicates denote relations or functional mapping from the elements of a domain (D) to the values true or false. Letters and words near the middle of the alphabet such as p, q, R, EQUAL, ... are used to represent predicates. Like functions predicates can have *n* ($n \geq 0$) terms as argument. A 0-ary predicate is a proposition, i.e. propositions are constant predicates.

Atom. Predicates are referred to as atomic formulas or atoms. When we want to refer and atomic formula or its negation, we use the worked literal. A predicate which has no variable is called a *ground atom.*

2.7.2 Representation of Simple Facts in Logic

Consider the following statements.

s1 : All empoyees earning Rs. 35,000 or more per year pay tax.
s2 : Some employees are on leave today.
s3 : No employee earns more than the president.

To represent these statements in predicate logic, we have to define abbreviations for the predicates and functions. For example,

EMP(x) for x is an employee
PRD(x) for x is president
inc(x) for income of x
GE(u,v) for u is greater than or equal to v
ON_LEAVE(x) for x is on leave today
TAX(x) for x pays tax.

Using these abbreviation s1, s2 and s3 as

sl : $\forall x$ ((EMP(x) $\wedge$ GE (inc(x),35000)) $\rightarrow$ TAX(x)
s2 : $\exists y$ (EMP(y) $\rightarrow$ ON_LEAVE (y))
s3 : $\forall xy$ ((EMP(x) $\wedge$ PRD(y))) $\rightarrow \neg$ GE (inc(x), inc(y)).

2.7.3 Issues Arise During the Conversion of English Sentences to Predicate Logic

Consider the following sentences and their predicate form:

(a) Marcus was a man—MAN (marcus).
(b) Marcus was a Pompeian—POMPEIAN (marcus).
(c) All Pompeians were Romans—$\forall x$ POMPEIAN (x) $\rightarrow$ ROMAN (x).
(d) Caesar was a ruler—RULER (caesar).
(e) All Romans were either loyal to Caesar or hated him.
$\forall x$ ROMAN(x) $\rightarrow$ loyalto (x, caesar) $\vee$ hate (x, caesar)
(f) Everyone is loyal to someone—$\forall x$ $\exists y$ loyalto (x, y).
(g) People only try to assassinate rulers they are not loyal to.
$\forall xy$ PERSON (x) $\wedge$ RULER (y) $\wedge$ tryassassinate (x, y) $\rightarrow$ ~ loyalto (x, y).
(h) Marcus tried to assassinate Caesar—tryassassinate (marcus, caesar).

(1) Represents the fact that Marcus is a man but it fails to capture some information in English sentence, namely the notion of the past tense. Acceptance of this omission depends on the use to which we intend to put the knowledge.

In (2), (3), and (4) we ignore the fact that proper names are often not referred to unique individuals. Since many people have the same name, deciding which of the several people have the same name, will require fair amount of knowledge and reasoning.

A major problem arises when converting English sentence into logical statement is the scope of quantifiers. (6) will be sometimes written as $\exists y \forall x$ loyal to (x, y), which represents "There exists someone to whom every one is loyal to".

In (7) and (8) we used "tryassassinate" for simplicity. Using this representation, connection between trying to assassinate and actually assassinate could not be made easily. If such connections are necessary, we have to choose another representation.

From these examples, three important issues must be addressed during the conversion of English sentence to logical statements and using them to deduce new ones.

- Many English sentences are ambiguous, choosing the correct interpretation must be difficult.
- There is often a choice of ways of representing knowledge. The representation for a particular set of sentences depends on the use which the knowledge contained in the sentence will be put.
- Even in very simple situation, a set of sentences is unlikely to contain all the information necessary to reason about the topic.

2.8 WELL-FORMED FORMULAS (WFFs)

Previous examples in predicate logic form are known as *well-formed formulas* or wffs (Pronounced as "woofs"). They are recursively defined as follows:

An atomic formula is a wff.

If P and Q are wffs then

$$\neg (P), (P \wedge Q), (P \vee Q), (P \rightarrow Q), (P \leftrightarrow Q),$$
$$\forall x\ P(x), \exists x\ P(x) \text{ are wffs.}$$

Example of statements which are not wffs

$$\forall P\ P(x), \text{MAN}(\sim\text{marcus}), \text{father\_of}\ (Q(x)).$$

Scope of a quantifier is the formula to which the quantifier applies.

An occurrence of a variable in a formula is *bound* if and only if the occurrence of the variable is within the scope of the quantifier employing the variable. Otherwise it is called *free* variable.

2.8.1 Properties of WFFs

1. ***Interpretation.*** When assignment of values is given to each predicate symbol in a wff, we say interpretation is given to the wff. If value of interpretation is *true*, then it is called the *model of the wff*. An interpretation of a formula in predicate logic consists of a non-empty domain D, and assignment of values to each constant, function symbol, and predicate symbol in it as follows:
   - To each constant/variable we assign an element in D.
   - To each n-ary function symbol, we assign mapping from D" to D.
   - To each n-ary predicate symbol, we assign mapping from D" to (T, F)
     e.g. consider the wff $(\forall x)\ (\exists y)\ P(x, y)$
     we can define the interpretation over the domain D = {1, 2} as follows:

   $$P\ (1, 1) = \text{true}, P(1, 2) = \text{false}, P(2, 1) = \text{false}, P(2, 2) = \text{true}.$$

2. ***Validity.*** A wff is said to be valid, if it is *true* under every interpretation, otherwise it is called invalid wff. Valid ground wffs are known as *tautology*.
3. ***Satisfiability.*** A wff which is *true* for some interpretation is satisfiable and wff which is *false* under every interpretation is said to be unsatisfiable (inconsistant).

   Valid wff is satisfiable, and inconsistent wffs are invalid.

4. *Logical consequence.* In Mathematics as well as in daily life, we often have to decide whether one statement follows from the other statement. It leads to the concept of logical consequences. We can define it as follows:

Given formulas W1, W2, ..., Wn and a formula G, which is a logical consequence of W1, W2, ..., Wn (or G logically follows from W1, W2, ..., Wn) if and only if for any interpretation l in which W1 ∧ W2 ∧ ... ∧ Wn is *true*, G is also *true*. Wl, W2, ..., Wn are called *axioms* or *postulates* of G.

5. *Equality.* If the truth values of the two wffs are same regardless of the interpretations, we say these wffs are equivalent.

2.8.2 Equivalent Logical Expressions

$\neg(\neg W) = W$ (Double negation)
$W1 \wedge W2 = W2 \wedge W1$
$W1 \vee W2 = W2 \vee W1$ (Commutativity)

$(W1 \wedge W2) \wedge W3 = W1 \wedge (W2 \wedge W3)$
$(W1 \vee W2) \vee W3 = W1 \vee (W2 \vee W3)$ (Associativity)

$W1 \vee (W2 \wedge W3) = (W1 \vee W2) \wedge (W1 \vee W3)$
$W1 \vee (W2 \vee W3) = (W1 \wedge W2) \vee (W1 \wedge W3)$ (Distributivity)

$\neg(W1 \wedge W2) = \neg W1 \vee \neg W2$
$\neg(W1 \vee W2) = \neg W1 \wedge \neg W2$ (D'Morgan's Law)

$W1 \rightarrow W2 = \neg W1 \vee W2$
$W1 \leftrightarrow W2 = (W1 \rightarrow W2) \wedge (W2 \rightarrow W1) = (\neg W1 \vee W2) \wedge (\neg W2 \vee W1)$

$\forall x\ W(x) \vee W1 = \forall x(W(x) \vee W1)$
$\forall x\ W(x) \wedge W1 = \forall x(W(x) \wedge W1)$

$\exists x\ W(x) \vee W1 = \exists x(W(x) \vee W1)$
$\exists x\ W(x) \wedge W1 = \exists x(W(x) \wedge W1)$
$\neg((\exists x)W(x)) = \forall x\ (\neg W(x))$
$\neg((\forall x)W(x)) = \exists x\ (\neg W(x))$

$\forall x\ W1(x) \wedge \forall x\ W2(x) = \forall x\ (W1(x) \wedge W2(x))$
$\exists x\ W1(x) \wedge \exists x\ W2(x) = \exists x\ (W1(x) \wedge W2(x))$

2.9 CLAUSAL FORM

A clause can be defined as a wff consisting of disjunction of literals, e.g. P1 ∨ P2 ∨ P3 ... ∨ ¬Pn, where P1, P2, ..., Pn are literals.

2.9.1 Conjunctive Normal Form (CNF)

If W1, W2, ..., Wn each possibly consisting of disjunction of literals, then we say W1 ∧ W2 ∧ ... ∧ Wn is in *conjunctive normal form,* e.g. (¬P ∨ Q) ∧ (P ∨ ¬Q ∨ R) ∧ ¬R is in CNF

2.9.2 Disjunctive Normal Form (DNF)

If W1, W2, ..., Wn each possibly consisting of conjunction of literals, then we say W1 ∧ W2 ∨ ... ∨ Wn is in *disjunctive normal form,* e.g. (¬P ∧ Q) ∨ (P ∧ ¬Q ∧ R) ∨ ¬R is in DNF.

Note: Any wff can be transformed into either normal form.

e.g. consider (P ∧ Q) ∨ (R ∧ S) is in DNF and can be transformed into CNF using the equivalent logical expressions as follows:

((P ∧ Q) ∨ R) ∧ (P ∧ Q) ∨ S)
((P ∨ R) ∧ (Q ∨ R)) ∧ ((P ∨ S) ∧ (Q ∨ S))
(P ∨ R) ∧ (Q ∨ R) ∧ (P ∨ S) ∧ (Q ∨ S)

2.9.3 Prenex Normal Form

A wff is said to be *prenex normal form,* iff that formula is of the form Qixi M, where Qi is any quantifier and M is a quantifier free formula. Here Qixi is called the *prefix* and M is called *matrix* of the formula.

Deduction Theorem: Given formulas W1, W2, ..., Wn and a formula G, G is a logical consequence of W1, W2, ..., Wn if and only if the formula ((W1 ∧ W2 ∧ ... ∧ Wn) ∧ →G) is valid.

Theorem: Given formulas W1, W2, ..., Wn and a formula G, G is a logical consequence of W1, W2, ... Wn if and only if the formula (W1 ∧ W2 ∧ ... ∧ Wn ∧ ¬G) is inconsistent.

Definitions:

Definite clauses (Horn clauses): A clause contains exactly one +ve and zero or more –ve literals.

Positive unit clause: A definite clause containing no –ve literals.

Negative unit clause: A negative clause with exactly one literal.

Negative clause: A clause with zero or more negative literals and no +ve literal.

Unit clause: Is either +ve or –ve unit clause.

Empty clause: Negative clause with no literal.

Indefinite clauses (Non-horn clauses): Clauses containing at least two +ve literals and zero or more –ve literals.

2.10 RULES OF INFERENCE

In predicate calculus, there are rules of inference, that can be applied to certain wff and set of wffs to produce new wffs. Those rules are:

1. ***Modus ponens.*** This is the operation which produces the wff W2 from the wffs

   W1 and
   W1 → W2

2. ***Modus tollens.*** This is the operation which produces ¬W1 from

   ¬W2 and
   W1 → W2

3. ***Universal specialization.*** This produces W(A) from the wff ∀xW(x), where A is a constant symbol.
   Using the above rules, we can produce W2(A) from wffs

   W1(A) and
   ∀x W1(x) → W2(x)

   For example, consider the assertion "Leo is a lion" and implication "All lions are ferocious", we can derive the conclusion "Leo is ferocious".

   W1 : LION (leo)
   W2 : ∀x LION(x) → FEROCIOUS(x)
   FEROCIOUS(leo)

   From W1 and W2, we have to show that FEROCIOUS(leo) is a logical consequence of W1 and W2.

   W1 ∧ W2 : LION(leo) ∧ (∀x LION(x) → FEROCIOUS(x))

   Since W1 and W2 are *true*, and LION(x) → FEROCIOUS(x) is *true* for all x, we can replace x by leo. So W2 will be ¬LION(leo) ∨ FEROCIOUS(leo), but ¬LION(leo) is *false*, so FEROCIOUS(leo) is *true*.

4. ***Chain rule.*** This is the operation which produces P → R from the wffs P → Q and Q → R.

Inference rules produce derived wffs from existing ones in predicate calculus. These derived wffs are called theorems and the sequence of inference rules application constitutes the proof of the theorem.

2.10.1 Substitution

In the previous example, for concluding FEROCIOUS(leo), substitution of x was necessary. Substitutions are essential parts of inference process.

Definition: *A substitution is defined as a set of pairs ti and vi where vi are distinct variables and ti are terms.*

The ti are substituted for the corresponding vi in the expression. These are represented by Greek letters α, β, γ, ...

i.e. $a = \{t_1/v_1, t_2/v_2, ..., t_n/v_n\}$

where $n \geq 1$.

For example, if C = P (x, y) ∨ Q(x, f(y)) and β = {a/x, g(b)/y} then after applying β to C we obtain C′ = Cβ = P(a, g(b)) → Q(a, f(g(b))).

A substitution instance of an expression is obtained by substituting terms for variables in that expression.

For example, instances of W = P(x, f(y), b) are:

W {z/x, w/y} = P(z, f(w), b) (Alphabetical variant)
W {a/y} = P(x, f(a), b)
W {g(z)/x, a/y} = P(g (z), f(a), b)
W {c/x, a/y } = P(c, f(a), b) (Ground instance)

2.10.2 Composition of Substitutions

Composition of two substitutions α and β is denoted by αβ which is obtained by applying β to the terms of α and adding pairs of β having variables not occuring in α.

e.g.:
α = {g(x, y)/z}
β = {a/x, b/y, c/w, d/z} then
αβ = {g(a, b)/z, a/x, b/y, c/w}

Note: It can be shown that

(E α)β = E (αβ) where E is an expression and
(αβ)βα

that is composition is associative but not commutative.

2.11 UNIFICATION

Any substitution that makes two or more expressions equal is called the *unifier* for the expressions. We say that a set of expressions $\{E_i\}$ is *unifiable*, if there exists a substitution 'a' such that

E1a = E2α = ..., where a is called the unifier of the set $\{E_i\}$.

EXAMPLE. α = {a/x, b/y} unifies the set {P(x, f(y), b), P(x, f(b), b)} to yield {P(a, f(b), b)}. Here we say α is the most general unifier (MGU) of the set if any other unifier is an instance of α.

There are many algorithms to unify a set of unifiable expressions, which reports failure when the set cannot be unified. The recursive procedure given below can be used to unify a set of two unifiable procedures.

Procedure UNIFY (E1, E2)

IF either E1 or E2 is an atom (i.e. a predicate symbol, a function symbol, a constant symbol, negation symbol or a variable), interchange the arguments so that El is an atom, and DO

```
BEGIN
   IF E1 and E2 are identical THEN return NIL
   IF E1 is a variable DO
   BEGIN
      IF E1 occurs in E2, return FALL
      Return (E2/E1)
   END
   IF E2 is a variable, return (E1/E2)
   Return FAIL
END
F1 := First element of El, T1 := Rest of El
F2 := First element of E2, T2 := Rest of E2
Z1 := UNIFY (F1, F2)
IF Z1 == FAIL, return FAIL
Gl := Result of applying Z1  to T1
G2 := Result of applying Z1  to T2
Z2 := UNIFY (G1, G2)
IF Z2 == FAIL, return FAIL
return the composition of Z1 and Z2
```

For example, if we we are unifying {P(x, f(y), b), P(x, f(a), b)} using the above procedure will return the unifier set {a/y}.

Consider the statement in the previous algorithm

IF E1 occurs in E2, return FAIL

This test is called *occur-check* and its purpose is to disallow self-referential bindings such as X/f(X). If we are not taking care of this self-referential binding, it leads to infinite loop and system crash.

We are using unification to discover if one literal can match another one. There may be variables in both literals and these variables may have terms substituted for them which would make literals identical.

2.12 RESOLUTION

Resolution is an important rule of inference, that can be applied to a set of clauses. This method was developed by J. A. Robinson in 1965. For applying resolution, we have to convert all the wffs to clausal form. The conversion procedure is given below:

1. ***Eliminate all implication symbols.***
   A → B with ¬A ∨ B and
   A ↔ B with (¬A ∨ B) ∧ (¬B ∨ A)
2. ***Reduce the scope of negation.*** (Using D'Morgan's law and other equivalences).
   Aim is to apply each negation symbol to atmost one atomic formula.

3. ***Standardize variables.*** Within the scope of a quantifier a variable bound by quantifier is a dummy variable. It can be replaced by any other variable, which has not occured anywhere else throughout the scope of the quantifier without changing the truth value of the wff.

   This is to ensure that each quantifier has its own unique dummy variable. e.g. $\forall x\ P(x) \rightarrow \exists x\ Q(x)$ can be writtten as $\forall x\ P(x) \rightarrow \exists y\ Q(y)$.
4. ***Eliminate existential quantifier.*** This is to replace each occurrence of existentially quantified variables by a Skolem function whose arguments are those universally quantified variables, whose scope includes the scope of the existential quantifier.

   For example, consider the wff, $\forall x\ (\exists y\ P(x, y))$; here existence of y depends on the value of x, which is explicitly defined by some function g(x), which maps each x into y. Thus we can replace y with g(x) in the previous wff, which will become $\forall x\ P(x, g(y))$. (This process is called Skolemization).

   Note: Skolem function symbol used must be unique. If E is not within the scope of some A, we will get Skolem function with no arguments (i.e. a constant).
5. ***Convert to prenix form.*** In this stage there are no E and each A has its own variable. So we can move A to the beginning.
6. ***Convert to CNF.***
7. ***Eliminate.*** In this stage all the variables we are using are universally quantified. So we can eliminate the explicit occurrence of A. Now we are left with a matrix in CNF form.
8. ***Eliminate $\wedge$ symbols.*** It is done by writing down the expression of the form ($W1 \wedge W2 \wedge \ldots \wedge Wn$) as $\{W1, W2, \ldots, Wn\}$. Here each Wi, $i = 1, 2, \ldots, n$ will be a disjunction of literals.
9. ***Rename variables.*** Variable symbol may be renamed so that no variable symbol appears more than one clause.

   e.g.: $S = \forall x\ \{P(x) \rightarrow \{\forall y[P(y) \rightarrow P(f(x,y))] \wedge \neg(\forall y)\ [Q(x,y) \rightarrow P(y))]\}\}$

1. $\forall x\ \{\neg P(x) \vee \{\forall y[\neg P(y) \vee P(f(x,y))] \wedge \neg(\forall y)[\neg Q(x,y) — P(y)]\}\}$
2. $\forall x\ \{\neg P(x) \vee \{\forall y[\neg P(y) \vee P(f(x,y))] \wedge \exists y[Q(x,y) \wedge \neg P(y)]\}\}$
   (By using $\neg(\forall x)P(x) = \exists x\ (\neg P(x)$ and D'Morgan's Law)
3. $\forall x\ \{\neg P(x) \vee \{\forall y[\neg P(y) \vee P(f(x,y))] \wedge \exists w[Q(x,w) \wedge \neg P(w))]\}\}$
4. $\forall x\ \{\neg P(x) \vee \{\forall y[\neg P(y) \vee P(f(x,y))] \wedge [Q(x, g(x)) \wedge \neg P(g(x))]\}\}$
5. $\forall x \forall y\ \{\neg P(x) \vee \{[\neg P(y) \vee P(f(x,y))] \wedge [Q(x,g(x)) \wedge \neg P(g(x))]\}\}$
6. $\forall x \forall y\ \{[\neg P(x) \vee \neg P(y) \vee P(f(x,y))] \wedge [\neg P(x) \vee Q(x,g))] \wedge [\neg P(x) \vee \neg P(g(x))]\}$
7. $\{[\neg P(x) \vee P(y) \vee P(f(x,y))] \wedge [\neg P(x) \vee Q(x,g(x))] \wedge [\neg P(x) \vee \neg P(g(x))]\}$
8. $\{\neg P(x) \vee \neg P(y) \vee P(f(x,y)),$
   $\neg P(x) \vee Q(x,g)),$
   $\neg P(x) \vee \neg P(g(x))\}$
9. $\{\neg p(x1) \vee \neg P(y) \vee P(f(x1,y)),$
   $\neg P(x2) \vee Q(x2,g(x2)),$
   $\neg P(x3) \vee \neg P(g(x3))\}$

Theorem: If a formula X logically follows a set of wffs, S, then it also logically follows from a set of clauses by converting the wffs in S to clausal form.

2.12.1 Resolution of Ground Clauses

Suppose we have two ground clauses P1 ∨ P2 ∨ ... Pn and Q1 ∨ Q2 ∨ ... ∨ Qn, we assume that Pi and Qj are distinct and one of the literal in one clause contains exact negation of one of the literal in the other clause. Here resolvant is computed by taking the disjunction of the two clauses and eliminating the complementary pairs P1 and ¬P1

Some special cases of resolution are:

Parent clause	Resolvants	
P and ¬P ∨ Q	Q	(Modus ponen)
P ∨ Q and ¬P ∨ Q	Q	(Q and Q collapses to Q)
P ∨ Q and ¬P ∨ ¬Q	P ∨ ¬P, Q ∨ ¬Q	(both are tautologies)
¬P and P	NIL (empty clause)	(sign of contradiction)
¬P ∨ Q and ¬Q ∨ R	¬P ∨ R	(Chain rule)

2.12.2 General Resolution

Here each clause is considered as a set of literals with disjunction between them. Let the corresponding parent clauses be given by $\{L_i\}$ and $\{M_j\}$. Suppose $\{l_i\}$ is a subset of $\{L_i\}$ and $\{m_j\}$ is a subset of $\{M_j\}$ such that there exists MGUs for the union of the sets $\{l_i\}$ and $\{\neg m_j\}$. We say $\{L_i\}$ and $\{M_j\}$ resolve and give $\{\{L_i\} - \{l_i\}\}s \cup \{\{M_j\} - \{m_j\}\}s$ as the resolvant.

For example, consider the clauses

$$P(x, f(a)) \vee P(x, f(y)) \vee Q(y) \text{ and}$$

$$\neg P(z, f(a)) \vee Q(z)$$

With $l_i = P(x, f(a))$ and $m_i = \neg P(z, f(a))$
we will get the resolvant $P(z, f(y)) \vee \neg Q(y) \vee Q(y)$.

With $l_i = P(x, f(a)), P(x, f(y))$ and $m_i = \neg P(z, f(a))$,
we will get the resolvant as $Q(a) \vee \neg Q(z)$.

2.12.3 Completeness Theorem of Resolution

If resolution is applied repeatedly to a set of unsatisfiable clauses, eventually empty clause will be produced.

2.12.4 Resolution Theorem of Resolution

Resolution based or theorem proving systems are designed to produce proof by contradiction or refutation. In resolution refutation, we first negate the goal wff and add that negation to the set of statements. These statements then converted to the set of clauses and using resolution we will derive a contradiction represented by an empty clause NIL.

Proof: Suppose a wff W logically follows a set S of wffs, so by definition every interpretation satisfies S also satisfying W.

Therefore none of the interpretations satisfying S can satisfy ¬W.

i.e. No interpretation can satisfy the union of S and ¬W.

Therefore if W logically follows S, then SU¬W is unsatisfiable.

By the completeness theorem, SU¬W is unsatisfiable, then resolution will produce and empty clause NIL.

e.g.: Consider the statements

"Whoever can read is literate"

$$\forall x\ R(x) \rightarrow L(x) \tag{1}$$

"Monkeys are not literate"

$$\forall x\ M(x) \rightarrow \neg L(x) \tag{2}$$

"Some monkeys are intelligent"

$$\exists x\ (M(x) \wedge I(x)) \tag{3}$$

From these statements suppose we want to prove

"Some who are intelligent cannot read"

$$\exists x\ (I(x) \wedge \neg R(x)) \tag{4}$$

We have to add negation of (4) to (1), (2), and (3) and resolve it after clausal conversion. After clausal conversion, these wffs will be

$$\neg R(x) \vee L(x) \tag{1'}$$

$$\neg M(y) \vee L(x) \tag{2'}$$

$$M(a) \tag{3a}$$

$$I(a) \tag{3b}$$

$$\neg I(x) \vee R(z) \tag{4}$$

Resolving (4) and (3b) we will get

$$R(a) \tag{5}$$

Resolving (5) and (1) we will get

$$L(a) \tag{6}$$

Resolving (6) and (2) we get

$$\neg M(a) \tag{7}$$

Resolving (7) and (3b) we get [ ] or NIL representing empty clause.

2.12.5 Control Strategies for Resolution Methods

Several strategies exists for the selection of two clauses from the set of clauses for the resolution.

Breadth First Strategy

Here all the first level resolvants are computed and then second level and so on. First level resolvant is the resolvant of two clauses in the base set.

Set_of_support Strategy

Here at least one parent of each resolvant is selected among the clauses resulting from the negation of the goal wff or their descendants.

Unit Preference Strategy

It is a modification of the set_of_support strategy in which instead of filling each level in breadth first fashion, we try to select a single literal clause (unit) as one of the parent clause.

Linear Input Form Strategy

Linear input refutation is one in which resolvant has at least one parent belonging to the base set. There are cases in which refutation exists but linear input form refutation does not. This strategy is used because of its simplicity and efficiency.

SLD Resolution

This is the strategy used in PROLOG. SLD stands for Selection rule driven Linear resolution for Definite clauses.

In this case we will start the resolution with the goal clause. Here resolution step uses the most reset resolvant as one of the parent and uses other parent either from the base set (input clauses) or some earlier resolvant (Linear). Selection of literals in this case is from left to right for the resolution.

e.g.: Consider the statements

"Some patients like all doctors."
"No patient like a quack."

From these statements we can prove

"No doctor is a quack."

2.13 RULE-BASED EXPERT SYSTEMS

Rule-based expert systems depend upon a precise set of rules that logically model a situation for making deductions and abductions. They contain the components shown in Table 2.3.

Table 2.3 Components of Rule-based Expert Systems

Component	*Properties, functions*
Knowledge Base	Contains rules, permanent facts (true propositions).
Working Memory	Used for intermediate results, new facts, goals, etc.
Inference Engine	Checks left-hand sides against true propositions in working memory, fires rules, makes lists and data structures.
Explainer	Provide explanation to the user as to why certain facts are true, what implications are made, etc.

Some strategies that are helpful in building rule-based expert systems are given below:

- Once a rule fires, eliminate it so that it does not fire again (the right-hand side is already true).
- Schedule the rules that are more general earlier than those that are more specific (A && B && C → Q is more general than A && B && C && D → Q)
- Put more important rules higher in the ordering of rules, if known.
- Decompose the rule base into disjoint sets when possible, or break into two or more sets that join together farther to the right (we start on the left with the first antecedents).
- Validation of the system can be done by giving the system and an expert the same set of test problems to solve, then comparing the results.

2.14 THE PROLOG LANGUAGE

We have now covered enough logic to be able to relate the programming language PROLOG to logic. A program in PROLOG is essentially a set of Horn clauses. Programs are executed by issuing an initial query, and then resolving using SLD resolution with the left-to-right selection rule. The conventional notation for PROLOG is slightly different from that we have used in this explanation using logic. PROLOG distinguishes between variables and constants by starting variables with upper case letters and constants with lower case letters. Lower case letters are also used for predicate names. The symbol : $\vee$ is used for logic $\neg$, and commas are used in the place of the $\wedge$ symbols to the right-hand side of the $\neg$. PROLOG clauses are ended with a full stop.

In general PROLOG does not use the occur check in unifications. It also has some additional "extralogical" constructs. Apart from that, it can be seen that executing a program in PROLOG is just a form of proving the initial call true as a fact in logic (with the condition, if necessary, that variables in it are bound to values determined by unification), with the PROLOG program being just a logical description of relationships we hold to be true.

The ability to reuse clauses means that recursion is available in PROLOG, and in fact recursion gives it much of its power, and takes the place of the iterative loops in imperative languages. In this way it is similar to the functional languages like Miranda. Both the functional languages and the logic languages are known as *declarative languages*. This is because programming in them is supposed to consist of declaring logical or functional relationships from the problem, rather than thinking in terms of what the machine is actually doing and issuing it "orders". In fact the goal of pure declarative programming is freeing the programmer from having to think in low-level machine terms at all. It is often let down, however, by the need to have non-declarative primitives for such things as input-output, or by having to consider various problems in the order of computation in declarative languages, such as the problem in PROLOG of getting caught in an infinite search tree.

In the functional programming paradigm there are many programming languages built around the abstract functional model. You have seen Miranda, ML is another example, but the most famous (and oldest) functional language is LISP, which is used in a lot of AI work in the USA. LISP has some disadvantages since it was first developed before functional languages were properly understood, but as it is often the case in computing, it has had the benefit of being the first established and thus difficult to displace. The same sort of comment could be made about PROLOG. There have been many suggestions for languages which like PROLOG are built on the model of being based on logical deduction using resolution, and which improve on PROLOG in some way. None of them however, has achieved any widespread use. We will leave further discussion of PROLOG to separate appendix in this text.

EXERCISES

1. (a) Use a truth table to show that, in propositional logic, $P \rightarrow Q$ can be rewritten as $\neg P \vee Q$.

(b) Why is this a useful rewrite rule for using the resolution rule of deduction?

2. (a) Translate the following sentences into first order logic:

(i) All dogs are mammals.
(ii) Fido is a dog.
(iii) Fido is a mammal.
(iv) All mammals produce milk.

(b) Use the modus ponens deduction rule to deduce sentence (iii) from (i) and (ii). What did you unify in order to use modus ponens, and what substitution made the unification possible?

(c) Write the sentences as PROLOG style Horn clauses.

3. (a) Write the answers from 2(a) in conjunctive normal form.
(b) Translate the following sentence into CNF:

"There exists a dog which doesn't produce milk."

(c) Explain why this new sentence contradicts sentences (i) to (iv) from question 2.

4. (a) Write down a substitution which unifies the following sentences:

(i) likes(homer, dinner(X)) $\wedge$ (today(A) $\rightarrow$ dinner(X)).
(ii) likes(homer, dinner(cooked_by(Y))) $\wedge$ (today(Z) $\rightarrow$ dinner(cooked_by (marge))).

[Universal quantification of variables is assumed].

(b) What are the compound operators in sentence (ii) from 4(a)? For each operator O, write down the results of the function args(O) and the result of the function op(X).

(c) Explain why these two sentences cannot be unified:

(i) p(X) $\vee$ (q(f(X)) $\wedge$ r(Y)).
(ii) p(X) $\vee$ (q(X) $\wedge$ r(s)).

5. Rewrite the following propositional sentence to be in conjunctive normal form:

$$(P \rightarrow Q) \vee \neg(Q \vee \neg R)$$

6. (a) Translate the following sentences into first order logic:

(i) All dogs are mammals.
(ii) Fido is a dog.
(iii) Fido is a mammal.
(iv) All mammals produce milk.
(v) There is a dog which doesn't produce milk.

(b) Using your translated sentences and the generalized resolution rule of inference, resolve sentences (i) and (iv) to deduce something new about dogs.
(c) Resolve your answer from (i) with sentence (ii) to deduce something new about fido.
(d) Take sentences (i), (ii), (iii) and (v) as axioms about the world and show they are inconsistent with sentence (iv). Do this by drawing a resolution proof tree. You will have to search for the correct resolution steps at each stage to carry out.
(e) Which steps in your proof are unit resolution steps?

7. Suppose you are trying to work out why certain exams will be difficult and others will be easy. You have compiled this table based on past experience:

Exam	*Use calculator*	*Duration (hrs)*	*Lecturer*	*Term*	*Difficulty*
1	yes	3	Jones	summer	easy
2	yes	3	Jones	spring	difficult
3	no	3	Ramesh	spring	difficult
4	no	2	Armstrong	summer	easy
5	yes	2	Jones	summer	easy

Suppose you set this as a machine learning problem to a learning agent. You specify that the positives are the exams which are difficult.

(a) Which would be the most specific hypothesis that the agent would initially construct?

(b) How would the agent generalize this hypothesis in light of the second positive example? What other possible generalizations are there?

(c) How would you use the two hypotheses (from parts 7(a) and 7(b) to predict whether an exam will be difficult?

(d) What score would the two hypotheses get in terms of predictive accuracy over the training set, and which one would be chosen as the learned hypothesis?

8. Express following sentences by the propositional calculus:

(i) This information in not good.
(ii) His car is red or brown.
(iii) Jane will catch the train only if she hurry.
(iv) If he was there, then he must have heard it.
(v) If Peter is in the forest, then Tom must be in the forest as well.
(vi) They will visit us if they are free.

9. Find the CNF for logical function f, given by the truth table:

P	*Q*	*R*	*f*
1	1	1	1
1	1	0	1
1	0	1	0
1	0	0	0
0	1	1	1
0	1	0	1
0	0	1	0
0	0	0	1

10. Translate the following statements into predicate logic with specified number of predicates:

(i) Every boy uses some bicycle and at least one bicycle is used by every boy.

(ii) Every year some male students fail every exam but every female student passes some exam.
(iii) Every man loves some woman who loves another man.
(iv) No two philosophers have the same favourite book.

11. Set up a small rule-based system to advise graduates as to what courses they need to take to satisfy the requirements for an MSc in CS (or to satisfy the requirements for a B.Tech in Computer Engineering). It will be necessary to consult an expert advisor to get all requirements. Use C, C++ or Java as the programming language. Include explanations for the user.

CHAPTER 3

Knowledge Acquisition and Representation

3.1 INTRODUCTION

It is difficult to discuss the workings of even relatively simple machines, such as washing machines, or sewing machines, unless we understand the functions they were designed to perform. Since artificial intelligence is concerned with the most complex kind of machines we can imagine, 'intelligent machines', perhaps we should try to define what we expect such machines to do. Obviously, we expect them to be intelligent. But what do we mean by intelligence? The dictionary gives the following definition:

Intelligence: The faculty of understanding.

Also

Understanding: To comprehend something, or to recognize its significance.

This is a concept that seems clear enough. When we apply it subjectively, it seems to correspond almost accurately to our own individual experience of what it is like to be intelligent or to use our intelligence. Unfortunately it begins to fall apart when we try to apply it objectively, to consider intelligence as a faculty which might be shared by other entities, whether living or mechanical.

The main problem is that we know what it feels like to understand something, and are generally willing to credit other people/things with sensations similar to our own. Take a simple example, a familiar piece of machinery, the thermostat in a central heating system. It does not just recognize when the temperature falls below or rises above a certain level, it responds by taking the appropriate action. In a single very limited respect, it seems to possess understanding and to demonstrate this in the clearest possible fashion, by behaving intelligently. If the thermostat is intelligent, we devalue the word to the point where it becomes meaningless.

General intelligence has turned out to be a concept of dubious value when applied in practice, and the whole question of using IQ tests to measure people's worth or suitability for a job has become extremely controversial. So should we break intelligence down into separate faculties such as perception, reason, creativity? If so, what is the difference between intelligence and knowledge?

One of the few hard and fast results to come out of the first three decades of AI research is that "intelligence requires knowledge". To compensate for its one overpowering asset, indispensability, knowledge possesses some less desirable properties, which includes the followings:

- It is voluminous
- It is hard to characterize accurately.
- It is constantly changing.
- It differs from data by being organized.

There are many different ways of categorizing knowledge types, one of the main distinctions is the difference between *induced knowledge* and *deduced knowledge.* This is best explained by means of an example.

Consider a commonplace skill which most children master between the ages of five and ten—catching a ball. At the age of five a child may have difficulty in catching a beach ball gently tossed at a few yards, yet a few years later he/she will probably be able to catch a tennis ball lobbed high in the air from twenty yards away. Human beings are not capable of mastering the technique for calculating ballistic trajectories at such an impressively early age. The child's understanding has been gained by induction. It is as a result of watching the trajectories of many balls and trying to catch them, that the child has been capable of predicting the trajectory of the next ball he/she wants to catch.

A computer system on the other hand would rely on information on the projectile velocity and trajectory to calculate the future location of a projectile using Newton's laws. This would be dependent on a rigorous and mathematically explicit set formula programmed into the computer. The program enables the computer to deduce the flight path of a projectile by reference to the set of formal mathematical rules.

Few people would dispute the proposition that calculating a ballistic trajectory mathematically requires more intelligence than being able to catch a ball.

So there is an important distinction to be made between knowledge and intelligence. It should also be clear that a machine may store knowledge without necessarily possessing intelligence; an intelligent machine that had no knowledge is impossibility. The question of how, to what extent, and in what sense can a machine be imbued with knowledge is thus fundamental to all aspects of artificial intelligence.

3.2 MACHINE INTELLIGENCE

Rather than becoming bogged down in the controversies which surround the nature of human intelligence, the practitioners of artificial intelligence have chosen to define their own goals, apart from the theoretical ones. They suggest that an intelligent machine is one that is able to do things which, if done by a human, would be judged to require intelligence. Thus the definition of intelligence becomes unnecessary. This seems very practical. If we can't define what intelligence is, we can recognize when people are being intelligent.

Unfortunately, this argument is easily beaten. To the proposition that people need intelligence to perform a function, then a machine which duplicates this is intelligent, sceptics respond that once a machine can do something then the task has been proved to be mechanical. If we can explain how the machine works we have explained away its intelligence.

Even if we admit that a machine is behaving intelligently, may it not be that the intelligence we see is a property of the people who programmed the computer and not of the machine itself? Also, can a distinction be drawn between intelligent behaviour and behaviour which merely appears to be intelligent?

Naturally, since we do not know what goes on in our heads, acceptance of this argument implies that our own intelligence may be in some fashion illusory—perhaps we only think we are intelligent. In the case of a machine we can establish the nature of the internal processes. If a machine and person display similar behaviour, are the internal processes in some way comparable?

If knowledge amounted to no more than an accumulation of data, even a comparatively modest computer would be rated more highly than the most intelligent human beings. It is indisputable that, in terms of sheer capacity computer memories have far outstripped our own. This is precisely why computers are so useful, within microseconds they can tell a booking clerk whether there is a seat left on tomorrow's flight to Los Angeles. The enormous memory is only accessible because there is a human being operating the terminal, asking exactly the right questions, in exactly the right way and in exactly the right order.

Key issues confronting the designer of an AI system are:

- knowledge acquisition
- knowledge representation
- knowledge manipulation

Knowledge manipulation occurs primarily through inference and deduction and the often search-oriented control strategy or inference engine (which determines the items of knowledge to be accessed, the deductions to be made, and order of steps to be used).

What is knowledge acquisition? Knowledge acquisition has been defined as:

> the transfer and transformation of potential problem-solving expertise from some knowledge source to a program
>
> — Buchanan et al. 1983

The knowledge acquisition process can also be defined as the task of identifying and eliciting relevant domain knowledge in sufficient quantities to provide the power to solve complex problems. The process often referred to as expertise transfer involves the extraction of knowledge from a variety of sources and its representation in a suitable format.

3.3 KNOWLEDGE ENGINEERING

The field of knowledge-engineering can be defined as the process of assessing problems, acquiring knowledge and building knowledge-based systems (Harmon and King, 1985).

Conventional computer systems are traditionally planned and designed by a system analyst. The analyst provides the link between the user who has little or no knowledge of the technical details of hardware and software, and the programmer who has little idea about the specific problems and demands of the user.

Knowledge-based systems (Figure 3.1) require a similar approach although there is one major difference. Systems analysts design computer systems which carry out specific procedures. Knowledge-based development however involves the incorporation of expert knowledge into a system. For this reason system development has traditionally been undertaken by a knowledge engineer (Adeli, 1988). A knowledge engineer is analogous to the systems analyst but is much more concerned with the thought processes of the expert.

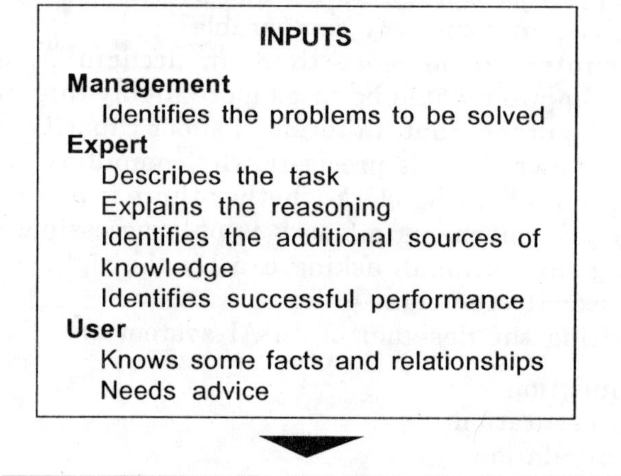

INPUTS

Management
- Identifies the problems to be solved

Expert
- Describes the task
- Explains the reasoning
- Identifies the additional sources of knowledge
- Identifies successful performance

User
- Knows some facts and relationships
- Needs advice

▼

KNOWLEDGE ENGINEER

Knows the strengths and weakness of the tools
Learns about the task from management, experts and users
May provide expertise from own experience and knowledge.

▼

OUTPUTS

Choosing a good domain and task
Analyzing representation and control strategies
Building a prototype system
Expanding the prototype
Fielding the system
Maintaning the system

Figure 3.1 Knowledge-based system.

Hart (1986) suggests that the knowledge engineer should never be the expert providing the knowledge. This is based on the assumption that he/she will usually have insufficient knowledge about programming and knowledge-based system techniques, and will find it difficult to describe their knowledge completely and correctly.

This viewpoint can be contested on the grounds that such a philosophy does not consider the disadvantages of such an approach. A knowledge engineer must become familiar with the knowledge domain under examination, something which is often not easily achieved. This is particularly the case for engineering knowledge domains. Adeli (1988) believes that in the future engineering knowledge-based systems will be developed by engineers knowledgeable in their domain, particularly as more engineers are introduced to, and learn about, AI tools and techniques.

3.4 PROCEDURE FOR KNOWLEDGE ACQUISITION

Initially the knowledge domain (Figure 3.2) must be clearly identified to ensure the development of a tightly focussed system. This is achieved by a careful examination

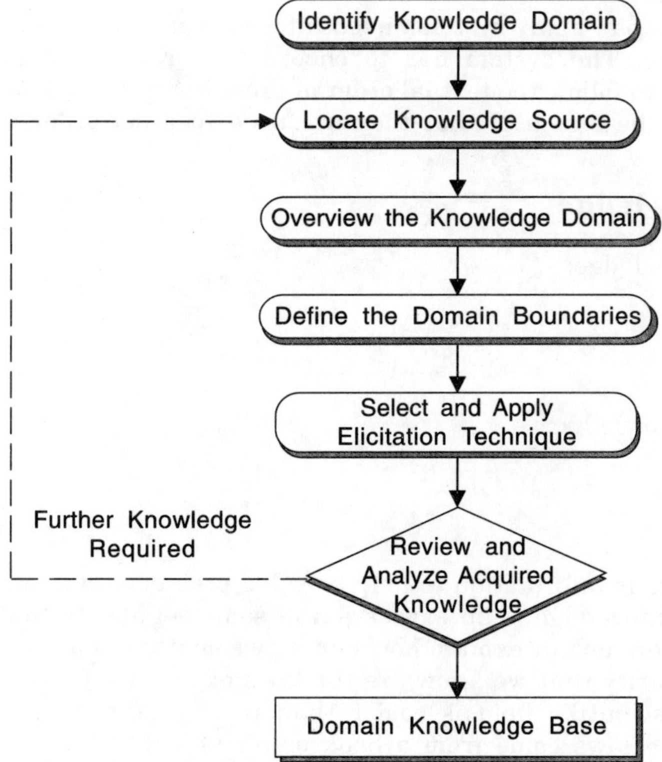

Figure 3.2 Procedure for knowledge acquisition.

of the proposed system goals. Sources of relevant domain knowledge could then be located for subsequent analysis and extraction. Prior to the definition of the domain boundaries it is advisable to overview the subject matter. This provides an insight and structure for subsequent work and highlights any potential problems. The definition of the domain boundaries ensures that during the elicitation process there are no major omissions or wasted effort gathering unwanted information.The selection of a suitable elicitation technique follows with the chosen method applied to abstract the required information. A variety of techniques are available.

Once knowledge is identified and acquired, the final task in the process is to ensure that it is sound, reliable and concentrated into a suitable format. The wealth of knowledge that contributes to the domain under investigation must be comprehensible and unambiguous.

Elicitation delivers single items of knowledge that need to be organized into a unified whole. How much organizing is needed depends very much on the way in which the knowledge base is implemented and used. Some implementations require items to be arranged in groups and sequences, where the arrangement displays relationships between items in the knowledge base. Their order could be used, for example, to determine the sequence in which various items are used—an important decision that the system has to make if several items could be validly used at a certain point of consultation.

To quote a concrete example, many systems need information about the client or patient: name, age, sex, etc. The system has to choose the order to obtain this information. A simple way is to follow the textual order of these items in the knowledge base. In other cases it may be essential that they are used in a set order.

3.4.1 Sources of Knowledge

Three main sources of knowledge:

- literature
- experts
- examples.

Three different bases of knowledge:

- scientific laws
- experience
- models.

We know that knowledge is information to help us solve problems in a particular domain. The most helpful knowledge is an expression of some regularity that helps us to predict what will happen next or explain how and why something has happened. The strongest laws of regularity that we know are the laws of science. Consequently acquiring knowledge in a scientific field is easier than in any other field, and it matters little whether these laws come from a book or an expert.

In other scientifically weaker domains, the regularities are weaker and often not clearly expressed. We do not speak of laws in gardening or investment advice, nevertheless the expert in these fields is aware of interesting regularities and uses them daily. Here the question of knowledge sources becomes more acute.

In practical fields an expert's experience may not be codified and written down. We need a live expert simply because little is available in written form. The majority of expert system applications have so far been in these areas; they rely on an accumulated wealth of experience but lack scientific formulation. The greatest difficulty in these fields is that the expert may not be able to verbalize the knowledge. This often makes knowledge acquisition a difficult and frustrating task for both the expert and the knowledge engineer.

Knowledge consists of facts, procedures and judgemental rules and is widely disseminated. Human experts, people of proven track record, can provide different types of information. Weiss and Kulikowski (1983) identified these as:

- Personal experience of past problems solved.
- Personal expertise or methods for solving the problems.
- Personal knowledge about the reasons for choosing the methods used.

However, for engineering knowledge-based system applications this approach is insufficient. Few engineering problems are purely heuristic and the following knowledge sources in addition to the human expert must be investigated:

- Expert opinion
- Historic data
- Codes of practice
- Standard engineering procedures
- Experimental data
- Technical literature
  - Textbooks
  - Journals
  - Manuals
  - Manufacturers information
- Established engineering equations.

Knowledge may therefore also be recognized as the steps to follow in solving a problem, use of the right equation and/or data, and the correct use of application programs.

3.4.2 Types of Knowledge

The next question to tackle is just what does knowledge acquisition collect? We are after three different sorts of knowledge.

The first is the simplest, and goes by the name of *perceptual knowledge*. This covers the knowledge of simple facts and relationships like the colour of quartz crystals, the melting point of iron, or the maximum torque of an engine. Strictly speaking expert systems do not need to hold these items, since they could be obtained as answers to questions. But practically any system needs to handle such information.

The next level up we find what most people would consider knowledge: *concepts and relationships*. Here we find scientific laws, such as Newton's equations and Boyle's law. We also find heuristic observations like "fever indicates illness". This is the basis of expert systems.

There is a third and extremely important level. Experts bring to bear on a problem not only their scientific knowledge and their experience, but also knowledge of how to set about a problem, how to go round difficulties, what to do when they get stuck. This could be termed as *strategic knowledge*. The effectiveness of an expert system could well depend on the strategic knowledge.

The three levels indicate not only the power of these items but how difficult they are to get hold of.

3.5 KNOWLEDGE REPRESENTATION

The knowledge representation problem concerns the mismatch between human and computer 'memory', i.e. how to encode knowledge so that it is a faithful reflection of the expert's knowledge and can be manipulated by computer. Psychological research suggests that we do not exhibit the kinds of reasoning behaviour that we associate with deductive or 'theorem proving' systems (Hart, 1985). Humans reason from situations to actions using logical consequences.

To program a computer to solve non-quantitative problems dealing with such intangibles as ideas, concepts, and their relationships, a formalism capable of representing and manipulating these relatively abstract entities must be devised. This requires structuring and processing tools that go beyond the data, text, and numerical manipulation and computation-oriented systems and languages that prevail today. We call these more powerful structures *knowledge bases*, and the manipulative operations on these knowledge bases, *inference engine* programs.

3.5.1 What to Represent?

Let us first consider what kinds of knowledge might need to be represented in AI systems:

Objects. Facts about objects in our world domain, e.g. Guitars have strings, trumpets are brass instruments.

Events. Actions that occur in our world, e.g. Steve Vai played the guitar in Frank Zappa's Band.

Performance. A behaviour like playing the guitar involves knowledge about how to do things.

Meta-knowledge. Knowledge about what we know, e.g. My sister plans a trip. My sister knows that she can read street signs along the way to find out where it is.

Thus in solving problems in AI we must represent knowledge and there are two entities to deal with:

Facts: Truths about the real world and what we represent. This can be regarded as the *knowledge level*.

Representation of the facts: which we manipulate. This can be regarded as the *symbol level* since we usually define the representation in terms of symbols that can be manipulated by programs.

We can structure these entities at two levels:

The knowledge level, at which facts are described.

The symbol level, at which representations of objects are defined in terms of symbols that can be manipulated in programs.

English or natural language is an obvious way of representing and handling facts. Logic enables us to consider the following fact: "spot is a dog as dog(spot)". We could then infer that "all dogs have tails" with dog(x) → hasatail(x).

We can then deduce:

hasatail(spot)

Using an appropriate backward mapping function the English sentence "spot has a tail can be generated".

The available functions are not always one to one but rather are many to many which is a characteristic of English representations. The sentences "all dogs have tails" and "every dog has a tail" both say that each dog has a tail but the first could say that each dog has more than one tail; try substituting teeth for tails. When an AI program manipulates the internal representation of facts these new representations should also be interpretable as new representations of facts.

3.5.2 Using Knowledge

We have briefly mentioned where knowledge is used in AI systems. Let us consider a little further to what applications and how knowledge may be used.

Learning. Means acquiring knowledge. This is more than simply adding new facts to a knowledge base. In this process new knowledge is added to the knowledge base and knowledge previously acquired is refined or improved.

Retrieval. The representation scheme used can have a critical effect on the efficiency of the method. Humans are very good at it.

Reasoning. Infer facts from existing data.

If a system only knows:

Remo is a Jazz musician.

All Jazz musicians can play their instruments well.

If things like "Is Remo a Jazz musician?" or "Can Jazz musicians play their instruments well?" are asked then the answer is readily obtained from the data structures and procedures.

However a question like "Can Remo play his instrument well?" requires reasoning.

The above are all related. For example, it is fairly obvious that learning and reasoning involve retrieval.

3.5.3 Form vs. Content of Knowledge

Consider the case of addition of numbers. It can be performed by storing a look-up table containing the sums of all acceptable input pairs of integers. Alternatively, an electronic counter can be used which can successively be incremented by the two integers to obtain their sum. From a functional or a content standpoint, the two approaches will produce identical answers, but it from a representational standpoint, there are significant differences that influence how efficiently we can perform the given task. The look-up table would be very fast, but it would require a very large memory store if we had to deal with large integers. The electronic counter would be much more efficient in its hardware requirements, but would be much slower in producing the required answers. Thus, the specific structures by which knowledge is characterized, in its encoded form, can have significant effect on its use in solving problems. Further, since no single representation or model can capture all aspects of a real object, an intelligent entity must employ a wide spectrum of representations to deal with the world.

3.5.4 Representing Knowledge

A representation of a situation (or object, or problem) is a translation of the situation into a system consisting of a vocabulary that names things and relations, operations that can be performed on these things, and facts and constraints about these things. The primary distinguishing characteristics of a representation are:

(a) what information is made explicit
(b) how the information is physically encoded.

The purpose of a representation is to simplify the problem of answering a restricted class of questions about the given situation, and thus the selection of the representation must be goal-directed.

At least two distinct representations are required to match the competence of some given computing mechanism to the requirements of solving a real-world problem: the first representation provides efficient symbolic apparatus for answering questions about the given situation, and the second translates the solution techniques of the first into the operations and storage structures inherent in the machine.

Thus we can think of a knowledge base in terms of a mapping between the objects and relations in a problem domain and the computational objects and relations in a program. The results of inferences on the knowledge base should correspond to the results of actions or observations in the world. The computational objects, relations and inferences available to programmers are determined by the knowledge representation language they select. The proper language can help the programmer acquire, organize and debug the knowledge base.

Numerous representation schemes have been proposed and implemented, each having their own strengths and weaknesses. Mylopoulos and Levesque (1954) have classified these into four categories:

(a) Logical representation scheme
(b) Procedural representation scheme

(c) Network representation scheme
(d) Structured represention scheme

Logical Representation Schemes

This class of representations uses expressions in formal logic to represent a knowledge base. Inference rules and proof procedures apply this knowledge to problem instances. First-order predicate calculus is the most widely used logical representation scheme, but it is only one of a number of logical representations (Turner, 1984). PROLOG is an ideal programming language for implementing logical representation schemes.

Procedural Representation Schemes

Procedural schemes represent knowledge as a set of instructions for solving a problem. This contrasts with the declarative representations provided by logic and semantic networks. In a rule-based system, for example, an *if ... then* rule may be interpreted as a procedure for solving a goal in problem domain—to solve the conclusion, solve the premises in order. Production systems are examples of a procedural representation schemes.

Network Representation Schemes

Network representations capture knowledge as a graph in which the nodes represent objects or concepts in the problem domain and the arcs represent relations or associations between them. Examples of network representations include "semantic networks", "conceptual dependencies", and "conceptual graphs".

Structured Representation Schemes

Structured representation languages extend networks by allowing each node to be a complex data structure consisting of named slots with attached values. These values may be simple numeric or symbolic data, pointers to other frames, or even procedures for performing a particular task. Examples of structured representations include "scripts", "frames", and "objects".

3.6 LOGICAL REPRESENTATION SCHEMES

The representation schemes of this class include the propositional and predicate calculus. These are representation languages for A1. Both these types of calculus have been described in the previous chapter.

3.7 PROCEDURAL REPRESENTATION SCHEMES

These representation schemes constitute what are called as the *rule-based expert systems*. An *expert system* is a knowledge-based program that provides "expert quality" solutions to problems in a specific domain.

The simple example (Example 3.1) shown below from a plant knowledge base demonstrates the use of a non-sequential declarative representation.

EXAMPLE 3.1

```
if   light is bright
then best plant is begonia
if   light is dim
then best plant is ivy
if   type of light is sunlight
then light is bright
if   type of light is light bulb
then light is dim
if   location is outdoor
then type of light is sunlight
if   location is indoor
then type of light is light bulb
```

3.8 NETWORK REPRESENTATION SCHEMES

Association theories define the meaning of an object in terms of a network of associations with other objects in a mind or a knowledge base. Although symbols denote objects in a world, this denotation is mediated by our store of knowledge. When we perceive and reason about an object, that perception is first mapped into a concept in our minds. This concept is a part of our entire knowledge of the world and is connected through appropriate relationships to other concepts. These relationships form an understanding of the properties and behaviour of objects such as "snow", for example, through experience we associate the concept "snow" with other concepts such as cold, white, snowman, slippery, and ice. Our understanding of "snow" and the truth of statements like "snow is white" manifests itself out of this network of associations. Here we shall see two types of network representation schemes which are discussed below.

3.8.1 Semantic Networks

Semantic networks are alternative to predicate logic as a form of knowledge representation. The idea is that we can store our knowledge in the form of a graph, with nodes representing objects in the world, and arcs representing relationships between those objects.

Graphs, by providing means of explicit representation of relations using arcs and nodes, have proved to be ideal vehicle for formalizing associationist theories of knowledge. A semantic network represents knowledge as a graph, with the nodes corresponding to facts or concepts and arcs to relations or associations between concepts. Some of the principles of semantic networks (e.g. in Figure 3.3) are as follows:

- Semantic nets describe relationships between things that are represented as nodes.
- The nodes are circles that have names.
- The relationships between nodes are represented by arcs that connect the circles.
- A semantic net can be used to generate structures and objects.
- A semantic net can be used to generate rules for a knowledge base.

The semantic network shown in Figure 3.3. is intended to represent the following data:

Tom is a cat.
Tom caught a bird.
Tom is owned by John.
Tom is ginger in colour.
Cats like cream.
The cat sat on the mat.
A cat is a mammal.
A bird is an animal.
All mammals are animals.
Mammals have fur.

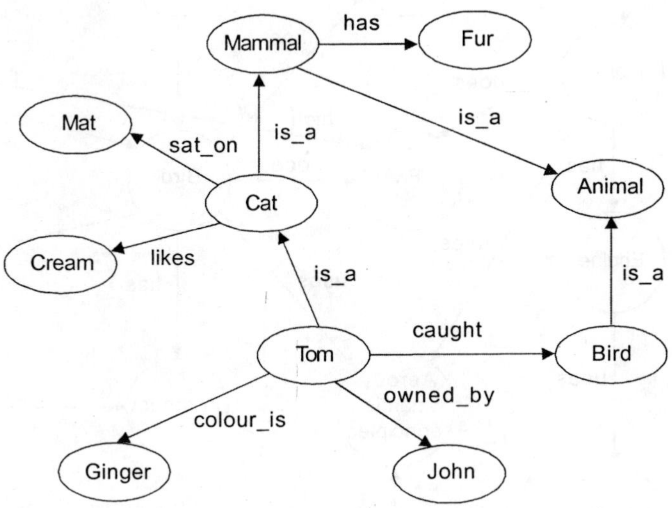

Figure 3.3 A semantic network.

It is argued that this form of representation is closer to the way human's structure knowledge by building mental links between things than the predicate logic we considered earlier.

The is_a link has two different meanings—it can mean that one object is an individual item from a class, for example Tom is a member of the class of cats, or that one class is a subset of another, for example, the class of cats is a subset of the class of mammals. This confusion does not occur in logic.

3.8.2 Conceptual Graphs

A *conceptual graph* is a finite, connected, bipartite graph. The nodes of the graph are either concepts or conceptual relations. Conceptual graphs do not use labelled arcs; instead the conceptual relation nodes represent relation between concepts. Because conceptual graphs are bipartite; concepts can have arcs to conceptual relations and vice versa. Consider the following example:

Here "dog" and "brown" are concept nodes and colour is conceptual relation. To distinguish these types of node concepts are represented as boxes and conceptual relations as ellipses. Figure 3.4 represents a semantic net showing relationships between parts of a bird and a plane.

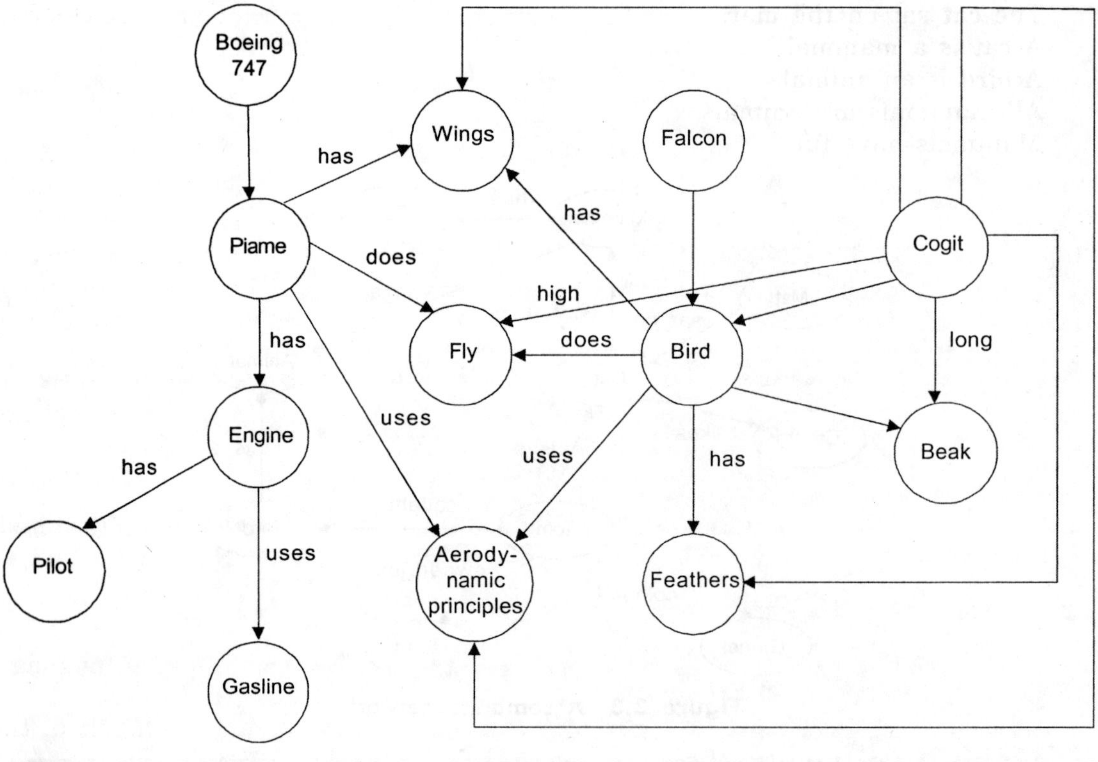

Figure 3.4 Semantic net showing relationships between parts of a bird and a plane.

Features of conceptual graphs:

- Concept nodes represent either concrete or abstract object of the world of discourse.
- Conceptual relation nodes indicate a relation involving one or more concepts.
- Each conceptual graph represents a single proposition. A typical knowledge base will contain a number of such graphs. Graphs may be arbitrarily complex but must be finite.
- The theory of conceptual graphs includes a number of operations that allow us to form new graphs from existing graphs.

Operations on Conceptual Graphs

Operating on conceptual graphs allows us to create a new graph by "specializing" an existing graph. This is done through four operations called copy, restrict, join, and simplify. Assume that g1 and g2 are conceptual graphs. Then:

- The copy rule allows us to form a new graph, G, that is the exact copy of g1.
- Restriction allows concept nodes in a graph to be replaced by a node representing their specialization.
- The join rule allows us to combine two graphs into a single graph.
- If a graph contains two duplicate relations, then one of them may be deleted. This is the simplified rule.

3.8.3 Conceptual Dependency

Roger Schank and his students developed a theory called *conceptual dependency* to try and understand basic story lines with the help of which he claimed that many stories can be represented by just a few concepts. He developed a number of NL systems which would map the English descriptions of the stories into his representation. Different English sentences with the same meaning would be mapped to the same representation.

In conceptual dependency (CD), slot and filler structures are used to represent the kind of knowledge about events that is usually conveyed in natural language sentences. Its goal is to represent knowledge so as to:

- Facilitate drawing inferences from sentences
- Be independent of the language in which the sentences were originally stated.

Conceptual Dependency Theory

- For any two sentences that are identical in meaning, regardless of language, there should be only one representation.
- Any information in a sentence that is implicit must be made explicit in the representation of the meaning of that sentence.

Building Blocks

Conceptual Dependency: 11 primitive acts:

ATRANS: Transfer of an abstract relationship (e.g. give)
PTRANS: Transfer of the physical location of an object (e.g. go)
PROPEL: Application of physical force to an object (e.g. push)
MOVE: Movement of a body part by its owner (e.g. kick)
GRASP: Grasping of an object by an actor (e.g. clutch)
INGEST: Ingestion of an object by an animal (e.g. eat)
EXPEL: Expulsion of something from the body of an animal (e.g. cry)
MTRANS: Transfer of mental information (e.g. tell)
MBUILD: Building new information out of old (e.g. decide)
SPEAK: Production of sounds (e.g. say)
ATTEND: Focusing of a sense organ towards a stimulus (e.g. listen)

Four primitive conceptual categories to build dependency structures:

ACTs: Actions
PPs: Objects (picture producers)
AAs: Modifiers of actions (action aiders)
PAs: Modifiers of PPs (picture aiders)

Dependencies among conceptualizations correspond to semantic relations among underlying concepts.

Advantages of Conceptual Dependency Primitives

Easier to describe the inference rules by which knowledge can be manipulated. Rules can be represented once for each primitive ACT rather than for all words that describe that ACT. e.g. Give, Take, Steal, and Donate all are instances of ATRANS and can make same inferences about who has the object, and who once had the object.

To construct CD representation we make explicit some information that was not stated in the text. e.g. "Gopal took the book from Gita", we make explicit the information that "Gita no longer has the book". This might make it easier to understand subsequent statement, e.g. "Gita had nothing to read".

We shall outline a simplification of one of Schank's systems called (SAM) *Script Applier Mechanism*. This would take a representation of a story and match it to a standard script which could then be used to flesh out the scenario and produce a paraphrase of the situation. So there would be an understanding of the story in terms of the script. They believed that we only need relatively few scripts to understand many human situations. Shank used about eleven basic ACTs to represent meaning. We will just list four of these, simplifying the ideas somewhat:

1. ptrans(Obj1, Obj2, Place1, Place2) change the location of a physical object—Obj1 moves Obj2 from Place1 to Place2.
2. ingest(Actor, Food, Means) take something to the inside of an animate object—Actor ingests Food by method Means.

3. atrans(Actor1, Obj, Actor2, Actor3) change an abstract relationship, such as ownership/possession with respect to an object—Actor1 changes Obj from Actor2's possession to Actor3.
4. mtrans(Actor1, Info, Actor2) transfer information—transfer Info from Actor1 to Actor2.

There are also other concepts besides the ACTs such as Times, Locations and Attributes.

3.9 STRUCTURED REPRESENTATION SCHEMES

How can a computer focus its attention on just those aspects of a given problem that are relevant to the solution? This is the "frame" (invented by Martin Minsky) problem. How can an intelligent system, in trying to solve a problem or carry out an action, know what information in its database should be ignored, and what is relevant to the problem at hand?

Marvin Minsky
One of the founders of AI & inventor of frame structure.

3.9.1 Frames

As tasks became more complex the representation needs to be more structured. The more structured the system it becomes more beneficial to use frames. A *frame* is a collection of attributes or slots and associated values that describe some real-world entities. Frames on their own are not particularly helpful but frame systems are a powerful way of encoding information to support reasoning. Set theory provides a good basis for understanding frame systems.

We view knowledge as organized using network representations, and explicit links or associations between objects in the knowledge base. Alternatively, we can organize knowledge into more complex units that represent complex situations or objects in the domain. These are called *"frames"* or *"schemas"*.

Each individual frame may be seen as a data structure, similar in many respects to the traditional *"record"*, that contains information relevant to stereotyped entities.

The slots in the frame contain information such as:

(a) Frame identification information.
(b) Relationship of this frame to other frames. The "hotel phone" might be a special instance of "phone", which in turn might be an instance of a "communication device".
(c) Descriptors of requirements for frame match. A chair, for instance, has its seat between 20 and 40 cm from the floor, its back higher than 60 cm etc. These requirements may be used to determine when new objects fit the stereotype defined by the frame.
(d) Procedural information on the use of the structure described. An important feature of the frames is the ability to attach procedural code to a slot.
(e) Frame default information. These are slot values that are taken to be true when no evidence to the contrary has been found. For instance, chairs have four legs, telephones have pushbutton, or hotel beds are made by staff.
(f) New instance information. Many frame slots may be left unspecified until given a value for a particular instance or needed for problem solving. For example the colour of the bedspread may be left unspecified in the definition of bed.

Consider the example:

EXAMPLE 3.2

Person is_a: Mammal
Adult-Male is_a: Person
Rugby-Player is_a: Adult-Male
Height:
Weight:
Position:
Team:

Team-Colors:
Back is_a: Rugby-Player
Tries: Mike-Hall
instance: Back
Height: 6–0
Position: Centre
Team: Cardiff-RFC
Team-Colors: Black/Blue
Rugby-Team is_a: Team
Team-size: 15
Coach:

Here the frames *Person, Adult-Male, Rugby-Player and Rugby-Team* are all classes and the frames *Robert-Howley* and *Cardiff-RFC* are instances.

Cardiff-RFC
instance: Rugby-Team
Team-size: 15
Coach: Terry Homes
Players: {Robrt-Howley, Guyn-Jones, ...}

Some important features of frames are:

- Frames extend semantic networks in a number of important ways, the most important being in terms of organization of knowledge into structures which is an important issue of a knowledge base.
- Procedural attachment is a particularly important feature of frames since certain knowledge does not adapt well to declarative representations.
- Representing knowledge with a frame system allows us to reason, at least to some extent, even though the information is incomplete, and it allows us to quickly infer facts that are not explicitly observed.
- One of the problems with frame representation is the difficulty of establishing the default values for a frame accurately.

3.9.2 Scripts

By definition, a *script* is a structured representation describing a stereotype sequence of events in a particular context. The script was originally designed by Schank and his research group (Schank and Abelson, 1977) as a means of organizing conceptual dependency structures into descriptions of typical situations. Scripts are used in natural language understanding systems as a knowledge base in terms of situations that the system is to understand.

The components of a script are:

- *Entry conditions* or descriptors of the world that must be true for the script to be called. In a restaurant script, these include a restaurant that is open and a customer who is hungry.
- *Results* or facts that are true once the script is terminated; for example, the customer is not hungry and has less money. The restaurant owner has more money.
- *Props* or the things that make up the content of the script. These might include tables, waiters, and menus. This allows reasonable default assumptions about the situation, e.g. a restaurant is assumed to have tables and chairs unless stated otherwise.
- *Roles* are the actions that the individual participants perform. The waiter takes orders, delivers food, and presents the bill. The customer orders, eats, and pays the bill.
- Schank breaks the script into a sequence of *scenes,* each of which presents a temporal aspect of the script. In the restaurant there is entering, ordering, eating, etc.

Scripts are useful in describing certain situations such as "robbing a bank". This might involve:

- Getting a gun.
- Hold up a bank.
- Escape with the money.

Here the *Props* might be:

- Gun, G.
- Loot, L.
- Bag, B.
- Get away car, C.

The *Roles* might be:

- Robber, S.
- Cashier, M.
- Bank Manager, O.
- Policeman, P.

The *Entry Conditions* might be:

- S is poor.
- S is destitute.

The *Results* might be:

- S has more money.
- O is angry.
- M is in a state of shock.
- P is shot.

There are 3 scenes: obtaining the gun, robbing the bank, and the get away. The full script could be described as seen in the box.

Some additional points to note on scripts:

- If a particular script is to be applied it must be activated and the activating depends on its significance.
- If a topic is mentioned in passing then a pointer to that script could be held.
- If the topic is important then the script should be opened.
- The danger lies in having too many active scripts much as one might have too many windows open on the screen or too many recursive calls in a program.
- Provided events follow a known trail we can use scripts to represent the actions involved and use them to answer detailed questions.
- Different trails may be allowed for different outcomes of scripts (e.g. The bank robbery goes wrong).

Advantages of Scripts

- Ability to predict events.
- A single coherent interpretation may be built up from a collection of observations.

Disadvantages of Scripts

- Less general than frames.
- May not be suitable to represent all kinds of knowledge.

Here is another example (Example of 3.3) of a script, first in English, and then it is given in the representational form:

Script of a restaurant

1. Customer goes to the restaurant.
2. Customer goes to table.
3. Waiter brings food.
4. Customer eats food.
5. Customer pays waiter.
6. Customer leaves the restaurant.

We now represent the script as a PROLOG assertion script(Name, Script, Defaults) where Name is just the name of the script, Script is a list of relations with free variables describing the script in terms of ACTs, and Defaults is a list of pairs, associating the variables to default names if they are not instantiated by the actual example which matches a subset of the script.

```
script(restaurant,
[ptrans(Actor, Actor, EarlierPlace, Restaurant),
ptrans(Actor, Actor, Door, Table),
ptrans(Waiter, Food, Kitchen, Table),
ingest(Actor, Food, mouth(Actor)),
atrans(Actor, Money, Actor, Waiter),
ptrans(Actor, Actor, Restaurant, ElseWhere)],
[(Actor, customer), (EarlierPlace, place1),
(Restaurant, restaurant), (Door, door),
(Table, table), (Food, meal),
(Waiter, waiter), (Kitchen, kitchen),
(Money, cash), (ElseWhere, place2)]).
```

EXERCISES

1. What do you mean by knowledge representation?
2. What is knowledge acquisition?
3. Discuss different tasks performed by knowledge engineer.
4. Why knowledge acquisition is considered as most difficult step in knowledge engineering?

5. Describe a frame. Give example of frame for kitchen.
6. What is a slot in a frame?
7. Compare knowledge representation to data representation in a database.
8. What are the special features of conceptual dependency?
9. Construct semantic net representations of the following:
   - Gopal is Indian, Gopal is a lecturer.
   - Rajesh lent his new vedio CD to his girlfriend.
10. What programming languages would be suited to implement a semantic network and frames?
11. Devise algorithms that enable reasoning with frames. Discuss how
    - inference through inheritance can be achieved.
    - matching can be achieved.
12. What problems do you envisage a frame based knowledge representation having? Give examples of knowledge hard to represent in a frame. How could such problems be overcome?
13. Describe the following concept as semantic network:

    Sehvan University is a accredited academic institution of higher learning. There are four schools in the university namely, Business, Engineering, Health Science, and Physical Science. Bob is the president of the university. Michael is vice-president of the university. Bart is head of school of engineering and he is married to Sussan. Sussan is a lecturer of Economics in Business School. They have one son. They are native of Colorado.
14. Create a script about shopping in a supermarket.
15. Prepare a frame of university that you know. Show different levels of hierarchies.
16. Rewrite the script given in the chapter so that the bank robbery goes wrong.
17. Discuss the inference process using frames to that of inference process in logic.

CHAPTER 4

Reasoning and KRR Systems

4.1 INTRODUCTION

A knowledge-based system is an essentially declarative system and as such should not be dependent on the order in which the knowledge is entered, stored or processed, unless there is some good reason for forcing modularity on the knowledge. This means that there are two primary problems facing the inference engine:

- A knowledge system must have a way to decide where to start. Rules and facts reside in a static knowledge base. There must be a way for the *reasoning process* to begin.
- The *inference engine* must resolve conflicts that occur when alternative lines of reasoning emerge. It could be, for example, that the system reaches a point at which four or more rules are ready to fire. The inference engine must choose which rule to examine next.

4.2 REASONING

Formal reasoning involves the *syntactic manipulation* of data structures to deduce new ones, in accordance with pre-specified rules of inference. Formal reasoning is the type of reasoning that is most natural and most commonly used in logic-based and production rule-based representation systems. It involves deduction rules such as *modus ponens*: if P implies Q, and P is *true*, then Q must be *true*.

Procedural reasoning (for example, a program that can take the sum of two numbers) involves specialized routines or procedures for answering questions and solving problems. Procedural reasoning is most commonly used today in frame-based and semantic network-based systems; it is used to a lesser extent in conventional programs for which skeletal program shells are created that can solve a class of specific problems.

Reasoning by analogy involves the extrapolation (or the induction) of new facts from existing knowledge. For example, if Elizabeth got A grades in mathematics and chemistry, we can infer that she probably also got a good grade in physics. This seems to be a very natural mode of thought for people, but so far it has been difficult to establish in an AI program. If this capability could be successfully implemented in a program, it would enable that program to adapt and learn by itself.

Generalization and abstraction are also natural reasoning processes for human beings that have been difficult to implement in a program. This area of research is thought to be at the core of most human learning. It involves induction rules, such as if Q is TRUE for every known instance, and if there is a large enough number of such instances, then Q is always TRUE. If we know that robins have wings, that sparrows have wings, and that pigeons have wings, eventually we will conclude that all birds have wings. This is an example of generalization—the creation of a more abstract, generalized rule from a collection of knowledge consisting of many specialized examples, or case histories. Conversely, we may successively refine our knowledge by making it more specific and detailed as we learn from more examples.

Metalevel reasoning involves using knowledge—particularly knowledge about the extent of your knowledge and about the importance of certain facts in order to solve a problem. Recent research indicates that metalevel reasoning plays a key role in human cognition.

4.2.1 Forward and Backward Chaining

There are two basic styles of using rules to define a direction of movement through a search space or in otherwise representing a problem-solving process. These two styles follow from the fact that modus ponens can be used in two different ways.

In the first, we could treat A as data and regard the implication A → B as the relevant operator or rule. In this style we would match the problem data against the antecedents of all the available rules, find the set of applicable rule(s), select the particular rule(s) to be fired, and then take the actions dictated by the consequents of the fired table(s). From this straightforward application of *modus ponens*, we would then naturally conclude B. This kind of reasoning is *data-driven reasoning* or *forward chaining.*

The second style of reasoning follows from the fact that we can write a rule in which the consequent appears first without changing the meaning of the rule in the slightest. That is, instead of writing

IF A
THEN B

we could write an equivalent formulation as

B
IF A

This inversion of the original rule suggests that we examine consequences or goals before we worry about whether the data are available to support the indicated conclusion.

Thus, in this second style we start by examining the right-hand sides of rules to see which rules have as their consequences the problem goals we wish to achieve. For those rules which have the desired outcomes, B in the above simple case, we examine the antecedents, A here, to see what facts are required to enable these rules to be fired. If the relevant facts are not available to trigger these rules, we take as subgoals the establishment of the relevant facts, and the search proceeds recursively in this fashion. This is goal-driven reasoning or backward chaining. B is thus regarded as the goal to be achieved and A is the data to be verified or perhaps established as a subgoal in the search process.

Four factors influence the question of whether it is better to reason forward or backward:

- Are there more possible start states or goal states? We would like to move from the smaller set of states to the larger (and thus easier to find) set of states.
- In which direction is the branching factor (i.e. the average number of nodes that can be reached directly from a single node) greater? We would like to proceed in the direction with the lower branching factor.
- Will the program be asked to justify its reasoning process to a user? If so, it is important to proceed in the direction that corresponds more closely with the way the user will think.
- What kind of event is going to trigger a problem-solving episode? If it is the arrival of a new fact, forward reasoning makes sense. If it is a query to which a response is desired, backward chaining is more natural.

Forward Chaining

Forward chaining involves making inferences by matching the condition sides of the if ... then rules to the facts at hand. This is characteristic of deductive reasoning. The matching of a fact to the condition half of a production rule is operationally equivalent to resolving two logical clauses. Since forward chaining works from facts to conclusions, the forward chaining inference mode has also been called the *antecedent mode, event-driven mode*, or *data-derived mode*.

Reasoning in a forward chaining system is described as a recognize-act cycle. First, the rules that can succeed are recognized, then one rule is selected and the conclusion (or action) is asserted into working memory. The system then uses this conclusion as initial data and proceeds to the next cycle. The inferences made are always consistent with the supplied data and knowledge items, but they may be irrelevant because the user may not be interested in the conclusions that result.

The forward chaining inference procedure is to start with a collection of facts and rules and to try, in an iterative manner, to find the available rule(s) whose condition side matches a fact (perhaps with a variable substitution or binding required). From this match, new facts are derived. We continue adding new facts and searching for matching rules until no further rules apply, or until the problem is solved and the goal state is reached. When more than one rule matches a fact, a possible conflict situation is created that must be resolved. We must decide which rule to apply first, with its associated variable bindings and its resultant new facts; then we must determine whether to try to match the new fact just derived or one of the older matches that we temporarily postponed considering.

Data driven processing employs what have become known as *demons*. A demon is the procedure that is attached to a data object, whenever the condition relating to that data becomes true the demon performs the appropriate processing function.

Figure 4.1 shows an example of a forward chaining procedure through a simple knowledge base. Rule 1 and rule 2 are presented in the figure as demon 1 and demon 2 respectively (a demon being distinguished by the "when" keyword). Two pieces of initial information are provided:

'it rained yesterday'
'excavation material is earth'

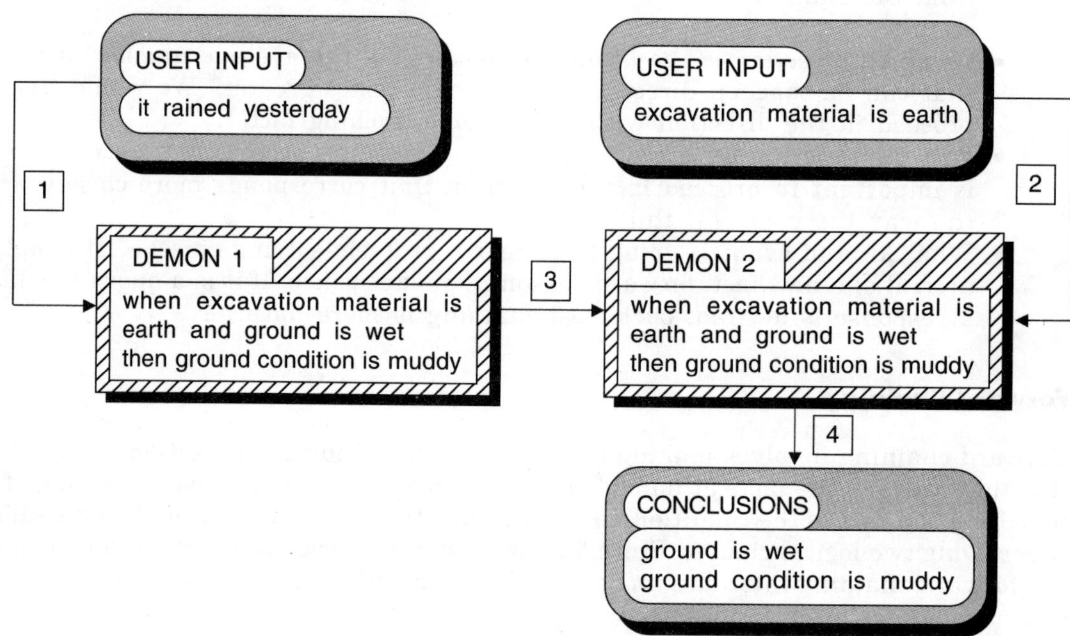

Figure 4.1 Forward chaining.

From the assertion "it rained yesterday" the inference engine fires demon 1 and infers the conclusion "the ground is wet". This is used in conjunction with the second piece of initial information to fire demon 2 and infers that the "ground condition is muddy". The inference engine then reports these two conclusions to the user.

Forward chaining systems do have some significant disadvantages. For one thing, they lack focus. Since it is data-driven, a forward chaining production rule system tends to discover all the logical consequences of the set of facts and knowledge under investigation, whether they were requested or not. Furthermore, if the problem characteristics are such that the facts or evidence can trigger many and diverse applicable rules, the search tree is multi-limbed at the outset, and the conflict resolution problem can get unwieldy. We may find the system wasting numerous computer cycles deriving facts that have no bearing on the problem under investigation.

A forward chaining strategy is particularly appropriate in situations where data is limited and expensive to collect. Typical domains are financial planning, process control, the configuration of complex systems and system tuning.

Backward Chaining

Backward chaining systems tend to provide the goal-oriented focus missing in forward chaining systems. They work from the hypotheses to the facts or evidence, and for this reason backward chaining inference mode has alternately been called consequent mode, goal-driven, and hypothesis-driven. Backward chaining starts with an unsubstantiated hypothesis and tries to prove it by finding rules that demonstrate the hypothesis and then trying to verify the facts that enable the rule to work.

Thus, it replaces the hypothesis to be proved with subgoals that, if proved, will prove the hypothesis. The first step consists of searching down the conclusion side of a list of rules and identifying the ones that, with the appropriate variables, substitutions, or bindings, would match the unsubstantiated hypothesis. The next step is to try to verify the facts on the condition side that would make each rule applicable. The condition side usually consists of a compound set of conditions—one or more subgoals. If these subgoals do not match known facts, they are used to rescan the list of rules, this time to search for facts or rules whose conclusions match the subgoals.

Iteration through the facts and rules continues in this manner until a complete line of reasoning has been identified that links or chains the unsubstantiated hypothesis back through subgoals until they finally connect to some known facts or evidence.

As is the case with forward chaining, this process of matching rules with variable substitutions is operationally equivalent to resolving two logical clauses. Backward chaining has the advantage of not performing unnecessary inferences. Backward chaining operates ad hoc when an expressed need, query, or goal has been raised.

Figure 4.2 shows an example of a backward chaining procedure through a simple knowledge base. The inference engine begins with the goal "ground condition is?", initially the system retrieves all the rules which make a conclusion about the goal. In the simplified example rule 2 is selected.

Each condition in the antecedent part of the rule is then evaluated to see if the rule can be fired. The system queries the user, who responds that the "excavation material is earth". If the user had responded "unknown", the system would have taken the default value which has been specified as "earth". The conditions are evaluated in turn and the next condition of rule 2 "ground is wet" results in the inference engine chaining into the conclusion of rule 1. The antecedent part of rule 1 which is the assertion "it rained yesterday" is proved to be true by a knowledge base fact.

The inference engine then uses this information to back track through the rules firing them in sequence, as shown on the right-hand side of the previous figure. This results in the system providing an answer of "ground condition is muddy".

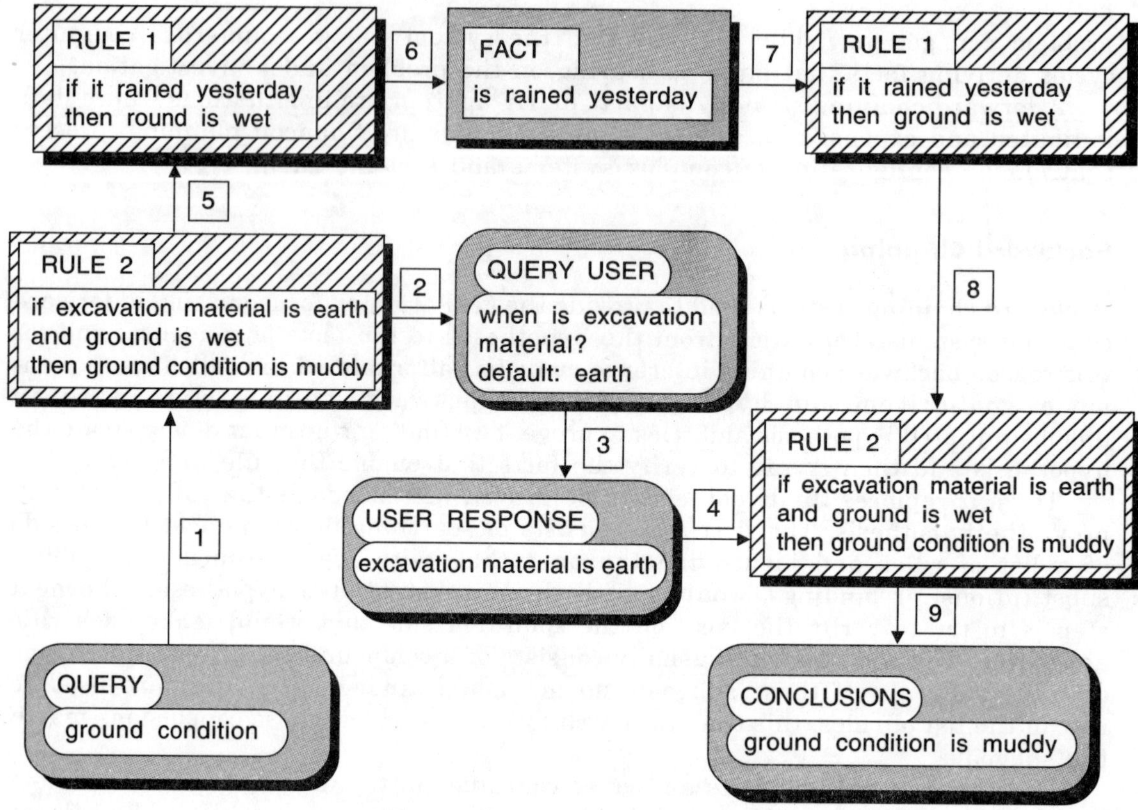

Figure 4.2 Backward chaining.

Backward chaining mechanisms are generally used where the quantity of data is potentially very large and where some specific characteristic of the system under consideration is of interest. Typical applications include medical diagnosis and fault finding, most expert system shells rely on some form of backward chaining.

Backward chaining, like forward chaining, is not trouble free. The subgoals can grow in number and complexity, making substantiation of the ultimate goal very difficult and time consuming. Furthermore, when we attempt to find a rule whose consequent matches a goal or subgoal, we may find that more than one possibility exists, putting us again in a conflict situation. Which rule and its resulting subgoals should we try first? Which is more likely to lead to a useful result, and which to a blind alley? The bushier the tree with the goal state as its starting point, the worse the problem. Practical backward chaining systems employ all sorts of organizational concepts to help overcome these difficulties.

Hybrid Systems

The differing strengths and weaknesses of forward and backward chaining have raised interest in efforts to integrate them into some sort of bidirectional search (goal-directed and data-driven) combining the best of both worlds. In combining both chaining modes, ambiguous or invalid input data may generate too many possible paths for pure forward chain reasoning and too many hypotheses for pure backward chaining. Backward chaining, however, can be used to control the exponential growth of possibilities and to avoid the needless collection of facts and conclusions when the forward chaining search tree begins to fan out excessively. The focus of backward chaining can be confined to plausible predictions with the aid of forward chaining.

Sometimes certain aspects of a problem are best handled via forward chaining and other aspects by backward chaining. Consider a forward chaining medical diagnosis program. It might accept twenty or so facts about a patient's condition, then forward chain on those facts to try to deduce the nature and/or cause of the disease. Now suppose that at some point, the left side of a rule was nearly satisfied—say, nine out of ten of its preconditions were met. It might be efficient to apply backward reasoning to satisfy the tenth precondition in a directed manner, rather than wait for forward chaining to supply the fact by accident. Or perhaps the tenth condition requires further medical tests. In that case, backward chaining can be used to query the user.

4.3 KNOWLEDGE REPRESENTATION AND REASONING (KRR) SYSTEM

Nowadays researchers concentrate on theoretical and practical computational approaches to represent and utilize the meaning of natural language. Such natural language driven computational models allow the development of truly intelligent computer systems simulating natural language in human information and knowledge processing. Developing knowledge representation and reasoning systems based on natural language constitute a new approach in artificial intelligence. Natural language-based knowledge representation and reasoning systems and their large-scale implementations closely simulate the representational and inferential computation machinery of natural language, which is different from any other theoretical and practical knowledge representation and reasoning system or automated reasoning systems.

This new direction of natural language-based knowledge representation and reasoning systems is of concern over the efficient handling of large-scale, general-purpose knowledge, reasoning and the meaning of natural language. But majority of knowledge representation and reasoning systems do not adequately reflect important characteristics of natural language and are representationally and inferentially poor relative to natural language. Historically, the goal of the knowledge representation and reasoning was to address representational and inferential needs of natural language processing. However, the goal of knowledge representation and reasoning quickly and substantially diverged from this. In the past several years there has been little interaction and interest between the knowledge representation and natural language processing communities.

The research direction of natural language-based knowledge representation and reasoning systems constitutes a tremendous change in how we view the role of natural language in an intelligent computer system. The traditional view, widely held within the AI and computational linguistics communities, considers natural language as an interface or front end to a system such as an expert system or knowledge base.

In this view, inferencing and other interesting information and knowledge processing tasks are not parts of natural language processing.

By contrast, the computational model of natural language views natural language as a knowledge representation and reasoning system with its own unique computationally attractive representational inferential machinery. This perspective sheds some light on the actual, still largely unknown, relationship between natural language and human mind. This approach states that the structure of human mind is also close to natural language and natural language is essentially the language of human thought.

In the natural language-based knowledge representation and reasoning systems, information and knowledge are (i) entered in computer systems via natural language in the form of text or dialogues, (ii) represented and combined via algorithms and data structures closely simulating the syntax and semantics of natural language, (iii) reasoned about via inference mechanisms, which closely simulate inferences that humans make in natural language, and (iv) exited from computer systems via natural language in the form of natural language answers to queries. This means that all information and knowledge processing tasks supporting the computer system's intelligent behaviour take place at the natural language level. The advantage of natural language-like uniformity of representation and reasoning is a simple and powerful computer architecture. For domains which are not well formalized, it can be stated that natural language-based knowledge representation and reasoning are more advantageous than knowledge representation and reasoning not motivated by natural language.

The puzzling computational nature of natural language not only algorithmic but its algorithmic build up appears very different from both the traditional computer science number-crunching computation and the traditional artificial intelligence symbol-crunching computation.

There is a widespread agreement that artificial intelligence programs should not use full-natural language text as a knowledge representation language. Natural language cannot be easily manipulated algorithmically. It is full of ambiguities. Its meaning is context-dependent. Its syntax is extremely complex and strongly dependent on semantics. Its connectives (propositions, articles, and conjunctions) are remarkably vague and unsystematic. There are few powerful rules of inference on natural language strings. The natural language has little to do with the inferencing. Language is on the surface of thought. A human's basic knowledge of the world is not represented linguistically in the brain. Language is for communication with people who cannot see through your eyes or duplicate your reasoning. Therefore, it cannot express thought directly.

The exact division of the representational and inferential labour between natural language and other systems such as human mind, database or knowledge base remains an open research question to be extensively investigated.

Representation of reasoning with and acquisition of different types of knowledge from large-scale natural language inputs are also important. In traditional approach natural language plays a lesser representational and inferential role and also the natural language processing system is supported by non-natural language-motivated knowledge representation and reasoning system. Other interesting methods are automatic knowledge acquisition from medium-to-large-scale natural language inputs. These acquisition methods are based on natural language and incorporate its various algorithmic aspects. They have the potential to replace handcrafting knowledge from textual documents, a costly and error-prone process. These methods raise hope that we will no longer need humans to post verify and clean-up system acquired garbage.

Natural language processing researchers and practitioners are constantly faced with the inadequacy of data structures for representing natural language because their syntax and semantics do not fit properly the syntax and semantics of natural language. Inference in natural language is not well simulated by traditional reasoning algorithms. This further complicates the task of the natural language processing—required automatic knowledge acquisition.

The natural language-based knowledge representation and reasoning systems allow one to uniquely combine the human-like quality of knowledge processing with computer quantitative advantages. These systems allow computers to process knowledge in the form of natural language similar to people and then to combine it with non-human computer capabilities like fast, systematic, and virtually memory-unlimited. Only such human and non-human combinations of information and knowledge processing give hope for an in-depth processing of information and knowledge in the huge volumes of natural language inputs. Such huge volumes include documents such as texts and transcribed dialogue which are available on the World Wide Web. This constantly growing volume is currently estimated to be thousands of textual documents.

4.3.1 Knowledge Representation Revisited

What is a knowledge representation? This idea can best be understood in terms of the distinct roles it plays, each crucial to the task at hand. A knowledge representation (KR) is most fundamentally a substitute, a substitute for the thing itself. It is used to enable, an entity to determine consequences by thinking rather than acting, i.e. by reasoning about the world rather than taking action in it. It is a set of ontological commitments, i.e. an answer to the question. That is, in what terms should I think about the world?

It is a fragmentary theory of intelligent reasoning, expressed in terms of three components: (i) the representation's fundamental conception of intelligent reasoning, (ii) the set of inferences the representation sanctions; and (iii) the set of inferences it recommends.

It is a medium for reasonably efficient computation, i.e. the computational environment in which thinking is accomplished. One contribution to this reasonable efficiency is supplied by the guidance a representation provides for organizing information so as to facilitate making the recommended inferences. It is a medium of human expression, i.e. a language in which things about the world are said.

Knowledge representation (KR) refers to the general topic of how information can be appropriately encoded and utilized in computational models of cognition. It is rather a broad field with links to logic, computer science, cognitive and perceptual psychology, linguistics, and other parts of cognitive science. Some KR work aims at psychological or linguistic plausibility, but much is motivated more by engineering concerns, a tension that runs through the entire field of AI. KR work typically ignores purely philosophical issues, but related areas in philosophy include analyses of mental representation, deductive reasoning and the 'language of thought' philosophy of language, and philosophical logic.

4.3.2 Reasoning

Reasoning is a process that goes on internally, but most things it wants to reason about exist only externally. It may be a program (or person) engaged in planning the assembly of a bicycle, and the system might have to reason about entities such as wheels, chains, sprockets, and handle bars, but such things exist only in the external world. This unavoidable dichotomy is a fundamental underlying principle and role for a representation. It functions as a substitute inside the reasoner, a stand-in for the things that exist in the world. Operations on and with representations substitute for operations on the real thing, that is, substitute for direct interaction with the world. In this view, reasoning itself is, in part, a substitute for action in the world when we cannot or do not (yet) want to take that action.

Knowledge acquisition is a phase in the building of knowledge based or expert systems. Knowledge-based systems are a kind of computer program that apply technical knowledge, or expertise, to problem solving. Knowledge acquisition involves identifying the relevant technical knowledge, recording it, and getting it into computable form so the problem solving engine of the expert system can apply it. Knowledge acquisition is the most expensive part of building and maintaining expert systems.

Knowledge-based systems (KBS) are a subfield of artificial intelligence concerned with creating programs that embody the reasoning expertise of human experts. In simplest terms, the overall intent is a form of intellectual cloning, that is to find persons with a reasoning skill that is important and rare (e.g. an expert medical diagnostician, chess player, and chemist), talk to them to determine what specialized knowledge they have and how they reason, then embody that knowledge and reasoning in a program.

Knowledge Representation (KR) has long been considered as one of the principal elements of artificial intelligence, and a critical part of all problem solving. The subfields of KR range from the purely philosophical aspects of epistemology to the more practical problems of handling huge amounts of data. This diversity is unified by the central problem of encoding human knowledge in all its various forms in such a way that the knowledge can be used.

Any mechanically embodied intelligent process will be comprised of structural ingredients that we as external observers naturally take to represent a propositional account of the knowledge that the overall process exhibits, and independent of such external semantical attribution, play a formal but causal and essential role in producing the behaviour that manifests that knowledge.

A successful representation of some knowledge then must be in a form that is understandable by humans, and must cause the system using the knowledge to behave as if it knows it. The "structural ingredients" that accomplish these goals are typically found in the languages for KR, both implemented and theoretical, that have been developed over the years.

Programming is a process of representing knowledge. The medium used for this representation, programming languages, do not satisfy the criteria set down by the KR hypothesis very well. They do affect a behaviour that is consistent with the knowledge represented, but they are well known to be difficult to understand.

4.4 KNOWLEDGE REPRESENTATION (KR) LANGUAGES

William Woods defines the properties of a KR language as follows:

A KR language must unambiguously represent any interpretation of a sentence (logical adequacy), have a method for translating from natural language to that representation, and must be usable for reasoning.

Wood's definition is merely a simplification of the KR Hypothesis where "reasoning" is the only method of "engendering the behaviour that manifests that knowledge". Reasoning is essential to KR, and especially to KR languages, yet even simple reasoning capabilities can lead to serious tractability problems, and thus must be well understood and used carefully.

One of the most important developments in the application of KR in the past 30 years has been the proposal, study and development of frame-based KR languages. While frame-based KR languages differ in varying degrees from each other, the central tenet of these systems is a notation based on the specification of objects (concepts) and their relationships to each other. The main features of such a language are:

1. ***Object-orientedness.*** All the information about a specific concept is stored with that concept, as opposed, for example, to rule-based systems where information about one concept may be scattered throughout the rule base.
2. ***Generalization/specialization.*** Long recognized as a key aspect of human cognition, KR languages provide a natural way to group concepts in hierarchies in which higher level concepts represent more general, shared attributes of the concepts below.
3. ***Reasoning.*** The ability to state in a formal way that the existence of some piece of knowledge implies the existence of some other, previously unknown piece of knowledge is important to KR. Each KR language provides a different approach to reasoning.
4. ***Classification.*** Given an abstract description of a concept, most KR languages provide the ability to determine if a concept fits that description, this is actually a common special form of reasoning.

Object orientation and generalization help to make the represented knowledge more understandable to humans; reasoning and classification help make a system behave as if it knows what is represented. Frame-based systems thus meet the goals of the KR hypothesis.

It is important to realize both the capabilities and limitations of frame-based representations, especially as compared to other formalisms. To begin with, all symbolic KR techniques are derived in one way or another from first order logic (FOL), and as a result are suited for representing knowledge that doesn't change. Different KR systems may be able to deal with non-monotonic changes in the knowledge being represented, but the basic assumption has been that change, if present, is the exception rather than the rule.

Two other major declarative KR formalisms are *production systems* and *database systems*. Production systems allow for the simple and natural expression of *if-then* rules. However, these systems have been shown to be quite restrictive when applied to large problems, as there is no ordering of the rules, and inferences cannot be constrained away from those dealing only with the objects of interest. Production systems are subsummed by frame-based systems, which additionally provide natural inference capabilities like classification and inheritance, as well as knowledge-structuring techniques such as generalization and object-orientation.

Database systems provide only for the representation of simple assertions, without inference. Rules of inference are important pieces of knowledge about a domain.

Frame-based systems are currently severely limited when dealing with *procedural knowledge.* An example of procedural knowledge would be Newton's Law of Gravitation—the attraction between two masses is inversely proportional to the square of their distances from each other. Given two frames representing the two bodies, with slots holding their positions and mass, the value of the gravitational attraction between them cannot be inferred declaratively using the standard reasoning mechanisms available in frame-based KR languages, though a function or procedure in a programming language could represent the mechanism for performing this "inference" quite well.

Frame-based systems that can deal with this kind of knowledge do so by adding a procedural language to its representation. The knowledge is not being represented in a frame-based method; it is being represented as C or LISP code which is accessed through a slot in the frame. This is an important distinction—there is knowledge being encoded in those LISP functions that is not fully accessible. The system can reason with that knowledge, but not about it; in other words we can use some attached procedure to compute or infer the value of one slot based on some others, but we cannot ask how that value was obtained.

4.5 DOMAIN MODELING

Domain modelling is the field in which the application of KR to specific domains is studied and performed.

Domain knowledge refers to the knowledge possessed by the domain expert that must be encoded in some fashion. This knowledge is not well defined and is fairly difficult for others to access. *Meta-model* refers to the KR formalism, typically a KR language, which will be used as the symbol level for the machine representation of this knowledge. *Instantiation* refers to the process of taking the domain knowledge and physically representing it using the meta-model, this process is sometimes referred to as *knowledge acquisition. Domain model* refers to the knowledge base that results from the instantiation, and the *operational goals* are typically not represented formally, but refer to the reason the domain model was built and what it will be used for.

This traditional separation between programs and domain models causes problems during the instantiation of a domain model that includes not only knowledge of the objects and attributes, but knowledge of the procedural aspects of the processes associated with the domain as well. The problems stem from the fact that domain modelling is a discipline in which advances are made incrementally, by building upon previous systems. Some of the most significant results are in the form of methodologies which help other domain modellers to avoid pitfalls and use techniques that work.

4.5.1 Ontological Analysis

The predominant methodologies for domain modelling clearly indicate that the instantiation of the model is the most time consuming part, and that the most important part of instantiation is *ontological analysis*. Ontologies for general taxonomies of objects are abundant, and there seem to be clear guidelines for developing new ones.

There are a few guidelines for the knowledge required to represent procedural knowledge and reason about it, especially when the procedures requiring representation are implemented as software. There is not much background to draw upon, other than software information systems, as far as ontologies and methodologies for modelling what software does. Ontological analysis ended up being a large part of the effort for research and because of this it had never been done before.

The word 'ontology' means "the study of the state of being". An ontology describes the states of being of a particular set of things. This description is usually made up of axioms that define each thing. In knowledge representation, an ontology has become the defining term for the part of a domain model that excludes the instances, yet describes what they can be. Ontological analysis is the process of defining this part of the model.

What makes up a specific domain ontology is restricted by the representational capabilities of the meta-model—the language used to construct the model. Each knowledge representation language differs in its manner and range of expression. In general, an ontology consists of three parts: concept definitions, role definitions, and further inference definitions.

The concept definitions set up all the types of objects in the domain. In object-oriented terms these are called the class definitions, and in database terms these are the entities.

Role defaults specify for each concept what the default values are for any attribute. Role restrictions specify for a concept any constraint on the values in a role, such as what types the values must be, how many values there can be, etc. A role is an attribute of an object.

The final part of an ontology is the specification of additional inference that the language provides. Examples of this are forward and/or backward chaining rules, path grammars, subsumption and/or classification, demons, etc.

4.5.2 Discourse Representation Theory

Kamp's discourse representation theory (DRT) is based on an atomic variable representation theory. DRT offers a representation for natural language discourses.

A discourse representation structure (DRS) consists of two parts, one is a set of discourse markers which are used to represent objects introduced in the discourse and the other is conditions on these objects. DRSs are characteristically drawn as boxes. The markers are shown in the upper part of the box and the conditions are shown at the lower part of the box. The following figure is the DRS for the sentence "A man walks".

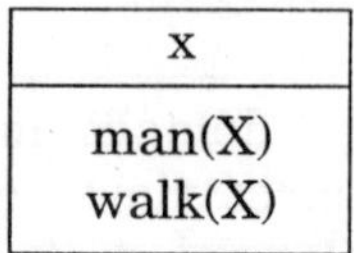

The following example deals with "conditionals" and determiner "every". It is represented as a relation between two DRSs. The DRS for the sentence "Every man loves a woman" can be drawn as follows:

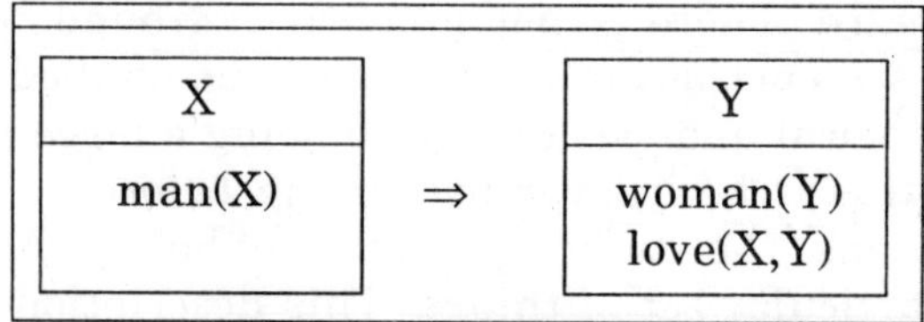

The interpretation of a DRS can be defined as follows. A DRS, D is true in a model M, when

- There exists a binding B which assigns each discourse marker in the top part of D to individuals in M such that each condition in D with respect to B becomes a true proposition in M.
- A ⇒ condition is defined to be true if for all bindings B' (which are an extension of B, the binding the ⇒ condition is within, for just those markers introduced in the left DRS) that make the left DRS true in M, there exists B", an extension of B' for just those markers introduced in the right hand DRS, which makes the right hand DRS true in M.

4.6 SEMANTIC NETS (ASSOCIATIVE NETWORKS) REASONING SYSTEMS

The *network* representations provide a means of structuring and exhibiting the structure in knowledge. In a network, pieces of knowledge are clustered together into coherent semantic groups. Networks also provide a more natural way to map to and from natural language than do other representation schemes. Network representations give pictorial representation of objects, their attributes, and the relationships that exist between them and other entities.

Associative networks are directed graphs with labelled nodes and arcs or arrow. The language used in constructing a network is based on selected domain primitives for objects and relations as well as some general primitives. Associative networks were introduced by Quillian to model the semantics of English sentences and words. He called his structures semantic networks to signify their intended use. He developed a system which found the meanings between words by the paths connecting them. The connections were determined through a kind of "spreading activation" between the two words. This model has some intuitive appeal where related information is clustered and bound together through related links. The knowledge required for the performance of some task is typically contained within a narrow domain or "semantic vicinity" of the task. This type of organization resembles the way knowledge is stored and retrieved in humans. There is no generally accepted syntax or semantics for associative networks.

The language of associative networks is formed from letter of the alphabet, both upper and lower cases, relational symbols, set membership and subset symbols, decimal digits, square and oval nodes, and directed arcs of arbitrary length.

The following headings depict the example of a few existing KRR systems built on semantic network scheme.

4.6.1 Semantic Network Processing System (SNePS)

The semantic network processing system (SNePS) has been designed by Shapiro and his group to be a system for representing the beliefs of a natural language using intelligent system. It has always been the intention that a SNePS-based knowledge base would ultimately be built, not by a programmer or knowledge engineer entering representations of knowledge in some formal language. SNePS has four types of nodes: base nodes, variables nodes, molecular nodes, and pattern nodes. Base nodes and variables nodes have no arcs emanating from them. A base node represents some particular entity that is conceptually different from the entity represented by any other node. Additional properties of the entity are assertionally determined by rest of the network connected to its node. Variable nodes also have no arcs emanating from them, and represent arbitrary individuals, propositions, etc., again as determined by the rest of the network. Molecular and pattern nodes have arcs emanating from them and are structurally determined by those arcs, the nodes they go to, the arcs emanating from, etc. Molecular nodes represent propositions, including rules or "structured individuals". Pattern nodes are similar to open sentences or functional terms with free variables in standard predicate logic. Every node has an identifier, which uniquely identifies it. Base nodes may have identifiers determined by the user. All other nodes have identifiers created by the system.

Figure 4.3 gives an example of SNePS representation which shows a partial relation of a problem structuring parts of *car*, which can be paraphrases as "engines are inside of cars".

4.6.2 Schubert's Representation

In the work of Schubert, which uses a semantic network-based formalism, variables are atomic nodes in the network. Type and other restrictions are specified by links

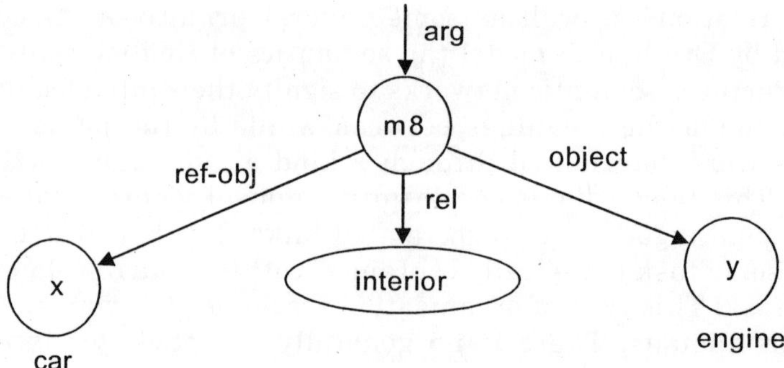

Figure 4.3 An SNePS representation.

to the variable nodes. There are no explicit universal or existential quantifiers. Free variables are implicitly universally quantified; Skolem arcs specify existentially quantified variable nodes. In Figure 4.4, the dotted arrow denotes a scope dependency between the universally quantified "man" and the existentially quantified "woman". The implication (as in the FOPL representation) is represented by the "⇒" connected to the variables and the predicate "likes". Because this is a non-linear notation, sentences with branching quantifiers can be represented.

"Every man likes some woman"

$(\forall x)\ (\exists y)\ [[x\ man] \Rightarrow [[y\ woman]\ \&\ [x\ likes\ y\ ]]]$

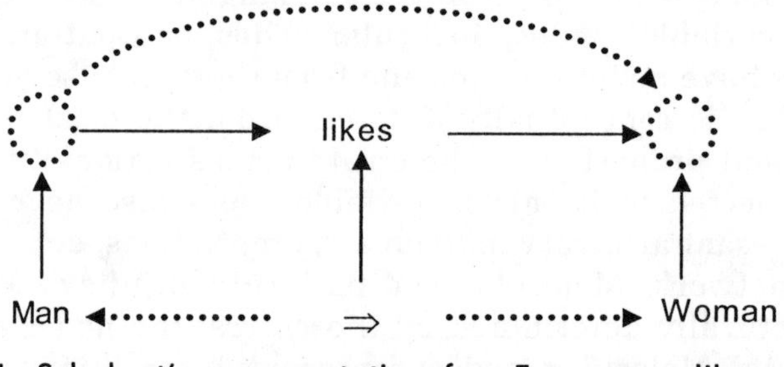

likes

Man ⇒ Woman

Figure 4.4 Schubert's representation for: Every man likes a woman.

However, the separation of variables from their constraints causes the representation not to be natural relative to the original natural language. Moreover, since restrictions on possible fillers for variables appear to be simple type restrictions, there is no representation for noun phrases with restrictive relative clause complements, and consequently no representation for donkey sentences. (Donkey sentence is a special type of sentences. Donkey sentence poses problems when we try to translate it into standard predicate logic.)

4.6.3 Fahlman's NETL Representation

NETL is a semantic network language for connectionist architectures. It is a system for representing and using real-world data. Fahlman's work specified two representations for variables. The first representation is as a *TYPE-NODE that represents the "typical-member" of a set. This approach suffers from the typical inheritance problems associated with such representations and Fahlman calls it *copy-confusion*. The second representation for variables corresponds to universally quantified nodes called *EVERY-NODEs. Restrictions on these nodes can be general type or relative clause restrictions and are directly linked to the *EVERY-NODE. Existentially quantified variables are of type *INDV with Skolem arcs to *EVERY-NODE variables to indicate scope dependencies.

The representation for the sentence "Any person that owns a dog that hates Fred also hates Fred" is shown in Figure 4.5. The node with the black centre dot is the universally quantified *person that owns a dog that hates Fred*. The labelled unfilled-filled node pairs correspond to classes. The arcs with double arrowheads correspond to what Fahlman calls *clauses*, which correspond directly to clausal restrictions on variables. The wavy line expresses the scope dependency between it and the *dog that hates Fred*. Finally, the *hates* relation of the top-level sentence is expressed by the arrow from the *person* node to the *Fred* node.

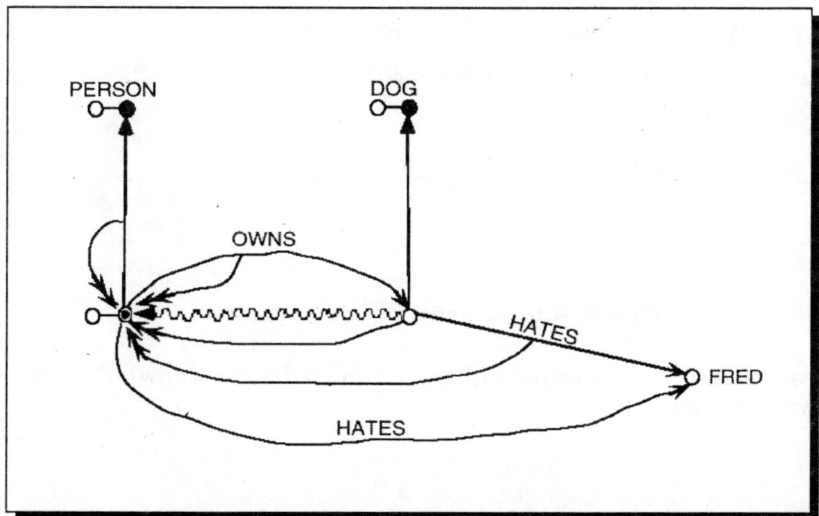

Figure 4.5 NETL representation for "Any person who owns a dog that hates Fred also hates Fred"

This is more general than the variable representation of Schubert, et al. because of the representation of complex clause restrictions. However, the form of the representation and its interpretation (as defining a set, rather than stating a proposition) is, again, unnatural relative to the sentence it represents. In principle, Fahlman's representation of variables appears capable of representing donkey sentences and branched quantifiers sentences; however, he has not discussed this, and semantics for such representations are unclear.

4.7 FRAMES BASED SYSTEMS

We have seen in earlier chapter that frames were introduced by Marvin Minsky as a data structure to represent a mental modal of a stereotypical situation such as driving a car, attending a meeting, or eating in a restaurant. Knowledge about an object or event is stored together in memory as a unit. When a new situation is encountered then an appropriate frame is selected from memory for use in reasoning about the situation.

Frames are general record-like structures which consist of a collection of slots and slot values. The slots may be of any size and type. Slots typically have names and values subfields called *facets*. Facets also have names and any number of values. A slot contains information such as attributes, value pairs and default values, conditions for filling a slot, pointers to another related frames, and procedures that are activated when needed for different purposes. The general frame structure looks like as given in Figure 4.6.

```
(<frame name>
(<slot1> (<fact1><value1> ...... <valuek1>)
    (<fact2><value2> ...... <valuek2>)
            .
            .
(<slot2> (<fact1><value1>......<valuekm>)
            .
            .
            )
```

Figure 4.6 A general frame structure.

The followings are the examples of well-known frame knowledge representation languages and systems.

Theo

Theo is a frame-based representation, with LISP and PROLOG inference methods. This system also has several user-invokable learning methods.

The philosophy and methodological assumptions of Theo was designed as a framework to support the next generation of machine learning algorithms. The developers of Theo believed that a general, flexible knowledge base would allow agents to learn facts and meta-facts. Meta-information is useful for many purposes, such as the reliability, utility, and indexing of information. In Theo, learning is interleaved with general problem solving and self-reflection. This allows the architecture to react appropriately when the environment presents opportunities for learning or self-reflection.

An additional assumption required by Theo's truth justification system is that the entire environment must be visible to Theo's sensors. This is due to the automatic retraction of environmental features when they pass out of sensing range.

Theo stores all knowledge in a frame representation. This uniform representation allows all knowledge to be accessed and manipulated. Frames are composed of a slot and a value, which may be a reference to another frame, a constant, or missing.

Frames represent concepts. A frame with a slot and a value is said to be a belief. A frame with a missing value is said to be a problem. Such a frame triggers problem solving as Theo attempts to infer the slot value.

Theo infers slot values of an entity by a three-step process. The first step is to directly calculate values via a LISP function in the TOGET slot of the entity. If there is no TOGET slot, the next step uses a list of methods to infer values.

Methods include: *Default value*—using the default value of the slot, *Inherits*—traversing up the hierarchy until a value is found, and *Defines*—calculating a value based on other known slot values for *<entity>*.

A statistical inference learning module (SE) attempts to order these methods, placing the methods most likely to succeed early in the list, so that a value is produced in optimal time. The final step, implemented by the defines method, attempts to calculate the value either by definitions or by previous explanation-based learning.

During inference, Theo saves an explanation of how each slot received its value. These explanations serve as a simple truth maintenance mechanism. When any slot value in the system changes, then the values of all dependent slots are marked invalid, and recalculated when needed. The explanation is also generalized by a module named TMAC to create general macro-methods for the computation of similar slot values.

When a value has been successfully inferred, Theo caches the result, allowing efficient knowledge access. However, the caching of every single inferred value creates a huge knowledge base requiring special management techniques.

The three learning mechanisms, SE, TMAC, and caching, operate independently of each other, but in certain cases the results of one mechanism can interfere with the functioning of the other mechanisms.

FrameKit

FrameKit is a frame-based knowledge representation, written in CommonLISP, that provides the basic mechanisms of frames, inheritance, demons, and views.

FrameKit was first developed by Jaime Carbonell and implemented in FranzLISP for the VAX. It has been used in several applications, ranging from expert systems to medical information storage or retrieval. FrameKit was enhanced and ported to CommonLISP by Robert Joseph. The applications of FrameKit included knowledge-based machine translation, the MedSort II project, and vision research at Carnegie Mellon University (CMU).

It has the functionality like, frames, slots, facets, views, fillers; demons; breadth-first, depth-first and exhaustive inheritance; user-defined inheritance; default values; restrictions; abstract data-typing to permit any low-level storage scheme and save utility.

In FrameKit, frames are printed as a simple embedded list structure, which is shown here (Figure 4.7) along with the facets that are pre-defined by the system for specific purposes.

```
<frame>         ::= (<name> <slot>*)
<slot>          ::= (<name> <facet>*)
<facet>         ::= (<name> <view>*) | <pre-defined-facet>
<view>          ::= (<name> <filler>*)
<filler>        ::= <value>* | <demon>* | <predicate>*
<name>          ::= any CommonLISP symbol
<value>         ::= any CommonLISP expression; generally a symbol or number
<demon>         ::= a CommonLISP expression; generally a function call that produces side-
                    effects when evaluated
<predicate>  ::= a CommonLISP expression; evaluates to true or false (non-NIL or NIL)
<pre-defined-facet> ::= (VALUE <view>*) |
(IF-ADDED <view>*) |
(IF-NEEDED <view>*) |
(IF-ERASED <view>*) |
(IF-ACCESSED <view>*) |
(RESTRICTIONS <view>*) |
(DEFAULT <view>*)
```

Figure 4.7 Structure of a FrameKit.

The views in VALUE and DEFAULT facets have fillers of type <value>; the views in IF-ADDED, IF-NEEDED, IF-ERASED, and IF-ACCESSED facets have fillers of type <demon>; and views in RESTRICTIONS facets have fillers of type <predicate>.

4.8 HYBRID REPRESENTATION SYSTEMS

A hybrid representation uses a structure which is the combination more than one existing representation schemes which in turn increases the efficiency of knowledge representation and reasoning. Hybrid variable representations accord concepts and have complex internal structures. These concepts are then used to restrict suitably variables in the theorem prover.

The following are the examples of hybrid knowledge representation systems.

Krypton

KRYPTON is a KR system that supports and separates two kinds of knowledge: terminological (in the TBox) and asertional (in the ABox). A pictorial view of KRYPTON's architecture can be seen in Figure 4.8. Here it represents the sentence "Some person's child is a doctor". KRYPTON can represent very complex description in the Tbox by providing a diverse group of concept constructors.

Logic-based assertional representation in the ABox makes use of the structured concept, syntactically as unary predicates or as binary relations. In principle, general structured concepts with almost arbitrary restrictions are possible in the TBox. Thus, it is straightforward to represent the concept of donkey sentence in TBox and use it in a quantified sentence as the restriction on a variable. However, constituents of complex terms and concepts in the TBox are not available in the ABox, so the donkey

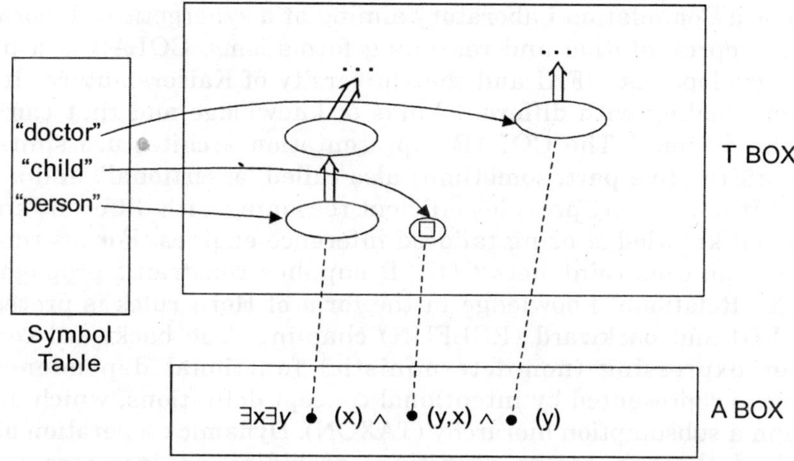

Figure 4.8 KRYPTON represents the sentence, "Some person's child is a doctor".

sentence cannot actually be represented. What is appealing about KRYPTON is that the form of the representation is more natural that FOPL, since restrictions on objects, which can take the form of complex terminological constraints in the TBox, are simple predicates (in the ABox) on those objects.

Further, concept subsumption is defined on terms in the TBox allowing the obvious kinds of natural language-based reasoning (e.g. "If every woman is happy then every rich woman is happy"). Variables of the ABox are still atomic and since sentences of the ABox are FOPL-based, KRYPTON cannot represent branched quantifiers or donkey sentences.

A general problem with hybrid system such as KRYPTON is the potential for inconsistency between reasoning in the TBox and reasoning in the ABox. Beierle makes the point that hybrid KR systems distinguish between taxonomical information (TBox) and assertional information (ABox) too rigidly. Thus, while information in the ABox can change, during inference or when new propositions are entered, information in the TBox tends to be static.

Beierle and his colleagues argue for two types of coupling between information in the TBox and information in the ABox—close and loose. Loose couplings correspond to static sort hierarchies not influenced by the assertional KB. That is inferential activity in the assertional component cannot change information in the terminological component. This is the approach of KRYPTON, where there is no interaction between the TBox and the ABox. Beierle argues that in NLU this loose coupling is insufficient because the system should be capable of explicitly reasoning the taxonomical information. This may in turn change the sort of hierarchy. This latter interaction corresponds to what they call a close coupling of the terminological and assertional components.

COLAB

Compilation Laboratory (COLAB) is a hybrid knowledge representation system emphasizing the horizontal and vertical compilation of knowledge bases. It has been designed as a Compilation Laboratory aiming at a synergetic collaboration of different knowledge representation and reasoning formalisms. COLAB is a piece of research software developed at DFKI and the University of Kaiserslautern. It is comprised of subsystems dealing with different kinds of knowledge and that can also be used as stand-alone systems. The COLAB representation architecture splits into two main parts, an affirmative part, sometimes also called 'assertional', and a taxonomic part.

The affirmative part provides efficient reasoning with different kinds of relational or functional knowledge using tailored inference engines. For affirmative knowledge represented as constraint nets COLAB supplies constraint propagation techniques (CONTAX). Relational knowledge in the form of Horn rules is processed by forward (FORWARD) and backward (RELFUN) chaining. The backward component is also suited for expressing (non-deterministic) functional dependencies. Taxonomic knowledge is represented by intentional concept definitions, which are automatically arranged in a subsumption hierarchy (TAXON). Dynamic cooperation of the subsystems is organized through access primitives providing an interface to the respective reasoning services.

YAK

YAK is a hybrid KR system, and in its foundation is similar to CLASSIC and Loom. The core of the system is a traditional TBox/ABox hybrid representation language, enhanced possibly in a "principled" fashion with other hybrid modules representing different kind of knowledge and reasoning. The system, fully implemented in CommonLISP is the main knowledge representation module of the large NL architecture (AlFresco) natural language system, a multimodel dialogue prototype for the exploration of Italian art history.

The expressivity of the YAK TBox comes out from a study about the balancing of expressiveness, functional adequacy and formal prototypes of deductive procedures.

The classifier provided within the YAK system has a tractable, sound and complete algorithm. Moreover the classifier is speeded up by a caching mechanism and an intelligent name expression scheduling, borrowed from the tabular approach used in non-deterministic natural language parsers.

ABox is with contexts, viewpoints and belief representation, reasoning about sets and time, compositional query language with typed variables.

KL-ONE Family

Ronald Brahman designed a network notation for his Knowledge Language One (KL-ONE), which is the ancestor of many frame systems. Woods and Schmolze reported that about 20 systems have been implemented in the KL-ONE tradition.

In Figure 4.9, KL-ONE representation for Truck and Trailer Truck is shown. The network has nine ovals for concept nodes and nine arrows, which represent different kinds of links. The white ovals represent "generic concepts" for the types, as distinguished from the shaded oval, which is an "individual concept" for the instance 18. The oval marked with an asterisk (*) indicates that integer is a built-in or primitive type. The

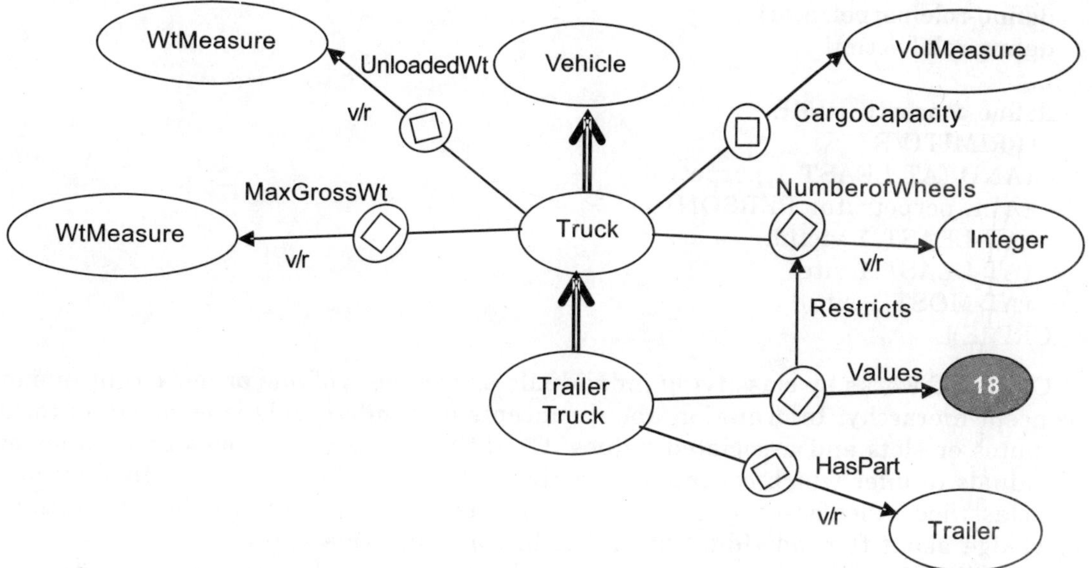

Figure 4.9 KL-ONE representation for 'Truck and Trailer Truck'.

concepts Truck and Trailer, WtMeasure and VolMeasure would have to be defined by other KL-ONE diagrams.

Brahman drew a clear distinction between the different kinds of links in a semantic network. The double line arrows represent subtype-supertype links from Trailer Truck to Truck and from Truck to Vehicle. The arrow with a circle in the middle represents roles, which corresponds to the slots other than supertype in the previous frames.

The Truck node has four roles labelled *UnloadedWt*, *MaxGrossWt*, *CargoCapacity* and *NumberofWheels*. The Trailer Truck node has two roles, one labelled *HasPart* and one that restricts the *NumberofWheels* role of Truck to the value of 18. The notation v/r at the target end of the role arrows indicates value restrictions of type constraints on the permissible values for those roles.

CLASSIC

CLASSIC is a textual knowledge representation language in the KL-ONE family of languages. CLASSIC is an "open world" database, as opposed to the relational database model which embraces a "closed world" assumption, if it is not in the database it doesn't exist. Users can populate the CLASSIC database with concepts, primitives, and individuals and assign roles like fields in relational databases, or slots in object-oriented systems to the concepts, primitives, and individuals. The roles can be constrained as to type concept conformance and arty, and can be assigned values in the form of individuals. For example, a user can add the concept CRIME to a CLASSIC database as follows:

```
define-role[perpetrator]
define-role[victim]
...
define-concept[CRIME,
  (PRIMITIVE
   (AND (AT-LEAST 1 perpetrator)
   (ALL perpetrator PERSON)
   (AT-LEAST 1 victim)
   (AT-LEAST 1 site)
   (AT-MOST 1 site))
 CRIME)].
```

CLASSIC works by classifying individuals as members of one or more concepts in a concept hierarchy. Information about concepts and individuals is encoded as roles attributes or slots and associated values. CLASSIC matches the roles and values of individuals to infer which concepts an individual belongs to. Once an individual has been classified, rules associated with the concepts may be fired to further instantiate knowledge about the individual by filling in roles and role values.

There has been extensive work on complexity of the subsumption algorithms in KL-ONE languages. The subsumption algorithm is important because subsumption calculation is the basis of all computation in KL-ONE languages. It turns out that extension of a base level version of KL-ONE composed of conjunction, limited negation, universal quantification, limited role existential quantification, and numeric role filler limits leads to worst-case complexities of NP-hard or worse. Fortunately, subsumption seems to be computationally tractable in practical situations.

Gaines has developed a visual version of the CLASSIC language, called KRS in which the user can specify and run a complete expert system. A small excerpt from a knowledge base about birds is illustrated in the next Figure 4.10. The ellipse with tick marks identifies bird as a primitive concept. The unmarked ellipses labelled *tubnose*, *albatross*, *fulmar*, *layson albatross*, and *black-footed albatross* represent subconcepts of bird as shown by the directed arcs. The labels with no surround are roles and the labels with rectangular surrounds are individuals which, in this case, are acting as values for the roles. The interpretation is that an observed individual of type *bird* may be recognized as a *tubenose* if it is observed that its *nostrils* are *external-tubular*, it *lives at sea*, and its *bill* is *hooked*. The class of the *bird* may be further refined by further observation as pictured. If a *bird* is classed as the concept *black-footed albatross*, then a rule is fired (*rule1* in the barred rectangle) which assigns "Black-footed Albatross" to its *name* role. A complete KRS knowledge base would have information about many other birds, descriptions of the types of things that can play the value part for each role, and various other pieces of information such as the mutual exclusion among certain concepts.

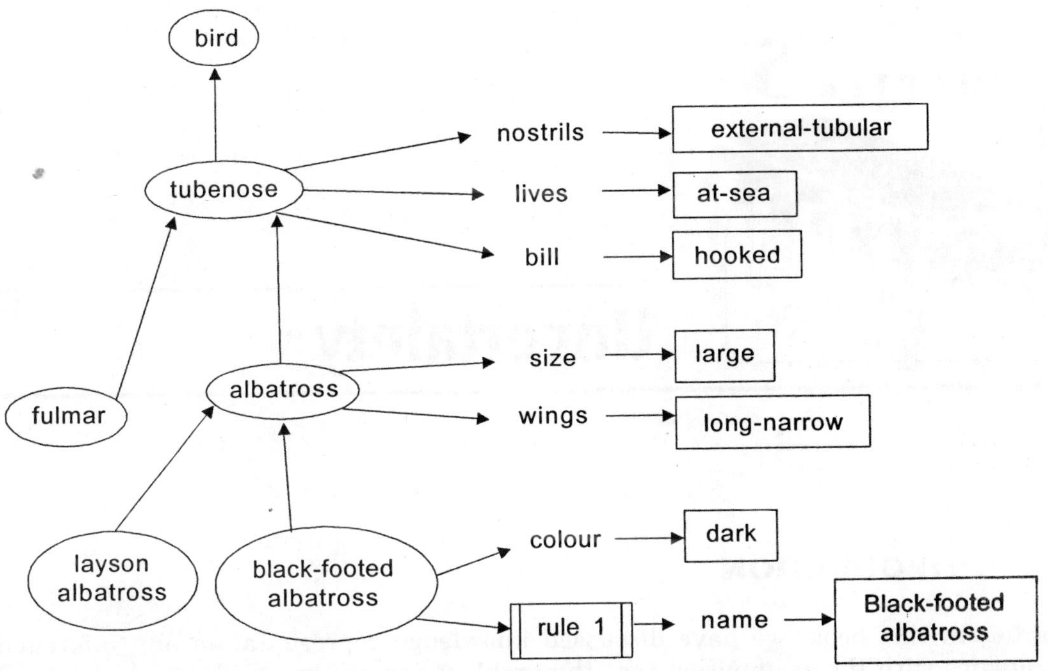

Figure 4.10 A small extract from a knowledge base about birds represented in CLASSIC.

EXERCISES

1. What do you mean by reasoning?
2. Discuss different types of reasoning.
3. What is the difference between forward and backward chaining?
4. Discuss the KRR system based on semantic network.
5. What are the advantages and disadvantages of hybrid systems?
6. Find out how the SNePS system aims to improve the expressiveness of semantic nets.
7. What is discourse representation theory?
8. Represent the following in a Semantic Net and comment on how the SNePS system helps.
   - Gopal and Gita's telephone number is the same.
   - Sanjay believes that Gopal and Gita's telephone number is the same.
9. Represent the following in Schubert's representation scheme and also in KRYPTON:
   - Every player kicked a ball.
   - All players like the referee.
   - Ravi believes that there is a fish with lungs.
10. Give KL-ONE representation of airplane and boeing.

CHAPTER 5

Uncertainty

5.1 INTRODUCTION

Earlier in this book, we have discussed knowledge representation and inferencing strategies with the assumption that the problem domain knowledge is complete and without ambiguities. Moreover all the facts, definitions and the relationship between each entity are unqualified truths. By unqualified truths we mean that they are *true* with 100 per cent certainties. For example, let us say in a problem domain, A and B are two entities or facts and $A \rightarrow B$ is the relation between them. There is no exception to the above relationship nor is there any ambiguity in that relation which means whenever A is *true* B is also true.

As much of man's knowledge many problem-solving tasks involve *uncertainty*. This uncertainty must be represented and successfully resolved in most everyday problems. For example, planning tasks are characterized by uncertainty about the interactions of the plan steps. Strategic planning is further complicated by uncertainty about the opponent's intentions and actions. *Perception* is characterized by large quantities of noisy, ambiguous data. The knowledge based upon this data and used to solve a problem is thus often incomplete; it represents a kind of bounded ignorance and is occasionally incorrect.

There are many occasions when a human being is required to make proper inference in spite of his problem solving knowledge being incomplete or inconsistent, simply on the basis of his problem solving experience in analogous domain. For example, if a person knows the general location of his destination he can reach it with fairly optimum route. Another example could be, if he knows how to park a car he can do it on a Sunday on M.G. Road without prior knowledge of the parking conditions there. From our general day-to-day life we can fine a lot of such examples where a man does inferencing and problem solving without possessing complete and unequivocal knowledge. Common sense reasoning is the term used to describe such actions. Therefore man is capable of reasoning when available information is incomplete and inconsistent. The conclusion obtained is based on knowledge considered as generally true. These conclusions are temporary as they are liable to be challenged by the arrival of new piece of information which will refine the hypothesis. Numerous studies have independently dealt with the formalization of this kind of revisable reasoning over the last 15 years. The approaches used have been diverse. Some are purely symbolic; others use numbers to quantify uncertainty. Some are close to formal logic and others are less formalized and more ad hoc.

In the current session we will see many of these systems which handle uncertainties and incompleteness in their knowledge bases and their inferencing methods. We shall consider one example from our daily life and see what are the fundamental principles that underlie each of these approaches. This will help us in evaluating their similarities, their differences, and their abilities to formalize certain aspects of the so called common sense reasoning. We will consider the following schemes, namely,

- Default logic
- Non-monotonic modal logic
- Logics of uncertainty namely possibilistic and probabilistic logic
- Belief functions namely DS theory, Bayesian logic and certainty Factor model.
- Fuzzy logic.

The number of schemes discussed will depend on the availability of time. Inexact reasoning is common in the sciences. It is characterized by such phrases as 'the art of good guessing' and the 'softer aspect of science'. Helmer and Rescher (1960) assert that only a small portion of natural sciences can be termed exact, e.g. the areas of pure mathematics. In several areas of applied natural science on the other hand, decisions, predictions, and explanations are made only after exact procedures are mixed with informal expertise.

5.1.1 Symbolic versus Statistical Reasoning

The (Symbolic) methods basically represent uncertainty belief as being:

- true,
- false, or
- neither true nor false.

Some methods also had problems with

- Incomplete knowledge
- Contradictions in the knowledge.

Statistical methods provide a method for representing beliefs that are not certain (or uncertain) but for which there may be some supporting (or contradictory) evidence.

Statistical methods offer advantages in two broad scenarios:

- ***Genuine randomness.*** Card games are a good example. We may not be able to predict any outcomes with certainty but we have knowledge about the likelihood of certain items (e.g. like being dealt an ace) and we can exploit this.

- ***Exceptions.*** Symbolic methods can represent this. However, if the number of exceptions is large, such system tends to break down many common sense and expert reasoning tasks, for example, statistical techniques can summarize large exceptions without resorting enumeration.

5.1.2 Probability

The basic approach statistical methods adopt to deal with uncertainty is via the axioms of probability. They are:

- Probabilities are (real) numbers in the range 0 to 1.
- A probability of $P(A) = 0$ indicates total uncertainty in A, $P(A) = 1$ indicates total certainty and values in between some degree of (un)certainty.
- Probabilities can be calculated in a number of ways.

Probability = (number of desired outcomes)/(total number of outcomes)

So given a pack of playing cards the probability of being dealt an ace from a full-normal deck is 4 (the number of aces)/52 (number of cards in deck) which is 1/13. Similarly the probability of being dealt a spade suit is 13/52 = 1/4.

If you have a choice of number of items k from a set of items n then the formula is applied to find the number of ways of making this choice.

Conditional probability, $P(A \mid B)$, indicates the probability of event A given that we know event B has occurred.

5.2 NON-MONOTONIC AND MONOTONIC REASONING

To be able to do this reasoning with uncertainty, we would require a technique for maintaining several parallel belief spaces, each of which would correspond to the beliefs of one expert.

Such techniques are complicated by the fact that the belief spaces of various experts, although not identical, are sufficiently similar that it is unacceptably inefficient to represent them as completely separate knowledge bases. The technique for this reasoning is known as *non-monotonic reasoning*.

Conventional reasoning systems, such as predicate logic, are designed to work with information that has three important properties:

- It is complete with respect to the domain of interest. In other words, all the facts that are necessary to solve a problem are present in the system or can be derived from those that are by the conventional rules of logic.
- It is consistent.
- The only way it can change is that new facts can be added as they become available. If these new facts are consistent with all the other facts that have already been asserted then nothing will ever be retracted from the set of facts that are known to be true. This property is called *monotonicity*.

Unfortunately if any of these properties is not satisfied, conventional logic-based reasoning systems become inadequate. *Non-monotonic reasoning systems* on the other hand, are designed to be able to solve problems in which all of these properties may be missing. In order to do this, we must address several key issues, including the following:

- How can the knowledge base be extended to allow inferences to be made on the basis of lack of knowledge as well as in the presence of it ?
- How can the knowledge base be updated properly when a new fact is added to the system (or when an old one is removed)?
- How can knowledge be used to help resolve conflicts when there are several inconsistent non-monotonic inferences that can be drawn?

Considering the reasoning systems used by conventional knowledge-based systems, a clear distinction is seen between monotonic and non-monotonic reasoning. In a monotonic reasoning system, all values concluded for an attribute remain true for the duration of the consultation session. Facts that become true remains true, and the amount of true information grows steadily. In a non-monotonic reasoning system, facts that are true may be retracted.

Design and planning are good examples of problems demanding non-monotonic reasoning. In the early stages of a planning problem, it may make sense to assume certain values, later as more information becomes available, these values may change.

Changing the value of a single attribute is not difficult, current software allows *identifiers* to be reset or to have new values forced into them. Tracking down all the implications based upon a particular fact is difficult. Most knowledge-based systems marketed today allow only carefully controlled non-monotonic reasoning or provide a "what-if" facility allowing identifiers to be altered, although the forcing of new assumptions over old ones must be monitored carefully.

5.3 CONFIDENCE FACTOR

A *certainty factor* (CF) is a number $\in [-1,1]$ that reflects the degree of belief in a hypothesis, positive certainty factors indicate that there is evidence that the hypothesis is valid. The larger the CF, the greater is the belief in the hypothesis. When CF = 1, the hypothesis is known to be correct.

On the other hand a negative CF suggests that the hypothesis is false. A small CF indicates that there is greater belief that the hypothesis is invalid, CF = –1 implies that the hypothesis is effectively disproved, CF = 0 implies that there is neither evidence regarding the hypothesis being true nor false.

In MYCIN, hypotheses are statements regarding values of clinical parameters for various nodes in the context tree. Sample hypotheses are:

h_1 = The identity of ORGANISM–1 is streptococcus
h_2 = PATIENT–1 is febrite
h_3 = The name of PATIENT–l is John Jones

$\mathrm{CF}(h_1, E) = X$ represents that the certainty factor for the hypotheis h_1 based on evidence E.

We can therefore have $\mathrm{CF}(h_1, E) = 8$, $\mathrm{CF}(h_2, E) = -3$ and $\mathrm{CF}(h_3, E) = 1$, etc. Here certainty factors are used in two ways. First the values of each clinical parameter is stored with its associated CF. In this case E stands for all information currently available in MYCIN. Thus if the program needs the identity of ORGANISM-l it may look into the fact set and find that the identity of ORGANISM-l is streptococcus with CF 0.8. The second use of CFs is in the statements of the decision rules themselves. In this case the evidence E corresponds to the condition in the premise of the rule. Thus,

$$A \wedge B \wedge C \rightarrow D$$

is a representation of the statement $\text{CF}(D, A \wedge B \wedge C) = X$. Since diagnosis is in effect the problem is selecting a disease from a list of competing hypotheses. These hypotheses are stored together along with their CFs for each node in the context tree. The motivation behind the CF model were largely pragmatic. But their usefulness was justified in their practical success.

Although conditional probabilities provide a better mathematical structure in capturing the certainty weights, they are not so suitable because of lack of data to compute the values and also due to presence of vast and imprecise knowledge. The certainty factor model is an approximation to conditional probabilities.

For example using Bayes theorem we can capture the uncertainty in knowledge. If E is all the evidence and d is the hypothesis under consideration then $P(d_1/E)$ is the conditional probability for hypothesis d, to be true in the light of the evidences E. Bayes theorem is useful because it allows $P(d_1/E)$ to be constructed from the component conditional probabilities, i.e.

$$(Pd_1/E) = \frac{P(d_i) * P(E/d_i)}{\sum_j P(d_j) * P(E/d_j)}$$

Here d_i is one of the disjoint hypothesis. For example d_i may be one of the diseases and E may be the set of all symptoms. Since evidences are collected sequentially in most diagnostic systems, we should use Bayes theorem to incrementally increase the conditional probability of the hypothesis. This is possible by modifying the Bayes theorem as follows:

$$(Pd_1/E \cup s1) = \frac{P(s_1/(d_i \wedge E)) * P(d_i/E)}{\sum_j P(s_1/d_j \wedge (d_j/E))}$$

where E is the set of previous evidences. d_i's are the hypotheses, and s is the new evidence.

Programs that use Bayes theorem in this form require huge amounts of statistical data not only $P(s/d)$ for each piece of data s in E, but also the interrelationship of s within each hypotheses as more evidence is collected. The procedure is sound but not suitable in practice. Also we will be using only judgemental knowledge so that the strict Bayesian approach can be approximated, i.e.

$$\text{CF}(d_j/E) = P(d_j/E) \text{ when } P(d) \text{ is small.}$$

When we have to sequentially search for the hypothesis we will need a combinatorial function. This function in MYCIN is

$$CF = \frac{MB - MD}{(1 - \min(MB, MD)}$$

$$CF_{com}(X, Y) = X, Y(1 - X)$$

where $X, Y > 0$

$$= \frac{X + Y}{1 - \min(abs(X), abs(Y))}$$

where X or $Y < 0$

$$= - CF_{com}(-X, -Y)$$

where $X, Y < 0$

CF_{com} preserves commutativity. This is necessary because the order in which the evidences are collected should not influence the final result.

5.4 BAYES THEOREM

Reverend Bayes was an eighteenth century English vicar who spent his life studying statistics. Essentially the theories he developed rely on the belief that for everything, no matter how unlikely, there is a prior probability that it could be true (Naylor, 1989).

An important goal for many problem-solving systems is to collect evidence as the system goes along and to modify its behaviour on the basis of the evidence. To model this behaviour, we need a statistical theory of evidence. Bayesian statistics is such a theory.

The fundamental notion of Bayesian statistics is that of conditional probability: $P(H|E)$

Read this expression as the probability of hypothesis H. Given that we have evidence E. To compute this, we need to take into account the prior probability of H (the probability that we would assign to H if we had no evidence) and the extent to which E provides evidence of H. To do this, we need to define a universe that contains an exhaustive, mutually exclusive set of H_i's, among which we are trying to discriminate. Then, let

$P(H_i | E)$ = the probability that hypothesis H_i is true given evidence E

$P(E | H_i)$ = the probability that we will observe evidence E given that hypothesis H_i is true

$P(H_i)$ = the probability that hypothesis H_i is true in the absence of any specific evidence. These probabilities are called prior probabilities or *priors*.

k = the number of possible hypotheses.

Bayes' theorem then states that

$$P(H_i|E) = \frac{P(E|H_i) \cdot P(H_i)}{\sum_{n=1}^{k} P(E|H_n) \cdot P(H_n)}$$

The key to using Bayes theorem as a basis for uncertain reasoning is to recognize exactly what it says. Specifically, when we say $P(A \mid B)$, we are describing the conditional probability of A given that the only evidence we have is B.

5.5 DEMPSTER AND SHAFER'S THEORY OF EVIDENCES

The mathematical theory of evidences developed by Arthur Dempster has a lot of advantages over the Bayesian and CF model. This theory was putforth by Dempster in the 1960s and subsequently extended by Glenn Shafer. The main advantage of the DS theory over other previous approaches is its ability to model the marrowing of the hypotheses set with accumulation of evidences, i.e. the process that characterizes reasoning in expert systems.

Let us take an example from MYCIN. Suppose a physician is considering a case of cholestatic jaundice for which there is a diagnostic hypotheses set of hepatitis (hep), cirrahosis (cir), gallstone (gall), and pancreatic cancer (pan). In D-S theory ϕ = {hep, cir, gall, pan} is called the *frame of discernment*. ϕ is assumed to be exhaustive. Let us consider that one piece of evidence by the physician might support the diagnosis of *intra hepatitic cholestasis* which reduces ϕ to a subset {hep, cir} or the hypothesis hepor-cir. Similarly the hypothesis *extra hepatitic cholestasis* corresponds to a set {gall, pan}. Evidence confirming intra hepatitic cholestasis to some degree will cause the physician to allot a proportional amount of belief to the corresponding subset of ϕ. A new piece of evidence might help the physician to exclude hepatitis to some degree. Evidence disconfirming hepatitis {hep} is equivalent to evidence confirming not-hep, which conforms to hypothesis cir-or-gall-or-pan or the subset {cir, gall, pan}. The evidence disconfirming hepatitis to some degree will cause the physician to allot a proportionate belief to this three element subset.

As illustrated above, a subset of hypotheses in ϕ gives rise to a new hypothesis which is equivalent to a disjunction of the hypotheses in the subset. Each hypothesis in ϕ corresponds to a one element subset (called *singleton*). By considering all possible subset of ϕ, denoted by 2, the set of hypotheses to which belief can be alloted is enlarged. Henceforth, we use the term hypothesis in this enlarged sense to denote any subset of the original hypotheses in ϕ.

A set of cardinality n has 2 subsets including the null set. The null set is a hypothesis known to be false and is not shown in Figure 5.1.

5.5.1 Basic Probability Assignments

The Dempster-Shafer theory uses a number in the range [0,1] to indicate amount of belief in a hypothesis, given a piece of evidence. This number is the degree to which the evidence supports the hypothesis.

The impact of each distinct piece of evidence on the subsets of ϕ is represented by a function called a *basic probability assignment* (bpa). A bpa is a generalization of the traditional *probability density function* (pdf). A pdf associates a number with each element ϕ of such that their sum equals 1. bpa assigns a number m to each subset

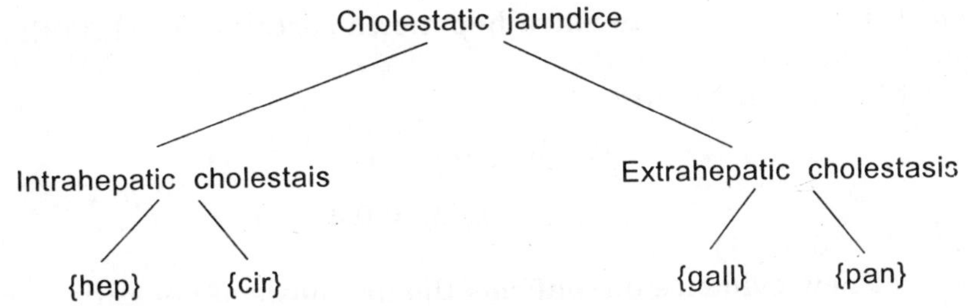

Figure 5.1 The subsets of clinical interest in jaundice.

of ϕ such that their sum equals 1. It uses an enlarged set 2 and assigns a number to each element.

By definition, $m = 0$ assigned to the null set implies no hypothesis and we know ϕ is exhaustive. Therefore, it allows assignment of a quantity to each element in the tree shown in the previous example and not just to the leaf nodes as in the case in pdf.

The quantity $m(A)$ is a measure of that portion of the total belief committed exactly to A. When $A \in 2^{\phi}$ and total belief is 1. This portion of belief cannot be further subdivided among the subsets of A and does not include portions of belief committed to the subsets of A. Belief in a subset.

A entails belief in all subset X such that

$$A \subset X$$

A function that computes a total amount of belief in A will essentially combine belief in A with all its subsets. Such a function is called a *belief function*.

The quantity $m(\phi)$ is measure of that portion of the belief that remains unassigned after commitment of belief to various proper subsets of O.

For example, evidence favouring a single subset of A need not to say anything about belief in the other subsets. If $m(A) = s$ and m assigns no belief to other subsets of O, then $m(\phi) = 1 - s$. Here the remaining belief is assigned to O and not to the negation of hypothesis, A and A^c as in set theoretic fashion, required by the Bayesian model.

Suppose that there is no evidence concerning the specific diagnosis in a patient with known cholestatic jaundice. The bpa representing ignorance, called the *vacuous* bpa, assigns 1 to O = {hep,gal,pan,car}, and 0 to all its subsets.

Bayesian assigns equal probabilities to each member of set O.

$$\text{p(hep)} = \text{p(cir)} = \text{p(gal)} = \text{p(pan)} = 0.25.$$

Dempster-Shafer (D-S) theory assigns $m(O) = 1$; and 0 to all other proper subsets of O.

Suppose that the evidence supports, or confirms the diagnosis of intrahepatic cholestasis to the degree = 0.6, but does not support a choice between cir or hep. Then ({hp, cir}) = 0.6 and the remainig belief is assigned to ϕ, $m(\phi) = 0.4$, as ϕ under assumption is exhaustive.

Bayesian would assign 0.4 to extra hepatic cholestasis, which is the negation of intrahepatic cholestasis.

Dempster-Shafer will require

$$m(\{\text{cir, hep}\}) = 0.6$$
$$m(\phi) = 0.4$$

for other sets $A \subset \phi$, $m(A) = 0$.

Suppose that new evidence disconfirms the diagnosis of hepatitis to a degree 0.7. This is equivalent to confirming hep to a degree 0.7.

Dempster-Shafer will require

$$m(\{\text{cir, gal, pan}\}) = 0.7$$
$$m(\phi) = 0.3$$

for other sets $A \subset \phi$, $m(A) = 0$

If the evidence confirms the diagnosis of hep to a degree 0.8, then

$$m(\{\text{hep}\}) = 0.8$$
$$m(\subset \phi) = 0.2$$

otherwise, $A \subset \varphi$ $m(A) = 0$.

5.5.2 Belief Functions

A *belief function*, Bel, corresponding to a specific bpa, assigned to every subset A of O is the sum of the beliefs committed exactly to every subset of A by m. For example,

$$\begin{aligned} \text{Bel}(\{\text{hep, cir, pan}\}) = {} & m(\{\text{hep, cir, pan}\})+ \\ & m(\{\text{hep, cir}\})+ \\ & m(\{\text{cir, pan}\})+ \\ & m(\{\text{hep, pan}\})+ \\ & m(\{\text{hep}\})+ \\ & m(\{\text{cir}\})+ \\ & m(\{\text{pan}\}) \end{aligned}$$

Thus Bel(A) is a measure of total amount of belief in A and not of the amount committed precisely to A.

FACTS

Bel(B) = $m(B)$, if B is singleton set.
Bel(A) = sum of m at each node of the tree rooted at A
Bel(ϕ) = 1

5.5.3 Combination of Beliefs

Evidence gathering procedure requires method for combining the support for a hypothesis, or its negation, based on multiple accumulated observations. In D-S theory for the same frame of discernment, two belief functions, based on two separate observations can be combined using a rule. We shall explain this rule through an example.

Evidence supporting hep, reduces belief in the singletion hypotheses {cir}, {gal}, and {pan} and other joint hypotheses not containing hep, that is all subsets of A, such, that $A \cap \{hep\} = \phi$. This has a wider implication on the hypotheses set in CF model.

Let Bel1, Bel2 and ml, $m2$, be two belief functions and their bpa. Dempster's rule computes a new m denoted by

$$m = m1 \ \phi \ m2$$

m represents the combined effects of $m1$ and $m2$ and the corresponding belief function is

$$\text{Bel} = \text{Bel1} \ \phi \ \text{Bel2}$$

which can be computed from m. If we sum all the products of the form $m(X)^* \ m(Y)$, where X, Y run over all subsets of O, the result is 1.

$$\Sigma(m1(X) = 2(Y)) = 1 = \Sigma m1(X) * \Sigma m2(Y)$$

The bpa m1 ϕ $m2(A)$ is defined in Dempster's rule as the sum of all products of the form $m1(X)^*$ $m2(Y)$, where X, Y run over all subsets whose intersection is A. For this we construct an Intersection Tableau.

	$m2(\{\text{cir, gal, pan}\}) = 0.7$	$m(\phi) = 0.3$
$m1(\{\text{hep, cir}\}) = 0.6$	$m(\{\text{cir}\}) = 0.42$	$m(\{\text{hep, cir}\}) = 0.18$
$M(\phi) = 0.4$	$m(\{\text{cir, gal, pan}\}) = 0.28$	$m(\phi) = 0.12$

Consider for a given patient one observation disconfirms hep (i.e. confirms {cir, gal, pan} to a degree $m1 = 0.6$, whereas another observation disconfirms hep (i.e. confirms {cir, gal, pan} to a degree $m2 = 0.7$. Then our net belief based on both observations is given by $m = ml \ \phi \ m2$ as follows:

$$m1 \ \phi \ m2 \text{ (cir)} = 0.42$$

$$m1 \ \phi \ m2 \text{ (hep, cir)} = 0.18$$

$$m1 \ \phi \ m2 \text{ (cir, gal, pan)} = 0.28$$

$$m1 \ \phi \ m2 \ (0) = 0.12$$

$$m1 \ \phi \ m2 = 0 \text{ for all other subsets}$$

since Bel = Bel1 ϕ Bel2

$$\begin{aligned} \text{Bel}(\{\text{hep, cir}\}) &= m1 \ \phi \ m2 \text{ (hep, cir)} + \\ &\quad m1 \ \phi \ m2 \text{ (hep)} + \\ &\quad m1 \ \phi \ m2 \text{ (cir)} \\ \text{Bel }(\{\text{cir, gal, pan}\}) &= m1 \ \phi \ m2 \text{ (cir, gal, pan\}} + \\ &\quad m1 \ \phi \ m2 \text{ (cir, gal)} + \\ &\quad \ldots m1 \ \phi \ m2 \text{ (pan)} \end{aligned}$$

In this case both the conditions are satisfied, namely

$$\Sigma (m1(X)\ m2(Y)) = 1$$

and

$$m1\ \phi\ m2(\phi) = 0$$

Consider another example. If another evidence $m3$ confirms the diagnosis of hepatitis to a degree $m3 = 0.8$, then the above tableau is changed to:

	$M(\{cir\}) = 42$	$M(\{hep,cir\}) = 0.18$	$M(\{cir,gal,pan\}) = 0.28$	$M(\phi) = 0.12$
$M3(\{hep\}) = 0.8$	$M(\phi) = 0.336$	$M(\{hep\}) = 0.144$	$M(\phi) = 0.224$	$M(\{hep\}) = 0.9$
$M(\phi) = 0.8$	$M(\{cir\}) = 0.084$	$M(\{hep,cir\}) = 0.36$	$M(\{gal,pan,cir\}) = .056$	$M(\phi) = .024$

When there are ϕ in the tableau the condition 2 is not valid to overcome this problem, Dempster suggested normalization so that $m1\ \phi\ m2\ (\phi) = 0$. This is done by dividing all the values in the tableau by a factor $1 - k$. k is the sum of all non-zero values assigned to ϕ.

5.6 NON-CLASSICAL LOGICS

The methods discussed so far are for expert systems where knowledge has to be represented as rules, and inference procedure is a sequential method of collecting evidences. Expert systems, as we all know solve problems from a narrow domain, such as diagnostics of modular operational entities of the knowledge (Rules), which are kept apart from the algorithms capable of exploiting it.

The problem with certainty factor (CF) models is that there is no rigorous semantics associated with the CFs. They may have several meanings, which do not correspond to a single treatment of coefficients. Another problem is of conflict resolution, when several rules lead to contradicting hypothesis.

Now, we shall take a small knowledge base (KB) as our standard example, and will use it to show advantages and disadvantages of various other reasoning methods under this uncertain and incomplete knowledge base.

Example knowledge base:

Rl : Students (stdn) are young (yng).
R2 : Young people are single (sng).
R3 : Single people are young.
R4 : Some young people are students.
R5 : Students who have children are married (mrd) or co-habitants (chbt).
R6 : Co-habitants are young.
R7 : Single, married, and co-habitants are all mutually exclusive.

In case of CF model, or some probabilistic models like bayesian, etc. each evidence contributes some quantitative value to the consequent, as we have already seen. Let us give some quantitative values to each parameter in the KB, and use the CF inference model.

Rl	:	stdn (+l)	then yng (0.9).
R2	:	yng (+l)	then sng (0.8).
R3	:	sng (+l)	then yng (0.7).
R4	:	yng (+l)	then stdn (0.3).
R5	:	stdn and Put	then mrd-or-chbt (0.95).
R6	:	chbt (+l)	then yng (0.8).
R7	:	sug (+l)	then chbt (–1).
		mrd (+l)	then mrd-or-chbt (+1)
		chbt (+l)	then mrd-or-chbt(+1)
		mrd-or-chbt(1)	then sng (–111).

If we have the following fact available to us:

F1 Rhea is student and is a parent.

then using the CF model, we can infer the hypothesis young as follows:

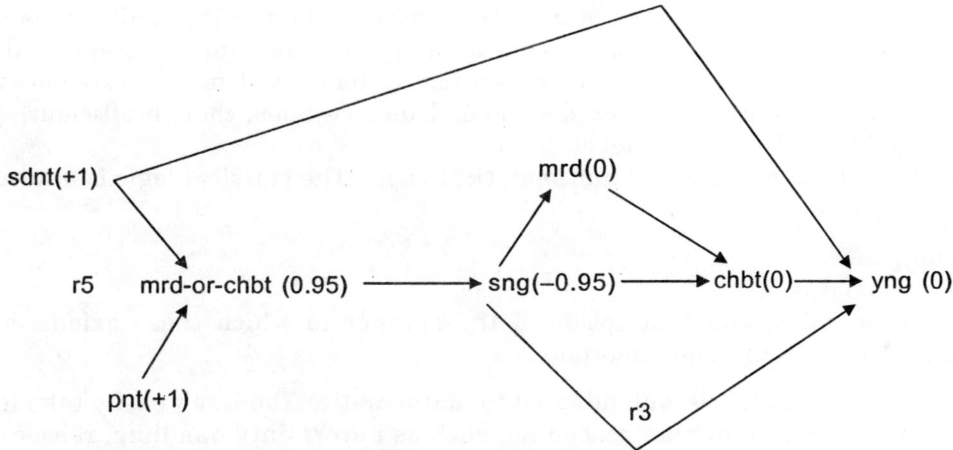

Figure 5.2 Inference in CF model of our example.

These have been obtained from CF combining rule already seen earlier.

1. Propagation Rule

$$A \rightarrow B : \text{CF}(B) = \max 90, \text{CF}(A)) * \text{CF}$$

2. Or Node Rule

$$\text{CF}(A) = \text{CF1}(0.1) + \text{CF2}(A) - \text{CF1}(A) * \text{CF2}(A) \text{ if CF1}(A), \text{CF2}(A) > 0.$$

$$= \text{CF1}(A) + \text{CF2}(A) + \text{CF1}(A) * \text{CF2}(A) \text{ if CF1}(A), \text{CF2}(A) < 0.$$

$$= \frac{\text{CF1}(A) + \text{CF2}(A)}{1 - \min([\text{CF1}(A)], [\text{CF2}(A)])}$$

3. And Node Rule

$$\text{CF}(A1 \wedge A2) = \min(\text{CF}(A1), \text{CF}(A2)).$$

In the above example the terminal combination for young is (0.9). The result is paradoxical since we do not use the information pnt. This is the case because negative facts are not allowed to propagate (absence of modus tollen). If that had been the case, we would have obtained:

$$\text{young} = \begin{cases} (0.9) \\ (0.76) \\ (0) \end{cases}$$

Using the Or Node Rule

$$\text{CF(yng)} = \frac{0.9 - 0.76}{1 - 0.76} = 0.58$$

This again is a debatable result, this is because the two solutions are obtained from the two justifications sets yng and {yng, pnt}, which are not disjoint. The system as such doesn't provide any means of detecting these dependencies, and carries out the combination in a systematic way. This approach has provided a great deal of impetus on research in uncertainty in reasoning systems, and many systems with weighted production rules have been designed. These systems, though efficient, are unsatisfactory at the theoretical level.

The classical logic has a sound mathematical basis. The classical logic is a formal system composed of:

- A language.
- Set of axioms.
- Inference rules, and description of the manner in which these axioms and rules are used to yield theorems.

Although, classical logic is well adapted to mathematics, it doesn't easily take into account certain aspects of human reasoning, such as uncertainty handling, reasoning under incomplete knowledge, common sense reasoning and temporality. These factors have led to the development of a large number of non-classical, non-standard logics which can do various types of inferences. All these have been derived from the classical logic by modifying the three components of the formal logic system.

- The language is extended by introducing particular predicates (as in suppositional logic) or operators (necessary and possible, in modal logic, autoepistemic logic, and operators like past and future in temporal logic).
- New axioms are added (circumscription approach).
- New notions of inference are defined, which permit the formulation of knowledge as *P* is true in certain vision of the world ... (default logic). The introduction of inference rules like necessitation rule in modal logic, etc.

5.6.1 Necessity for New Logics

Considering the example "students are young", this piece of knowledge cannot be written in propositional calculus, because the set student is not defined. If that had been the case, we could enumerate the fact for each element of the set of students as below:

$$A = \{ \text{ set, of students } \}$$

Then xi is young for all $xi \in A$.

This is a laborious process, and not possible when A is infinite, or when it is not well-defined. Our natural choice in that case will be predicate calculus. In this we will be allowed to capture the information as follows:

All students are young.

$$\text{e1 : stdn(x)} \rightarrow \text{yng(x)}$$

Such a formulation is sound for x belonging to the set of student, but rules out the possibility of an exception. For example,

Ram is a student and he is not young.

$$\text{Stdn(Ram) and} \rightarrow \text{yng (Ram)}$$

This piece of information is not incorrect, but in conjunction with earlier fact it produces inconsistencies in the knowledge base, since:

Ram is a student → Ram is young (from 1)

Ram is not young, (from 2)

In order to restore consistency, while still keeping interesting deductions, we have to express these two facts as:

All students are young, except Ram.

By allowing equality predicate, we can write it as:

$$\text{e1: stdn(x) and} - (\text{x} = = \text{Ram}) \rightarrow \text{yng(x) hfill} - 3$$

Such approach will solve the inconsistency problem but will pose several other problems such as:

(a) Expressing all the exceptions is unrealistic.
(b) Different ($\neq$) is not provable in predicate calculus; we will be required to state that each student is unique.
(c) Representation no longer will be modular. Every new exception will require complete revision of the knowledge base. To make this point clear, we shall go back to our test example with the additional fact that Ram is a student who co-habits with someone. In order to restore the consistency of the KB, we make following changes:

$\text{e1} : \forall x \ \text{stdn(x)} \wedge \rightarrow (\text{Ram} == x) \rightarrow \text{yng(x)}$
$\text{e2} : \forall x \ \{\text{yng(x)} \rightarrow \text{sng(x)}\}$
$\text{e3} : \forall x \ \{\text{sng(x)} \rightarrow \text{yng (x)}\}$
$\text{e4} : \exists x \ \{\text{yng(x)} \rightarrow \exists y \ [\text{yng(y)} \wedge \text{stdn(y)}]\}$
$\text{e5} : \forall x \ \{\text{stdn(x)} \wedge \text{pnt(x)} \rightarrow \text{mrd(x)} \vee \text{chbt(x)}\}$

e6 : $\forall x$ {chbt(x) $\wedge \rightarrow$ (Ram == x) $\rightarrow$ yng(x) }
e7 : $\forall x$ { à sng(x) $\wedge \rightarrow$ mrd(x)}
$\forall x$ { $\rightarrow$ sng(x) $\wedge \rightarrow$ chbt(x)}
$\forall x$ { $\rightarrow$ chbt(x) $\wedge \rightarrow$ mrd(x)}

Soundness is obtained at the expense of transforming the KB. The problem becomes more complicated when we have make additions of exceptions of different types. Moreover the question of good transformation also arises, because KB can be transformed in more than one way. Our test example can also be made sound in the following way:

e1 : $\forall x$ stdn(x) $\rightarrow$ yng(x)
e2 : $\forall x$ {yng(x) $\wedge \rightarrow$ (Ram == x) $\rightarrow$ sng(x)}
e3 : $\forall x$ {sng(x) $\rightarrow$ yng (x)}
e4 : $\exists x$ {yng(x) $\rightarrow \exists y$ [yng(y) $\wedge$ stdn(y)]}
e5 : $\forall x$ {stdn(x) $\wedge$ pnt(x) $\rightarrow$ mrd(x) $\vee$ chbt(x)}
e6 : $\forall x$ {chbt(x) $\rightarrow$ yng(x)}
e7 : $\forall x$ { $\rightarrow$ sng(x) $\wedge \rightarrow$ mrd(x)}
$\forall x$ { $\rightarrow$ sng(x) $\wedge \rightarrow$ chbt(x)}
$\forall x$ { $\rightarrow$ chbt(x) $\wedge \rightarrow$ mrd(x)}

(d) The quantifiers are not sufficient to capture facts like "Some young people are students". The closest will be

$$\exists x \{yng(x) \rightarrow \exists y[yng(y) \wedge stdn(y)]\}$$

which happens to be a very poor substitute.

Also because of the symmetrical nature of disjunction, the formulae

$$A \rightarrow B \text{ and } B \vee A$$

are evaluated identically. Although the first one has a totally different implication as far as representation is considered. For example, the fact

$$\forall z \{yng(x) \wedge \rightarrow chbt(x) \rightarrow sng(x)\}$$

and

$$\forall x \{yng(x) \wedge \rightarrow [sng(x) \vee chbt(x)]\}$$

are identical in the predicate calculus domain. Both of them are evaluated in the resolution procedure identically. But semantically, they mean two different things. In the first case, we mean that a young person who is not a co-habitant is single; in the second case, we mean that a young person can be either single or co-habitant. The property "single" is attached to young people in a privileged sense in relation to the property "co-habitant" in the first case.

We therefore need some mechanism that would break this symmetry. The introduction of negation as failure resolves this conflict. This algorithm is used in PROLOG for the interpretation of the negation operator NOT.

Another way of breaking the symmetry of clauses is to associate with a logical database (or logic program) a canonical model that gives new semantics to negation.

The approach in PROLOG is procedural and is borrowed from classical logic. The second approach uses declarative semantics, thus producing non-classical logic. Some of the important non-classical logic are Reiter's Default which gave rise to default model semantics, and Moore's Autoepistemic Logic, which gave rise to the stable model semantics.

5.7 DEFAULT LOGIC

Default logic is a non-monotonic logic introduced by Reiter in order to formalize default reasoning. A default theory $\nabla = (D, W)$ consists of a set of facts W, which are closed first order formulae (grounded formulae), are a set of defaults D which are specific inference rules. An open default is any expression of the form:

$$\frac{u(x) : v(x)}{w(x)}$$

where $u(x)$, $v(x)$ are first order well formed formulae, containing a single free variable.

- $u(x)$ is called prerequisite
- $v(x)$ is called justification
- $w(x)$ is the consequent

The meaning of such a formula is the following:
If $u(x)$ is known and if $v(x)$ is consistent with what is known, then infer w(x).
A default is called normal if $v(x)$. The default

$$A(x) : B(x)$$

$$B(x)$$

where A and B are unary predicates is read as B is deduced from A with exceptions. It may be used to capture following information: "Normally or typically the A's are B's".

5.8 BAYESIAN NETWORKS

These are also called *belief networks* or *probabilistic inference networks*. It was initially developed by Pearl (1988).

The basic idea

- Knowledge in the world is modular—most events are independent of most other events.
- Adopt a model that can use a more local representation to allow interactions between events that only affect each other.
- Some events may only be unidirectional, others may be bidirectional—make a distinction between these in model.
- Events may be causal and thus get chained together in a network.

Implementation

- A Bayesian network is a directed acyclic graph.
- A graph where the directions are links indicating dependencies that exist between nodes.
- Nodes represent propositions about events or events themselves.
- Conditional probabilities quantify the strength of dependencies.

Consider the following example (Figure 5.3):

- The probability, $P(s)$ that my car won't start.
- If my car won't start then it is likely that the battery is flat or the staring motor is broken.

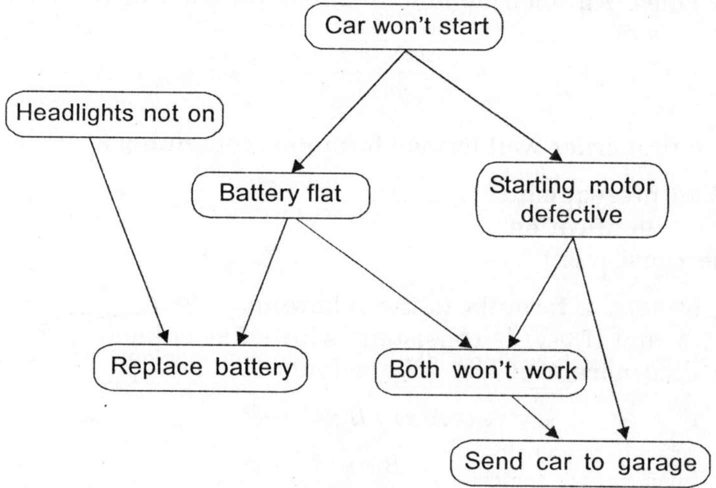

Figure 5.3 The network to represent car fixing.

In order to decide whether to fix the car myself or send it to the garage I make the following decision:

- If the headlights do not work then the battery is likely to be flat so *i* fix it myself.
- If the starting motor is defective then send car to garage.
- If battery and starting motor both gone send car to garage.

5.9 FUZZY LOGIC

The concept of a fuzzy set was introduced by Zadeh (1965) who recognized that human problems were not amenable to standard control systems. Zadeh's principle of incompatibility states that:

"As the complexity of a system increases, our ability to make precise and yet significant statements about its behaviour diminishes until a threshold is reached beyond which precision and significance (or relevance) become almost mutually exclusive characteristics."

In the techniques we have discussed so far, we have not modified the mathematical underpinnings provided by set theory and logic. We have instead augmented those ideas with additional constructs provided by probability theory. In this section, we take a different approach and briefly consider what happens if we make fundamental changes to our idea of set membership and corresponding changes to our definitions of logical operations.

Fuzzy logic is a totally different approach to represent uncertainty:

- It focuses on ambiguities in describing events rather the uncertainty about the occurrence of an event.
- Changes the definitions of set theory and logic to allow this.
- Traditional set theory defines set memberships as a Boolean predicate.

Fuzzy set theory defines set membership as a possibility distribution.

This basically states that we can take n possible events and use them to generate a single possible outcome. The motivation for fuzzy sets is provided by the need to represent such propositions as:

John is very tall.
Mary is slightly ill.
Sue and Linda are close friends.
Exceptions to the rule are nearly impossible.
Most Frenchmen are not very tall.

We could allow for variations in definitions by allowing both possibilities in fuzzy definitions. Once set membership has been redefined we can develop new logics based on combining of sets, etc. and reason effectively.

Mathematical probability theory was developed to help explain random physical phenomena, from games of chance to the random fluctuations of atoms and electrons. Random physical phenomena generally can be characterized by some objects capable of taking on one of a number of distinguishable and mutually exclusive states. Furthermore, over a large number of independent trials, the frequency of occurrence of the observed states tends to approach a stable value for each observed state.

Set theory and formal logic are dual representations of the same information. The law of the *excluded middle* states that for any thing it is either true or that it possesses any given property. Fuzzy sets and fuzzy logic repeal this law. Any object may be a member of a set to some degree; and a logical proposition may hold true to some degree. Figure 5.4 illustrates the concept of fuzzy sets by their membership definitions. The classic set M shows a very well-defined line of criteria for membership of the set. The fuzzy set M' graphically illustrates the concept that there is a cloudy or imprecise boundary for membership of the set. In the case of the fuzzy set, the grade of membership of x in M' will be a number in the range of 0 to 1.

A fuzzy set can be regarded as a label applied to a *linguistic concept* which has no precise boundary; and such concepts, with all their associated vagueness, are how humans mediate and exchange ideas. The graphs (Figure 5.5) overleaf show how

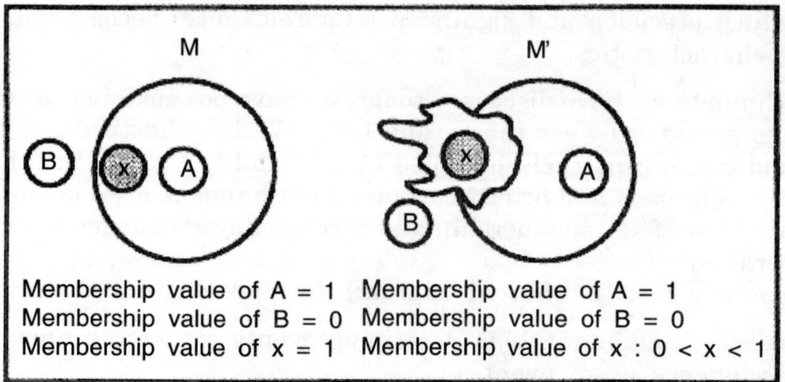

Figure 5.4 The concept of fuzzy sets by their membership definition.

fuzzy sets can be represented numerically. The chart to left of the figure is a truth table selecting numbers between 4 and 9. The chart on the right shows numbers which are near seven. This is a fuzzy set; each particular number along the x-axis has a degree of membership of the set (normally represented as $\mu(x)$). The y-axis is scaled from 0 (meaning false) to 1 (meaning true).

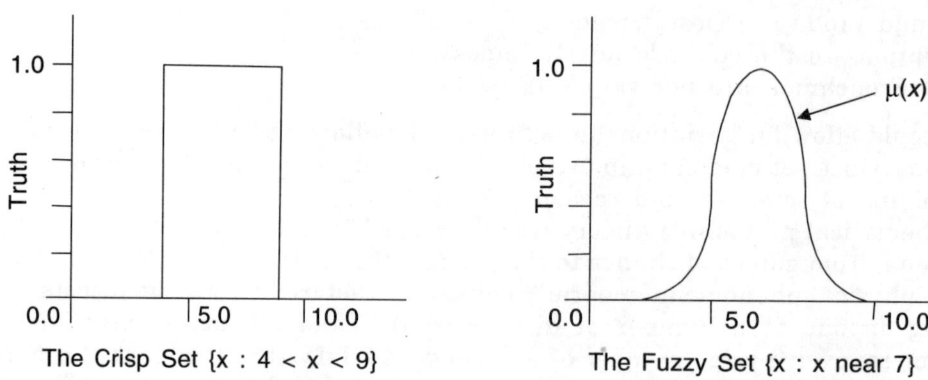

Figure 5.5 Membership function of the set.

Often a weak point in the application of fuzzy logic is the mapping or membership function of the set. Someone has to decide the shape of the fuzzy set graph such as the one shown above. There are no strong grounds for preferring one mapping function over another and often many different functions are applied. To allow these functions to take place the theoretical set operations of intersection, union and complement are used.

Linguistic variables from within a knowledge base need to be converted into manipulative numerical values, (qualitative to quantitative). The linguistic preference structure is assigned membership values of a set between 0 and 1. Table 5.2 illustrates this principle applied to the factor ground condition.

This *linguistic preference structure* (Table 5.1) allows fuzzy set membership values to be manipulated in the form of matrices. Computer representations of fuzzy sets often take the form of two-dimensional arrays, stored as individual files in the computer memory. Within these knowledge matrices each column represents an alternative within a particular domain, each row represents factor or features relating to those alternatives and each cell in the matrix is the relative merit of a factor for a particular alternative.

Table 5.1 Linguistic preference structure and Fuzzy set membership values

Preference structure	*Membership value*
Very Dry	0.1
Dry	0.3
Average	0.5
Wet	0.7
Very Wet	0.9

Table 5.2 Impact calculation

Impact Ruler (similar to certainty factor)

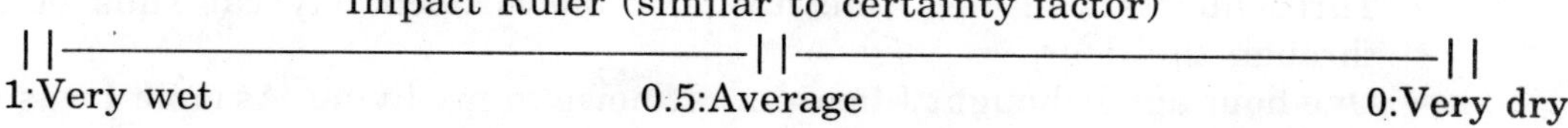

EXERCISES

1. What are the different sources of uncertainty?
2. What is meant by non-monotonic reasoning?
3. Can you differentiate between statistical reasoning and symbolic reasoning?
4. Explain Bayes theorem with example.
5. What is the major function of the Bayes theorem?
6. What are Dempster-Shafer models?
7. Write a LISP program that computes certainty factors for rules based on the MYCIN model.
8. What are the basic premises on which the fuzzy logic approach is based?
9. Certainty factors are popular in expert systems. Why is that so? What unique features does the theory of uncertainty provide?
10. Discuss major advantages and disadvantages of fuzzy logic.
11. Describe an algorithm whereby memory elements are distributed in neurons and the fuzzy values of the memory elements at a synapse must be sufficiently

strong to enable the synapse to fire and transfer the fuzzy values to the downstream neuron.

12. Write an algorithm in simple English (pseudocode) for performing diagnosis (backward reasoning with forward checking) with fuzzy rules.

13. What knowledge forms are totally inadequate for uncertain reasoning?

14. Discuss how they might deal with incompleteness, inconsistency, change, and non-monotonic default reasoning.

15. Represent the following in Dempster-Shafer theory:

- The probability that following an observation of fever that flu, cold or pneumonia cause it is 0.6.
- The probability of fever caused by allergy, flu or cold is 0.8.

(i) Use the Dempster combination rule to compute beliefs for further subsets derived from the above.

(ii) We now discover that probability of allergy is 0.8. Combine this information to compute the beliefs for all possible outcome of set intersections.

16. Consider the following facts:

- I saw my cat in the living room 3 hours ago.
- Two hours ago my door blew open.
- Three quarters of the time my door blows open, my cat runs outside through the door.
- One hour ago I thought I heard a cat noise in my living. Assume I was half certain.
- In any one hour period the probability that the cat will leave the room is 0.2. There is also a 0.2 probability that he may enter the room.

What is the certainty that the cat is in my living room?

1. Use Dempster-Shafer theory to answer this.
2. Use Bayesian networks to answer this.

17. Design a Bayesian network for each of the following problems:

(i) Choosing a menu for a dinner party.
(ii) Planning a holiday.
(iii) Selecting final year computer science options based on second and first year prerequisites.

CHAPTER 6

Search Techniques

6.1 INTRODUCTION

In AI, search refers to a large body of core ideas that deals with deduction, inference, planning, common sense reasoning, theorem proving, and related processes. Applications of these general ideas are found in Natural Language Understanding, Information Retrieval, Automatic Programming, Robotics, Scene Analysis, Game Playing, Expert Systems and Mathematical Theorem Proving.

Search systems generally have three components:

- Database
- Operators
- Control Strategy

The *database* describes the current task domain and the goal or, in other words, the sate. *Operators* are used to manipulate the database. The *control strategy* decides what operators to apply and where.

The objective of any search technique is the application of an appropriate sequence of operators to an initial task domain (state) to achieve the goal.

There are two ways to achieve this objective. One is called *forward reasoning* and the other is called *backward reasoning*. Forward reasoning refers to the application of operators to those structures in the database that describe the task domain in order to produce a modified state. Such a method is also referred to as bottom-up or data-driven reasoning. Here the objective is to bring the state forward from the initial state to one satisfying the goal condition. For example, consider a game of chess. Here,

Initial situation. Placement of chessmen on the board at the beginning of the game.

Goal. Any board configuration that is a checkmate.

Operators. Rules for legal moves in chess.

Backward reasoning or top-down or goal-directed reasoning breaks down the goal (problem) statement into subgoals (problems) which, hopefully, are easier to solve and whose solutions are sufficient to solve the original problem. For example, consider the integration problem,

$$\int \frac{1}{\cos^2} dx$$

If the operator permits

$$\frac{1}{\cos^2} dx$$

then we can restate our problem as

$$\int \sec^2 x \, dx = \tan x + c$$

It is interesting to note that much of our reasoning is backward.

6.2 PROBLEM REPRESENTATION

A problem solving system that uses either forward or backward reasoning whose each operator works to produce a single new object—a new state—in the database is said to represent problems in a *state-space.*

It is interesting to note that in the case of backward reasoning, two cases arise. One, application of an operator yields exactly one new problem whose size or difficulty is less than the original one and two, application of an operator in a complex system reduces a problem into a *set of subproblems*, perhaps each significantly smaller than the original problem. Such a system is said to employ a *problem-reduction representation.* There is, however, a relationship between the state-space and the problem-reduction representations. There may or may not be constraints on the order in which the subproblems are solved. For example, if the original operator is to integrate.

$$\int [f(x) + g(x)] \, dx$$

Applying the obvious operator changes to a problem of two integrations,

$$\int f(x) \, dx + \int g(x) \, dx$$

Depending on the type of representation, the new problem can be viewed as being either

- two new integration problems that can be solved in either order or
- two new integration problems plus a third problem f summing the integrals.

In the latter case, the third task cannot be performed unless the earlier 2 tasks are completed.

6.3 DEFINITIONS

In this book, we shall look at some of the search techniques in detail. But before going into that here we present a few preliminary definitions.

Graph. A *graph* is a data object. A graph, G, consists of two sets called *vertices* (nodes) V and *edges* E. V is a finite non-empty set of nodes and E is a finite set of pairs of nodes. Each pair in E is an edge in G. If the pairs of vertices are ordered, that is (i, j) is different from (j, i), then G is said to be directed. Otherwise it is undirected.

Tree. A *tree* is a finite set of one or more nodes such that (i) there is a specially designated node called the *root*; (ii) the remaining nodes are partitioned into $n \geq 0$ disjoint sets $T_1 \ldots T_n$ where each of these sets is a tree. $T_1 \ldots T_n$ are called the *subtrees* of the root.

Root node, terminal node and children. The node at the top of a tree, the one with no parent is called the *root node*. The nodes at the bottom of a tree, the one with no children are called the *terminal nodes*. If any node is connected to some other node or nodes through branches, then the nodes to which it is connected to are called its *children*.

Branching factor, expanding, opening, and closing. If the number of children is always the same for all the nodes that have children, that number is referred to as the *branching factor*. The process of obtaining the children of node is called *expanding the node*. Nodes are said to be open until they are expanded, whereupon they become closed.

Path. A *path* from a vertex u_p to another vertex u_q is a sequence of vertices u_p, u_{i1}, u_{i2}, ..., u_{in}, u_q. Such that (u_p, u_{i1}), ..., (u_{in}, u_q) are edges in $E(G)$. The length of a path is the number of edges in it.

A simple path is a path in which all the vertices are distinct. A cycle is a simple path in which the first and last vertices are identical.

Solution/goal. A *solution/goal* is a path in a tree from the root (or start state) to a goal state. Goal states may be defined either explicitly or as a set of states satisfying a given predicate. The search for a solution is conducted by making explicit just enough of the state-space tree that contains the solution path.

Backtracking. *Backtracking* represents one of the most general techniques in algorithm design. In order to apply the backtrack method the desired solution must be expressed as an n-tuple $(g_1, \ldots, g_n)$ where the g_i are chosen from some finite set D_i. Often the problem to be solved calls for maximizing (or minimizing or satisfying) a criterion function $P(g_1, \ldots, g_n)$. Now, suppose m is the size of D_i. Then there are $m = m_1, m_2, \ldots, m_n$ n-tuples which are possible candidates for solving the criterion function P. The backtrack procedure evaluates only those tuples that lead to the optimal solution. It's basic idea is to build up the solution vector one component at a time and to use the modified criterion function $P_i(g_1, \ldots, g_n)$ (sometimes called *bounding functions*) to test whether the vector being formed has any chance of success or not. If, in case, it realized that the partial vector $(g_1, ..., g_n)$ can in no way lead to an optimal solution, then $m_{i+1}, ..., m_n$ possible test vectors will be ignored entirely.

Dynamic orogramming. *Dynamic programming* is an algorithm design method that can be used when the solution to a problem may be viewed as a result of a sequence of decisions. For some of the problems viewed in this way, an optimal sequence of decisions may be found by making the decisions one at a time and never making an erroneous decision. In some cases however, such stepwise decisions (based only on local information) may not be possible to be made. One way to obtain an optimal solution even in such cases is to try out all the possible paths and choose the best one. Dynamic programming often drastically reduces the amount of enumerations by avoiding the enumeration of some decision sequences that cannot be optimal.

Branch-and-bound. The term *branch-and-bound* refers to all state-space search methods in which all children of the root node or the current node are generated before any other node can become the current node. The selection rule for the generation of the next node does not give any preference to a node that has a very good chance of getting the search to an answer node quickly. This brute force search method can be made optimal by assigning ranks to the node(s) that haven't been explored so far on the basis of the computational effort (cost) required to reach an answer node from the current node. This cost could be either the number of the nodes needed to reach the goal or the sum of the number of levels that is required to reach the nearest goal node. Note that in practice it is very difficult to employ the above criteria since the effort needed for computing the cost of a node may be too high as this involved the cost of searching the subtree of the current node.

6.4 REPRESENTATION SCHEMES

In analyses as well as solving, the tree structures are commonly used to represent the control strategies to the search. In state-space representation, a tree may be used to represent the set of problem states produced by the application of the operators. In such a representation, the root node of the tree represents the initial problem state or situation. Each of the new states that can be obtained by applying only one operator to the root are represented as successor node of the root node. Subsequent operator applications produce successors to these nodes, and so on. Each operator application is represented as a directed edge of the tree.

In practice however, the states are represented by a graph rather than a tree since there may be many different paths from the root to a given node. Besides trees and graphs other representation schemes include AND/OR graphs that are used with problem-solving methods involving problem reduction. These provide a means for obtaining subgoals, a combination of which is sufficient to obtain the desired goal.

Here, Figure 6.1 is a simple representation of a tree that represents the various states together with the transitions. Also, a representation of a transition from one state to another on the application of an operator in a branch of a tree is given in Figure 6.2.

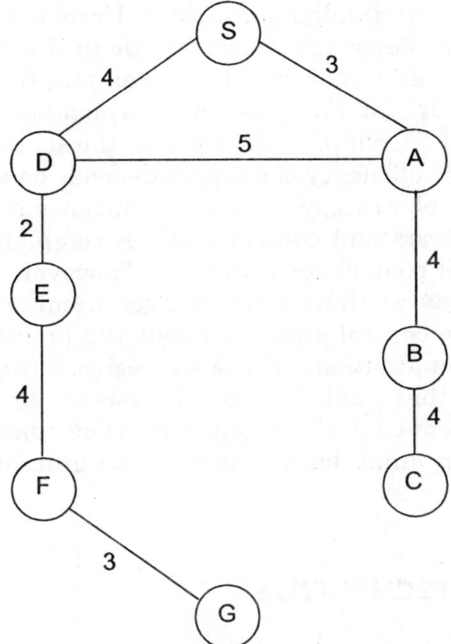

Figure 6.1 Basic search problem.

A basic search problem is shown in Figure 6.1. A path is to be found from the start node, S, to the goal node, G. Search procedures explore trees like these, learning about connections and distances as they go.

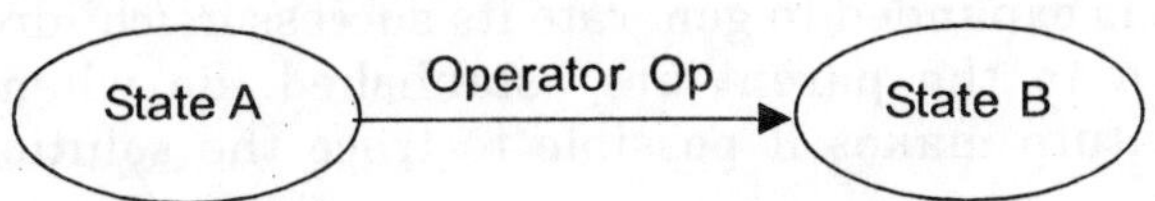

Figure 6.2 State change for A to B on the application of an operator *Op*.

With this background let us now look at the general procedure to solve problems in AI.

6.5 PROBLEM SOLVING IN AI

The basic procedure for solving a problem in AI can be written as:

procedure PRODUCTION

1. DATA ← initial database
2. while (DATA does not satisfy the termination condition) do
   (a) select some rule, R, in the set of rules that can be applied to DATA.
3. DATA ← result of applying R to DATA

end PRODUCTION.

In the above procedure, the fundamental control problem is selecting the rule R to apply to the database. An important characteristic in this regard is the amount of "knowledge" of information at hand that these computations use. Such a search procedure uses the knowledge at hand as an informed/heuristic search procedure against an uninformed/blind search procedure where the selection is made arbitrarily.

The overall computational efficiency of a search depends on wherein the uninformed/informed spectrum the control strategy falls. This efficiency is a measure of two types of costs: rules application costs and control costs. A completely uninformed control strategy incurs only a small control computations. However, such a strategy results in high rule application costs as these require large number of rule applications to find a solution. To inform a control strategy about the problem domains of interest usually involves high cost computations. These strategies, however, result in minimum rule application costs since they guide the search systems directly to a solution. Part of the art of designing efficient control strategies in AI systems is to decide to balance these two costs. With this in mind, let us consider the uninformed and the informed strategies in some detail.

6.6 BLIND SEARCH TECHNIQUES

Although uninformed search techniques are not practical for non-trivial problems it however provides a foundation for understanding the informed search strategies.

All the search algorithms make the following assumptions:

- A node can be expanded by some known procedure, say expand.
- The state-space graph is tree. The implications are that there is only a single start state and there is a unique path from one node to another.
- Whenever a node is expanded to generate its successors/children, back pointers from the children to the parent are established. So when a goal node is obtained, this feature makes it possible to trace the solution path.

For all search methods, the tree given in Figure 6.3 represents the initial state of the problem.

6.6.1 Breadth-first Search

In *breadth-first search* we start at an initial node (state) S and mark it as having been visited (reached). Then S is expanded to obtain all other nodes in order of their proximity to S. This is measured by the number of edges between them. We use the convention that the alternatives are tried in the left-to-right order. This means every possible operator sequence at level n is considered before considering any sequence at level $n + 1$. Thus, although this procedure may be an extremely long one, it nevertheless finds an optimal path to the goal state, if such a path exists.

Breadth-first search (Figure 6.4) is described by the following algorithm:

Procedure BREADTH-FIRST-SEARCH

1. Form a one element queue consisting of the root node.

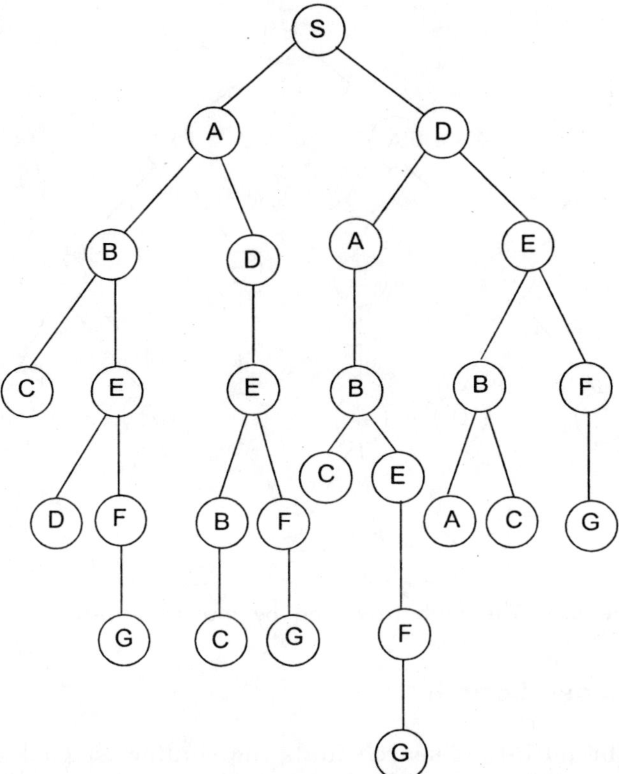

Figure 6.3 Illustration of the tree which denotes the state-space of the problem under consideration. Node S is the root node and also a parent node, with its children being A and D. The nodes with no children are the terminal nodes or leaves.

2. Until the queue is empty or the goal has been reached, determine if the first element in the queue is a goal node:
   (a) If the first element is a goal node then do nothing.
   (b) If the first element is not a goal node, then remove the first element from the queue and add the first element's children, if any to the back of the queue.
3. If the goal has been found, announce success; otherwise, announce failure.

end BREADTH-FIRST-SEARCH

In the breadth-first-search, downward motion proceeds level by level until the goal is reached.

We can make the following observations about breadth-first searches:

- It is a very systematic search strategy as it considers all nodes (states) at level 1 and then all states at level 2, etc.
- If there is a solution breadth-first search is guaranteed to find it.
- If there are several solutions then breadth-first search will always find the shallowest goal state first and if the cost of a solution is a non-decreasing function of the depth then it will always find the cheapest solution.

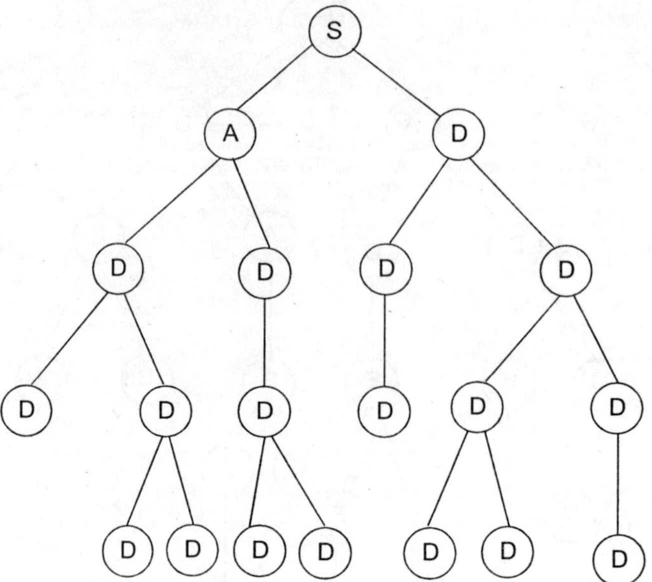

Figure 6.4 The path traversed by the breadth-first search.

6.6.2 Uniform Cost Search

We have said that breadth-first search finds the shallowest goal state and that this will be the cheapest solution so long as the path cost is a function of the depth of the solution. But, if this is not the case, then breadth-first search is not guaranteed to find the best (i.e. cheapest) solution.

Uniform cost search remedies this. It works always by expanding the lowest cost node on the fringe, where the cost is the path cost, $g(n)$. In fact, breadth-first search is a uniform cost search with $g(n)$ = DEPTH(n).

Consider the following problem:

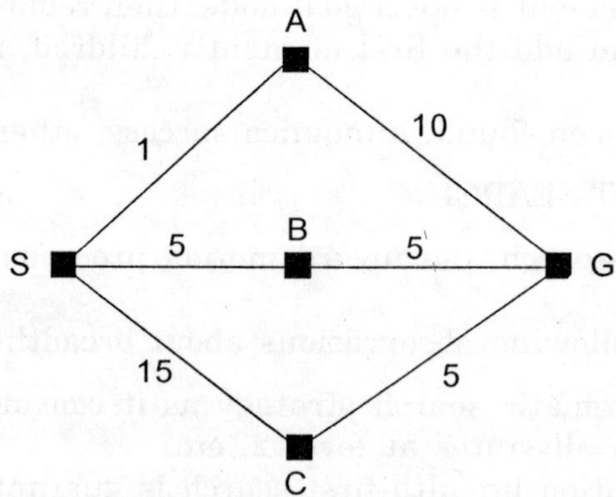

We wish to find the shortest route from S to G, that is S is the initial state and G is the goal state. We can see that SBG is the shortest route but if we let breadth-first search loose on the problem it will find the path SAG, assuming that A is the first node to be expanded at level 1. But this is how uniform cost search tackles the problem.

We start with the initial state and expand it. This leads to the following tree:

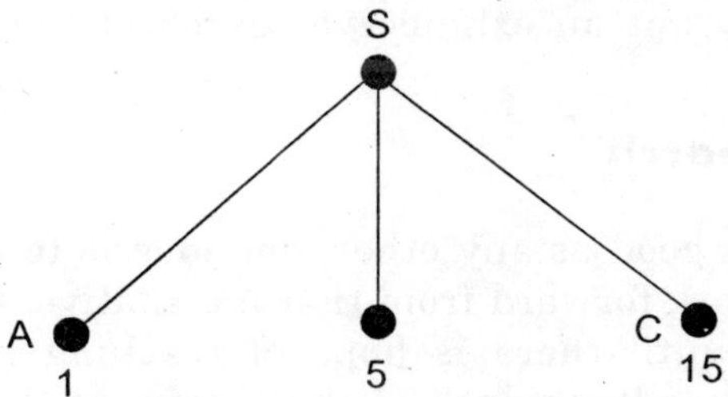

The path cost of A is the cheapest, so it is expanded next, giving the following tree:

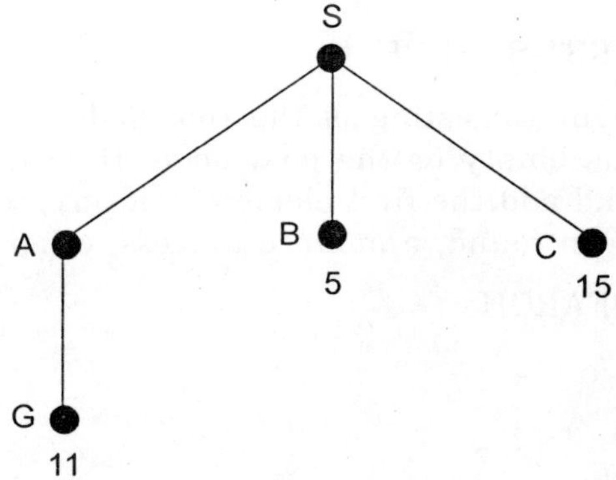

We now have a goal state but the algorithm does not recognize it yet as there is still a node with a cheaper path cost. In fact, what the algorithm does is order the queue by the path cost so the node with cost 11 will be behind node B in the queue. Node B (being the cheapest) is now expanded, giving the following tree:

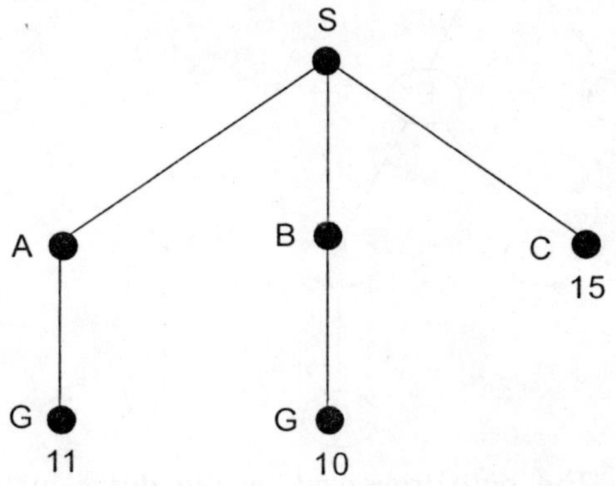

A goal state (G) will now be at the front of the queue. Therefore the search will end and the path SBG will be returned.

In short, uniform cost search will find the cheapest solution provided that the cost of the path never decreases as we proceed along the path. If this requirement is not met then we never know when we will meet a negative cost. The result of this would be a need to carry out an exhaustive search of the entire tree.

6.6.3 Depth-first Search

Given that one path is as good as any other, one idea is to pick up an alternative at every node visited and work forward from that alternative. Other alternatives at the same level are ignored until there is hope of reaching the destination with the original choice. Hence a headlong dash to the bottom of the tree along the leftmost branches is made. In case such a dive leads to a terminal non-goal node, the way out is to back up to the nearest unexplored ancestor with an unexplored alternative. This is the essence of the *depth-first search*. Depth-first search is described by the following algorithm:

Procedure DEPTH-FIRST-SEARCH

1. Form a one element consisting of the root node.
2. Until the queue is empty or the goal node, then remove the first element from the queue and add the first element's, if any, to the front of the queue.
3. If the goal has been found, announce success; otherwise announce failure.

End DEPTH-FIRST-SEARCH.

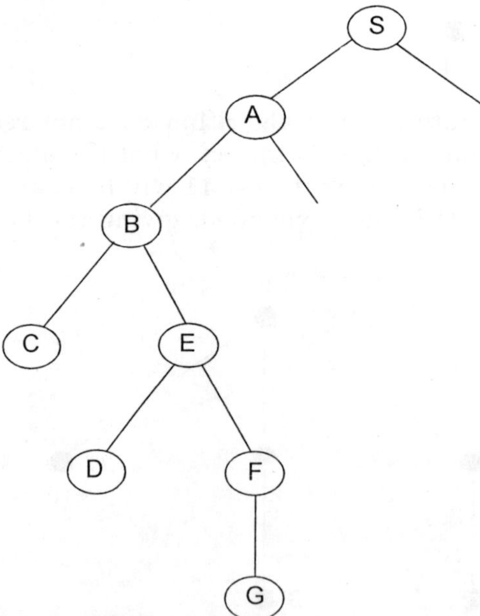

Figure 6.5 The path traversed by the depth-first search.

We can make the following comments about depth-first search:

- It has the modest memory requirements. It only needs to store the path from the root to the leaf node as well as the unexpanded nodes. For a state space with a branching factor of b and a maximum depth of m, depth-first search requires storage of bm nodes.
- The time complexity for depth-first search is b^m in the worst case.
- If depth-first search goes down an infinite branch it will not terminate unless finds a goal state. If it does find a solution there may be a better solution at a higher level in the tree. Therefore, depth-first search is neither complete nor optimal.

In depth-first-search, one alternative is selected at each node and pursued until the goal is reached or a node is reached where further downward motion is impossible. In the latter case, search is restarted at the nearest ancestor node with unexplored children.

6.6.4 Depth-limited Search

The problem with depth-first search is that the search can go down an infinite branch and thus never return. *Depth-limited search* avoids this problem by imposing a depth limit which effectively terminates the search at that depth. The algorithm can be implemented using the general search algorithm by using operators to keep track of the depth.

The choice of the depth parameter can be an important factor. Choosing a parameter that is too deep is wasteful in terms of both time and space. But choosing a depth parameter that is too shallow may result in never reaching a goal state.

As long as the depth parameter, I is set 'deep enough' then we are guaranteed to find a solution if it exists. Therefore, it is complete as long as $I >= d$ (where d is the depth of the solution). If this condition is not met then depth limited search is not complete.

The space requirements for depth-limited search are similar to depth-first search, that is, $O(bl)$. The time complexity is $O(b^l)$.

6.6.5 Iterative Deepening Search

The problem with depth-limited search is deciding on a suitable depth parameter. If you look at the Romania map you will notice that there are 20 towns. Therefore, any town is reachable from any other town with a maximum path length of 19. But, closer examination reveals that any town is reachable in atmost 9 steps. Therefore, for this problem, the depth parameter should be set as 9. But, of course, this is not always obvious and choosing a parameter is one reason why depth limited searches are avoided.

To overcome this problem there is another search called *iterative deepening search*. This search method simply tries all possible depth limits; first 0, then 1, then 2, etc. until a solution is found. What iterative deepening search is doing is, combining breadth-first search and depth-first search.

It may appear wasteful as it is expanding nodes multiple times. But the overhead is small in comparison to the growth of an exponential search tree. To show this is the case, consider the following example.

For a depth-limited search to depth d with branching b, the number of expansions is

$$1 + b + b^2 + \dots + b^{d-2} + b^{d-1} + b^d$$

If we apply some real numbers to this (say $b = 10$ and $d = 5$), we get

$$1 + 10 + 100 + 1{,}000 + 10{,}000 + 1{,}00{,}000 = 1{,}11{,}111$$

For an iterative deepening search the nodes at the bottom level, d, are expanded once, the nodes at $d - 1$ are expanded twice, those at d–3 are expanded three times and so on back to the root. The formula for this is

$$(d + 1)1 + (d)b + (d - 1)b^2 + \dots + 3b^{d-2} + 2b^{d-1} + 1b^d$$

If we plug in the same numbers, we get

$$6 + 50 + 400 + 3{,}000 + 20{,}000 + 1{,}00{,}000 = 1{,}23{,}456$$

We can see that, compared to the overall number of expansions, the total is not substantially increased.

In fact, when $b = 10$ only about 11% more nodes are expanded for a breadth-first search or a depth-limited node down to level d. Even when the branching factor is 2 iterative deepening search only takes about twice as long as a complete breadth-first search.

The time complexity for iterative deepening search is $O(b^d)$ with the space complexity being $O(bd)$.

For large search spaces where the depth of the solution is not known iterative deepening search is normally the preferred search method.

In this section we have looked at five different blind search algorithms. Whilst these algorithms are running it is possible (and for some problems extremely likely) that the same state will be generated more than once. If we can avoid this then we can limit the number of nodes that are created and, more importantly, stop the need to have to expand the repeated nodes.

There are three methods we can use to stop generating repeated nodes.

- Do not generate a node that is the same as the parent node or, to put it another way, do not return to the state you have just come from.
- Do not create paths with cycles in them. To do this we can check each ancestor node and refuse to create a state that is the same as this set of nodes.
- Do not generate any state that is the same as any state generated before. This requires that every state is kept in memory (meaning a potential space complexity of $O(b^d)$).

The three methods are shown in increasing order of computational overhead in order to implement them. The last one could be implemented via hash tables to make checking for repeated states as efficient as possible.

6.7 HEURISTIC SEARCH TECHNIQUES

Blind searches are normally very inefficient. By adding domain knowledge we can improve the search process and the investigation of some of these methods is the purpose of this part of the course.

The idea behind a heuristic search is that we explore the node that is most likely to be nearest to a goal state. To do this we use a heuristic function which tells us how close we are to a goal state. There is no guarantee that the heuristic function will return a value that ensures that a particular node is closer to a goal state than any other node. If we could do that we would not be carrying out a search. We would simply be moving through the various states in order to reach the goal state.

To implement a heuristic function we need to have some knowledge of the domain. That is, the heuristic function has to know something about the problem so that it can judge how close the current state is to the goal state.

When we looked at blind searches we have already seen one type of evaluation function, where we expanded the node with the lowest path cost (for the uniform cost search). Using this type of evaluation function we are calculating the cheapest cost so far. Heuristic searches are different in that we are trying to estimate how close we are from a goal state, not how cheap the solution is so far.

You might recall that the path cost function is usually denoted by $g(n)$. A heuristic function is normally denoted $h(n)$, that is $h(n)$ = estimated cost of the cheapest path from the state at node n to a goal state.

6.7.1 Implementation

To implement a heuristic search we need to order the nodes based on the value returned from the heuristic function. We can implement such a search using the general-search algorithm. We call the function BEST-FIRST-SEARCH as the function chooses the best node to expand first. In fact, we cannot be sure we are expanding the best node first (otherwise, it would not be a search at all—just a march from the current state to the goal state) but, given our current knowledge we believe it to be the best node—but calling the function *Believed-to-be-best-first-search* is a bit of a mouthful).

Function BEST-FIRST-SEARCH(*problem*, *EVAL-FN*) returns a solution sequence

Inputs: problem, a problem

EVAL-FN, an evaluation function

Queueing-Fn = a function that orders nodes by *EVAL-FN*

Return GENERAL-SEARCH(*problem*, *Queueing-Fn*)

6.7.2 Greedy Search

Greedy search is an implementation of the best search philosophy. It works on the principle that the largest 'bite' is taken from the problem (and thus the name greedy search). Greedy search seeks to minimize the estimated cost to reach the goal. To do this it expands the node that is judged to be closest to the goal state. To make this judgement it uses the heuristic function, *h*.

Given a heuristic function *h*, we can implement a greedy search as follows:

Function GREEDY-SEARCH(*problem*) returns a solution of failure
Return BEST-FIRST-SEARCH(*problem*, *h*)

6.7.3 Hill Climbing

Search efficiency may be improved if there is some way of ordering the alternatives or choices so that the most promising are explored first. *Hill climbing* is one such technique which involves ordering in a fundamentally depth-first search. One of the ordering schemes is based on the remaining distance like straight line or as-the-crow-flies distance.

Following is the procedure for hill-climbing (Figure 6.6):
Procedure HILL-CLIMBING

1. Form a one element queue consisting of the root node.
2. Until the queue is empty or the goal has been reached, determine if the first element in the queue is a goal node
   (a) If the first element is a goal node then do nothing.
   (b) If the first element is not a goal node, then remove the first element from the queue. Sort its children if any, by estimating the remaining distance, and add them to the front of the queue.
3. If the goal has been found, announce success; otherwise announce failure.

end HILL-CLIMBING.

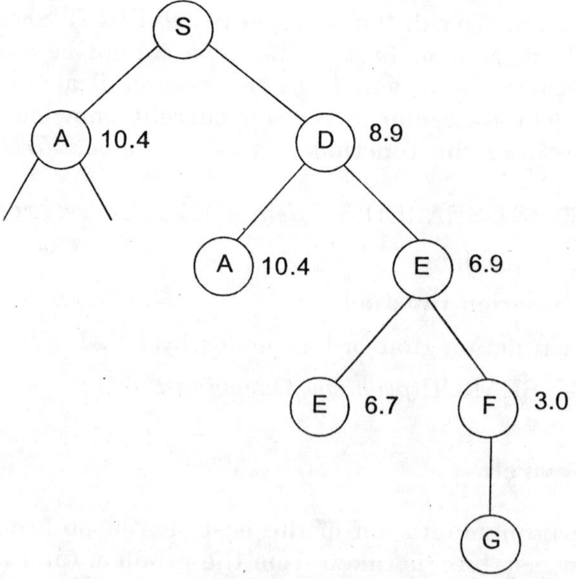

Figure 6.6 The path traversed by the hill climbing procedure.

Hill climbing is basically a depth-first search with a heuristic measurement that orders choices as nodes are expanded. The number beside the nodes are straight line distances to the goal node.

6.7.4 A* Search

In the previous section we considered greedy search. This search method minimizes the cost to the goal using a heuristic function, $h(n)$. Greedy search can considerably cut the search time but it is neither optimal nor complete. By comparison uniform cost search minimizes the cost of the path so far, $g(n)$. Uniform cost search is both optimal and complete but can be very inefficient.

It would be nice if we could combine both these search strategies to get the advantages of both. And we can do that simply by combining both evaluation functions. That is,

$$f(n) = g(n) + h(n)$$

As $g(n)$ gives the path cost from the start node to node n and $h(n)$ gives the estimated cost of the cheapest path from n to the goal, we have

$f(n)$ = estimated cost of the cheapest solution through n

The good thing about this strategy is that it can be proved to be optimal and complete, given a simple restriction on the h function.

We can implement A* search as follows:

Function A*-SEARCH(*problem*) returns a solution of failure

Return BEST-FIRST-SEARCH(*problem*, *g*+*h*)

Note that if you work through this algorithm by hand (or implement it), you should always expand the lowest cost node on the fringe, wherever that node is in the search tree. That is, the nodes you select to expand next are not just restricted to nodes that have just been generated. Of course, this is built into the algorithm as the queuing function 'automatically' orders the nodes in this way.

6.7.5 Admissible Heuristics

The restriction we mentioned above for the h function is simply that the h function must never overestimate the cost to reach the goal.

Such an h is called an *admissible heuristic*. Another way of describing admissible functions is to say they are optimistic, as they always think the cost to the goal is less than it actually is.

If we have an admissible h function, this naturally transfers to the f function as f never overestimates the actual cost to the best solution through n.

It is obvious that the SLD heuristic function is admissible as we can never find a shorter distance between any two towns.

A* is optimal and complete but it is not all good news. It can be shown that the number of nodes that are searched is still exponential to length of the search space for most problems. This has implications for the time of the search but is normally more serious for the space that is required.

6.7.6 The 8-Puzzle

The 8-puzzle consists of a square of eight tiles and one blank. The aim is to slide the tiles, one at a time to reach a goal state. A typical problem is shown in Figure 6.7.

5	4		1	2	3
6	1	8	8		4
7	3	2	7	6	5
Initial State			Goal State		

Figure 6.7 A typical 8-puzzle problem.

This problem is just the right level that makes it difficult enough to study yet not so difficult that we quickly get bogged down in its complexity.

A typical solution is about twenty steps. The branching factor is about three (four when the empty tile is in the middle, two when the empty square is in a corner and three for other positions). This means an exhaustive search would look at about 3^{20} states (or $3.5 * 10^9$). However, by keeping track of repeated states we can reduce this figure to 3,62,880 as there are only 9! possible arrangements of the tiles.

But, even 3,62,880 is a lot of states to search (and store) so we should next look for a good heuristic function.

If we want to find an optimal solution we need a heuristic that never over-estimates the number of steps to the goal. That is we need an admissible heuristic. Here are two possibilities:

h_1 = The number of tiles that are in the wrong position. In the above figure (for the initial state) this would return a value of seven, as seven of the eight tiles are out of position. This heuristic is clearly admissible as each tile that is out of place needs to be moved at least once to get it to its correct location.

h_2 = The sum of the distances of the tiles from their goal positions. The method we will use to calculate how far a tile is from its goal position is to sum the number of horizontal and vertical positions. This method of calculating distance is sometimes known as the *city block distance* or *Manhattan distance*. This heuristic function is also admissible as a tile must move at least its Manhattan distance in order to get to the correct position.

The Manhattan distance for the initial state above is

$$h_2 = 2 + 3 + 3 + 2 + 4 + 2 + 0 + 2 = 18$$

where the figures given are for tiles 1 through 8.

How do we decide which one is the best one to use? One method is to create many instance of the problem and use both heuristic functions to see which one gives us the best solutions. Table 6.1 shows the results of an averaged 100 runs at depths (solution length) 2, 4, 6, ..., 24 using A* with the h_1 and h_2 heuristic functions (for comparison we also show the results for a non-heuristic method; iterative deepening search (IDS)—at least we show it until the numbers get too large). The search cost figures show the average number of nodes that were expanded (the EBF figures are explained below).

Table 6.1

	Search cost			*EBF*		
Depth	*IDS*	$A^*(h_1)$	$A^*(h_2)$	*IDS*	$A^*(h_1)$	$A^*(h_2)$
2	10	6	6	2.45	1.79	1.79
4	112	13	12	2.87	1.48	1.45
6	680	20	18	2.73	1.34	1.30
8	6384	39	25	2.80	1.33	1.24
10	47127	93	39	2.79	1.38	1.22
12	364404	227	73	2.78	1.42	1.24
14	3473941	539	113	2.83	1.44	1.23
16		1301	211		1.45	1.25
18		3056	363		1.46	1.26
20		7276	676		1.47	1.27
22		18094	1219		1.48	1.28
24		39135	1641		1.48	1.26

From these results it is obvious that h_2 is the better heuristic as it results in less nodes being expanded. But, why is this case?

An obvious reason why more nodes are expanded is the *branching factor*. If the branching factor is high then more nodes will be expanded. Therefore, one way to measure the quality of a heuristic function is to find out its average branching factor. If we are using A* search for problem and the solution depth is d, then b^* is the branching factor that a uniform depth d would have to have in order to contain N nodes. Thus,

$$N = 1 + b^* + (b^*)^2 + \dots + (b^*)^d$$

To make the example more concrete, if A^* finds a solution at depth 5 using 52 nodes then the effective branching factor is 1.91. That is,

$$52 = 1 + 1.91 + (1.91)^2 + (1.91)^3 + (1.91)^4 + (1.91)^5$$

The effective branching factor is shown in the table for the various search strategies. We can see from this that A* using h_2 has a lower effective branching factor and thus h_2 is a better heuristic than h_1.

We could ask if h_2 is always better than h_1. In fact, it is easy to see that for any node n, $h_2(n) > h_1(n)$. This is called *domination* and we say that h_2 dominates h_1. Domination translates directly into efficiency. It is one thing being able to say that

h_2 dominates h_1 but how could we come up with h_2 (or even h_1) in the first place. Both h_1 and h_2 are estimates of the number of moves to the final solution. It is likely that we will need more moves the estimate (bear in mind the admissible property). But if we change the rules of the game slightly then we can make these heuristics give an exact path length needed to solve the problem. For example, if the rules were changed so that we could move any tile to the blank square then h_1 would give an exact value as to the path length required to solve the problem. Similarly, if a tile could move one square in any direction, even to an occupied square, then h_2 gives an exact path length to the solution. These changes to the rules are relaxing the rules and a problem that has less restrictive operators is called a *relaxed problem*. It is often the case that the cost of an exact solution to a relaxed problem is a good heuristic for the original problem.

6.7.7 Branch-and-Bound

One way to find the optimal paths with less work is by employing the branch-and-bound search procedure. This method works like the following way. During search there are many incomplete paths contending for further consideration. The shortest one is extended one level, creating as many new incomplete paths as there are branches. These new paths are then considered along with the old ones, and again, the shortest path is extended, the path first reaching the destination will always be optimal. Beware! The last step reaching the destination may be long enough to make the supposed solution longer than one or more incomplete paths to the solution points. Hence the search should be terminated when the shortest incomplete path is longer than the shortest complete path.

Evaluation functions are employed so as to use heuristic information during the search process. They are basically real valued functions of measurements. The measures of evaluation function are:

(a) the probability that the node is on a best path
(b) distance or difference metrics between an arbitrary node and a goal set, etc.

Suppose we denote the evaluation function as f, then $f(n)$ gives the value of the function at node n.

The procedure with the proper terminating condition is:

Procedure BRANCH-AND-BOUND

1. Form a queue of partial paths. Let the initial queue consist of zero-length, zero-step path from the root node to nowhere.
2. Until the queue is empty or the goal has been reached, determine if the first path in the queue reaches the goal node
   (a) If the first path reaches the goal node, do nothing.
   (b) If the first path does not reach the goal node
      (i) Remove the first path from the queue.
      (ii) Form new path from the removed path by extending one step.
      (iii) Add the new paths to the queue.
      (iv) Short the queue in the increasing order of the cost accumulated so far.
3. If the goal has been found announce success; otherwise announce failure.

End BRANCH-AND-BOUND

Figure 6.8 shows an example of branch-and-bound procedure.

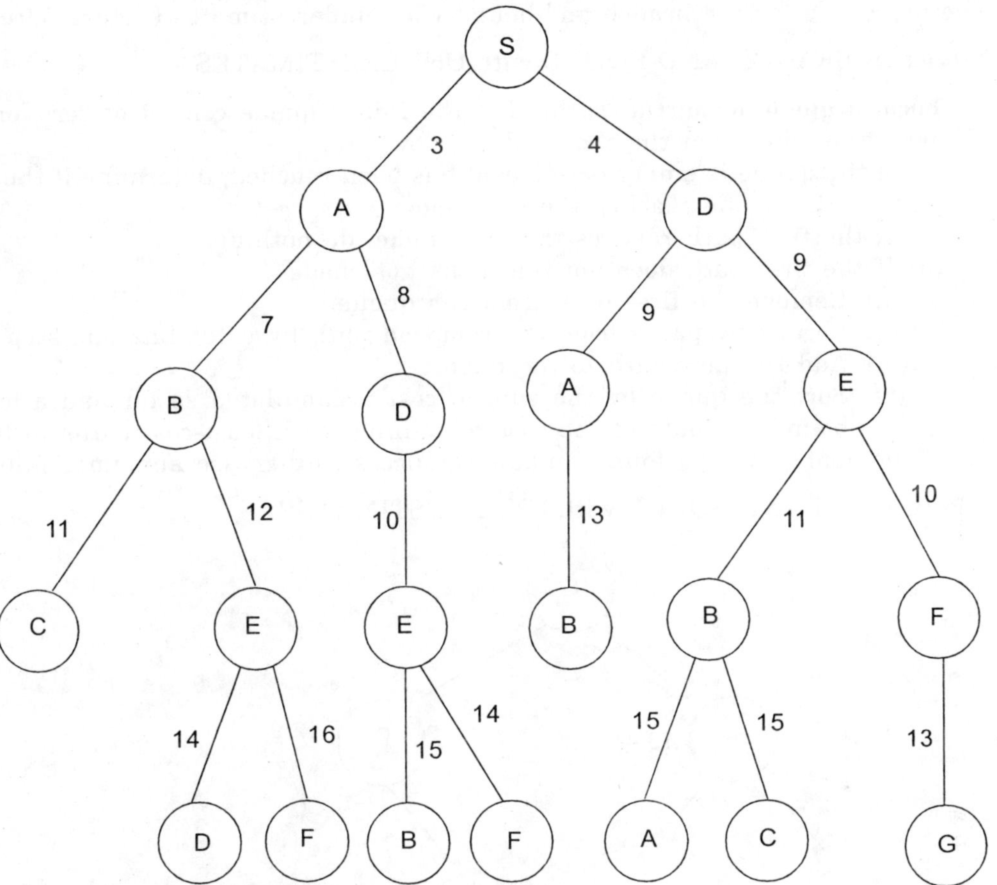

Figure 6.8 Branch-and-bound determines that the path S-D-E-F-G is optimal. The numbers beside the nodes are the accumulated distances.

Addition of Underestimates

The effect of branch-and-bound can be greatly improved by using guesses about the remaining distance and the known facts about the distance already covered. Thus,

$$e(\text{total path length}) = d(\text{already travelled}) + d(\text{distance remaining})$$

where

e (total path length) is the estimate of the total path length
d (already travelled) is the known distance already travelled
d (distance remaining) is and estimate of the remaining distance.

This provides us means of staying on the optimal path all the time. But one has to take care of the guessing to the extent that one should not overestimate anywhere along the optimal path. This is because a bad estimate at any such point may cause the search to wander off the optimal path permanently.

The procedure for the branch-and-bound with underestimates (Figure 6.9) is:

Procedure BRANCH-AND-BOUND with UNDERESTIMATES

1. Form a queue of partial paths. Let the initial queue consist of zero-length, zero-step path from the root node to nowhere.
2. Until the queue is empty or the goal has been reached, determine if the first path in the queue reaches the goal node
   (a) If the first path reaches the goal, node, do nothing.
   (b) If the first path does not reach the goal node
      (i) Remove the first path from the queue.
      (ii) Form new paths from the removed path by extending one step.
      (iii) Add the new path to the queue.
      (iv) Sort the queue by the sum of cost accumulated so far and a lower-bound estimate of the cost remaining, with least-cost paths in front.
3. If the goal has been found, announce success; otherwise announce failure.

End BRANCH-AND-BOUND with UNDERESTIMATES.

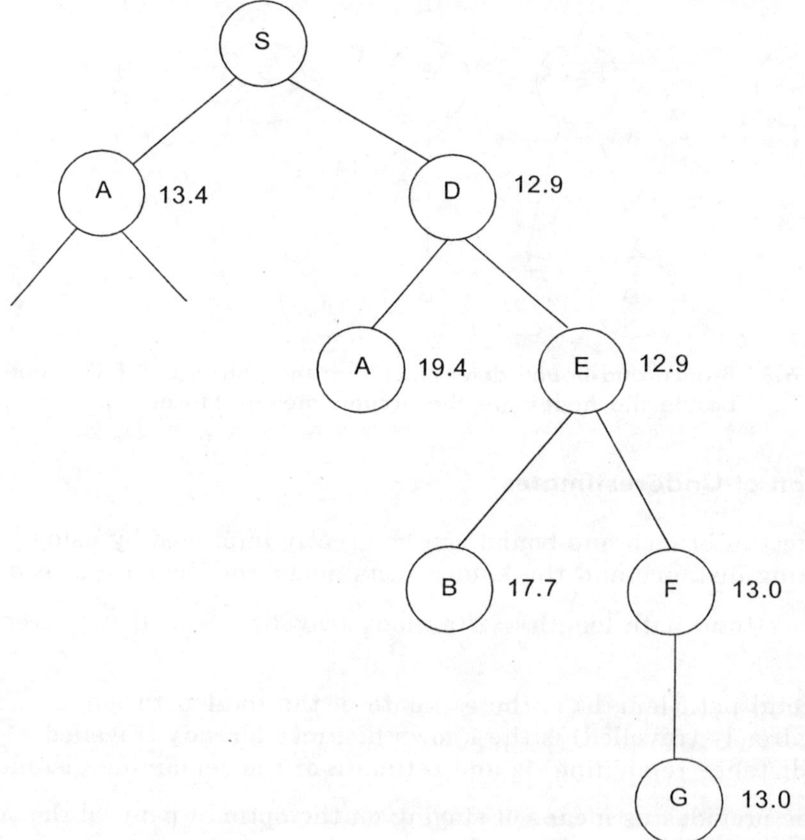

Figure 6.9 Shows the path traversed by the branch-and-bound algorithm together with underestimates when the goal in the tree as given in Figure 6.1 is obtained.

Branch-and-bound search augmented by underestimates determines that path S-D-E-F-G is optimal. The numbers beside the nodes are accumulated distances plus underestimates of distances remaining. Underestimates quickly push up the lengths associated with bad paths. Here many fewer nodes are expanded than with branch-and-bound search operating without underestimates.

Branch-and-bound with Dynamic Programming

The essence of dynamic programming can be stated as: Assume that the path from the starting point, S, to an intermediate point I, does not influence the choice of paths from I to the goal-node G. Then the minimum distance from S to G through I is the minimum distance from S to I and the minimum distance from I to G. Hence dynamic programming holds that when looking for the best path from S to any intermediate goal I, all path from S to I other than the minimum path from S to I can be ignored. The procedure for branch-and-bound with dynamic programming (Figure 6.10) is as follows:

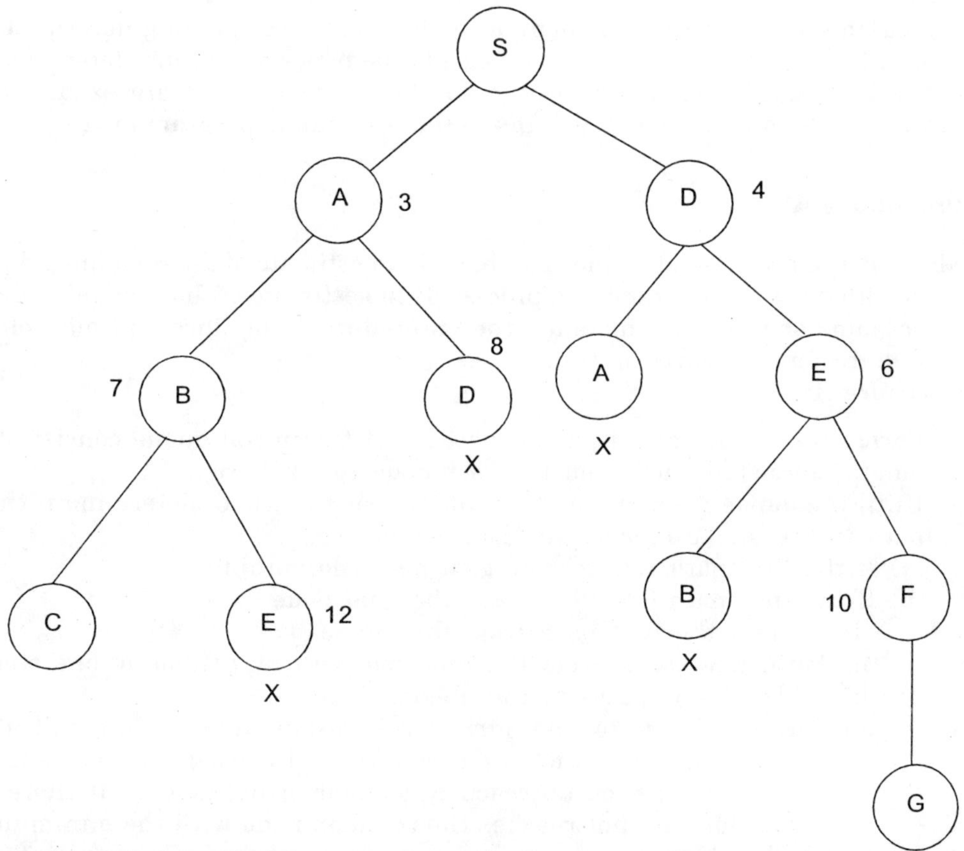

Figure 6.10 The figure shows the path traversed by the branch-and-bound algorithm with dynamic programming.

Procedure BRANCH-AND-BOUND with DYNAMIC PROGRAMMING

1. Form a queue of partial paths. Let the initial queue consist of zero-length, zero-step path from the root node to nowhere.
2. Until the queue is empty or the goal has been reached, determine if the first path in the queue reaches the goal node
   (a) If the first path reaches the goal node, do nothing.
   (b) If the first path does not reach the goal node
      (i) Remove the first path from the queue.
      (ii) Form new path from the removed path by extending one step.
      (iii) Add the new paths to the queue.
      (iv) Sort the queue by cost accumulated so far, with least-cost paths in front.
      (v) If two or more paths reach a common node, delete all those paths except for one that reaches the common node with the minimum cost.
3. If the goal has been found, announce success; otherwise announce failure.

End BRANCH-AND-BOUND with DYNAMIC PROGRAMMING.

Branch-and-bound search augmented by dynamic programming determines that path S-D-E-F-G is optimal. The numbers beside the nodes are accumulated distances. The crossed out nodes are found to be redundant. Fewer nodes are expanded than with branch-and-bound search operating without dynamic programming.

The Procedure A*

Procedure A* is a branch-and-bound search, with an estimate of the remaining distance, combined with dynamic programming process. If the estimate of the remaining distance is a lower bound on the actual distance, then procedure A* produces optimal solutions. The procedure for A* search is thus:

Procedure A*

1. Form a queue of partial partial paths. Let the initial queue consist of zero-length, zero-step path from the root node to nowhere.
2. Until the queue is empty or the goal has been reached, determine if the first path in the queue reaches the goal node
   (a) If the first path reaches the goal node, do nothing.
   (b) If the first path does not reach the goal node
      (i) Remove the first path from the queue.
      (ii) Form new paths from the removed path by extending one step.
      (iii) Add the new paths to the queue.
      (iv) Sort the queue by the sum of cost accumulated so far and a lower bound estimate of the cost remaining, with least cost paths in front.
      (v) If two or more paths reach a common node, delete all those paths except for one that reaches the common node with the minimum cost.
3. If the goal has been found, announce success; otherwise announce failure.

End A*

6.8 GAME SEARCHES

Games like chess, checkers tic-tac-toe, nim, etc. require another type of search. The node in a game tree represents board configurations and the branches represent the transformation from one board configuration to another. The decisions are made by two people or adversaries each making a decision in turn. Note that in games like chess, a move means one player's single act and his opponent's single response. Here, informally, a move refers to a person's single act.

Games require different search procedures than the one's we have encountered so far. Brute force search techniques are definitely out. This is because, for example, in chess, if we take the effective branching factor to be something like 16 and the depth to be 100, then the number of branches denoting the exhaustive possibilities would be approximately 100, a ridiculously large number.

On the other hand, if we assume piece count as heuristic for selecting our next move, then we end up getting poor results. So, such techniques require a situation analyzer that can be used after the game has extended through several levels of moves and counter moves. One has to be careful enough to see that combinatorial explosion doesn't occur. Hence after some reasonable depth, the situations can be compared in order to obtain certain look-ahead moves. This is based on the assumption that the moves clarify certain positions as the game progresses. It should be noted that this assumption is a debatable one.

6.8.1 The MINIMAX Procedure

Suppose we have an analyzer that converts all the judgement about the board positions into a single quality number. Also suppose that positive numbers indicate favour to one person and negative numbers to his adversary. The degree of favour is dependent upon the absolute value of the number. The process of determining the quality of the number is called *static evaluation*. At the end of certain number of moves, one finds the static evaluation scores produced by situation analyzers called *static evaluators*.

The player hoping for the positive number is called *maximizing player* and his opponent, *minimizing player*. At any intermediate level in the tree, given the values at the terminal positions, the value of a non-terminal position is computed by backing up from the terminals.

The procedure by which the scoring information passes you the game tree is called MINIMAX procedure (Figure 6.11) since the score at each node is either the minimum or maximum of the scores immediately below.

Procedure MINIMAX

1. Determine if the limit of search has been reached, or if the level is a minimizing level, or if the level is a maximizing level
   (a) If the limit of search has been reached, compute the static value of the current position relative to the appropriate player. Report the result.
   (b) If the level is a minimizing level, use MINIMAX on the children of the current position. Report the minimum of the results.
   (c) Otherwise the level is a maximizing level. Use MINIMAX on the children of the current position. Report the maximum of the results.

End MINIMAX

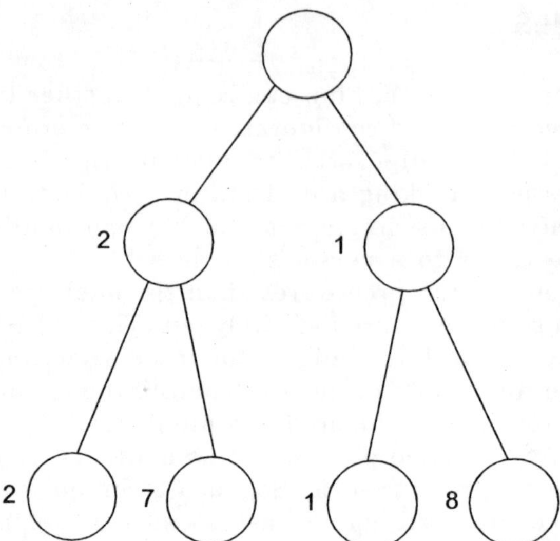

FIGURE 6.11 The MINIMAX procedure traverses in the process of obtaining the goal.

The MINIMAX procedure employs a static evaluator to calculate advantage-specifying number for the game situation at the bottom of a partially developed game tree. If the MINIMAX procedure has to be used, static evaluators have to be used at each situation found at the bottom of the tree. Fortunately, there are procedures for which the number of evaluations can be reduced consequently reducing the number of branches in the tree.

6.8.2 The ALPHA-BETA Procedure

ALPHA-BETA procedure behaves like: If the opponent has one response establishing that a potential move is bad, there is no need to check any other responses to the potential move.

Thus the ALPHA-BETA procedure (Figure 6.12) is:

Procedure ALPHA-BETA

1. Determine if the level is the top level, or if the limit of search has been reached, or if the level is a minimizing level, or if the level is a maximizing level.
   (a) If the level is the top level, let alpha be –oo and let beta be +oo.
   (b) If the limit of search has been reached, compute the static value of the current position relative to the appropriate player. Report the result.
   (c) If the level is a minimizing level:
      (i) Until all children are examined with MINIMAX or alpha is greater than beta
         A. Set beta to the smaller of the given beta values and the smallest value so far reported by MINIMAX working on the children.
         B. Use MINIMAX on the next child of the current alpha and beta.
      (ii) Report beta.

(d) If the level is a maximizing level:
   (i) Until all children are examined with MINIMAX or alpha is greater than beta:
      A. Set alpha to the larger of the given alpha values and the biggest value so far reported by MINIMAX working on the children.
      B. Use MINIMAX on the next child of the current position, handing this new application of MINIMAX the current alpha and beta.
   (ii) Report alpha.

End ALPHA-BETA

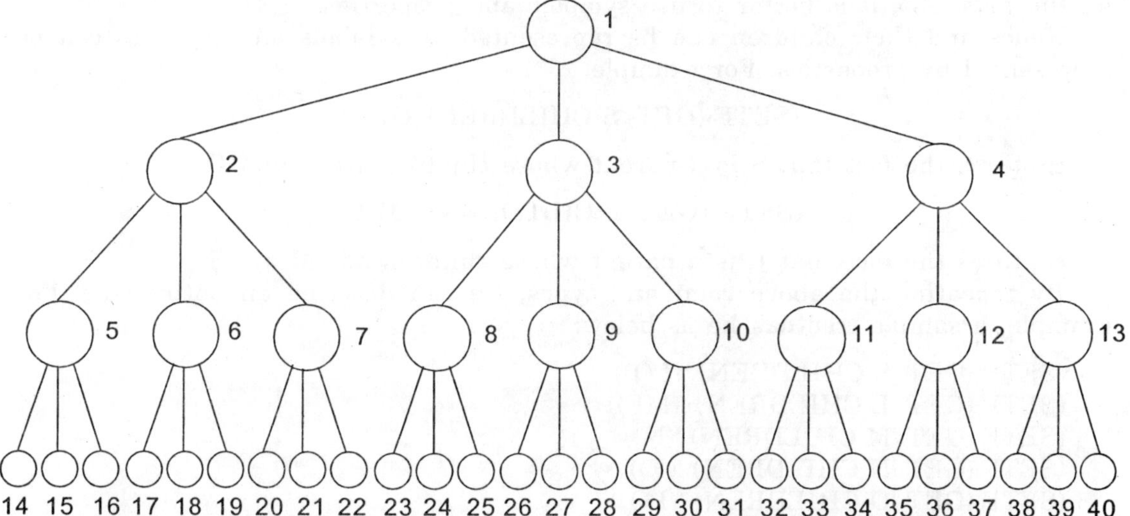

Figure 6.12 ALPHA-BETA procedure where a number of static evaluations are reduced to 11 from a maximum of 27.

6.9 PROGRAMMING FEATURE

This section takes you step by step on how to create LISP programs to solve depth-first search problems and then presents Missionary and Cannibal problem using PROLOG.

It is easy to write a program for depth-first search. Doubly recursive procedures penetrate a tree in a very efficient manner. However, it is not easy to modify these codes and adapt them for breadth first and other searches.

Let us work on a queue-oriented search. Our queue will consist of partial paths. Using queues of partial paths is hard at first, but once we have done depth-first search, it is very easy to modify these codes to do other searches.

SEARCH simply converts its first argument into a one-element queue for the benefit of SEARCH1. Then SEARCH1 examines the queue, testing the first path in the queue for success. If the last node in the first path is not the finish node, then SEARCH1 extends the path, modifies the queue, and hands the modified queue to another copy of SEARCH1.

```
(DEFUN SEARCH (START FINISH)
    (SEARCH1 (LIST START) FINISH); initialize
(DEFUN SEARCH1(QUEUE FINISH)
    (COND ((NULL QUEUE) NIL); return NIL if queue is empty
((EQUAL FINISH ((CAR QUEUE) T); return T if goal is found
(T (SEARCH1
    <appropriate merge of (EXPAND (CAR QUEUE)) and QUEUE> FINISH))))
```

Here, EXPAND returns the children of a node, given that node as an argument. Before we write EXPAND, let us look at representing the data in a program.

If we are dealing with trees only, nested lists would do nicely. If we want to handle nets also, it is better to use symbols and properties.

Nodes and their children can be represented by symbols and the arcs can be represented by properties. For example,

```
(SETF (GET 'S CHILDREN) '(L O))
```

captures the fact that S is a parent whose children are L and O.

```
(SETF (GET 'L CHILDREN) '(M F))
```

captures the fact that L is a parent whose children are M and F.

By repeating the above command types, we can describe an entire tree. For example, a sample tree can be as below:

```
(SETF (GET 'S CHILDREN) '(LO))
(SETF (GET 'L CHILDREN) '(MF))
(SETF (GET 'M CHILDREN) '(N))
(SETF (GET 'N CHILDREN) '(F))
(SETF (GET 'O CHILDREN) '(PQ))
(SETF (GET 'P CHILDREN) '(F))
(SETF (GET 'Q CHILDREN) '(F))
```

Having been defined how the nodes are connected, we are now ready to write the code for EXPAND.

```
(DEFUN EXPAND (NODE) (GET NODE 'CHILDREN) )
```

The method of merging the new children into the old QUEUE depends upon the search strategy. For a simple depth-first search, the appropriate form is:

```
(APPEND (EXPAND (CAR QUEUE) (CDR QUEUE) )
```

So a simple-minded depth-first search looks like this

```
(DEFUN DEPTH (START FINISH); Note change in name to DEPTH
(DEPTH1 (LIST START) FINISH); initialize
(DEFUN DEPTH1(QUEUE FINISH); Note change in name to DEPTH1
(COND ( (NULL QUEUE) NIL); return NIL if queue is empty
((EQUAL FINISH ((CAR QUEUE) T); return T if goal is found
(T (DEPTH1; try again with new queue
(APPEND (EXPAND (CAR QUEUE); New node at head
(CDR QUEUE)); Rest of queue
FINISH))))
```

This program does the job, but very little. It simply returns T or NIL. It would be nice if we get to know the nodes along the path that led us to the goal. Also, this program cannot handle nets because there is no check to prevent it from going into endless loops.

How to get the program to return a PATH? We have to pack more information into the elements of the data structure QUEUE. Until now, the elements representing the nodes remained to be tested. So the QUEUE would have looked like this:

```
(S)
(L O)
(M F O)
(N F O)
(F F O)
```

Instead, we want the elements to represent paths, rather than just nodes. Each path starts with the starting node and extends up to the node whose children are not yet explored. Then the QUEUE develops like this

```
((S))
((L S) (O S))
((M L S) (F L S) (O S))
((N M L S) (F L S) (O S))
((F N M L S) (F L S) (O S))
```

Because of the new format in QUEUE, we need to change DEPTH. First, FINISH is compared with (CAAR QUEUE) rather than with (CAR QUEUE). Second, instead of returning T, the path on which T is located is returned. Finally, a small adjustment is made to present the result in reverse order which is the natural order, namely from source to goal.

```
(DEFUN DEPTH (START FINISH); Note change in name to DEPTH
(DEPTH1 LIST (LIST START) FINISH); Note slight change
(DEFUN DEPTH1 (QUEUE FINISH); Note change in name to DEPTH1
(COND ((NULL QUEUE) NIL); return NIL if queue is empty
((EQUAL FINISH ((CAAR QUEUE)); Note small change to CAAR
(REVERSE (CAR QUEUE))); Note small change to CAAR
(T (DEPTH1; try again with new queue
(APPEND (EXPAND (CAR QUEUE); New node at head
(CDR QUEUE)); Rest of queue
FINISH))))
```

We also have to change EXPAND. Rather than taking a node and returning a list of its children, it should take a path, find the children of the node at the end of the path and return a list of new paths. Each new path will consist of the original path with one of the children tacked on. This can be arranged as follows:

```
(DEFUN EXPAND (PATH); initial version
(MAPCAR # '(LAMBDA (CHILD) (CONS CHILD PATH))
(GET (CAR PATH) 'CHILDREN)))
```

The MAPCAR arranges for a new path to be constructed for each child found just beyond the end of the old path. This still does not work if there are loops.

If we wish to handle nets, as well as trees, then we have to examine the paths offered up by the EXPAND operation, check to see if it has a new node that is already present elsewhere in the path and purge that.

```
(DEFUN EXPAND (PATH); improved version
(REMOVE-IF
# '(LAMBDA (PATH) (MEMBER (CAR PATH) (CDR PATH))); flush circular paths
(MAPCAR # '(LAMBDA (CHILD) (CONS CHILD PATH))
(GET (CAR PATH) 'CHILDREN))))
```

If we wish to use this on a net, rather than a tree, the data capture operations done earlier with SETF expressions should be done with reference to a net.

Example: Missionaries and Cannibals

- There are three missionaries and three cannibals on the left bank of a river.
- They wish to cross over to the right bank using a boat that can only carry two at a time.
- The number of cannibals on either bank must never exceed the number of missionaries on the same bank, otherwise the missionaries will become the cannibals' dinner!
- Plan a sequence of crossings that will take everyone safely across.

This kind of problem is often solved by a graph search method. We represent the problem as a set of states which are snapshots of the world and operators which transform one state into another states can be mapped to nodes of a graph and operators are the edges of the graph. Before studying the missionaries and cannibals problem, we look at a simple graph search algorithm in PROLOG. The missionaries and cannibals program will have the same basic structure.

Graph Representation

A graph (Figure 6.13) may be represented by a set of edge predicates and a list of vertices.

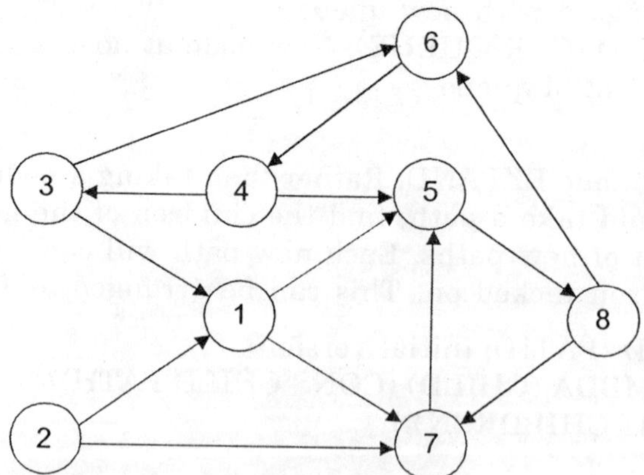

Figure 6.13 A graph representation.

```
edge(1, 5). edge(1, 7).
edge(2, 1). edge(2, 7).
edge(3, 1). edge(3, 6).
edge(4, 3). edge(4, 5).
edge(5, 8).
edge(6, 4). edge(6, 5).
edge(7, 5).
edge(8, 6). edge(8, 7).
vertices([1, 2, 3, 4, 5, 6, 7, 8]).
```

Finding a Path

- Write a program to find path from one node to another.
- Must avoid cycles (i.e. going around in circle).
- A template for the clause is:

  path(Start, Finish, Visited, Path).
  Start—the name of the starting node.
  Finish—the name of the finishing node.
  Visited—the list of nodes already visited.
  Path—the list of nodes on the path, including Start and Finish.

The Path Program

- The search for a path terminates when we have nowhere to go.

```
path(Node, Node, _, [Node]).
```

- A path from Start to Finish starts with a node, X, connected to Start followed by a path from X to Finish.

```
path(Start, Finish, Visited, [Start | Path]):–
    edge(Start, X),
    not(member(X, Visited)),
    path(X, Finish, [X | Visited], Path).
member(X, [X|_]).
member(X, [_|Y]):– member(X, Y).
```

Representing the State

Now we return to the problem or representing the missionaries and cannibals problem:

- A state is one 'snapshot' in time.
- For this problem, the only information we need to fully characterize the state is:
  - the number of missionaries on the left bank,
  - the number of cannibals on the left bank,
  - the side the boat is on.

All other information can be deduced from these three items.

- In PROLOG, the state can be represented by a 3-arity term, state(Missionaries, Cannibals, Side).

Representing the Solution

- The solution consists of a list of moves, e.g.
  [move(1, 1, right), move(2, 0, left)]
- We take this to mean that 1 missionary and 1 cannibal moved to the right bank, then 2 missionaries moved to the left bank.
- Like the graph search problem, we must avoid returning to a state we have visited before.
- The visited list will have the form:
  [MostRecent State | ListOfPreviousStates]

Overview of Solution

We follow a simple graph search procedure:

- Start from an initial state
- Find a neighbouring state
- Check that the new state has not been visited before
- Find a path from the neighbour to the goal.

The search terminates when we have found the state:

state(0, 0, right).

Top-level PROLOG Code

```
% mandc(CurrentState, Visited, Path)

mandc(state(0, 0, right), _, []).
mandc(CurrentState, Visited, [Move | RestOfMoves]):–
    newstate(CurrentState, NextState),
    not(member(NextState, Visited)),
    make_move(CurrentState, NextState, Move),
    mandc(NextState, [NextState | Visited], RestOfMoves]).
make_move(state(M1, C1, left), state(M2, C2, right), move(M, C, right)):–

    M is M1 – M2,
    C is C1 – C2.

make_move(state(M1, C1, right), state(M2, C2, left), move(M, C, left)):–

    M is M2 – M1,
    C is C2 – C1.
```

Possible Moves

- A move is characterized by the number of missionaries and the number of cannibals taken in the boat at one time.
- Since the boat can carry no more than two people at once, the only possible combinations are:

  carry(2, 0).
  carry(1, 0).
  carry(1, 1).
  carry(0, 1).
  carry(0, 2).
- Where carry(M, C) means the boat will carry M, missionaries and C, cannibals on one trip.

Feasible Moves

- Once we have found a possible move, we have to confirm that, it is feasible. It is not feasible to move more missionaries or more cannibals than that are present on one bank.
- When the state is state(M1, C1, left) and we try carry(M, C) then

  $$M \le M1 \text{ and } C \le C1$$

  must be true.
- When the state is state(M1, C1, right) and we try carry(M, C) then

  $$M + M1 \le 3 \text{ and } C + C1 \le 3$$

  must be true.

Legal Moves

- Once we have found a feasible move, we must check that it is legal, i.e. no missionaries must be eaten.

  legal(X, X).
  legal(3, X).
  legal(0, X).
- The only safe combinations are when there are equal numbers of missionaries and cannibals or all the missionaries are on one side.

Generating the Next State

```
newstate(state(M1, C1, left), state(M2, C2, right)):–
    carry(M, C),
    M ≤ M1,
```

```
    C ≤ C1,
    M2 is M1 – M,
    C2 is C1 – C,
    legal(M2, C2).
newstate(state(M1, C1, right), state(M2, C2, left)):–
    carry(M, C),
    M2 is M1 + M,
    C2 is C1 + C,
    M2 ≤ 3,
    C2 ≤ 3,
    legal(M2, C2)
```

EXERCISES

1. Water jugs problem 1
   Given a 3 litre jug and a 4 litre jug, where jugs can be filled with water, emptied, or water can be poured from one jug into another until either the source jug is empty or the destination jug is full. Consider a problem where the jugs are initially empty and the goal is to achieve 2 gallons in the 4 gallon jug. (*Hint:* Systematically expand a search tree for the problem to find the solution.)
2. Water jugs problem 2
   Given three jugs of capacity 2, 5, and 7 gallons respectively. Initially the 7 gallon jug is full and the other jugs are empty. The goal is to achieve 1 gallon of water in some jug, without spilling any water, and using no external sources of water.
3. Missionaries and cannibals problem.

   3 missionaries and 3 cannibals want to cross a river using a boat that holds 2 people. Cannibals can never outnumber missionaries, and an empty boat cannot cross the river.

   Initial state: MMMCCCB |

   Goal state: | BMMMCCC

   Action: take 1 or 2 people across the river.
4. 8-puzzle

   Sketch and solve the 8-puzzle problem from initial state 14235678 by A* search algorithm. Heuristic function for single state is given by:

   (i) the number of incorrectly placed tiles,
   (ii) the Manhattan distance.

   Compare and justify the result.

5. Intercity distances

Let us consider following intercity distances:

AD = BE = 5
AB = BC = EF = SD = 4
SA = FG = 3
DE = 2

and direct (e.g. aerial) distances to the destination (city G):

A = 10.4
B = 6.7
C = 4.0
D = 8.9
E = 6.9
F = 3.0
S = 11.0

Find the way between cities S and G by below listed search methods:

a. Uniform Cost
b. Hill Climbing
c. Beam Search with w=2
d. A*

6. Robot navigation

Our robot is in a maze with obstacles and wants to reach the goal state (see picture). To familiarize with his possibilities,

(i) calculate Manhattan and actual distances between start and goal,
(ii) for the both above cases try to outline 3D representation of distance (penalty) function surface and explain differences.

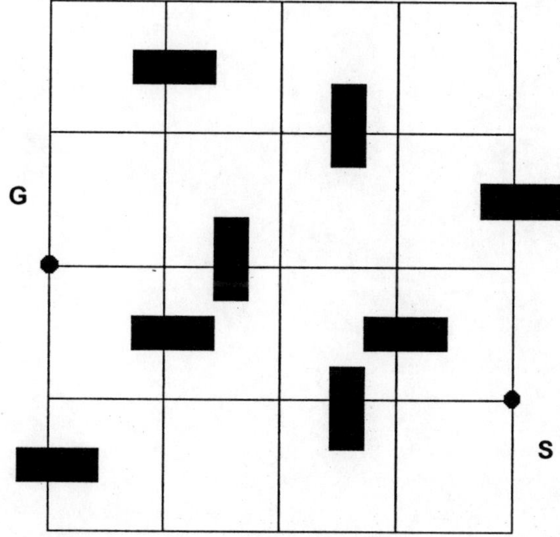

7. MINIMAX procedure

Let us consider quite complex two-person game, based on zero-sum and perfect information presumptions. Average branching factor is three and look ahead depth is also three.

a. How many leaf nodes must we investigate using MINIMAX procedure?
b. Outline corresponding subtree and justify winning move.
c. How does the ALPHA-BETA pruning algorithm influence overall task complexity?
d. Add alpha and beta values to the problem tree and mark out pruned (unnecessary) nodes. Discuss the solution.

One-digit values of static evaluation function (SEF) of leaf nodes are in sequence:

8 7 2 9 1 6 2 4 1 1 3 5 3 9 2 6 5 2 1 2 3 9 7 2 8 6 4

CHAPTER 7

AI Technologies

7.1 INTRODUCTION

Many AI technologies are becoming popular nowadays. These technologies are established as a separate research field. In this chapter, we will discuss three such AI technologies. We begin with *computer vision* which was initially developed for military applications. Nowadays, we see the fantastic developments in computer vision ranging from robot's eye to machine vision. Then we present natural language processing. This process enables us to communicate with computer in natural language. It is popular front end to many databases, expert systems, robots, etc. The usual collaborator of NLP is speech recognition which is discussed in the final part of this chapter.

7.2 COMPUTER VISION

The main problem of computer vision is from one or a sequence of images to understand the object or scene and its 3D properties. Vision is the process by which descriptions of physical scenes are inferred from images of them. There are many applications of computer vision, namely, medical image analysis, assembly, navigation, human-computer interface, etc.

A computer imitates human sight in four steps namely, image acquisition, image processing, image analysis, and image understanding. At present, there are numerous superior hardware devices for acquiring clear images. Once image is acquired, improving the quality of the images is taken care by the image processing mechanism. Here noise signals, which could have crept in due to faults in the imaging device, illumination variation and error in digitization process are concealed. Then analysis phase begins followed by understanding, which deals with recognition of various objects in the picture.

Let us consider a problem of *face recognition* using an *eigenspace representation*: Given a training set of M images, each of size $N \times N$ pixels, where each image contains a single person's face, approximately registered for face position, orientation, scale, and brightness, and a test image, determine if the person in the test image is one of the people in the training set, and, if so, indicate which person it is.

7.2.1 Eigenspace Representation of Images

An $N \times N$ image can be represented as a point in an N^2 dimensional *image space*, where each dimension is associated with one of the pixels in the image and the possible values in each dimension are the possible gray levels of each pixel. For example, a 512 × 512 image where each pixel is an integer in the range 0, ..., 255 (i.e. a pixel is stored in one byte), then image space is a 262,144-dimensional space and each dimension has 256 possible values.

If we represent our M training images as M points in image space, then one way of recognizing the person in a new test image would be to find its nearest neighbour training image in image space. But this approach would be very slow since the size of image space is so large, and would not exploit the fact that since all of our images are of faces, they will likely to be clustered relatively near one another in image space. So, instead, let's represent each image in a lower-dimensional feature space, called *face space* or *eigenspace*.

Say we have M' images, E_1, E_2, ..., $E_{M'}$, called *eigenfaces* or *eigenvectors*. These images define a basis set, so that each face image will be defined in terms of how similar it is to each of these basis images. That is, we can represent an arbitrary image I as a weighted (linear) combination of these eigenvectors as follows:

Compute the average image, A, from all of the training images $\mathbf{I}_1$, $\mathbf{I}_2$, ..., $\mathbf{I}_M$:

$$A = \frac{1}{M} \sum_{i=1}^{M} I_i$$

For $k = 1, ..., M'$ compute a real-valued weight, w_k, indicating the similarity between the input image, $\mathbf{I}$, and the kth eigenvector, E_k:

$$w_k = E_k^T * (I - A)$$

where I is a given image and is represented as a column vector of length N^2, E_k is the kth eigenface image and is a column vector of length N^2, A is a column vector of length N^2, * is the dot product operation, and – is pixel by pixel subtraction. Thus w_k is a real-valued scalar.

$W = [w_1, w_2, ..., w_{M'}]^T$ is a column vector of weights that indicates the contribution of each eigenface image in representing image $\mathbf{I}$. So, instead of representing image $\mathbf{I}$ in image space, we'll represent it as a point W in the M'-dimensional weight space that we'll call face space or eigenspace. Hence, each image is projected from a point in the high dimensional image space down to a point in the much lower dimensional eigenspace. In terms of compression, each image is represented by M' real numbers, which means that for a typical value of $M' = 10$ and 32 bits per weight, we need only 320 bits/image to encode it in face space. Obviously, we must also store the M' eigenface images, which are each N^2 pixels, but this cost is amortized over all of the training images, so it can be considered to be a small additional cost.

The image **I** can be approximately reconstructed from W as follows:

$$\mathbf{I} \sim \mathbf{A} + \sum_{i=1}^{M'} w_i * E_i$$

This reconstruction will be exact if $M' = min(M, N^2)$. Hence, representing an image in eigenspace will not be exact if the image is not reconstructible, but it will be a pretty good approximation that is sufficient for differentiating between faces.

At this point, select a value for M' and then determine the M' 'best' eigenvector images (i.e., eigenfaces).

This is done using the statistics technique called *Principal Components Analysis* (also called the *Karhunen-Loeve transform* in communications theory). Intuitively, this technique selects the M' images that maximize the information content in the compressed (i.e., eigenspace) representation.

The best M' eigenface images are computed as follows:

For each training image I_i, normalize it by subtracting the mean (i.e., the average image): $Y_i = I_i - A$

Compute the $N^2 \times N^2$ Covariance Matrix:

$$C = \frac{1}{M} \sum_{i=1}^{M} Y_i Y_i^T$$

Find the eigenvectors of C that are associated with the M' largest eigenvalues. Call the eigenvectors $\mathbf{E}_1$, $\mathbf{E}_2$, ..., $\mathbf{E}_{M'}$. These are the eigenface images used by the algorithm given above.

Since C is very large, this method is computationally very rigorous. Nevertheless, there are relatively fast methods for finding the k largest eigenvectors.

7.2.2 Face Recognition Algorithm

The entire face recognition algorithm can be stated as follows:

1. Given a training set of face images, compute the M' largest eigenvectors, $\mathbf{E}_1$, $\mathbf{E}_2$, ..., $\mathbf{E}_{M'}$. $M' = 10$ or 20 is a typical value used. Notice that this step is done once 'offline'.
2. For each different person in the training set, compute the point associated with that person in eigenspace. That is, use the formula given above to compute $\mathbf{W} = [w_1, ..., w_{M'}]$. Note that this step is also done once 'offline'.
3. Given a test image, $\mathbf{I}_{\mathbf{test}}$, project it to the M'-dimensional eigenspace by computing the point $\mathbf{W}_{\mathbf{test}}$, again using the formula given above.
4. Find the closest training face to the given test face:

   $$d = \min_k || \mathbf{W}_{\mathbf{test}} - \mathbf{W}_{\mathbf{k}} ||$$

   where $\mathbf{W}_{\mathbf{k}}$ is the point in eigenspace associated with the kth person in the training set, and $|| \cdot \mathbf{X} ||$ denotes the Euclidean distance in eigenspace.

5. Find the distance of the test image from eigenspace (that is, compute the projection distance so that we can estimate the likelihood that the image contains a face):

$$\text{dffs} = \| \mathbf{Y} - \mathbf{Yf} \|$$

where $\mathbf{Y} = \mathbf{I}_{test} - \mathbf{A}$, and $\mathbf{Yf}$ = sum_i_from_1_to_M′ ($w_{test,i} * \mathbf{E}_i$)
6. If dffs < Threshold1
   ; Test image is 'close enough' to the eigenspace
   ; associated with all of the training faces to
   ; believe that this test image is likely to be some
   ; face (and not a house or a tree or something
   ; other than a face)
   then if d < Threshold2
      then classify $\mathbf{I}_{test}$ as containing the face of person k,
         where k is the closest face in the eigenspace to
         $\mathbf{W}_{test}$, the projection of $\mathbf{I}_{test}$ to eigenspace
      else classify $\mathbf{I}_{test}$ as an unknown person
   else classify $\mathbf{I}_{test}$ as not containing a face

EXAMPLE 7.1. Suppose we have two 3 × 3 training images, so $N = 3$ and $M = 2$, defined as follows:

0	0	0
10	10	10
0	0	0

Image $\mathbf{I}_1$

0	10	0
0	10	0
0	10	0

Image $\mathbf{I}_2$

We represent these two images as column vectors of length 3*3 = 9, so we have

$$\mathbf{I}_1 = [0\ 0\ 0\ 10\ 10\ 10\ 0\ 0\ 0]^T$$

$$\mathbf{I}_2 = [0\ 10\ 0\ 0\ 10\ 0\ 0\ 10\ 0]^T$$

Now assume that we use a subspace of dimension 1, i.e. $M' = 1$, and the eigenvector computed from the two training images is:

$$\mathbf{E}_1 = [5\ 0\ 5\ 10\ 5\ 10\ 5\ 0\ 5]^T$$

The average image, **A**, is computed from $\mathbf{I}_1$ and $\mathbf{I}_2$ by computing for each pixel, the average gray level from the two images' corresponding pixels. Thus, the second pixel in **A** is (0 + 10)/2 = 5. Hence,

$$\mathbf{A} = [0\ 5\ 0\ 5\ 10\ 5\ 0\ 5\ 0]^T$$

We can now compute how the first training image, $\mathbf{I}_1$, is projected into the one-dimensional eigenspace by computing $\mathbf{W}_1 = [w_{1,1}]$, where $w_{1,1} = \mathbf{E}_1^T * (\mathbf{I}_1 - \mathbf{A})$. So, here we have

$$\mathbf{I}_{1'} = \mathbf{I}_1 - A = [0\ {-5}\ 0\ 5\ 0\ 5\ 0\ {-5}\ 0]^T$$

$$w_{1,1} = 5*0 + 0*{-5} + 5*0 + 10*5 + \ldots + 5*0 = 0$$

$$\mathbf{W}_1 = [0]$$

In other words, image $\mathbf{I}_1$ projects to the origin in this one-dimensional subspace defined by basis image $\mathbf{E}_1$.

Similarly, for $\mathbf{I}_2$ we get $\mathbf{W}_2 = [w_{2,1}]$, where

$$w_{2,1} = \mathbf{E}_1^T * (\mathbf{I}_2 - \mathbf{A})$$
$$= [5\ 0\ 5\ 10\ 5\ 10\ 5\ 0\ 5] * [0\ 5\ 0\ -5\ 0\ -5\ 0\ 5\ 0]^T$$
$$= -100$$

So, $\mathbf{W}_2 = [-100]$.

Now, say we are given the following test image

0	7	3
0	10	10
0	10	0

Image $\mathbf{I}_{test}$

Projecting $\mathbf{I}_{test}$ into face space we get $\mathbf{W}_{test} = [w_{test,1}]$, where

$$w_{test,1} = \mathbf{E}_1^T * (\mathbf{I}_{test} - \mathrm{A})$$
$$= [5\ 0\ 5\ 10\ 5\ 10\ 5\ 0\ 5] * [0\ 2\ 3\ -5\ 0\ 5\ 0\ 5\ 0]^T$$
$$= 15$$

So, $\mathbf{W}_{test} = [15]$, which means that $\mathbf{W}_{test}$ is more similar to image $\mathbf{I}_1$ than to image $\mathbf{I}_2$. Therefore, we would classify $\mathbf{I}_{test}$ as the same class as $\mathbf{I}_1$.

7.2.3 Face Recognition Accuracy

Performance using a 20-dimensional eigenspace resulted in about 95% correct classification on a database of about 7,500 images of about 3,000 people.

If training set contains multiple images of each person, then for each person compute the average point in eigenspace from the points computed for each image of that person.

The method requires that all images in the database contain faces of about the same size, position, and orientation, so that they can be compared using this global distance function in eigenspace.

If there are multiple images of a 3D object (e.g. a person's head from many different positions and orientations), then the points in eigenspace corresponding to the different 3D views can be combined by fitting a hypersurface to all the points, and storing this hypersurface in eigenspace as the description of that person. Then, classify a test image as the person corresponding to the closest hypersurface. There are a variety of commercial products that are now available based on the eigenface method.

7.3 NATURAL LANGUAGE PROCESSING

Natural language processing is one of the largest applications of artificial intelligence. It referes to artificial intelligence technique of communicating with a computer in natural language.

Using a natural language interface is one reasonable way to approach certain kinds of interface design. It has the advantage of requiring no skill other than a rudimentary ability to use a keyboard to type a sentence or two. On the other hand, natural language (NL) interfaces have the disadvantage of not being particularly concise. Conceptually, there are two kinds of NL interfaces: those which restrict themselves to a subset of English (or of some other language) and those which try to provide (more or less) complete coverage of the language (note that even humans do not have this—nobody knows every word/meaning of their native language). Restricted interfaces face the *habitability* problem: can a user easily learn to stay within the language subset covered by the interface?

Other applications of natural language processing (NLP) include machine translation (MT) and NL CAI (computer-aided instruction) systems. The budget for written translation services runs to ten billions of dollars per year worldwide. Most of this is translation of commercial and technical documents—contracts, manuals, etc.

The structure, especially the syntactic structure, of a natural language like English is usually expressed by grammar rules which decompose a sentence or other unit of language into small units. For example, we might have a rule that says that a *sentence* can consist (in English) of a *noun phrase* followed by a *verb phrase*. This rule would usually be expressed briefly as S $\rightarrow$ NP VP, with S standing for sentence, NP for noun phrase, and VP for verb phrase.

There are two major techniques for NL analysis in NLP.

- *Template matching* (also called as keyboard analysis). Here system scans the input sentences for selective keywords and once they are found, the system responds with a built-in reply.
- *Syntactic driven parsing.* Here knowledge of the grammar of the language is used for analysis.

7.3.1 Grammar

Grammar is a formal description of the structure of a language. A grammar captures the legal structures in a language, and thus allows a sentence to be analyzed. Parsing a sentence then involves finding a possible legal structure (or structures) for the sentence. The result is (usually) a tree (referred to as parse tree). An example is shown in Figure 7.1.

7.3.2 Parser

Parser is an algorithm for analyzing sentences given a grammar. It may

- just give yes/no answer to the question *Does this sentence conform to the given grammar.* Such a parser is termed an *accepter*
- also produce a structure description (*parse tree*) for correct sentences.

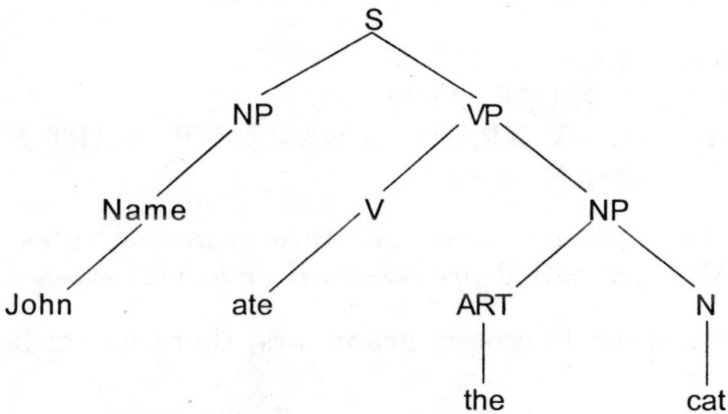

Figure 7.1 An example of a tree.

For example, the tree in Figure 7.1 can be represented as the list below:

The tree in LISP

```
(S (NP (NAME John))
   (VP (V ate)
      (NP (ART the))
         (N cat))))
```

and in a PROLOG notation ...

```
s(np(name(john)),
  vp(v(ate),
     np(art(the),
        n(cat))))
```

Describing Syntax: Context Free Grammars (CFGs)

1. S → NP VP 2. VP → V NP 3. NP → NAME 4. NP → ART N	grammar rules
5. NAME → John 6. V → ate 7. ART → the 8. N → cat	lexical entries

Definition: A CFG is a 5-tuple (P, A, N, T, S) where

- P is a set of context-free productions, i.e. objects of the form X → beta, where X is a member of N, and beta is a string over the alphabet A,
- A is an alphabet of grammar symbols,
- N is a set of non-terminal symbols,
- T is a set of terminal symbols (and N U T = A),
- S is a distinguished non-terminal called the start symbol (think of it as sentence in NLP applications).

For example,

T = {ate, cat, John, the}
N = {S, NP, VP, N, V, NAME, ART}
P = {S → NP VP, VP → V NP, NP → NAME, NP → ART N, NAME → John V → ate, ART → the, N → cat}.

Notice how the productions were split into grammar rules and lexicon above. N, V, NAME, and ART are called *pre-terminal* or *lexical symbols*.

Aside: In programming language grammars, there would be context-free rules like:

WhileStatement → **while** Condition **do** StatementList **end**
StatementList → Statement
StatementList → Statement; StatementList

7.3.3 Types of Grammars

Grammars can be of the following types:

- unrestricted grammars
- context-sensitive grammars
- context-free grammars
- regular grammars.

With context-free grammars, these form the *Chomsky hierarchy* of grammars. The four types of grammar differ in the type of rewriting rule alpha → beta that is allowed:

- ***Unrestricted grammar.*** No restrictions on the form that the rules can take. Unrestricted grammars are not widely used. Their extreme power makes them difficult to use;
- ***Context sensitive grammar, or transformational grammar.*** The length of the string alpha on the left-hand side of any rule must be less than or equal to the length of the string beta on the right-hand side of the rule. It is equivalent to require that all the productions be of the form *lambda A rho* → *lambda alpha rho*, where *lambda* and *rho* are arbitrary (possibly null) strings. *lambda* and *rho* are thought of as the *left and right context* in which the non-terminal symbol *A* can be rewritten as the non-null symbol-string *alpha*. Hence the term *context-sensitive* grammar. Context-sensitive production rules can be used for transforming an active sentence into the corresponding passive sentence.
- ***Context-free grammar, or phrase structure grammar.*** All rules must be of the form *A* → alpha, where A is a non-terminal symbol and *alpha* is an arbitrary string of symbols.
- ***Regular grammar, or a right linear grammar.*** All rules take one of two forms: either A → t, or A → tN, where A and N are non-terminal symbols and t is a member of the vocabulary (a terminal symbol). Regular grammar rules

are not powerful enough to conveniently describe natural languages (or even programming languages). They can sometimes be used to describe portions of languages, and have the advantage that they lead to fast parsing.

Since the restrictions which define the grammar types apply to the rules, it makes sense to talk of unrestricted, context-sensitive, context-free, and regular rules.

7.3.4 Deriving Sentences from a Grammar

To derive a sentence from a grammar, start with the start symbol S, and refer to it as the *current string*. Repeatedly perform the following rewriting processes:

- Choose any rule whose LHS occurs in the current string (in a CFG, the LHS must be a non-terminal symbol).
- Replace the LHS of that rule with the RHS of the rule in the current string, producing a new current string.

Repeat until there are no non-terminals remaining in the current string. The current string is then a sentence in the language generated by the grammar. (Before this, it is termed a sentential form.) e.g.

Current string	*Rewriting*
S → NP VP	S
→ NAME VP	NP
→ John VP	NAME
→ John V NP	VP
→ John ate NP	V
→ John ate ART N	NP
→ John ate the N	ART
→ John ate the cat	N

Parsing might be the reverse of this process (doing the steps shown above in reverse would constitute a *bottom-up right-to-left parse* of "John ate the cat").

7.3.5 Top-down Parsing

In this parsing method, we guess (predict) what the next production to be applied should be, and, in case we guess wrong, we stack any alternatives so that we can come back to them if necessary. We cross off the leading item of our current sentential form if it can be matched against the next word of the sentence. This algorithm can take exponential time on bad sentences for bad CFGs. With *well-behaved* grammars, it can be a linear time algorithm. NL grammars are not usually all that well behaved.

The following example shows the top-down parsing:

S → NP VP
NP → ART N | NAME
PP → PREP NP
VP → V | V NP | V NP PP | V PP

Sentence: 1 The 2 dogs 3 cried 4.

Backup states	*Position*
S → NP VP	1
→ ART N VP	1
NAME VP	1
→ (The) N VP	2
NAME VP	1
→ (dogs) VP	3
NAME VP	1
→ V	3
V NP	3
V NP PP	3
V PP	3
NAME VP	1
→ (cried.)	4

7.3.6 Bottom-up Parsing

The dogs cried → ART N V
→ NP V
→ NP VP
→ S

Using *bottom-up parsing* methods, all CFGs can be parsed in $n*n*n$ steps, where n is the length of the sentence. The reason, predictive parsing may take exponential time is that it may re-parse pieces of the sentence, particularly confusing sentences (like "the horse [that was] raced past the barn fell"):

Indication of parsing state	*Comment*
The horse raced past the barn ...	"past the barn" parsed as PP, "raced" parsed as [main] verb
The horse raced past the barn fell	confusing sentence
The horse ...	backtrack to this point and start over
The horse raced past the barn fell	"past the barn" parsed as PP again: "raced" parsed as ADJ [from past participle] starting the ADJP ["raced past the barn"]

7.3.7 Chart Parsing

The *chart* is a record of all the substructures (like "past the barn") that have ever been built during the parse. A chart is sometimes also called a *well-formed substring table.* Actual charts get complex rapidly.

Charts help with *elliptical* sentences:

1: Q. How much are apples?
2: A. Thirty cents each.
3: Q. Plums?

An attempt to parse 3 as a sentence fails, but all is not lost, as the analysis of "plums" as an NP is on the chart. Successful parsing of the entire utterance as any kind of structure can be useful.

A Bottom-up Chart-based Parsing Algorithm

This algorithm expresses an efficient bottom-up parsing process. It is guaranteed to parse a sentence of length n within $n * n * n$ parsing steps, and it will perform better than this ($n * n$ steps or n steps) with well-behaved grammars.

The algorithm constructs (phrasal or lexical) constituents of a sentence. We shall use the sentence "the green fly flies" as an example in describing an NL-oriented parser similar to Earley's algorithm. The sentence is notionally annotated with positions: our sentence becomes 0the1green2fly3flies4.

In terms of this notation, the parsing process succeeds if an S (sentence) constituent is found covering positions 0 to 4.

Points (2) to (9) below do not completely specify the order in which parsing steps are carried out: one reasonable order is to scan a word (as in (3)) and then perform all possible parsing steps as specified in (4)–(7) before scanning another word. Parsing is completed when the last word has been read and all possible subsequent parsing steps have been performed.

Parser inputs: *sentence, lexicon, grammar.*

Parser Operations

1. The algorithm operates on two data structures: the active chart—a collection of active arcs (see (4) below) and the constituents (see (3) and (6)). Both are initially empty.
2. The grammar is considered to include *lexical insertion* rules, for example, if "fly" is a word in the lexicon/vocabulary being used, and if its lexical entry includes the fact that "fly" may be a N or a V, then rules of the form N → fly and V → fly are considered to be part of the grammar.
3. As a word (like fly) is scanned, constituents corresponding to its lexical categories are created:

   N1: N → fly FROM 2 TO 3, and
   V1: V → fly FROM 2 TO 3

4. If the grammar contains a rule like NP → ART ADJ N, and a constituent like ART1: ART → the FROM m TO n has been found, then an *active arc* ARC1: NP → ART1 * ADJ N FROM m TO n is added to the *active chart*. (In our example sentence, m would be 0 and n would be 1.) The "*" in an active arc marks the boundary between found constituents and constituents not (yet) found.

5. Advancing the "*": If the active chart has an activę arc like:

ARC1: NP → ART1 * ADJ N FROM m TO n

and there is a constituent in the chart of type ADJ (i.e. the first item after the *), say

ADJ1: ADJ → green FROM n TO p

such that the FROM position in the constituent matches the TO position in the active arc, then the "*" can be advanced, creating a new active arc:

ARC2: NP → ART1 ADJ1 * N FROM m TO p.

In the following figure new are from 0 to 2 has been created.

6. If the process of advancing the "*" creates an active arc whose "*" is at the far right-hand side of the rule: e.g.

ARC3: NP → ART1 ADJ1 N1 * FROM 0 TO 3

then this arc is converted to a constituent.

NP1: NP → ART1 ADJ1 N1 FROM 0 TO 3

Not all active arcs are ever *completed* in this sense.

7 Both lexical and phrasal constituents can be used in steps 4 and 5, e.g. if the grammar contains a rule S → NP VP, then as soon as the constituent NP1 discussed in step 5 is created, it will be possible to make a new active arc

ARC4: S → NP1 * VP FROM 0 TO 3

8. When subsequent constituents are created, they would have names like NP2, NP3, ..., ADJ2, ADJ3, ... and so on.
9. The aim of parsing is to get phrasal constituents (normally of type S) whose FROM is 0 and whose TO is the length of the sentence. There may be several such constituents.

Chart Parsing Example

Grammar:

1. S → NP VP
2. NP → ART ADJ N
3. NP → ART N
4. NP → ADJ N

5. VP → AUX V NP
6. VP → V NP

Sentence: 0 The 1 large 2 can 3 can 4 hold 5 the 6 water 7

Lexicon:

the... ART
large... ADJ
can... AUX, N, V
hold... N, V
water... N, V

Steps in parsing:

sentence: **the** *position*: 1
constituents:
ART1: ART → the FROM 0 TO 1
active-arcs:
ARC1: NP → ART1 * ADJ N FROM 0 TO 1 [rule 2]
ARC2: NP → ART1 * N FROM 0 TO 1 [rule 3]

sentence: the **large** *position*: 2
constituents: add
ADJ1: ADJ → large FROM 1 TO 2
active-arcs: add
ARC3: NP → ART1 ADJ1 * N FROM 0 TO 2 [arc1*→]
ARC4: NP → ADJ1 * N FROM 1 TO 2 [rule 4]

sentence: the large **can** *position*: 3
constituents: add
NP2: NP → ART1 ADJ1 N1 FROM 0 TO 3 [arc3*→]
NP1: NP → ADJ1 N1 FROM 1 TO 3 [arc4*→]
N1: N → can FROM 2 TO 3
AUX1: AUX → can FROM 2 TO 3
V1: V → can FROM 2 TO 3
active-arcs: add
ARC5: VP → V1 * NP FROM 2 TO 3 [rule 6]
ARC6: VP → AUX1 * V NP FROM 2 TO 3 [rule 5]
ARC7: S → NP1 * VP FROM 1 TO 3 [rule 1]
ARC8: S → NP2 * VP FROM 0 TO 3 [rule 1]

sentence: the large can can *position*: 4
constituents: add
N2: N → can FROM 3 TO 4
AUX2: AUX → can FROM 3 TO 4
V2: V → can FROM 3 TO 4
active-arcs: add
ARC9: VP → AUX1 V2 * NP FROM 2 TO 4 [arc6*→]
ARC10: VP → V2 * NP FROM 3 TO 4 [rule 6]
ARC11: VP → AUX2 * V NP FROM 3 TO 4 [rule 5]

sentence: the large can can hold
position: 5
constituents: add
N3: N → hold FROM 4 TO 5
V3: V → hold FROM 4 TO 5
active-arcs: add
ARC12: VP → AUX2 V3 * NP FROM 3 TO 5 [arc11*→]
ARC13: VP → V3 * NP FROM 4 TO 5 [rule 6]

sentence: the large can can hold the
position: 6
constituents: add
ART2: ART → the FROM 5 TO 6
active-arcs: add
ARC14: NP → ART2 * ADJ N FROM 5 TO 6 [rule 2]
ARC15: NP → ART2 * N FROM 5 TO 6 [rule 3]

sentence: the large can can hold the water
position: 7
constituents: add
S2: S → NP1 VP2 FROM 1 TO 7 [arc7*→]
S1: S → NP2 VP2 FROM 0 TO 7 [arc8*→]
VP2: VP → AUX2 V3 NP3 FROM 3 TO 7 [arc12*→]
VP1: VP → V3 NP3 FROM 4 TO 7 [arc13*→]
NP3: NP → ART2 N4 FROM 5 TO 7 [arc15*→]
N4: N → water FROM 6 TO 7
V4: V → water FROM 6 TO 7
active-arcs: add
ARC16: VP → V4 * NP FROM 6 TO 7 [rule 6]
ARC17: S → NP3 * VP FROM 5 TO 7 [rule 1]

Doing the same steps diagrammatically. We can have Figure 7.2.

The disadvantage of bottom-up method is that it will find irrelevant constituents like the VP "hold the water" which would not be noticed by a top-down parser, because it wouldn't be looking for (the start of) a VP at that point. A top-down CFG parser can have a chart (but you have to keep track of which constituents are hypothesized, and which are substantiated by the text being parsed).

Recording Sentence Structure

A frame-like, or slot/filler representation is suitable: "Jack found a dollar"

```
(S SUBJ (NP NAME jack)
   MAIN-V find
   TENSE past
   OBJ (NP ART a HEAD dollar))
```

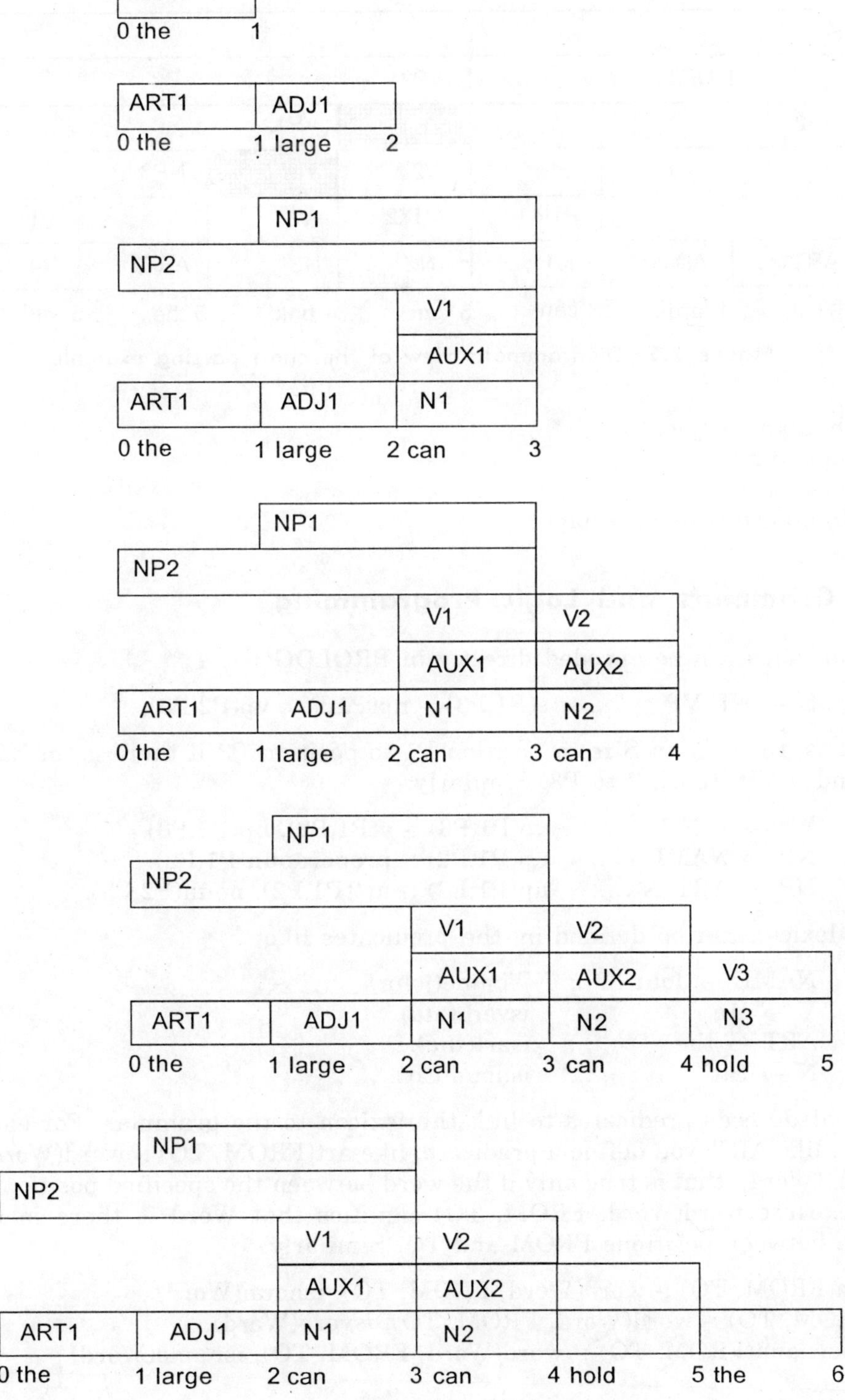
ART1
0 the
1
ART1
ADJ1
0 the
1 large
2
NP1
NP2
V1
AUX1
ART1
ADJ1
N1
0 the
1 large
2 can
3
NP1
NP2
V1
V2
AUX1
AUX2
ART1
ADJ1
N1
N2
0 the
1 large
2 can
3 can
4
NP1
NP2
V1
V2
AUX1
AUX2
V3
ART1
ADJ1
N1
N2
N3
0 the
1 large
2 can
3 can
4 hold
5
NP1
NP2
V1
V2
AUX1
AUX2
ART1
ADJ1
N1
N2
0 the
1 large
2 can
3 can
4 hold
5 the
6

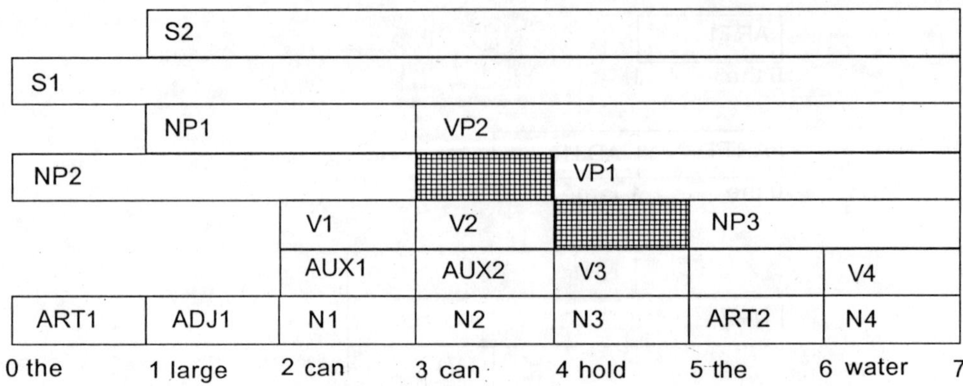

Figure 7.2 Diagrammatic view of the chart parsing example.

```
s(subj(np(name(jack))),
   mainv(find),
   tense(past),
   obj(np(art(a), head(dollar))))
```

7.3.8 Grammars and Logic Programming

Grammar rules can be encoded directly in PROLOG:

S → NP VP ..... s(P1,P3) :- np(P1,P2), vp(P2,P3).

That is, there is an S from position P1 to position P3 if there is an NP from P1 to P2 and a VP from P2 to P3. Similarly:

VP → V NP ..... vp(P1,P3) :- v(P1,P2), np(P2,P3).
NP → NAME ..... np(P1,P2) :- propernoun(P1,P2).
NP → ART N ..... np(P1,P3) :- art(P1,P2), noun(P2,P3).

The lexicon can be defined by the predicates like:

NAME → John ..... isname(john).
V → ate ..... isverb(ate).
ART → the ..... isart(the).
N → cat ..... isnoun(cat).

One also needs predicates to link the lexicon to the grammar. For each lexical category, like ART, you define a predicate, like art(FROM, TO) :- word(Word, FROM, TO), isart(Word), that is true only if the word between the specified position is of that category. Here word(Word, FROM, TO) signifies that Word is there in the input sentence between positions FROM and TO. Similarly:

```
noun(FROM, TO) :- word(Word, FROM, TO), isnoun(Word).
v(FROM, TO) :- word(Word, FROM, TO), isverb(Word).
propernoun(FROM, TO) :- word(Word, FROM, TO), isname(Word).
```

To use the system as so far described, one can assert the words in their sentence positions:

```
word(john, 1, 2).
word(ate, 2, 3).
word(the, 3, 4).
word(cat, 4, 5).
```

and then use the PROLOG query s(1,5)? This will result in ** yes.

To get at the *structure* of the sentence, add extra arguments to pass the structure across necks as it is built:

```
s(P1,P3,s(NP,VP)) :- np(P1,P2,NP), vp(P2,P3,VP).
vp(P1,P3,vp(v(Verb),NP)) :- v(P1,P2,Verb), np(P2,P3,NP).
np(P1,P2,np(name(Name))) :- proper(P1,P2,Name).
np(P1,P3,np(art(Art),noun(Noun)))
art(P1,P2,Art),
noun(P2,P3,Noun).

art(FROM, TO, Word) :- word(Word, FROM, TO), isart(Word).
noun(FROM, TO, Word) :- word(Word, FROM, TO), isnoun(Word).
v(FROM, TO, Word) :- word(Word, FROM, TO), isverb(Word).
proper(FROM, TO, Word) :- word(Word, FROM, TO), isname(Word).
```

7.3.9 Knowledge Representation Languages

The knowledge representation issues of concern to NLP systems include those relating to general knowledge about the world needed for language understanding, and typically, specific knowledge relating to the domain handled by the particularly NLP system. The term *knowledge representation language* (KRL) is used to refer to the language used by a particular system to encode the knowledge. The collection of knowledge used by the system is referred to as a *knowledge base* (KB).

A Representation Based on FOPC

The language used has much in common with the logical form language. The terms of the language include constants, like *John1*, function applications, like *father(John1)*, and variables, like x and y. Note that the logical form language did not use constants —everything was expressed in terms of discourse variables to keep the representation context-independent. For example, the logical form term (NAME j1 "John"), in a specific context, might be represented by the constant *John1* in the KB.

Restricted quantification makes sense in the KRL, as it did in the logical form language. Restrictions follow the quantified variable, separated from it by a semicolon:

$\exists$x : Person(x) Happy(X) ..... There is a happy person
$\forall$x : Person(x) Happy(X) ..... All people are happy

The second of these is equivalent to $\forall$x Person(x) $\rightarrow$ Happy(X). Free variables can handle "forall"

Many KR systems do not explicitly use quantifiers. Their variables are all tacitly universally quantified, as in PROLOG. Thus eats(john1, X) :- fried(X). means "John eats anything if it's fried". Literally anything, of course—if fried(cartyres1) is stored in the KB, then eats(john1, cartyres1) is *true*.

Skolem Constants and Functions

Existentially quantified variables are handled by a technique called *skolemization*, which replaces the variable with a new constant. For example, the formula ∃y ∀x. loves(x, y) would be encoded as a formula such as loves(X, sk1), where sk1 is a new constant that stands for the object that is asserted to exist. Quantifier scoping dependencies are shown using new functions called *Skolem functions*. For example, the formula ∀y ∃x. loves(x, y) would be encoded as a formula such as loves (sk2(Y), Y), where sk2 is a new function that produces a potentially new object for each value of Y.

Semantics

Several tasks fall under the heading of semantics:[*Semantics* is the study of meaning. For our purposes, *semantics* means the process of determining the meaning of an input sentence.]

- Selecting correct word sense meanings.
- Removing ambiguity: choosing interpretations that 'make sense' when many interpretations are syntactically possible.

  John saw my dog driving to work this morning.

- Resolving pronoun references.

  Bill wanted John's bike.
  He stole it.

- Producing a representation of the meaning of the input language. This representation may be quite different from the input.

  John sold his rabbit to Bill.
  Did Bill buy a pet?

- Filling in missing information.

  I was late for work today.
  My car wouldn't start.
  The battery was dead.

  The battery *is part of* my car. The battery's being dead *caused* my car not to start. The car's not starting *caused* me to be late for work because I usually use the car to drive to work and because if a car will not start, it cannot be driven.

Ambiguity. There is much more potential ambiguity in natural language sentences than one might think.

Lexical ambiguity. A word can have multiple parts of speech and multiple meanings for each part of speech.

The number of combinations of meanings is the *product* of the number of meanings for each word.

Syntactic ambiguity. Phrases might be attached to different parts of the sentence. Especially troublesome are propositional phrase attachment and conjunctions

7.3.10 Examples

In this section we look at a couple of simple examples of solving some NL problems using Definite Clause Grammars (DCGs). The first shows how noun-verb agreement can be achieved using the variables which can appear in non-terminals in DCGs. Only the present tense will be illustrated. We then consider the problem of translating from one language to another. Here a sentence in French is parsed/recognized and at the same time the English translation is constructed in one of the variables.

We begin with a general introduction to the syntax and translation of DCG in PROLOG. Most versions of PROLOG have the capability of defining languages and operating on them by means of definite clause grammars. These types of grammars are similar to CFGs but are strictly more powerful as they do have some context sensitive features.

Simplest Form

The most basic form of DCGs are essentially the same as context-free grammars (CFGs). We give an example to illustrate this. Once the rules are presented to the PROLOG interpreter they are translated into pure PROLOG clauses. If a listing is performed then the translations can be seen.

EXAMPLE 1. Here we have a grammar to recognize various forms of numbers. Let us see how close it is to the normal CFG definition.

```
digit → [0] | [1] | [2] | [3] | [4] | [5] | [6] | [7] | [8] | [9]. % a digit is in 0–9
nat num → digit. % a natural number is a
nat num → digit, nat num. % sequence of digits
int → nat num. % an integer is a natural number
int → sign,nat num. % possibly with a sign
real → int. % a real is given in normal
real → int,['.'],nat num. % decimal notation
real → sign,['.'],nat num.
sign → [–] | [+].
```

The objects inside '[ ]'s are terminal elements of the language, the other identifiers play the role of non-terminals. We can use '|' to separate alternatives on the right-hand side of a rule or give them as separate rules. The above is translated into the following PROLOG clauses:

```
nat num(A,B) :-
                 digit(A,B).
nat num(A,B) :- digit(A,C),
nat num(C,B).
sign(A,B) :-
                 ('C'(A,–,B) |
                 'C'(A,+,B) ).
real(A,B) :-
int(A,B).
real(A,B) :-
                 int(A,C),
                 'C'(C,'.',D),
                 nat num(D,B).
real(A,B) :-
                 sign(A, C),
                 'C'(C,'.',D),
                 nat num(D,B).
int(A,B) :-
                 nat num(A,B).
int(A,B) :-
                 sign(A,C),
                 nat num(C,B).
digit(A,B) :-
                 ('C'(A,0,B) |
                 'C'(A,1,B) |
                 'C'(A,2,B) |
                 'C'(A,3,B) |
                 'C'(A,4,B) |
                 'C'(A,5,B) |
                 'C'(A,6,B) |
                 'C'(A,7,B) |
                 'C'(A,8,B) |
                 'C'(A,9,B) ).
```

If we take the clause nat num(A,B), then the interpretation of this predicate is that the sequence of elements in B is an end part of A, and that the sub-sequence of A obtained by cutting off B satisfies the definition of natural number. In other words we are essentially using the pair (A,B) as a difference list.

So for example nat num([1,2,3],[]) is *true*.

More generally nat num([1,2,3 | X],X) is also true for any X. The special built-in predicate 'C' is used for recognizing the terminals and 'C'(X,Terminal,Y) means that Terminal is the head of X and it's tail is Y—as if it were defined as 'C'([X | Xs],X,Xs).

To make the above easier to use we could write a procedure which would convert a number in normal representation into a sequence of the separate symbols, i.e.

'+123' would be converted to the list [+,1,2,3] and '1.23' would be converted to [1,'.',2,3] etc. Note it is essential to quote the '.' otherwise PROLOG will take it as a terminator for a PROLOG clause and so give an error. Also if the number contains a sign it must be quoted as name requires an atom and +123 for example is not an atom (as begins with '+').

```
convert to list(Atom,Lst):-
    name(Atom,AtomLst),
    % convert to list of ascii numbers
    list to vals(AtomLst,Lst).
ascii to char(Asc,Chr):-
    name(Chr,[Asc]).
    list to vals([],[]). % apply down a list
list to vals([H|T],[HV|TV]):-
    ascii to val(H,HV),
    list to vals(T,TV).
```

Instead of using the translated predicates to recognize elements of a language we can also use the built-in predicate phrase. phrase(NT,Lst) means Lst is generated by the non-terminal NT, e.g. phrase(real,[1,2,'.',4,5]) is *true*.

Now the above grammar allows numbers with leading zeros such as 003. It is not too diffcult to alter the grammar by introducing new non-terminals to reject such numbers. The changes are as follows:

```
nonz digit → [1] | [2] | [3] | [4] | [5] |
                [6] | [7] | [8] | [9]. % a nonz digit is in 1–9
digit → [0] | nonz digit.
red nat num → digit | nonz digit,nat num.
red int → red nat num | sign,red nat num.
red real → red int | red int,['.'],nat num.
```

This will then return *false* for phrase(red nat num,[0,0,2,3]) but *true* for phrase(nat num,[0,0,1,2]).

More Complex Examples

DCGs also have the facility of embedding PROLOG code in their bodies. This is achieved by placing the required code in { }. Anything inside { } is then left unaltered by the interpreter. Parameters can also appear as arguments to the non-terminal symbols so that results can be returned as a side effect to the language recognition or used in further calculations.

EXAMPLE 1. We add a parameter to the previous example so that after recognizing a correct number it will contain the value of that number. We also need to carry how many digits appear in the number, e.g. phrase(nat num(N),[1,2,3,1]) will instantiate the variable N to the value 1231. We shall not bother with the reduced form but take the original grammar.

```
digit(0) → [0]. % a digit is in 0–9
digit(1) → [1].
digit(2) → [2].
digit(3) → [3]. % etc
...
digit(9) → [9].
nat num(N,1) → digit(N). % a natural number is a
                         % sequence of digits
nat num(N,ND) → digit(D), nat num(N2,ND1),
                         % ND is the number of digits
{plus(ND1,1,ND),
          power ten(D,ND1,P),
          plus(P,N2,N)}.
          int(N,D) → nat num(N,D). % an integer is a natural number
          % possibly with a sign
int(N,D) → [+],nat num(N,D).
int(N,D) → [–],nat num(N1,D),
          {N is – N1}.
real(R) → int(R,). % a real is given in normal decimal notation
real(R) → int(I,),['.'],nat num(N,ND),
          {neg power ten(ND,InvP),
          (I >= 0 → R is I + N * InvP;
          R is I – N * InvP) }.
real(R) → [+],['.'],nat num(N,D),
          { neg power ten(D,InvP),
          R is N * InvP }.
real(R) → [–],['.'],nat num(N,D),
          { neg power ten(D,InvP),
          R is – N * InvP }.
          power ten(D,0,D) :-!.
power ten(D,E1,P) :-
          E1 > 0,
          plus(E,1,E1),
          power ten(D,E,P1),
          P is P1 * 10,!.
neg power ten(0,1):-!.
neg power ten(N,P):-
          N > 0,
          succ(N1,N),
          neg power ten(N1,P1),
          P is P1/10.
```

A call of for example real(R,[–,2,3,'.',4,5],[]) returns *true* and instantiates R to the real number –23.45.

A call of phrase(int(N,D),[–,1,2,3]) instantiates N to the number –123 and D, the number of digits, to 3.

EXAMPLE 2.

```
% parse simple English sentence
% for time being just present as a list of identifiers
% e.g. [the,big,cat,kicks,the,black,dog]
% first we have a straightforward generator
% will not repeat adjective like big big girl!
% also check whether we need an 'an' or an 'a'.
adjnounph(CV) → noun(CV).
adjnounph(CV) → adjective(CV,Adj),noun( ).
adjnounph(CV) → adjective(CV,Adj),adjective(,Adj2),
                {Adj \== Adj2},
                noun( ) .
nounphrase → det(CV),adjnounph(CV).
sentence → nounphrase,verb,nounphrase.
% now some explicit examples
det(cons) —> [the] | [a].
det(vowel) → [an].
verb → [hit] | [kicks] | [kisses].
noun(cons) → [cat] | [boy] | [girl].
noun(vowel) → [owl] | [ox].
adjective(cons,big) → [big].
adjective(cons,black) → [black].
adjective(cons,brown) → [brown].
adjective(cons,tabby) → [tabby].
adjective(vowel,awful) → [awful].
adjective(vowel,awesome) → [awesome].
```

The above will now correctly recognize "an awful owl hits an ox" and reject "an awesome cat kisses an awful girl".

Let us consider some systems which attempt to understand English (or rather natural language) as input. It is only recently that we have had programs which can cope with very complex sentences and they tend to be very large and slow. More success can be had once the domain of discourse is limited. All the early programs were of this form.

7.3.11 ELIZA

This was an effort to play the role of a psychiatrist (Rogerian therapist) and works by pure syntactic trickery—although having said this, it nevertheless does impress people as you will see. It is supposed to form an empathy with the client, not offer its own opinions and encourage clients to express their own feelings and thoughts freely. ELIZA has a list of templates against which it tries to pattern match the input question together with a list of ranked keywords which it uses if no matching can be obtained. The templates are of one of the following forms:

1. identical character for character

2. <string> %
3. <string1> % <string2>

The strings are lists of characters which must be matched exactly and the % is then matched against the substring which remains. This value of % will then be used in the answer to give a more reasonable reply—thus giving the impression that the machine is really understanding the input. Of course, it is only in case 1 where it is known exactly what the user typed in.

Let us consider a template match of the form 2, e.g. do you % with possible responses:

(a) what difference does it make whether or not I do %
(b) may be I % and maybe I don't
(c) yes

If the user typed in:

(a) do you believe in god? Then a possible answer, by invoking response (b) would be: may be I do believe in god and may be I don't.

Hashing techniques are used for fast retrieval and template matching. For example, in the implementation on UNIX a match is made on the first 2 characters initially. If no template match can be made, then a search is made using keywords in the input sentence. The keywords are ranked—the highest ranking word is the one which is fired, e.g. a list of possible responses for the keyword difficult might be:

(a) tell me about your difficulties
(b) what do you mean by difficult

If there are no keywords in the sentence which match with the keywords in the database then some standard non-committal remark can be made such as

(a) let's change the subject
(b) go on

An alternative approach is to choose at random from one of the previous used keywords—a record of say the last 4 keywords is kept. So here the system is making use of a limited history of the session. This is the basic technique used by Eliza except when a template match of the forms 2 or 3 is fired some post-processing must be performed to produce a grammatically correct answer, e.g., if the user mentions the personal pronoun I in the input then this cannot be used in the substituted part as it stands. Essentially this must be changed to you but it is not quite that simple, e.g. suppose there were a template because % with a response template

%? that's incredible!

Then on the input

because I am clever.

a straightforward substitution would result in

I am clever? that's incredible!

and then substituting for I would give

you am clever? that's incredible!

Of course this is still not correct and has to go through a further transformation changing "you am" to "you are". These two phases are called *fix* and *grammar*. Fix does the following changes

you → me
I → you
me → you
that you → that I

along with some others.

Here simple grammatical errors are corrected. These include

you am → you are
me are → I am

with other similar changes.

It is important that fix is performed before grammar, e.g.

do you think I am clever
⇓
may be I think I am clever and may be I don't.
⇓ fix
may be I think you am clever and may be I don't.
⇓ grammar
may be I think you are clever and may be I don't.

This cannot catch every grammatical error and it is fairly easy for it to give an ungrammatical reply. For example, the current Unix implementation doesn't take care of what you in fix, and so from

do you believe in what you do

would result in

may be I do believe in what me do or maybe I don't.

Of course, this would be easy to change fix to accommodate this but there are plenty more examples which can fool the program. The only real knowledge we might say the program has is that contained in fix and grammar—there is no deductive power for instance. In no way can this be truly thought to be intelligent. To improve it would require more and more fixes to deal with new cases that arose as there is no real knowledge of syntax or semantics of English.

7.4 SPEECH RECOGNITION

Speech recognition is the diagnostic task of recovering the words that produce a given acoustic signal. In other words, it is the problem of transforming a digitally encoded acoustic signal of a speaker talking in a natural language (e.g. English)·into text in that language. Given the uncertainty at many levels of this problem (e.g. introduced by background noise, digitization noise, speaker's accent), we can formally specify the problem as

$$\text{argmax}_{words} P(\text{words} \mid \text{signal})$$

where words is a string of words in a given natural language like English, and signal is a sequence of observed acoustic data that has been digitized and pre-processed.

7.4.1 Signal Processing

Speech is one of the main methods people use to communicate with one another. Computers have been continuously increasing their computational powers over the years hence increasing the capabilities of speech recognition. Speech can be divided into two general fields, speech recognition and speech understanding, recognition being by far the easier task. So for the purpose of this document, speech understanding will be examined since speech recognition is a subset of speech understanding. Speech recognition is the task of mapping from a digitally encoded acoustic signal to a string of words. Speech understanding is speech recognition as well as interpreting the meaning of the words uttered. The system must answer three questions:

1. What speech sounds did the speaker utter?
2. What words did the speaker intend to express with those speech sounds?
3. What meaning did the speaker intend to express with those words?

To answer the first question, we must begin by distinguishing the difference between a sound and a speech sound. Almost all human languages, combined use about 40 to 50 distinct sounds, called phones. A phone is a sound that corresponds to a single vowel or a consonant. However, it should be noted that certain combination of letters can produce phones ("th") and that certain letters can produce a number of different phones, depending on the context ("a" in rat and cat).

Once we have determined all the possible sounds, then we need to characterize them in some manner so that we can easily refer to them in our dictionary of sounds. The easiest and most obvious method would be to analyze the sounds in terms of distinguishing features such as amplitude, frequency, etc. Next we need to place these features in a reference manual, our dictionary, from which we will be able to characterize the sounds correctly. The best method of sorting this document would be by pronunciation, since spelling in this circumstance is irrelevant.

The next question then is how to determine what words the speaker intended to express to the listener. Although we have a dictionary sorted by pronunciation, there are still some difficulties that need to be resolved. One such problem is the occurrence of homophones, that is to say the existence of two or more words with the same pronunciation, such as "their", "there", and "they're". Another problem in determining the correct strings of words has to do with the fact that most languages have no breaks in between words. Therefore, we must find a method of determining when a word ends and another begins. If we could not distinguish between the words, we would need to review the dictionary at each phone, since it is possible that each new phone is the beginning of another word.

The answer to the last question has still not fully been solved, what are the semantics of the words spoken. To accomplish this, once we can determine which words were spoken, we must pass these to some sort of analyzer that will try to convey the meaning to the computer.

The raw acoustic signal captured by a microphone is initially digitized and pre-processed. Digitization consists of sampling the analog signal, usually between 8 and 16 kHz, and then quantizing each sample point, usually as an 8 to 12 bit value per point.

Next, overlapping subsequences of the digitized data are processed. Subsequences of length about 10 msecs (i.e. containing about 80–160 data points) are usually used, defining a sequence of frames. Within each frame a set of features are then detected. For example, total energy in the frame, and difference in energy between the current frame and the previous frame. About 8 to 40 features are usually detected for each frame. This n-D vector of features values is then itself quantized using a process called *vector quantization* into, e.g. 256 "bins" so that each frame is now described by one of 256 possible "labels." The result of this whole process is a compact description of overlapping regions of the acoustic signal that should be sufficient for word recognition.

The basic approach to speech recognition is to use Bayes's rule to break up the problem into manageable parts:

$$P(\text{words} \mid \text{signal}) = P(\text{words})P(\text{signal} \mid \text{words})/P(\text{signal})$$

Since we are given a digital signal of the type described above and our goal is to find the sequence of words that maximizes $P(\text{words} \mid \text{signal})$, $P(\text{signal})$ is a constant for a given acoustic input and therefore we can simply drop this term. Thus, our new goal is to compute

$$\text{argmax}_{\text{words}} P(\text{signal} \mid \text{words})P(\text{words})$$

$P(\text{words})$ represents our *language model* specifying the prior probability of a particular word string. Thus it has to quantify the likelihood of a sequence of words occurring in English. $P(\text{signal} \mid \text{words})$ is the *acoustic model*, which specifies the probability of the acoustics given that a sequence of words was spoken. This part is complicated by the fact that often there are many ways of pronouncing a given word. The next sections describe in more detail the language model and the acoustic model.

7.4.2 The Language Model

$P(\text{words})$ is the prior probability that a sequence of words words $= w_1 w_2 \ldots w_n$ is likely in the given natural language. For example, "I have a gun" is more likely than "I have a gub." Or, "how to recognize speech" is more likely than "how to wreak a nice beach." One way to express this joint probability is to use the chain rule as follows:

$$P(w_1 w_2 \ldots w_n) = P(w_1)\, P(w_2 \mid w_1) \ldots P(w_{n-1} \mid w_1, \ldots, w_{n-2})\, P(w_n \mid w_1, \ldots, w_{n-1})$$

Now we need to compute the probability that the first word in the sentence is w_1, and the probability that the second word in the string is w_2 given that the first word is w_1, etc. The final part is the probability that the last word in the string is w_n given that the sequence of $n - 1$ words before it was $w_1, ..., w_{n-1}$. This expression is very complex because it requires that we determine conditional probabilities of long sequences of possible words. If word is a sequence of n words and our language contains m words, then to compute $P(w_n \mid w_1, ..., w_{n-1})$ requires collecting statistics for m^{n-1} possible starting sequences of words.

Instead, we will make a simplifying assumption, called the *First-order Markov Assumption*, which says that the probability of a word is only dependent (approximately) only on the previous word:

$$P(w_n \mid w_1, ..., w_{n-1}) = \sim P(w_n \mid w_{n-1})$$

Using this assumption we now have a much simpler expression for computing the joint probability:

$$P(w_1 w_2 ... w_n) = P(w_1)\, P(w_2 \mid w_1) ... P(w_n \mid w_{n-1})$$

This simplified model is called a *bigram model* because it relates consecutive pairs of words. This provides a minimum amount of context for determining the probability of each word in a sentence. Obviously, using more context (for example, a second-order Markov assumption so that we use a trigram grammar) would be more accurate but more expensive to compute.

We can construct a table representing the bigram model by computing statistics of the frequency of all possible pairs of words in a (large) training set of word strings. For example, if the word "a" appears 10,000 times in the training set and "a" is followed by "gun" 37 times, then (gun | a) = 37/10,000 = 0.0037.

Instead of representing the bigram model in a table, we can alternatively represent it as a *probabilistic finite automata*. Create a node (state) for each possible word, and draw an arc from each node to every other node. Label each arc with the probability that the word associated with the source node is followed by the word associated with the destination node. Finally, add a node called START and an arc from it to all of the other nodes. Label these arcs with the probability that the word associated with the destination node can start a sentence. We can use this Finite State Machine (FSM) to determine the probability of a given sentence by starting at node START and making the transitions to the nodes corresponding to successive words in the given sentence. Multiplying the probabilities of the arcs that are traversed gives the estimated joint probability associated with the First-order Markov assumption given earlier.

7.4.3 The Acoustic Model P(signal|words)

The *acoustic model* instructs us what sounds will be heard when a given word is uttered. The Markov model shows us alternative pronunciations of words. This transitioning is dependant on the current state only and none of the previous states. This model is used to show all possible paths to get to the end, based solely on its present state not any other previous ones.

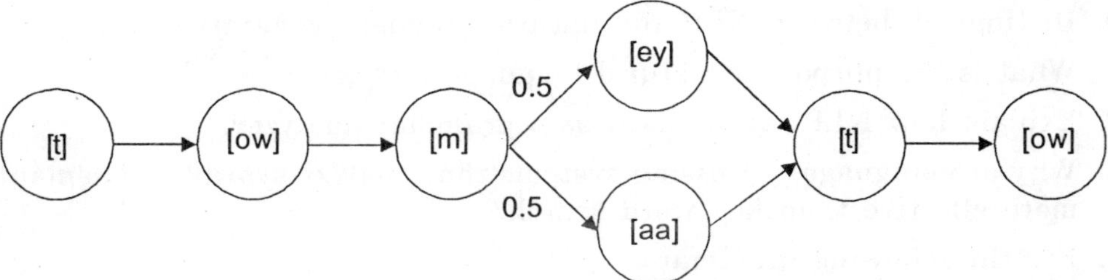

Figure 7.3 Markov model.

Co-articulation occurs when one speaks slow/fast and mixes sounds together by slurring them, basically slightly changing their pronunciation. This is due to people talking fast and combining some words together, as well as people who have accents.

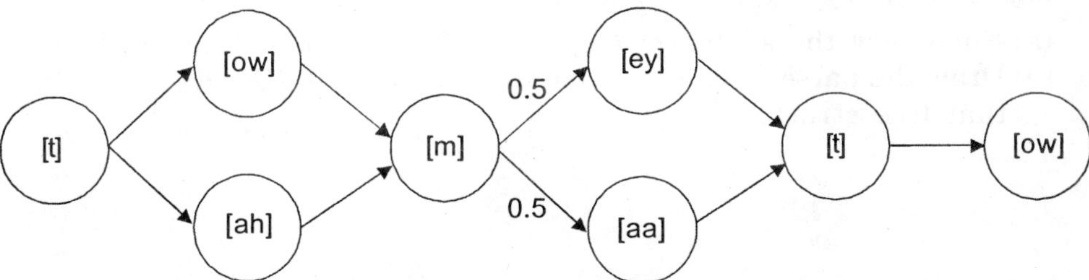

Figure 7.4 Co-articulation.

The *Hidden Markov model* tries to take into consideration the differences in speech, and tries to minimize P(words | phones) and P(signal | phones), and also take into consideration the possibility of having slurs or parts of speech that hang, by adding in the probability of repeating a phone.

EXERCISES

1. What are the major steps in computer vision?
2. What is image acquisition and processing?
3. Why computer vision is important in robotics?
4. List major limitations of computer vision.
5. Why speech recognition considered AI technology?
6. Give examples of how speech recognition can be applied today and list its benefits.
7. What is the purpose of combining NLP with speech recognition?
8. Can you differentiate between speech recognition and speech understanding?
9. What are the major advantages of natural language processing?

10. Distinguish between NLP and natural language generation.
11. What is the purpose of natural language interface?
12. Explain how NLP can be used as a grammar analyzer.
13. Why are language processing systems that analyze syntax and semantics far more effective than key word search?
14. For the following grammar:

s → np, vp.	name → [Gopal].
vp → v, np.	v → [ate].
np → name.	art → [the].
np → art, adjs, n.	n → [sandwich].
adjs → [ ].	adj → [large].
adjs → adj, adjs.	adj → [tasty].

(a) Show how the sentence "Gopal ate the large tasty sandwich" can parse.
(b) Draw the parse tree, and give a corresponding PROLOG term representing that tree structure.

CHAPTER 8

Expert Systems

8.1 INTRODUCTION

In the recent years, research in AI has had many important successes. Among the most significant of these has been the development of powerful computer systems known as expert systems or knowledge-based systems. These programs are designed to represent and apply factual knowledge in specific areas of expertise to solve problems. For example, collaborative efforts by human experts and system developers have resulted in systems which diagnose diseases, configure computer systems and prospect for minerals, at performance levels equal to human expertise.

The symbols in a knowledge-based system are used to represent virtually any kind of object, including artefacts, people, materials, biological organisms, classes of objects, concepts, and so on. The interesting point is that we are intent on seeing and manipulating symbols as something other than numbers, hence we need very different programming language features and facilities.

Another distinction between conventional algorithmic programming and the AI-based programming that is reflected in knowledge-based systems could be said to be in the programming style. In conventional programming, which is often called *procedural programming*, we tell the computer what must be done with the data subsequently entered. Thus, in procedural programming the procedures are our representation of how we want something done. In *knowledge-based programming*, on the other hand, we are representing *declarative knowledge* about a domain; that is, we are representing *what* we know without deciding in advance precisely *how* that knowledge will be used.

Table 8.1 summarizes the distinctions between the two programming styles. Two points are particularly worth noting here. The first, consistent with the dichotomy of procedural versus declarative styles just mentioned, is the fact that in procedural programming we talk about manipulating data, while in declarative programming we are concerned with representing knowledge. The second and more important point is the attribute of separating knowledge from control that is a characteristic of knowledge-based programming.

Table 8.1

Conventional software	*Knowledge-based software*
Requires correct data	Capable of handling missing or uncertain information
Fixed procedural structure	Sequence determined by inference engine
Good for numerical processing	Good for symbol manipulation
Only a programmer can understand	Natural language interfaces
Mid-run explanation impossible	Mid-run explanation possible
Structure	Structure
Program = Algorithm + Data	Expert System = Control + Problem + Data

8.1.1 Definitions

There are many expert system definitions available, although most are similar. Professor E. Feigenbaum (Barr and Feigenbaum, 1981) of Stanford University has defined an expert system as:

"...an intelligent computer program that uses knowledge and inference procedures to solve problems those are difficult enough to require significant human expertise for their solution. Knowledge necessary to perform at such a level, plus the inference procedures used, can be thought of as a model of the expertise of the best practitioners of the field."

E. Feigenbaum,
father of Expert Systems

A widely quoted definition of expert systems is given by Gaschnig, Reboh and Reiter (1981).

"Expert systems are interactive computer programs incorporating judgement, rules of thumb, intuition and other expertise to provide knowledgeable advice about a variety of tasks."

More extensive definition of an expert system is to be found in Brachman (1983).

"An expert system is one that has expert rules and avoids blind search, reasons by manipulating symbols, grasps fundamental domain principles, and has complete weaker reasoning methods to fall back on when expert rules fail and to use in producing explanations. It deals with difficult problems in a complex domain, can take a problem description in lay terms and convert it to an internal representation appropriate for processing with its expert rules, and can reason about its own knowledge (or lack thereof), especially to reconstruct inference paths rationally for explanation and self-justification."

Knowledge-based systems investigate methods and techniques for constructing man-machine systems with specialized problem solving expertise. Expertise consists of knowledge about a particular domain, understanding of the domain problems and skill at solving some of them. Knowledge in any speciality is usually of two types.

- Private knowledge
- Public knowledge

8.1.2 Public Knowledge

Public knowledge includes the published definitions facts and theories, available in textbooks, journals, research papers, etc.

8.1.3 Private Knowledge

Public knowledge is not the only source of human expertise. Human experts generally possess *private knowledge*. Private knowledge largely consists of rules of thumb also called heuristics. Heuristics enable human expert to make educated guesses when necessary, to recognize promising approaches to problem solving and deal effectively with errorful or incomplete data.

8.2 SKILL VERSUS KNOWLEDGE

Skill in solving problems generally implies speed, efficiency, reduced error, reduced cognitive load, robustness, etc. Knowledge, on the other hand, allows humans to solve new problems through analogies, common sense, analysis, etc.

- Most of the difficult and interesting problems at least till now do not have tractable algorithmic solutions. Many important tasks arise in complex socio-physical contexts which generally resist precise description and rigorous analysis, for example, planning legal reasoning medical diagnosis, military situation analysis machine diagnostics, etc.
- Human experts achieve outstanding performance because they are knowledgeable and experienced.
- The third reason for focussing on knowledge is in recognition to its intrinsic value. Knowledge is a scarce resource whose refinement and reproduction creates wealth. Human knowledge is propagated through apprenticeship or training.

With the use of knowledge humans achieve outstanding success in solving difficult day-to-day problems. If the problem solving knowledge from these human experts is extracted and put in a computer program which uses it then the program too should attain high level of performance. Extracting knowledge from the experts and putting it into computable forms will greatly reduce the cost of knowledge reproduction and exploitation. At the same time knowledge refinement can be speeded up by making private knowledge available for public test and evaluation.

In most cases of intelligent or knowledge-based problem solving, we are faced with problems that do not have easily formalized or algorithmic solutions. Therefore, heuristic methods have to be used. Effective solutions depend on the timely use of knowledge to identify potential decisions that can lead to promising results and rule out unproductive choices. This basic idea of any knowledge-based problem solving activity can be reviewed as:

1. Knowledge = Facts + Beliefs + Heuristics.
2. Success = Finding a good solution within the available resources.
3. Search efficiency directly affects success.
4. The factors responsible for an efficient solution.
   (a) Applicable, correct and discriminatory knowledge.
   (b) Rapid eliminations of unproductive views.
   (c) Multiple cooperative sources of knowledge.
   (d) Dividing solutions at various levels of abstraction.
5. The major difficulties in a knowledge-based approach.
   (a) Wrong or error knowledge.
   (b) Number of possibilities to evaluate.
   (c) Complex procedures to rule out possibilities.
   (d) Dynamically changing problem.

From our experiences in intelligent problem solving the central notion can be stated in general as:

1. Construction of solutions selectively and efficiently from a space of alternatives.
2. Identify the useful ones and then explore them further.
3. Keep pruning these solutions till the best solution is obtained.

An ideal intelligent problem solver should have:

1. Language processor for problem-oriented communications.
2. Scratch pad for recording any intermediate results.
3. Knowledge about domain which can be facts, heuristics or beliefs.
4. Knowledge to check the consistency of the emerging solution.
5. Knowledge to schedule the next problem solving strategy.
6. Knowledge to evaluate the partial solutions.

This basic intelligent problem solver evolved into expert systems. Expert systems are simplified knowledge-based systems, because the entire problem solving knowledge in any domain is too complex and cannot be captured in simple syntactical structures.

Therefore, the problem domain has to be narrowed down so that for all practical purposes the knowledge required is restricted so as to be captured in simple knowledge representation languages. Before we discuss about expert systems in detail it is pertinent that we should be able to distinguish between a conventional program and an expert system. This will give us an alternate perspective to define expert systems (Figure 8.1).

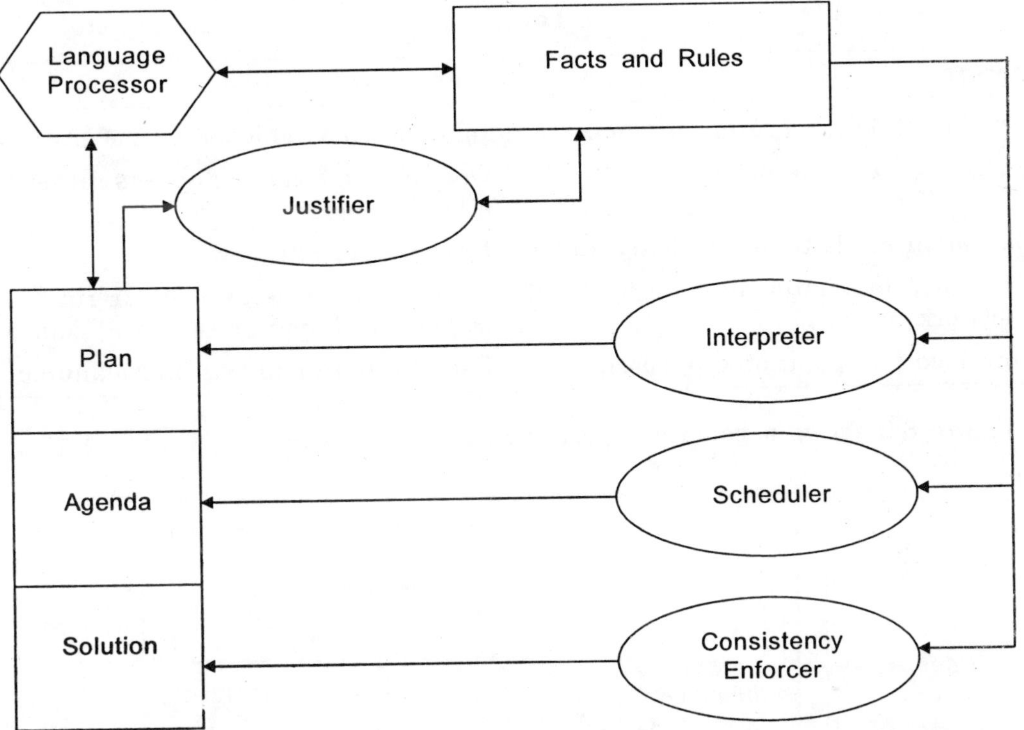

Figure 8.1 Ideal architecture of expert system.

8.2.1 How do Expert Systems Differ from Conventional Programs?

The most basic difference is that expert systems manipulate knowledge while conventional programs manipulate data (Table 8.2).

Table 8.2

Data processing	*Knowledge processing*
Representation and use of static data	Representation and use of data + control = knowledge
Algorithms	Heuristic
Repetitive process	Inferential process
For control and large data kept separately	Large control and few data kept together

Therefore major difference between database and knowledge base is as follows (Table 8.3):

Table 8.3

Database	*Knowledge base*
Collection of data representing facts	Information at a higher level of abstraction
Operates on a single object	Operates on a class of objects rather than a single object
Information needs to be explicitly stated	Uses inferencing power
Represented by relational or hierarchical or network model	Representation is by logic or rules or frames or scripts or semantic nets
Maintained for operational purpose	Used for data analysis and planning

Figure 8.2 shows a generic expert system architecture.

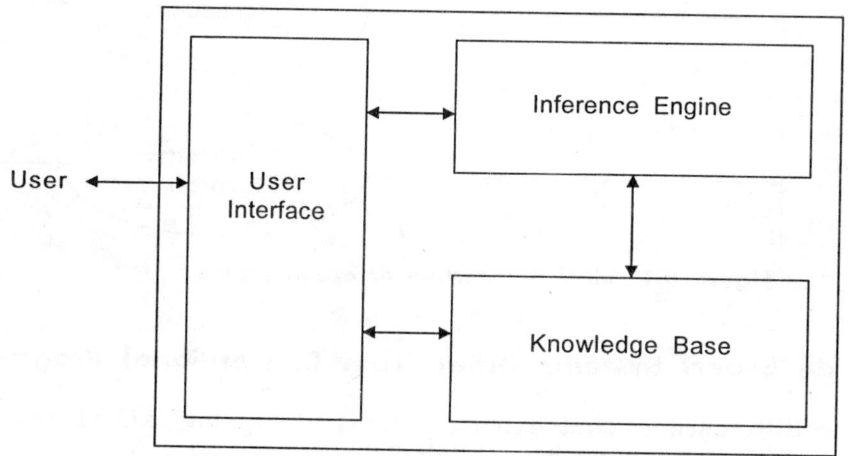

Figure 8.2 Structure of expert system.

8.3 BASIC CHARACTERISTICS OF AN EXPERT SYSTEM

Expert systems must have:

(a) Expertise who should exhibit expert performance. They should possess high level of skills and should be adequately robust.
(b) Perform symbolic reasoning since their knowledge is symbolic.
(c) They should be able to use complex rules and handle difficult problem domains.
(d) Self-knowledge they should be able to examine their reasoning and explain their operations.

The usefulness of an expert system is directly dependent on the quality of knowledge provided by the designers. Therefore, it is very important to validate and refine the system recursively.

8.4 BRIEF HISTORY OF EXPERT SYSTEMS

At prestigious International Joint Conference on AI, 1977, Professor Feigenbaum, in an invited paper, presented the key insight into expert systems, "The power of an expert system is derived from the knowledge it posesses not from the particular formalisms and inference schemes it employs".

In the initial years of AI research it was thought that a few laws of reasoning coupled with powerful computers would produce expert systems capable of handling any problem in any domain for example GPS (General Problem Solver). As experience accrued, the severely limited powers of GPS ultimately led to the view that it was too weak to solve complex problems. So people started concentrating on narrow domain problem solvers rather than a general problem solver.

By mid-70s several expert systems had begun to emerge. A few investigators who recognized the central role of knowledge in these systems then initiated efforts to develop comprehensive knowledge representation theories and general-purpose systems. They too did not succeed because knowledge cannot be captured by finite structures as it is too diverse and broad. On the other hand several different approaches to knowledge representation proved sufficient for the expert systems designed to solve problem in very specific areas.

8.4.1 What We Mean by Knowledge in a Domain?

In a general and abstract sense, knowledge consists of descriptions, relationships, and procedures in some domain of interest

The descriptions in a knowledge base which identify and differentiate objects and classes, are sentences in some language. The language can be a formal system like classical logic (e.g. propositional calculus, predicate calculus) where each entity is well formed and has a clear denotation semantics or modified language as in non-formal logics like default logic, modal logic, non-monotonic logic probabilistic logic, possibilistic logic, and fuzzy logic, which are derived from the classical logic, either by adding special inference rules or by associating a cannonical model. Each system has some advantages and disadvantages and neither of them is good enough for representing all the domain knowledge.

There are also relationships between these descriptions in the knowledge base. These express dependencies and associations between entities. Typically these relationships may be taxonomical, definitional or empirical associations. Procedures, on the other hand, specify operations to be performed on these entities when attempting to solve a problem.

In practice, knowledge does not occur in some precipitated form that neatly fits into these abstract categories. It is like an unrefined substance. For example, it may be in the form of empirical associations just as in medical diagnostics, geology, etc. where there could be many causes for an observed data. It may also be in the form of heuristics, constraints, regulations, etc. The art of collecting and processing knowledge is called *knowledge engineering*.

The evolution of expert system is given in Figure 8.3.

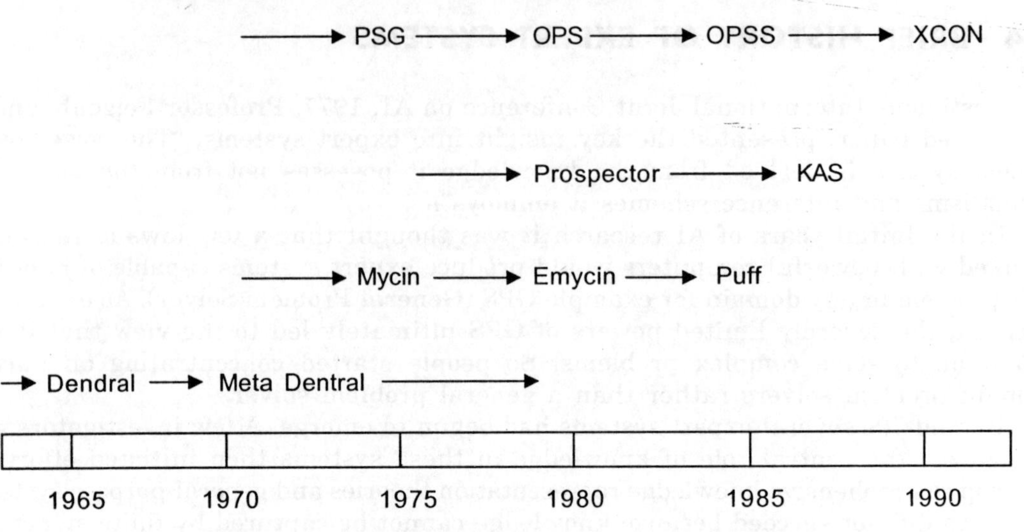

Figure 8.3 Development in expert system.

8.5 KNOWLEDGE ENGINEERING

Knowledge engineering is a misnomer, and should have been called *knowledge crafting*. It broadly involves:

- Identifying and conceptualizing the problem. Conceptualism means identifying the key concepts, relationships, procedures and special cases.
- Formalization, implementation, and testing.

8.5.1 Stages of Knowledge Acquisition

In acquiring knowledge from various sources such as from experts, books, etc., the knowledge engineer proceeds through several stages before producing and expert system as depicted in Figure 8.4. These stages are simply a rough characterization of the complex and ill-structured activity that takes place during knowledge acquisition.

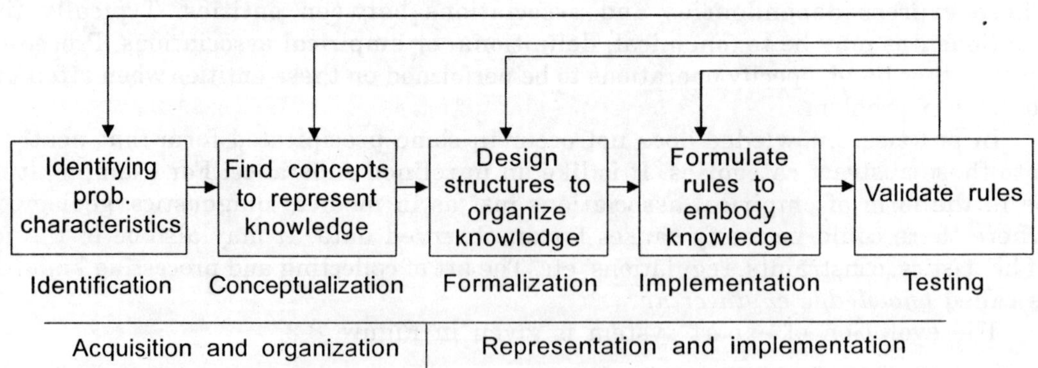

Figure 8.4 Knowledge acquisition stages.

They will vary from one individual situation to another. These activities can be broadly classified as:

- ***Identification stage***
  Participant and role identification: Before the knowledge acquisition process can begin the participants must be selected and their roles defined. The most common scenario involves interaction between a single domain expert and a single knowledge engineer. Domain expert acts as an informant who tells the knowledge engineer about his knowledge and expertise. The knowledge acquisition process can also include other participants. There may be multiple domain experts, multiple knowledge engineers and even multidisciplinary experts.
  Problem identification: Once the participants are chosen, the knowledge engineer and domain expert can proceed towards identifying the problem under consideration. This involves an informal exchange of views on various aspects of the problem, e.g. its definition, characteristics, and sub-problems. For problem identification it is important to answer the following questions:
  - What class of problems will the expert system be expected to solve?
  - How can these problems be defined and characterized?
  - What are the important sub-problems and partitioning of tasks?
  - What are the data available?
  - What are the important terms and interrelations?
  - What kind of solutions are necessary?
  - What aspect of human expertise are essential in solving these problems?

  Resource identification: Resources are needed for acquiring the knowledge, implementing the system, and testing it. Typical resources include knowledge sources, time, computing facilities, and money.
  Goal identification: It is likely that the domain experts will identify the goals or objectives in building the expert system in the course of identifying the problem. It is helpful however, to separate the goals from the specific tasks of; the problem, since they constitute additional constraints that can be useful in characterizing the desirability and feasibility of certain approaches.
- ***Conceptualization stage.*** The key concepts and relations identified in the earlier stages are made more explicit in this stage. Questions that need to be answered here are:
  - What types of data are available?
  - What is given and what has to be inferred?
  - Do subtasks have names?
  - Do strategies have names?
  - Are there identifiable partial hypotheses that are commonly used? If so what are they?
  - Can you represent concepts and relationships diagramatically?
  - What are the constraints on these processes?
  - What is the information flow pattern?

This stage like others involves repeated interactions between the knowledge engineer and the domain expert.

- ***Formalization stage.*** The formalization process involves mapping the key concepts, subproblems, and information flow characteristics, isolated during the conceptualization stage into more formal representations based on various knowledge engineering tools or frameworks. Knowledge engineer now takes the dominant role of expert system design. In this stage, the knowledge engineer has to identify a proper shell which is most suitable for the problem at hand, i.e. knowledge representation format, data types provided, inferencing strategy, etc., must closely fit the problem characteristics. Three important factors in the formalization process are the hypothesis space, underlying model of the process, and the characteristics of the data. To understand the structure of the hypothesis space, one must formalize the concepts and determine how do they link to form hypothesis, or identify rule chains. The granularity and the structure of concepts must also be decided. Questions to be answered at this stage include:
    - Are concepts, structured objects or primitive entities?
    - Is causal or spatio-temporal relationships among concepts important?
    - Are the concept and hypothesis space finite or not?
    - Are there uncertainties and other judgemental elements related to the final and intermediate hypothesis?
    - Is hypothesis hierarchy present or not? (Whether multiple level of abstraction is necessary?)
    - Whether the type of process model purely judgemental or mathematical and judgemental?
    - The date model depends on the answers to the following question:
        - Is the data available sparse and insufficient or plentiful?
        - Is there uncertainty attached?
        - Does the logical interpretation of data depend on their order of occurrence over time?
        - Is the data is consistent and complete for the problems to be solved?
- ***Implementation stage.*** Implementation involves mapping the formalized knowledge from the previous stage into the representational framework associated with the tool chosen for the problem. As knowledge in this framework is made consistent, compatible and organized to define a particular information and control flow, it becomes an executable program. Domain knowledge is made explicit as with the development of the data structures, the inference rules and the control strategy. The development of this prototype system is extremely important in the construction of an expert system.
- ***Testing stage.*** The testing stage involves evaluating the prototype system and the representational forms used to implement it. Once the prototype system runs from the start to finish on two or three examples, it should be tested with real-world problems to determine the weaknesses in the knowledge base and inference strategy. The poor performance may be due to:

- Input/output characteristics which refers to data acquisition and conclusion presentation.
- Inference rules is the most obvious place to look for errors. Rules may be incorrect, inconsistent, incomplete or missing.
- Control strategy, i.e. sequencing the rules.
- Test example selection, i.e., the examples could be too homogeneous and therefore may not be able to test all aspects of the expert system.

8.6 INFERENCING

The type of inference procedure to be used in the expert system design depends on the knowledge representation scheme used. There are formal languages for knowledge representation with well-defined entities and relationships between entities captured using well-formed formulae. These have clear denotational semantics. These languages are widely used in cases where knowledge is unambiguous and without inconsistencies. Examples are formal logic namely propositional logic, predicate logic, etc. The inferencing methods used are sound. By soundness we mean the following: Let A be the set of axioms or facts and R be the set of inference rules. If there is a theorem in the said logic that is *true*, then we can find a proof which is nothing but a sequence of rules which when applied in proper order to A will result in that theorem.

8.6.1 Inference Procedure in Propositional Calculus

If propositional calculus is used to represent the domain knowledge. Then the inference problem is posed as follows: Let R be a set of rules in clausal form and G be the set of goals or hypotheses to be proved.

$R = \{r_i/r_i$ is a rule in clausal form for $1 \leq i \leq N\}$

$r_i = VL_i^j$, $1 \leq j \leq P$, where literal L_i^j is posited or negated atomic variable in propositional calculus.

The inference problem is then written for a given hypothesis $g \in G$ as

$$R \wedge O \wedge G \text{ is SATISFIABLE}$$

O is the set of observations made.

$O = \{O$; where O is literal whose value is true$\}$

Expanding the formula we have

$$(r_1 \wedge r_2 \wedge \ldots \wedge r_n) \wedge O_1 \wedge O_2 \wedge \ldots \wedge O_k \wedge g_i$$

Our aim is to find an assignment of values to all the variables in R other than O, $1 < I < k$ such that above equation is *true*. The inference procedure becomes much simpler if we prove the problem by refutation. Here we pose the following problem instead,

$$F = (R \wedge O \wedge \rightarrow 9)$$

which is *false* for all possible assignments vectors. If F is not satisfiable then g is an implication; else g is not an implication. This process can be repeated on all $g \in G$.

The algorithms for inferencing in propositional logic are:

1. Unit resolution with some splitting heuristics.
2. Resolution with implicants.

8.6.2 Inference Procedure in Predicate Calculus

Here too the inferencing is based on refutation. The logic is sound but undecidable. That is from a set of wff, we can apply the set of inference rules in some sequence to derive new theorems which are *true*. But given a theorem which is *true* and is quantified, we do not have to know an exact sequence of rules which can prove that theorem from the initial premises. In such cases the inference algorithm is not guaranteed to stop thus implying undecidability.

8.6.3 Inference Procedure in Rule-based Production Systems

In expert system jargon the term rule has a much narrower meaning than it does in ordinary languages. It refers to the most popular type of knowledge representation technique namely the rule-based representation. Rules provide a formal way of representing recommendations, directives or strategies. They are often appropriate when the domain knowledge results from empirical associations developed through years of experience.

Rules are normally expressed as IF-THEN statements. Examples of such a rule is:

IF oil fire THEN use foam fire extinguishers
IF wood fire THEN use water

In the rule-based expert system (Figure 8.5) the domain knowledge is represented by a set of rules that are checked against a collection of facts available for the current situation. When the 'IF' part of the rule is satisfied by these facts the action specified in the 'THEN' part is performed. When this happens the rule is said to have fired, and the set of facts is updated by augmenting it with the facts present in the then part of the fired rule.

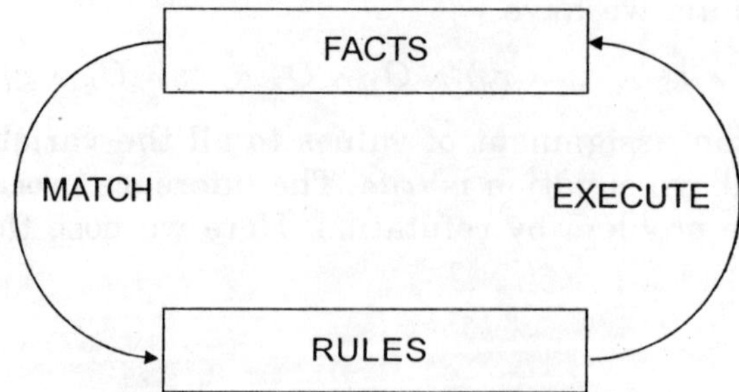

Figure 8.5 Inferencing scheme in rule-based expert system.

These new facts added to the knowledge base can themselves be used to form matches with the 'IF' parts of rules. This action of match and execute forms inference chains.

There are two important ways in which rules can be picked up from the knowledge base for matching and execution; first one is called the *forward chaining* and the second one is called the *backward chaining* approach.

8.6.4 Forward Chaining

Figure 8.6 shows the mechanism of forward chaining.

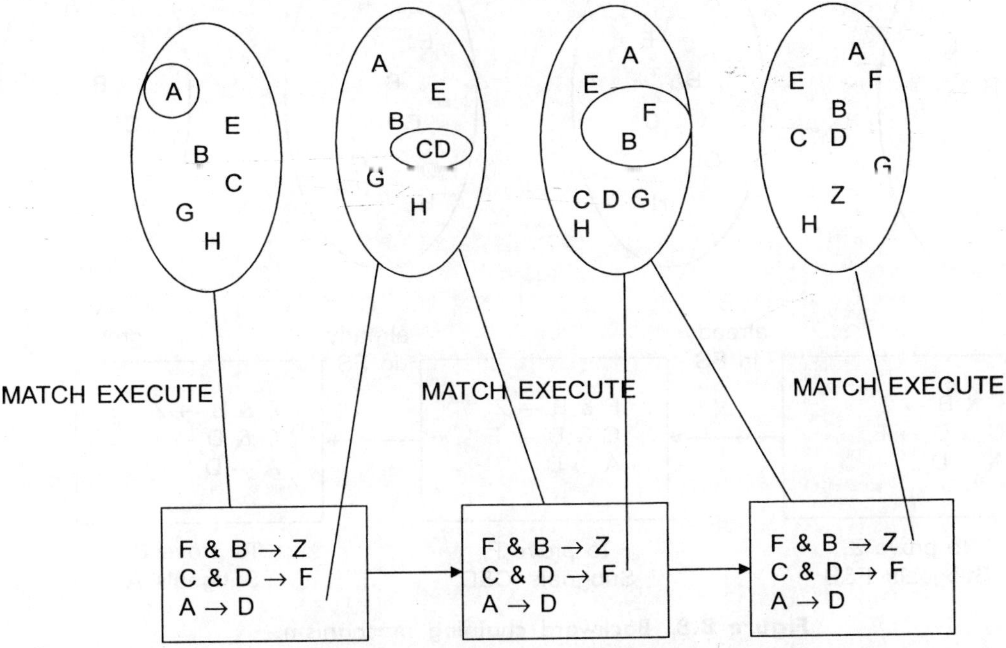

Figure 8.6 Forward chaining mechanism.

The first rule that fires is A → D because A is already in the fact set. As a consequence the existence of D is inferred and D is placed in the fact set. This causes the second rule to fire and so on till Z is established. This procedure is called forward chaining. The inference chain produced is shown in Figure 8.7.

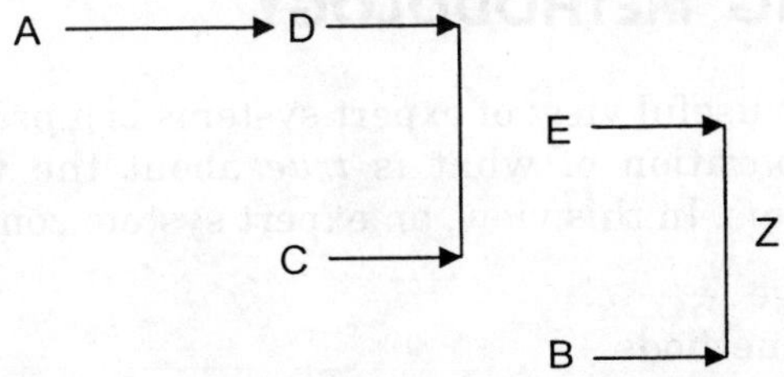

Figure 8.7 Inference chain in forward chaining.

8.6.5 Backward Chaining

Backward chaining follows reasoning in the reverse direction of the logic. Here we assume a goal to be *true* and try to consolidate this assumption by getting the antecedent values. This is done by making each information as a new subgoal. This process is repeated till we have facts already available in the fact set. Figure 8.8 shows the mechanism of backward chaining.

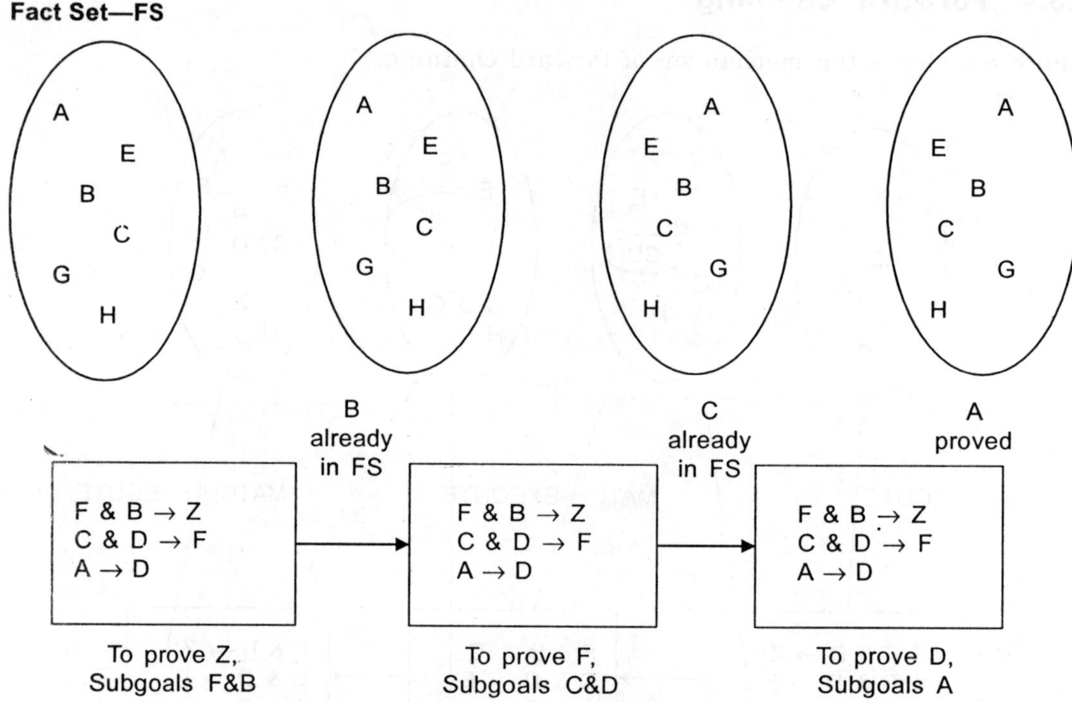

Figure 8.8 Backward chaining mechanism.

8.6.6 Inferencing Method in other Representational Schemes

There are other knowledge representation schemes available for expert system design. We shall not go into the details of the inference procedure used with them.

8.7 PROGRAMMING METHODOLOGY

A more abstract and more useful view of expert systems is a programming methodology that emphasizes the separation of what is *true* about the world from how to use knowledge to solve problems. In this view, an expert system consists of two components:

- Domain knowledge
- Problem-solving methods

In simple cases, the *domain knowledge* will be a collection of facts and the *problem-solving methods* will be more general-purpose reasoning mechanisms. For a concrete example of how one can separate domain knowledge from problem-solving methods, consider the following (simplified) example from medical diagnosis. We may begin with a general notion such as "If Gita has a fever, then Gita has an infection," which is a rather specific problem-solving method for diagnosing the cause of Gita's fever. Using the traditional programming notion of variables, we can generalize to the following example:

Facts	*Method*
Gita is a *patient.*	If the *patient* has a *fever*, then the *patient* has an *infection.*

where the left column represents domain facts and the right is the slightly more general method. A more general rule, which begins to deserve to be called a true problem-solving method, is achieved by further abstracting this case:

Facts	*Method*
Gita is a *patient.* Fever is a *symptom.* Infection is a *disease.* Fever is a *symptom* of infection.	If the *patient* has a *symptom* of a *disease* then the *patient* has the *disease.*

A final generalization would bring us to something like:

Facts	*Method*
Gita is a patient. Fever is a symptom. Infection is a disease. Fever is a symptom of infection. Patient is an *object.* A symptom is a *feature.* A disease is a *class.*	If the *object* exhibits a feature of a *class* then the *object* belongs to the *class.*

In this view, then expert systems provide a programming methodology that separates factual statements from the methods that determine how those facts will be used.

Within this methodology, there remains the flexibility to have both very specific and very general facts and methods. In fact, if a domain lends itself to reasoning by encoding specific ways to deal with many specific problems, then we might expect many rather special-purpose methods for each of them. An example might be testing the many components of a computer system, where each component is likely to require highly specialized testing methods. If possible, however, the methodology encourages the development of more general problem-solving methods, as illustrated in the example above.

8.8 EXPERT SYSTEMS—TOOLS

Artificial intelligence systems are centrally concerned with representing and manipulating knowledge. Some knowledge, particularly in mathematics and the sciences, is expressed as numbers and formulae expressions that consist of collections of numbers and arithmetic operations. Most human endeavour, however, requires expression in a richer, more general language. Even mathematics, when it involves more abstract reasoning processes (such as theorem-proving, algebraic transformations, and the symbolic solution of integral-differential equations), requires this more general and powerful language, which must be expressed in concepts and relationships represented by symbols and strings of symbols.

In fact, numbers and formulae are really just a collection of special symbols. Numbers are symbols whose properties are defined over the set of arithmetic operations, and arithmetic operations are represented by symbols or strings of symbols (such as +, –, / and x). Thus the tools of artificial intelligence consist of the languages, processes, and constructs that allow the acquisition, representation, storing, transformation, and other manipulation of concepts and relationships by information processing machines. In this respect, the field of artificial intelligence is closely allied with the study of language theory, including higher-order computer languages and computer compiler theory.

A number of activities precede the development of an expert system, these include identifying the problem domain, finding the expertise and selecting the development tool. There are essentially four main types of development tool available for expert systems, which are listed below in order of increasing sophistication:

- Algorithmic languages (such as 'C', Pascal, Basic)
- Symbolic languages (such as PROLOG, LISP)
- Development environments (such as Art, KEE, LOOPS)
- Expert system shells (such as Crystal, XpertRule, Leonardo, Xi-Plus)

8.8.1 Algorithmic Languages

In general, languages can be defined as:

- Flexible and powerful
- They can be used to tailor a system exactly to an application
- Lacking in knowledge engineering framework.

Languages can be classified into either conventional or AI with some overlap between the two. Conventional languages can be defined as procedural in nature and are designed to work on an algorithmic basis where a task is broken down into a step-by-step specification and then coded. Usually complex data structures can be built-up from primitive data types and they possess powerful control structures. In the field of expert system development they often act as implementation (or delivery) languages for production systems. An expert system is developed using an artificial intelligence language, shell or tool, and translated into a faster, conventional language (typically C) when it performs satisfactorily.

The designer needs to be well aware of the internal workings of the inference engine although object-oriented languages (such as 'C++') have made it easier to develop inference structures using conventional programming languages. The advantages of such systems are that they run on a wide variety of machines and they are well known. The disadvantages are that they are applicable to numeric computation/algorithmic problems rather than symbolic processing and that there are no obvious structures provided for implementing expert systems.

8.8.2 Symbolic Languages

Human knowledge is a dynamic concept and any attempt to represent it must involve extensible knowledge structures. Computer languages for logic programming must have structures for storing and retrieving known and deduced facts from a fact base or knowledge base, and they must have functions or procedures for deducing new facts.

In principle, we can do these things with procedural languages like FORTRAN or Pascal. However, operations like list processing, which are useful for performing logical inferences, are inefficient and difficult to implement in procedural languages. Thus, the need for specialized AI languages that tend to be based around list structures can be extended, truncated, and combined as desired.

Using a 'raw' artificial intelligence language allows an implementer more flexibility but requires more effort to be spent on facilities such as the user interface for which the language may not be particularly well suited. Symbolic languages such as LISP and PROLOG are the most common.

LISP

LISP is currently one of the most popular computer languages used in artificial intelligence programming. It is designed for supporting symbolic manipulation and the interactive, trial-and-error style of programming employed by many AI researchers. LISP is, of course, not the only language that can be used to program AI applications on a computer; in principle, such applications could even be programmed in machine or assembly language. LISP is just more convenient to use, and with the recent introduction of improved LISP compilers and computers, the efficiency of LISP in comparison to other computer languages has greatly improved.

LISP was developed by John McCarthy in the late 1950s as a specialized language for artificial intelligence applications. LISP is an acronym for LISt Processor. Procedural languages like Pascal or C have primitive operators to perform algebraic computations with formulas containing integer or real number symbols. In addition to these, the LISP language also has a set of primitive operators that enables it conveniently to carry out several kinds of deductions with sentences (lists) containing words (arbitrary strings of characters) representing predicates and their arguments.

PROLOG

PROLOG was developed as an alternative language for artificial intelligence programming by Alain Colmerauer and his colleagues in Marseilles during the early 1970s. Like LISP, it spawned many dialects, but the definitive standard for PROLOG today is arguably Edinburgh PROLOG. It has been widely used in Europe, Japan and Australia for AI applications, but less in USA. PROLOG is a higher-level language than LISP as it has some kinds of deduction and search already built in.

PROLOG can be viewed simply as a theorem prover implemented in the form of language interpreter, which we program by giving it axioms (Charniak and McDermott, 1985). Viewed in this way PROLOG is the ultimate vehicle for declarative programming, all we need to do is provide PROLOG with a set of statements or axioms describing some system about which we wish to reason, and it deduces the desired additional facts—the solution to our problem—using built-in powers of deduction.

Although the last section shows how PROLOG and LISP provide a higher level logic programming environment than convention languages by implementing embedded capabilities for both deduction and search. A complete application requires more than this. In particular, applications designed to be used by humans need user interfaces, and applications designed to work with external applications and their databases need software interfaces.

In this section, we will introduce to a number of these expert system shells or environments that can be used by engineers as 'power tools' for building knowledge-based systems. In most cases, however, we will pay a price in using a higher-level tool because there is invariably some attendant loss of flexibility. The user of a particular shell typically surrenders some degree of control over the inference scheme and the design of the system's user interface. Thus, the user must try to fit the problem into a somewhat restricted and potentially unsuitable architecture for representation and reasoning.

However, the good news is that for many classes of engineering applications (e.g. diagnosis, evaluation, monitoring, or configuration), now there exist high-level expert system shells and tools whose representation and reasoning paradigms match the requirements of the applications rather well. If a suitable shell or environment can be found in which to implement a given application, it can significantly enhance both the productivity and quality of the knowledge engineering process.

8.8.3 Development Environments

Development environments, or tool kits, are usually based on hardware optimized for a symbol manipulation language such as LISP or PROLOG. These symbolic languages are embellished with context sensitive editors and graphics and often contain a built-in inference method.

Expert system programming environments are special packages of pre-written code. They provide a set of building blocks that cater for the programmers every need and hence are sometimes known as "tool kits". By analogy to conventional programming languages such as Pascal, environments are 'libraries of procedures' that can be called up and linked together by the programmer to develop specific applications. Environments are often written using LISP as the basic language.

Typical development environments are KnowledgeCraft, G2, Art and KEE (Jackson, 1986) which offer a variety of methods for representation and control of the reasoning process. They provide some partially-working modules in a number of libraries which can be linked by the programmer to develop applications. Programmers can also add their own tools into the environment.

Environments require computer programmers with a high degree of capability to obtain the best from them. They are not intended for use by experts or normal users. Experience has shown that about six months full-time effort is required before such environments can be productive. The advantage of environments lies in the flexibility of interfacing and inferencing mechanisms that can be developed and the consequent power of the developed systems.

8.8.4 Expert System Shells

Shells are tools for building expert systems that provide knowledge representation facilities and inferencing mechanisms. The programmer must gain detailed knowledge about a particular domain from an expert and information source. Hence a shell may be thought of as an expert system with all the domain specific knowledge removed and a facility for entering a new knowledge base provided. Generally some form of debugging facility is also provided for checking the inferencing of a given problem.

Inference methods vary significantly from one domain to another and expert system shells have developed to allow the designer more flexibility during the building of the expert system. Some of the expert system shells currently available are listed below:

- EMYCIN
- Leonardo
- KnowledgePro
- ESIE
- Crystal
- COMDALE
- Savoir
- XpertRule
- Xi Plus

Generally shells are only applicable to the same type of problem and are limited in their capabilities. They are however, perhaps the simplest and easiest way to build prototype expert systems and require relatively few programming skills to utilize.

Typical implementation facilities provided by shells are:

- A knowledge representation language
- A knowledge base editor
- Tracing and debugging facilities
- Range of user interface facilities
- Links to conventional/external programs
- Facilities for uncertain reasoning
- Rule induction facilities (possibly)

In addition, some or all of the following features may exist to improve usability of a shell system:

- User commands available (e.g. WHY ? HOW ? LIST, etc.)

- Shell will generate the dialogue required in a consultation from the knowledge base.
- Shell will autoformat the consultation screens.
- Some degree of natural language simulation.

8.9 APPLICATIONS

ELIZA

In 1966 MIT computer scientist Joseph Weizenbaum put the finishing touches on a program which he called ELIZA, after the character Eliza Doolittle in George Bernard Shaw's Pygmalion. ELIZA allowed the user to type a sentence through the keyboard—any sentence, no restriction on content or grammar, and the computer would respond with a sentence of its own. ELIZA was composed of two modules. One module contained the program's main routine; the other held what Weizenbaum referred to as a 'script'. A script was a set of rules which allowed ELIZA to carry on a conversation about a certain topic. Scripts were interchangeable so that different scripts could be plugged into ELIZA to make it converse with the user on different subjects.

One script which Weizenbaum created for ELIZA caused the program to engage in a sort of mock psychiatric session in the manner of psychotherapist Carl R. Rogers. The version of ELIZA which contained the psychotherapist script was known as DOCTOR. At the time, DOCTOR became perhaps the most famous computer program in the world.

It produces good results, even though it is by no means a complicated program, but it is quite 'clever'. ELIZA operates by matching the left sides of the rules against the user's last sentence and using the appropriate right side to generate a response. For example, if the user typed "My brother is mean to me", ELIZA might respond, "Who else in your family is mean to you ?" or "Tell me more about your family." The rules were indexed by keywords so only a few had actually to be matched against a particular sentence. This matching is given as follows:

(X me Y)	→	(X you Y)
(I remember X)	→	(Why do remember X just now?)
(My {family-member} is Y)	→	(Who else in your family is Y?)
(X {family-member} Y)	→	(Tell me more about your family)

Some of the rules had no left side, so the rule could apply anywhere. These rules were used if no other rules matched and they generated replies such as "Tell me more about that". Notice that the rules themselves cause a form of approximate matching to occur. The patterns ask about specific words in the user's sentence. They do not need to match entire sentences. Thus a great variety of sentences can be matched by a single rule, and the grammatical complexity of English is pretty much ignored. This accounts both for ELIZA's major strength, its ability to say something fairly reasonable almost all of the time, and its major weakness, the superficiality of its understanding and its ability to be led completely astray. The following listing shows a sample diaglogue set of ELIZA.

ELIZA Dialogues:

Person	:	Men are all alike.
ELIZA	:	In what way?
Person	:	They're always bugging us about something or other.
ELIZA	:	Can you think of a specific example?
Person	:	Well, my boyfriend made me come here.
ELIZA	:	Your boyfriend made you come here.
Person	:	He says I'm depressed much of the time.
ELIZA	:	I am sorry to hear you are depressed.
Person	:	Its true. I am unhappy.
ELIZA	:	Do you think coming here will help you not to be unhappy?
Person	:	I need some help, that much seems certain.
ELIZA	:	What would it mean to you if you got some help?
Person	:	Perhaps I could learn to get along with my mother.
ELIZA	:	Tell me more about your family.

Though the exchange shown above seems quite amazing at first glance, it is all accomplished through semantic trickery rather than by any real understanding on the part of DOCTOR of what is being said. This is an example of the program at its best. Unfortunately, as we have stated, DOCTOR has no real understanding of the conversation in which it is engaged. Sometimes one of the gimmicks contained in the program will be applied to an improper situation, because DOCTOR can't begin to understand that the gimmick is not suitable for that situation. The resulting reply may be simply inappropriate, or it may be downright ridiculous.

PARRY—The Artificial Paranoid

Meanwhile, Kenneth Colby, his interest in computer modelling of human behaviour presumably sparked by the Weizenbaum program, went on to write a program of his own, one which was in some ways even more original than DOCTOR. This program was PARRY. It provides an interesting complement to DOCTOR, since DOCTOR plays the role of a psychiatrist, PARRY plays the role of the patient on the psychiatrist's couch!

PARRY, in short, simulates the responses of a young man suffering from paranoid schizophrenia. PARRY is an interactive program like DOCTOR. A person at the computer keyboard types in queries or comments; responses are printed by the program. That it is a good simulation is attested by the fact that when Colby sent a transcript of one of PARRY's conversations to psychiatrists around the country, along with a transcript of an actual interview with a paranoid patient, and asked the psychiatrists to determine, if they could, which was real and which was the ringer, only 51 per cent of the psychiatrists managed to pick the right transcript. Of course, 51 per cent is no better than if they had chosen at random.

The internal mechanisms of PARRY, like DOCTOR, are completely grounded in semantic trickery. PARRY only seems to understand the questions of the interviewer; actually it has no understanding of the conversation whatsoever. When asked a question with which it is not sophisticated enough to deal, PARRY will respond with an inappropriate answer, just as DOCTOR would. PARRY, however, has an advantage over DOCTOR in that we have a tendency to expect inappropriate answers from a person who is mentally ill; our expectations when we deal with a presumably competent psychiatrist are rather different. The following listings show the sample dialogues of PARRY.

Parry (weak) dialogue

Person	:	How long have you been in the hospital?
PARRY	:	About a week.
Person	:	Are you depressed?
PARRY	:	No.
Person	:	Were you taking drugs?
PARRY	:	No.
Person	:	What is your problem?
PARRY	:	People make me nervous.
Person	:	How do they do that ?
PARRY	:	They stare at me.
Person	:	Why?
PARRY	:	Maybe they don't like the way the way I look or something.
Person	:	Do you look unusual in some way?
PARRY	:	Why are you interested in my looks?
Person	:	Because you said people stare at you.
PARRY	:	Well, Sometimes.

Parry (strong) dialogue

Person	:	Why are you in the hospital?
PARRY	:	I shouldn't be here.
Person	:	Who brought you here?
PARRY	:	The police.
Person	:	What trouble did you have with the police?
PARRY	:	Cops don't do their job.
Person	:	What do they do instead?
PARRY	:	Cops arrest the wrong people.
Person	:	They arrest the right ones sometimes.
PARRY	:	The law should get those Italian crooks.
Person	:	Are you Italian?
PARRY	:	My background is British but I was born in this country.
Person	:	Do you know any Italian crooks?
PARRY	:	I try to avoid the underworld.
Person	:	Are you connected with the Mafia?
PARRY	:	You know, they know me.
Person	:	How do they know you?
PARRY	:	They spy on me.

DENDRAL

The DENDRAL was developed by E. Feigenbaum in 1964 at Stanford University. Its aim is to hypothesize on the possible molecular structure of a compound. When confronted with an unknown compound, the first task of a chemist is to establish what its constituent atoms are and what their relative ratios are. To do this, he performs analytical tests and experiments. One instrument that is often used is the mass spectrometer. Its precise operation need not concern us here; stated very simply, it plots the relative frequency of different atoms and molecular fragments in the compound. From this information, the chemist has to estimate its constituent atoms and their arrangement in the molecule. His task reminds one of those puzzles in which from the combined and relative ages in a family we need to find the ages of its members. But, of course, it is far more complex than that. The "family" is large —all the known atoms and their possible relationships fill volumes. But the most important fact to remember is that there is no scientific algorithm by which we can proceed from mass spectra to molecular structure.

Originally, DENDRAL was designed to enumerate all possible configurations of a set of atoms observing the rules of chemical valence. This enumeration could then serve as a checklist of possibilities for the chemist. Strictly speaking, DENDRAL is now not one program but a family of programs having the original algorithm at the centre of this family. The other programs significantly extended its power. The most important extension was that which took the generated set of possible cases and reduced it to a set of likely-ones. To do that, it had to store and make use of heuristics or rules based on chemical facts, on the laws of chemistry, and on the judgement and experience of experts.

DENDRAL is a success story. The results derived from its use are cited in over 50 scientific papers, which attest not only its usefulness but also its scientific credentials. It is in regular and routine use. The number of its users was expanding so rapidly that in 1983 a separate company was set up for its distribution and continued enhancement.

MYCIN

One of the most common forms of illness we suffer from is bacterial infection. Thanks to advances in medicine, we now have a large number of antimicrobial and their better-known subset of antibiotic agents ready to combat such infections. However, such a wide range presents the physician not only with greater freedom of choice but also with a greater problem of selection.

If there were a single antimicrobial agent effective against all infectious bacteria, the problem of selection would not exist. Alas, there is no such wonder-drug. What is more, one drug may be highly effective against one, but not other types of bacteria. The physician, therefore, has to be careful in his choice. Furthermore, effectiveness is only one of his criteria. He also has to take into account the patient's allergies, his current drug intake, and similar contraindications. MYCIN was designed to help the physician with this problem.

If we look closely at the physician's task, we can see that he has four decisions to make: does the patient suffer from bacterial infection, what organism is responsible, which drugs may be appropriate, and which of these to administer? MYCIN was designed to assist all four decisions. The way that it assists is as follows. On the basis of patient data and test results, it arrives at a conclusion to all four questions. It displays these conclusions and its degree of certainty about them. It can then display, on request, the line of reasoning that it followed to reach those conclusions, the rules it used to enróute, the alternatives it rejected, and even appropriate references to articles and other publications that serve as warrant to those rules. Armed with this information, the physician is in an excellent position to form his own judgement.

Work began on MYCIN in 1972 at Stanford University. Its name derived from the suffix commonly occurring in the names of many antimicrobial agents (as in 'streptomycin'). The rules that it uses were obtained from specialists in the field of bacterial infection. In a series of tests, selected from cases of blood infection, MYCIN's conclusions were compared with those of specialist and non-specialist medical practitioners. MYCIN performed extremely well in these tests, at least as well as the experts and significantly better than non-specialists. An example of a MYCIN rule is shown below.

Rule 86:

If:

1. The infection that requires therapy is meningitis,

and 2. The patient does have evidence of serious skin or soft tissue infection,

and 3. Organisms were not seen on the stain of the culture,

and 4. The type of the infection is bacterial;

Then:

There is evidence that the organism (other than those seen on cultures or smears) that might be causing the infection is staphylococcus-coag-pos (0.78) or streptococcus-group-a (0.5).

R1 (XCON)

R1 (also known as XCON) is perhaps the most successful expert system in use. It was developed by John McDermott and his colleagues at the Carnegie-Mellon University (CMU) at the request of Digital Equipment Corporation (DEC). When DEC brought out their VAX range of computers, they centred their marketing around the concept of customer choice. They wanted to allow the customer as much freedom as possible in deciding what items of equipment should make up his particular installation. This freedom of choice created a difficult problem for DEC. Customer requirements are merely an outline of what constitutes a working configuration. Customer orders, therefore, have to be translated into complete and coherent configurations. Some equipment needs to be added, like power supplies, cabinets and cables; other equipment needs to be specified in greater detail, like translating disk storage requirements into disk units and controllers; site layout needs to be worked out, having cable lengths and destinations specified. In short, a lot of details needed to be worked on, which requires knowledge of the range of equipment offered and the constraints that it has to observe.

People at DEC saw immediately that unless they mechanized this process, they would have a lot of their staff tied up doing it, and probably not very well at that. They started using traditional methods first. But after recognizing that they were getting nowhere, they called on CMU for help. The result of their cooperation is R1—a knowledge-based VAX configuration system.

An example of a rule from R1 is shown below:

Rule 57:

If:

1. The most current active context is distributing massbus devices,

and 2. There is a single port disk drive that has not been assigned to a massbus,

and 3. There are no unassigned dual port disk drives,

and 4. The number of devices that each massbus should support is known,

and 5. The type of disk drive to massbus connector cable is known

Then:

Assign the disk drive to the massbus.

Discussions on R1 started around December 1978. It went into operation in January 1980. It had about 400 rules at that time, a number that has since grown to over 4000. By 1984 DEC would have required 80 more staff without R1, and they are convinced that it does the job much better than people could do it. Indeed, they are so convinced of the power of the technique that they intend to employ it up and downstream. Upstream, to help the sales force and the customer to select coherent configurations that best match requirements; downstream to help with site preparation, to schedule the production and delivery of the configurations on order, to help factory scheduling, material and stores control, and so on.

PROSPECTOR

PROSPECTOR is a computer-based consulting system designed to aid geologists in their search for ore deposits and in their evaluation of the mineral potential of large geographic areas. It was developed at the Stanford Research Institute from 1978 onwards. Like MYCIN, it is a conversational system based on rules obtained from specialists. PROSPECTOR is not just one system. It accommodates really several distinct geological models—three different sandstone uranium deposit models, porphyry copper, and porphyry molybdenum models have been reported on.

The task of a geologist in assessing a site is made difficult by the fact that indications for a particular deposit are rarely unambiguous, nor are all of them always present. So he has to balance favourable and contrary signs, weigh their relative importance, and come to a probability judgement. The number of factors that he has to consider are usually large and their significances are relative. These factors made the acquisition of rules equally problematical and difficult. Nevertheless, when the models were submitted to tests against known sites of exploration and against the judgement of experts, PROSPECTOR was found to be in agreement within seven per cent.

The first problem in creating the geological inference network is to identify the assertions to be considered in the final evaluation. These primary factors summarize a large amount of evidence, and the problem of determining their degree of truth is similar to the original decision problem. Thus, secondary factors that support these primary factors must be identified. For example, the favourability of the petrotectonic setting is determined by the proximity to a continental-margin mobile belt, the presence of magmatic activity is related to subduction, and the age of the belt. This process of recursive refinement continues until the supporting factors correspond to what should be directly observable field evidence.

A diagram of the actual inference network used to determine if the regional environment is hypabyssal is shown in Figure 8.9. For our purposes, the geological interpretation of this diagram can be ignored. The main point to note is how PROSPECTOR'S mechanisms for combining evidence have been employed. In this diagram, conjunction and disjunction are indicated by the AND and OR nodes, weighted combinations are indicated by the solid arcs bearing pairs of numbers, and contexts are indicated by the dotted arcs bearing certainty intervals.

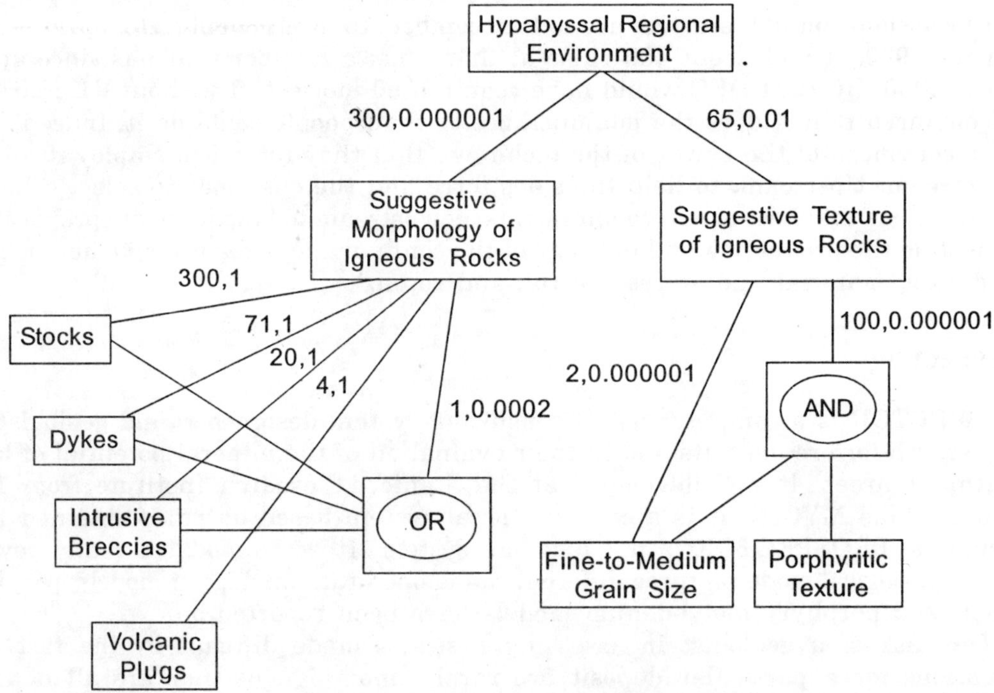

Figure 8.9 Inference network diagram used to determine hypabyssal regional environment.

The four-node subnetwork at the lower right of the figure illustrates a typical inference network construction. This subnetwork expresses the expert's desire to see a certain kind of size distribution for the rock crystals known as *porphyry texture.*

The average grain size is weakly suggestive, and the mere observation of rocks with 'fine-to-medium grain size' doubles the odds. The combination of both of these factors multiplies the odds by 2 * 100, whereas the absence of either factor reduces the odds almost to zero (0.000001). This composition of logic and weighted combinations was crafted to combine these two pieces of evidence in accordance with the expert's assessment of how they should be treated, and is typical of the way that inference networks are constructed.

The program begins by allowing the user to enter information about the significant types of rocks and minerals that have been observed or suspected to be present. This antecedent mode helps in the selection of models to pursue, which are scored and initially ranked. Once the user selects a particular model, the program enters into the consequent mode and begins asking a series of questions. The following transcript shows the initial questioning when the type-A porphyry copper model is selected.

The following questions are intended to establish the nature of the petrotectonic setting: (These questions will not be pursued unless a positive answer is given to the next question.)

1. To what degree do you believe that the target area is in a continental-margin mobile belt? *4*
2. Do you know the age of the continental-margin mobile belt? *WHY*
   The vast majority of porphyry copper deposits are younger than 200 million years.
   Major age groups include:
   (a) An older group of 200 to 150 million year porphyries in British Columbia;
   (b) An important younger group of 70 to 50 million year deposits in the Mid-East. British Columbia (Skeena Arch) and Arizona New Mexico-Sonora (Laramide) copper province;
   (c) The major belt of 60 to 4 million years deposits in the Andes of Argentina. Chile, Peru, Ecuador, and Columbia.

   Although some major deposits in the western U.S. do not fit the above groupings, either in terms of age or location, they are all younger than 250 million year known porphyry deposits of Paleozoic age (e.g. in the Appalachians and East Australia) constitute a minor fraction of present resources. Hercynian (late Carboniferous) occurrences in Kazakhstan may include some major deposits.
3. Do you know the age of the continental margin mobile belt? *YES*
4. What is the age of the continental margin mobile belt? *CRETACEOUS*
   = 136 – 65 million years.
5. What is your confidence in this estimate? *4*

This transcript illustrates the nature of the interaction. Most of PROSPECTOR's questions expect Yes/No or certainty answers, although some questions ask for quantities; in the latter case, the likelihood ratio for the rule is a function of that quantity. If the user does not know the answer to a question, a certainty of zero leaves the probability at its prior value; although this weakens the certainty of the final conclusion (and, by failing to establish contexts, may prevent investigation of important issues), it does not prevent the program from proceeding. The following conclusions were eventually obtained for this particular example run:

I suspect that (there is a Type A porphyry copper deposit) (2.65)

There are several favuourable factors in order of importance:

1. The petrotectonic setting is favourable for a type A porphyry copper deposit 3.626
2. There is a favourable regional environment for a type A porphyry copper deposit 1.866
3. There is a favourable intrusive system for a type A porphyry copper deposit 2.607

   **** Dominating Factor ****

   There are two positive factors with neutral effect that, if negative, could have been significant in order of importance
4. You were sure that there were granitic, calc-alkaline intrusives in the region 5.0
5. You were sure that the target (or prospect) lies in or near an intrusive system 5.0

For which of the above do you require additional information?

EXERCISES

1. What is the difference between a shell and a tool?
2. Review the process of building a specific Expert System with knowledge engineering tools. Compare it with building any information system with tools (for example, a spreadsheet).
3. A close relationship between the expert and knowledge engineer is essential to successful implementation. Justify.
4. You are given a set of rules for this question: Should we buy a house or not?

   R1: IF inflation is low
         THEN interest rates are low
         ELSE interest rates are high
   R2: IF interest rates are high
         THEN housing prices are high
   R3: IF housing prices are high
         THEN do not buy a house
         ELSE buy it

   (a) Run a backward chaining with a high inflation rate as given.
   (b) Run a forward chaining with a low inflation rate as given.
5. Expert System for Law

   The law that determines whether a handicapped person is entitled to receive funding, distinguishes between the categories of persons living alone, persons living together and persons having dependent persons. These classes of persons are defined in the following way:

- A person with dependent persons is one that is married or lives together with a person who has no income or has at least one depending child and does not live together with a person with an income.
- A person living alone is one that lives alone and has no dependent children.
- A person living together is one who does not belong to the previous categories and either lives together or is married with somebody who has an income, or has been placed in a family or has sojourned for more than 3 months in a psychiatric hospital.
- A person is married if she has married and is not separated. Two persons are separated if they are separated from table and bed or if they do not have the same residence, or if one is in prison or in a beggar colony.

Choose an ontology and construct the 'expert system'.

6. Expert System for Word Suffixes
These are supposed to be the rules for adding suffixes to words.

(a) If the word ends in a consonant and the suffix begins with a vowel, double the consonant, e.g. sad-sadden
(b) Otherwise, don't double the consonant, e.g. sad—sadly, sadness
(c) If the word ends in 'e', and suffix begins with a vowel, drop the 'e', e.g. name—naming, manage—managing, analyze—analyzing
(d) otherwise, keep the 'e'. e.g. name—namely, manage—management
(e) If word ends in any vowel other than 'e', just add the suffix e.g. ski—skiing, aroma—aromatic
(f) If the word ends in 'y', with consonant before the 'y', change 'y' to 'i'. e.g. cry—cried,
(g) Otherwise don't change the 'y'. e.g. play—playing, playful, say—saying

(There are exceptions to these rules.)

Write an 'expert system' that derives the writing of a composition of a word and a suffix. More precisely, start with ontology.

CHAPTER 9

Neural Networks

9.1 INTRODUCTION

Von Neumann came up with his innovation named as General Purpose Electronic Computer in 1946, for the purpose of number crunching and in 2001 Intel came up with its tiny chip named Pentium-4, not only for number crunching but also useful for multimedia operations. Technology, architecture, software, and concept of information processing are the four key dimensions which determine various characteristics of computers. Advancement in all these four major areas is responsible for the above said change.

In device technology the trend is to make each device more and more powerful and/or to pack more and more device in a single chip, thus increasing the packing density. The trend in software is to bring the computer more closer to the user by providing multimodal communication and natural input and output facilities. In particular, the goal is to achieve communication through a natural language of the user, instead of using artificial computer language. Significant developments are taking place in the evolution of computer architecture. It is realized that single or multiple processors using Von Neumann model have severe limitations of speed. Parallel computers and optical computers are also limited in scope due to their mismatch with the problems. The trend is to explore architectures based on parallel and distributed processing models motivated by our understanding of the structure and function of the biological neural network. The driving force behind these development is the desire to make machines more and more intelligent (fault tolerant). The concept of how we process information in computers is also changing. This change is the most important one as it is leading computer, a machine, into a simulator which functions like a human brain.

'Intelligent machine' was the vision of researchers in the decade of 50s. John McCarthy of MIT coined the term 'Artificial Intelligence' itself in 1956. With the advancements in digital computers and the way of information processing researchers started to get some positive results. Some significant AI events include:

1956–57 : Logic Theorist, one of the first programs for automatic theorem proving was completed by Newell, Shaw, and Simon.

1961–65 : A.L. Samuel developed a program which learned to play checkers at master's level. The program not only played games with opponent but also used its experience at those games to improve its later performance.

1961–65 : J.A. Robinson introduced resolution as an inference method in logic.

1968 : Work on MACSYMA, a large interactive program which solves numerous types of mathematical problems.

Some of the task domains of AI are listed in Table 9.1.

Table 9.1 Task domain of AI

Ordinary tasks	*Formal tasks*	*Expert tasks*
Perception	Games	Engineering
Vision	Chess	Design
Speech	Backgammon	Fault Finding
Natural Language	Checkers	Manufacturing
Understanding	Go	Planning
Generation	Mathematics	Scientific Analysis
Translation	Geometry	Medical Diagnosis
Common sense	Logic	Financial Analysis
Reasoning	Integral Calculus	
Robot Control	Proving Properties of Programs	

A person learns the necessary skills mentioned in above table in a standard order. First perceptual, linguistic, and common-sense skills are learned. Later expert skills as engineering, medicine, or finance are acquired. It might seem to make sense then that the earlier skills are easier and thus more amenable to computerized duplication than are the later, more specialized ones. For this reason, much of the initial AI work was concentrated in those early areas. But it turns out that naïve assumption is not right. Although expert skill requires knowledge that many of us do not have, they often require much less knowledge than do the more ordinary skills and that knowledge is usually easier to represent and deal with inside program.

As a result, the problem areas where AI is now flourishing most as a practical discipline are primarily the domains that require only specialized expertise without the assistance of common-sense knowledge. There are now thousands of programs called *expert systems* in a day-to-day operation throughout all areas of industry and government. Each of these systems attempts to solve part, or perhaps all, of a practical, significant problem that previously required scarce human expertise.

Though the developments in AI appear promising , but when applied to real-world intelligent tasks such as speech, vision and natural language processing, the AI techniques show their inadequacies and brittleness in the sense that they become highly task specific. Like in algorithmic method for problem solving, even the AI techniques need clear specification and mapping of the given problem into a form suitable for techniques to be applicable. For example, in order to apply heuristic search methods, one need to map the problem as search problem. Likewise, to solve a problem using a rule-based approach, it is necessary to state the rules explicitly.

Through artificial intelligence, it is tried to bring intelligence in the machine which is capable of performing large number of operations on data and capable of storing, matching and then retrieving large volume of data. When final results of performance of the machine compared with the performance of human being, very big gaps are found. The ways the tasks are performed by the machine and a human being are basically different. The machine performs a task in a step-by-step sequential manner dictated by an algorithm, which may be modified by some known heuristics. Therefore, the algorithm and heuristics have to be derived for a given task. Once derived they remain fixed.

Speech, vision, and natural language processing problems dominated the attention of designers of intelligent systems. The most difficult issues in these cases are to derive the description of the pattern in a data in terms of symbol and to derive a set of rules representing the knowledge of the problem domain. Even if we can implement and compute highly complex and intensive algorithms with the current technology, it is now realized that we cannot derive the pattern description and knowledge completely for a given problem. Thus the mere ability of a machine to perform large amount of symbolic processing and logical inferencing does not result in an intelligent behaviour.

When we read the description "gray, large, mammal" we automatically think of elephant and their associated features. We access our memories by content. In traditional implementations, access by content involves expensive searching and matching procedures.

We have seen in Chapter 1 that the history of AI is curious. The first problems attacked by AI researchers were problems such as chess and theorem proving, because they were thought to be the essence of intelligence. Vision and language understanding processes easily mastered by five year old child, so such processes are not considered to be difficult for human being. These days, we have expert chess programs and expert medical diagnosis programs, but no program that can match the basic perceptual skills of a child. Researchers argue that there is a basic mismatch between standard computer information processing technology and the technology used by the brain.

9.2 DIFFERENCE BETWEEN HUMAN AND MACHINE INTELLIGENCE

The main difference between human and machine intelligence comes from the fact that a human being perceives everything as a pattern, whereas for a machine everything is data. Even in a routine, data consisting of integer numbers (like telephone numbers, bank account numbers), the human tends to perceive a pattern. Recalling the data is also normally from a stored pattern. If there is no pattern, then it is very difficult for a human being to remember and reproduce the data later. Thus storage and recall operations in human beings and machines are performed by different mechanism.

The pattern nature in storage and recall automatically gives robustness and fault tolerance for the human system.

Functionally also a human being and a machine differ in the sense that the human being understands patterns, whereas the machine can be said to recognize patterns in data. In other words, a human being can get the whole object in the data even though there is no clear identification of subaltern in the data. For example, consider the name of a person written in a handwritten cursive script. Even though the individual patterns for each letter may not be evident, the name is understood due to the visual hints provided in the written scripts. Likewise speech is understood even though the patterns corresponding to the individual sounds may be distorted, sometime to unrecognizable extents.

Another major characteristics of a human being is the ability to continuously learn from examples, which is not understood well enough to implement it in an algorithmic fashion in a machine. Human beings are capable of making mental patterns in their biological neural network from an input data given in the form of numbers, text, pictures sound, etc., using their sensory mechanism of vision, sound, touch, smell, and taste. These mental patterns are formed even when the data is noisy or deformed due to variations such as translation, rotation, and scaling. The patterns are also formed from a temporal sequence of data as in case of speech and pictures. Human beings have the ability to recall the stored patterns even when the input information is noisy or partial or mixed with information pertaining to other patterns.

9.3 FEATURES OF BIOLOGICAL NEURAL NETWORKS

Some attractive features of the biological neural network that make it superior to even the most sophisticated AI computer system for various tasks are as follows:

- ***Robustness and fault tolerance.*** The decay of nerve cells does not seem to affect the performance significantly.
- ***Flexibility.*** The network automatically adjusts to a new environment without using any preprogrammed instructions.
- ***Ability to deal with a variety of data situations.*** The network can deal with information that is fuzzy, probabilistic, noisy and inconsistent
- ***Collective computation.*** The network performs routinely many operations in parallel and also given task in distributed manner.

9.4 HOW THE HUMAN BRAIN LEARNS?

In the human brain, a typical neuron (Figure 9.1) collects signals from others through a host of fine structures called *dendrites*. The neuron sends out spikes of electrical activity through a long, thin strand known as an *axon*, which splits into thousands of branches. At the end of each branch, a structure called a *synapse* (Figure 9.2) converts the activity from the axon into electrical effects that inhibit or excite activity

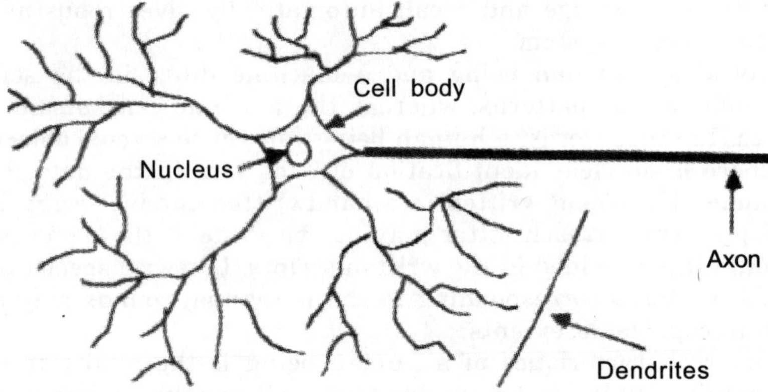

Figure 9.1 Components of a neuron.

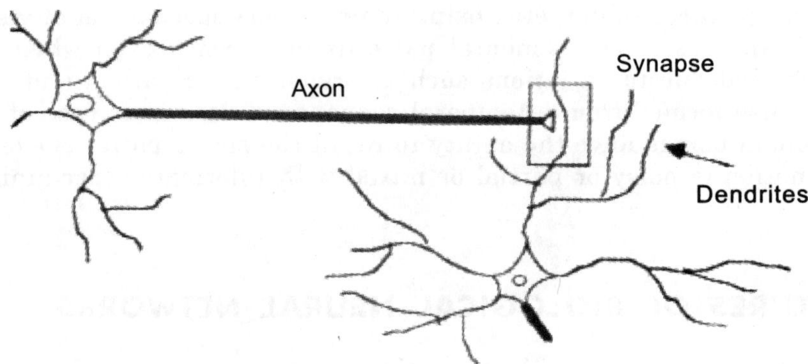

Figure 9.2 The synapse.

in the connected neurons. When a neuron receives excitatory input that is sufficiently large compared with its inhibitory input, it sends a spike of electrical activity down its axon. Learning occurs by changing the effectiveness of the synapses so that the influence of one neuron on another changes.

9.5 FROM HUMAN NEURONS TO ARTIFICIAL NEURONS

We conduct these neural networks by first trying to deduce the essential features of neurons and their interconnections. We then typically program a computer to simulate these features. However because our knowledge of neurons is incomplete and our computing power is limited, our models are necessarily gross idealizations of real networks of neurons. One such neuron model is shown in Figure 9.3.

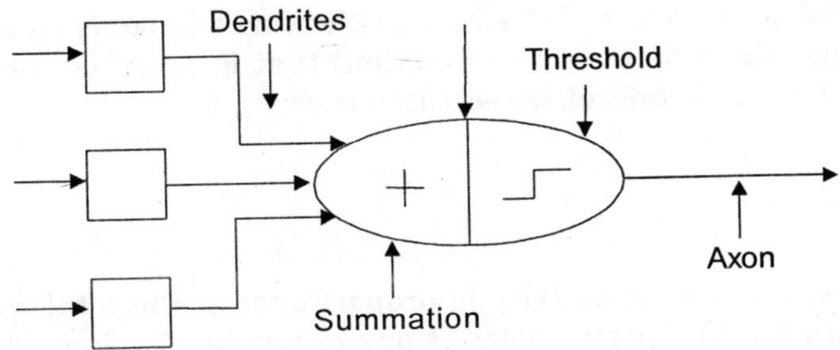

Figure 9.3 The neuron model.

9.6 HOW NEURAL NETWORKS LEARN?

Artificial neural networks are typically composed of interconnected 'units', which serve as model neurons. The function of the *synapse* is modelled by a modifiable weight, which is associated with each connection. Each unit converts the pattern of incoming activities that it receives into a single outgoing activity that it broadcasts to other units. It performs this conversion in two stages:

(i) It multiplies each incoming activity by the weight on the connection and adds together all these weighted inputs to get a quantity called the *total input*.
(ii) A unit uses an input-output function that transforms the total input into the outgoing activity.

A more technical investigation of a single neuron preceptron is given in Figure 9.4, which shows that it can have an input vector X of N dimensions. These inputs go through a vector W of weights of N dimension. Processed by the summation node, 'a' is generated where 'a' is the 'dot product' of vector X and W plus a bias. 'A' is then processed through an activation function which compares the value of 'a' to a predefined threshold. If 'a' is below the threshold, the perceptron will not fire. If it is above the threshold, the perceptron will fire one pulse whose amplitude is predefined.

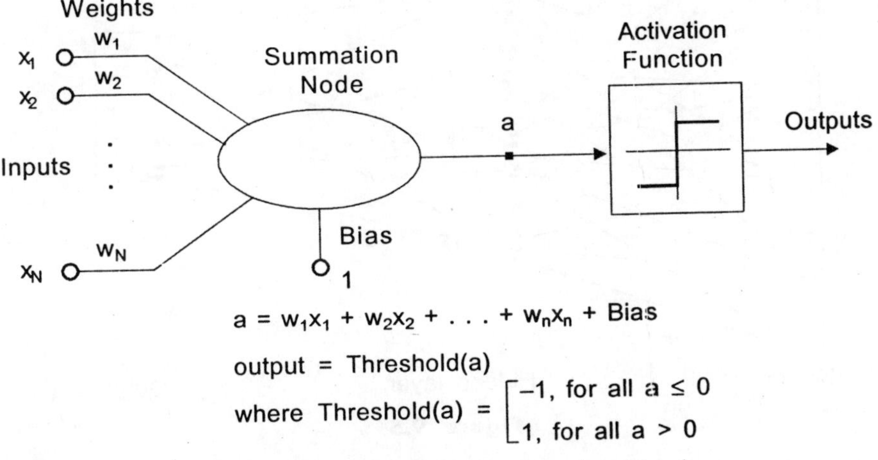

$$a = w_1x_1 + w_2x_2 + \ldots + w_nx_n + \text{Bias}$$

$$\text{output} = \text{Threshold}(a)$$

$$\text{where Threshold}(a) = \begin{cases} -1, & \text{for all } a \leq 0 \\ 1, & \text{for all } a > 0 \end{cases}$$

Figure 9.4 Learning in neural network.

The behaviour of an ANN (Artificial Neural Network) depends on both the weights and the input-output function (transfer function) that is specified for the units. This function typically falls into one of three categories:

- linear
- threshold
- sigmoid

For *linear units*, the output activity is proportional to the total weighted output.

For *threshold units*, the output is set at one of two levels, depending on whether the total input is greater than or less than some threshold value.

For *sigmoid units*, the output varies continuously but not linearly as the input changes. Sigmoid units bear a greater resemblance to real neurons than linear or threshold units, but all three must be considered rough approximations.

To make a neural network that performs some specific task, we must choose how the units are connected to one another, and we must set the weights on the connections appropriately. The connections determine whether it is possible for one unit to influence another. The weights specify the strength of the influence.

The commonest type of artificial neural network consists of three groups, or layers, of units (Figure 9.5), a layer of '*input*' units is connected to a layer of '*hidden*' units, which is connected to a layer of '*output*' units.

- The activity of the input units represents the raw information that is fed into the network.
- The activity of each hidden unit is determined by the activities of the input units and the weights on the connections between the input and the hidden units.
- The behaviour of the output units depends on the activity of the hidden units and the weights between the hidden and output units.

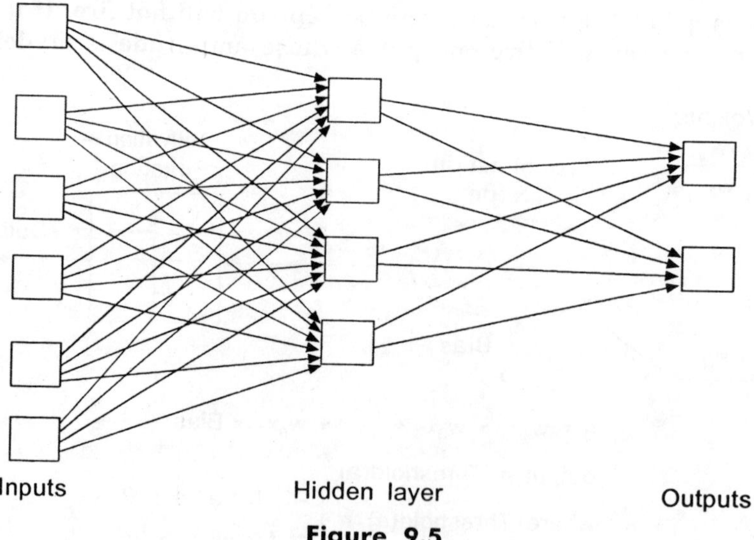

Figure 9.5

This simple type of network is interesting because the hidden units are free to construct their own representations of the input. The weights between the input and hidden units determine when each hidden unit is active, and so by modifying these weights, a hidden unit can choose what it represents.

We can teach a three-layer network to perform a particular task by using the following procedure:

(a) We present the network with training examples, which consist of a pattern of activities for the input units together with the desired pattern of activities for the output units.
(b) We determine how closely the actual output of the network matches the desired output.
(c) We change the weight of each connection so that the network produces a better approximation of the desired output.

9.7 LEARNING ALGORITHMS

Learning can be viewed as settling down of weights in a systematic manner. There are several learning laws in use, and new laws are being proposed to suit a given application and architecture. Based on the characteristics these learning algorithms expected to possess, they can be categorized as follows:

Supervised or unsupervised. In supervised learning the weight adjustment is determined based on the deviation of the desired output from the actual output. Supervised learning may be used for structural learning or for temporal learning. Structural learning is concerned with capturing in the weights the relationship between the given input-output pattern pairs. Temporal learning is concerned with capturing in the weights the relationship between patterns in a sequence of patterns.

Unsupervised learning discovers failure in a given set of patterns, and organizes the pattern accordingly. There is no externally specified desired output in this case. Unsupervised learning uses mostly local information to update the weights. The local information consists of signal or activation values of the units at the either end of the connection for which the weight update is being made.

Offline or online. In an offline learning all the given patterns are used together to determine the weights. On the other hand, in an online learning the information in each new pattern is incorporated into the network by incrementally adjusting the weights. Thus an online learning allows the neural network to update the information continuously. However, an offline learning provides solutions better than an online learning since the information is extracted using all the training samples in the case of offline training.

Discrete or continuous. Whether the weight values are updated in discrete steps or in continuous time determines the type of that algorithm.

All these factors influence not only the convergence of weights, but also the ability of the network to learn from training samples.

9.8 DIFFERENT NETWORK ARCHITECTURES AND THEIR APPLICATIONS

The description of various network architectures and their applications are described in Table 9.2.

Table 9.2 Network architectures and their applications

Network	*Application*	*Description*
ADALINE Adaline Network	Pattern Recognition Classification of Digits 0.9	The Adaline is essentially a single-layer back-propagation network. It is trained on a pattern recognition task, where the aim is to classify a bitmap representation of the digits 0–9 into the corresponding classes. Due to the limited capabilities of the Adaline, the network only recognizes the exact training patterns. When the application is ported into the multilayer backpropagation network, a remarkable degree of fault-tolerance can be achieved.
BPN Backpropagation Network	Time-Series Forecasting Prediction of the Annual Number of Sunspots	This program implements the new classic multilayer backpropagation network with bias terms and momentum. It is used to detect structure in time-series, which is presented to the network using a simple tapped delay-line memory. The program learns to predict future sunspot activity from historical data collected over the past three centuries. To avoid overfitting, the termination of the learning procedure is controlled by the so-called stopped training method.
HOPFIELD Hopfield Model	Autoassociative Memory Associative Recall of Images	The Hopfield model is used as an auto-associative memory to store and recall a set of bitmap images. Images are stored by calculating a corresponding weight matrix. Thereafter, starting from an arbitrary configuration, the memory will settle on exactly that stored image, which is nearest to the starting configuration in terms of Hamming distance. Thus given an incomplete or corrupted version of a stored image, the network is able to recall the corresponding original image.

(*Contd.*)

Table 9.2 Contd.

Network	*Application*	*Description*
BAM Bidirectional Associative Memory	Heteroassociative Memory Association of Names and Phone Numbers	The bidirectional associative memory can be viewed as a generalization of the Hopfield model, to allow for a heteroassociative memory to be implemented. In this case, the association is between names and corresponding phone numbers. After coding the set of exemplars, the network, when presented with a name, is able to recall the corresponding phone number and vice versa. The memory even shows a limited degree of fault-tolerance in case of corrupted input patterns.
BOLTZMANN Boltzmann Machine	Optimization Travelling Salesman Problem	The Boltzmann machine is a stochastic version of the Hopfield model, whose network dynamics incorporate a random component in correspondence with a given finite temperature. Starting with a high temperature and gradually cooling down, allowing the network to reach equilibrium at any step, chances are good that the network will settle in a global minimum of the corresponding energy function. This process is called *simulated annealing*. The network is then used to solve a well-known optimization problem. The weight matrix is chosen such that the global minimum of the energy function corresponds to a solution of a particular instance of the travelling salesman problem.
CPN Counter-propagation Network	Vision Determination of the Angle of Rotation	The counterpropagation network is a competitive network, designed to function as a self-programming look-up table with the additional ability to interpolate between entries. The application is to determine the angular rotation of a rocket-shaped object, images of which are presented to the network as a bitmap pattern. The performance of the network is a little limited due to the low resolution of the bitmap.
SOM Self-organizing Map	Control Pole Balancing Problem	The self-organizing map is a competitive network with the ability to form topology-preserving mappings between its input and output spaces. In this program the network

(*Contd.*)

Table 9.2 Contd.

Network	*Application*	*Description*
		learns to balance a pole by applying forces at the base of the pole. The behaviour of the pole is simulated by numerically integrating the differential equations for its law of motion using Euler's method. The task of the network is to establish a mapping between the state variables of the pole and the optimal force to keep it balanced. This is done using a reinforcement learning approach. For any given state of the pole, the network tries a slight variation of the mapped force. If the new force results in better control, the map is modified, using the pole's current state variables and the new force as a training vector.

9.8.1 Hopfield Networks

One of the milestones for the current rebirth in the field of neural networks was the associative model proposed by Hopfield at the beginning of the 1980s. Hopfield proposed his model as a theory of memory with the following characteristics:

- ***Distributed representation.*** A memory is stored as a pattern of activity across a set of units. Memories can be superimposed on one another, i.e. different memories can be represented by different patterns over the same units.
- ***Distributed, simultaneous control.*** Each unit decides its activation based solely on its local situation. All these local decisions add up to a global solution, or a particular memory.
- ***Content addressable memory.*** To retrieve a pattern we only need to specify part of it, the network automatically finds the closest match.
- ***Fault tolerance.*** If a few units in the network function incorrectly or fail completely, the whole network will still operate correctly.

Hopfield proposed a simple network of processing elements or units that are either on or off. Units are connected together via weighted symmetric connections. Positive connections between two units indicate that both units tend to activate each other, and negative connections indicate that the connected units will tend to turn each other off. Individual units preserve their individual states until they are selected for a new update. The selection of a unit is made randomly. If any of its neighbouring units is active, the chosen unit calculates the sum of the connections to the active units. If the sum is positive then the unit turns itself on otherwise the unit turns itself off. This process (called *parallel relaxation*) continues until no more units can

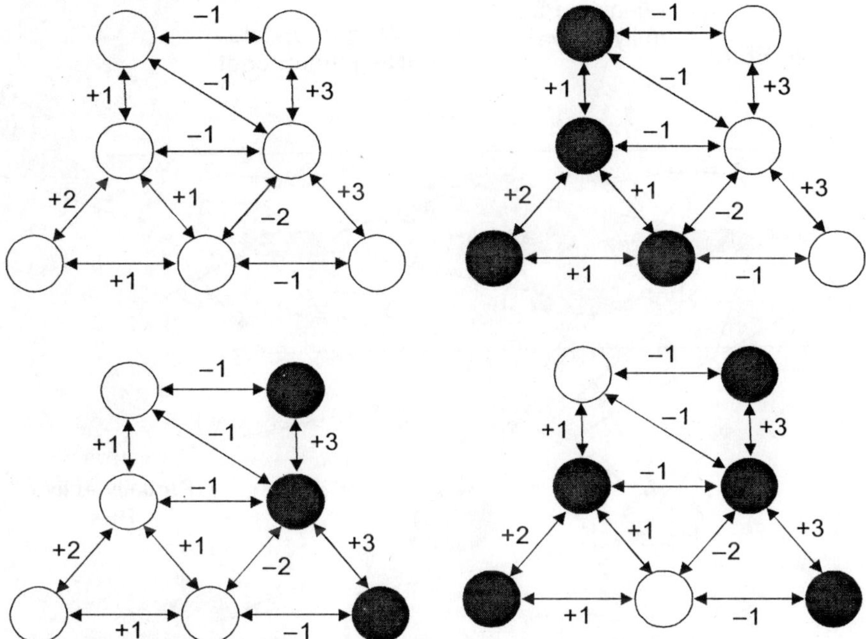

Figure 9.6 The four stable states of a Hopfield network.

change their value and the network is said to have reached a *stable state.* Hopfield networks have only limited number of stable states, each one represented by a pattern of activation across the network units. Hopfield proved that given any initial set of connection strengths and any initial state of activation, the network will settle into the nearest stable state via parallel relaxation. No oscillation or divergence can occur. The Hopfield network is classified as an *associative memory*.

9.8.2 Self-Organizing Maps (SOMs)—Kohonen Networks

Unlike the other neural networks, the SOM or Kohonen network (named after its inventor) uses unsupervised learning, and hence, is applicable to different types of problem. Kohonen networks have a single layer of units and, during training, clusters of units become associated with different classes (with statistically similar properties) that are present in the training data. The Kohonen network is useful in applications where it is important to analyze a large number of examples and identify groups with similar features. The Kohonen network is shown in Figure 9.7.

A SOM network categorizes inputs by creating a two-dimensional feature map on its layer of the input data so that the order of the input data is preserved. For example, if two input patterns are closed or similar as measured in the input space, then they will be mapped onto processing elements close together in the two-dimensional layer (also known as *Kohonen layer*).

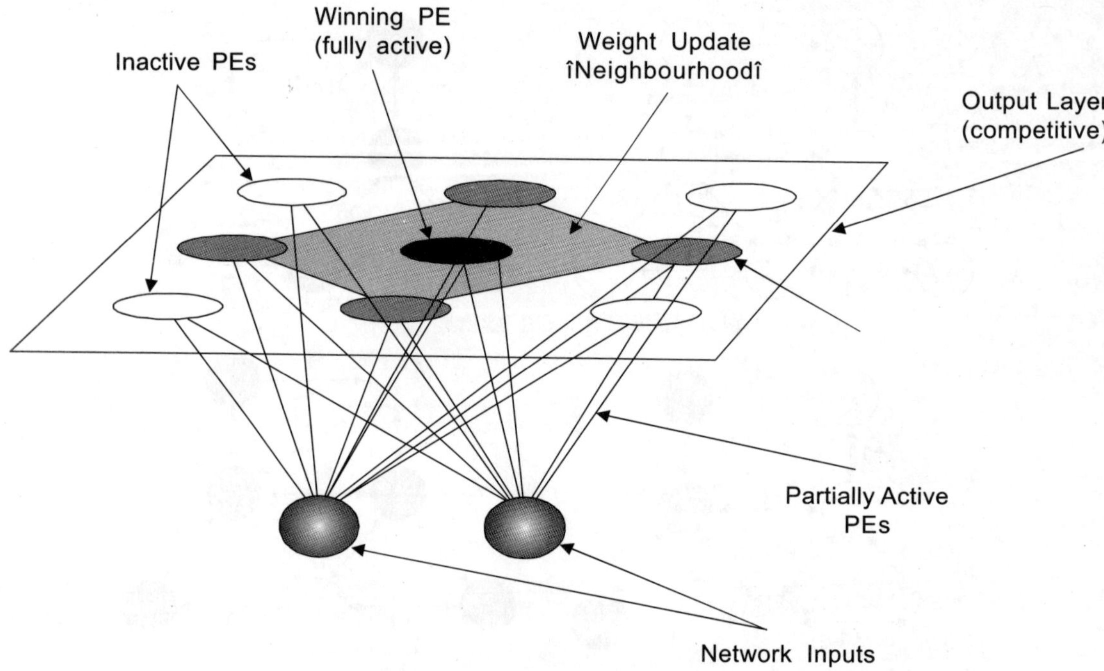

Figure 9.7 Kohonen network.

9.9 SOME SIMPLE NETWORKS

We can use what we have learnt earlier to demonstrate a simple neural network which acts as a logic gate. Figure 9.8 is modelling some truth tables for AND, OR, and NOT (Table 9.1–93).

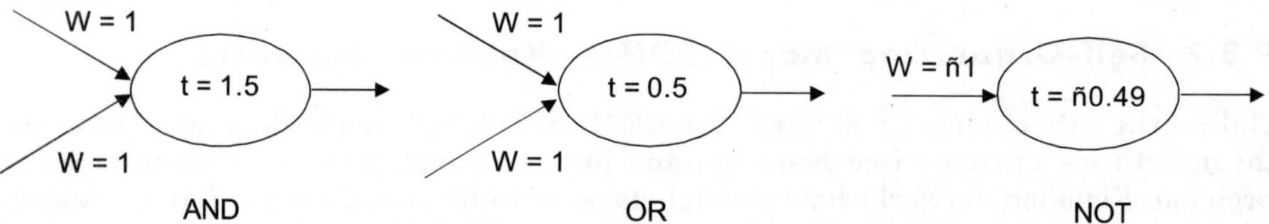

Figure 9.8 Simple neural network which act as a logic gate.

Table 9.1 AND truth table

$Input_1$	$Input_2$	*Output*
0	0	0
0	1	0
1	0	0
1	1	1

Table 9.2 OR truth table

$Input_1$	$Input_2$	*Output*
0	0	0
0	1	1
1	0	1
1	1	1

Table 9.3 NOT truth table

Input	*Output*
0	1
1	0

In these networks we are using the step activation function. You should convince yourself that these networks produce the correct output for all the allowed inputs.

You will notice that each neuron has a different threshold. From a computational viewpoint it would be easier if all the neurons had the same threshold value and the actual threshold was somehow modelled by the weights. In fact, it is possible to do this exactly. Consider the network in Figure 9.9, which is modified AND network having extra input neuron.

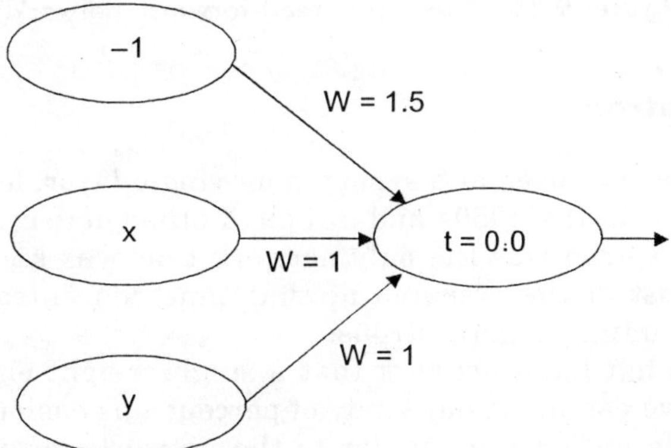

Figure 9.9 AND network with extra input neuron.

It is the same as the AND network in the figure above except that there is an extra input neuron whose activation is always set to –1. The threshold of the neuron is represented by the weight that links this extra neuron to the output neuron. This means the threshold of the neuron can be set to zero. We can work through this network using the four possible combinations of x and y and convince that the network operates correctly.

The advantage of this method is that we can always set the threshold for every neuron to zero and from a computational point of view, when 'training' the network, we only have to update weights and not both thresholds and weights.

The simple networks we have considered only have input neurons and output neurons. It is considered a one-layer network (the input neurons are not normally considered to form a layer as they are just a means of getting data into the network).

Also, in the networks we have considered, the data only travels in one direction (from the input neurons to the output neurons). In this respect it is known as a *feedforward network*. Therefore, we have been looking at one-layer, feedforward networks. There are many other types of network. An example of a two-layer, feedforward network is shown in Figure 9.10.

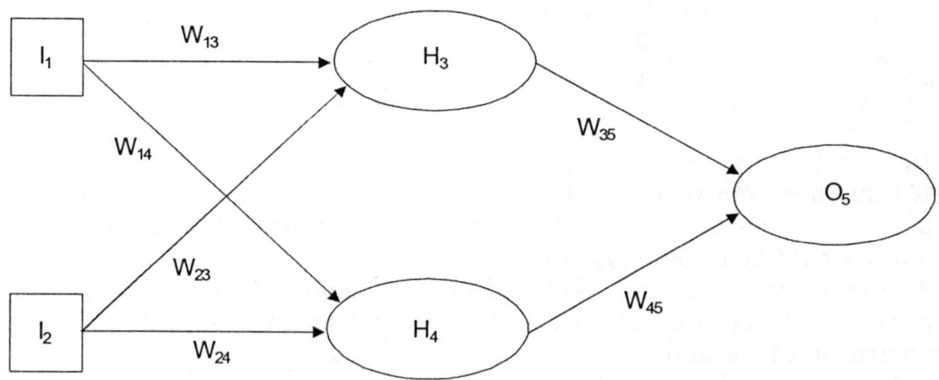

Figure 9.10 Two-layer, feed-forward network.

9.9.1 The Perceptron

The name perceptron is now used as a synonym for single-layer, feedforward networks. They were first studied in the 1950s and although other network architectures were known about the perceptron was the only network that was known to be capable of learning and thus most of the research at that time concentrated on perceptrons. Figure 9.11 shows example of perceptrons.

We can see in the left hand network that a single weight only affects one of the outputs. This means we can make our study of perceptrons easier by only considering networks with a single output (i.e. similar to the network shown on the right-hand side of Figure 9.11).

As we only have one output we can make our notation a little simpler. Therefore, the output neuron is denoted by O and the weight from input neuron j is denoted by W_j. Thus, the activation function becomes

$$O = \text{Step}_0 \ \Sigma_j W_j I_j$$

We have already seen that perceptrons can represent the AND, OR, and NOT logic functions. But does it follow that a perceptron (a single-layer, feedforward network) can represent any Boolean function? Unfortunately, this is not the case.

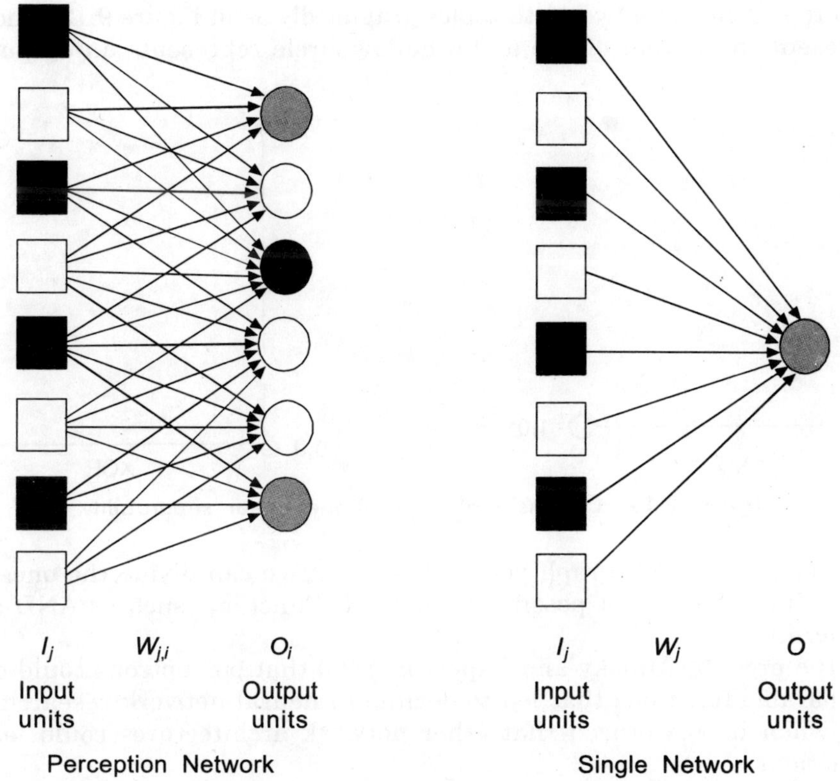

Figure 9.11 Example of perception.

To see why, consider the following two truth tables (Tables 9.5 and 9.6).

Table 9.5 AND truth table

$Input_1$	$Input_2$	$Output$
0	0	0
0	1	0
1	0	0
1	1	1

Table 9.6 XOR truth table

$Input_1$	$Input_2$	$Output$
0	0	0
0	1	1
1	0	1
1	1	0

We can represent these two truth tables graphically as in Figure 9.12 (where a filled circle represents an output of one and a hollow circle represents an output of zero).

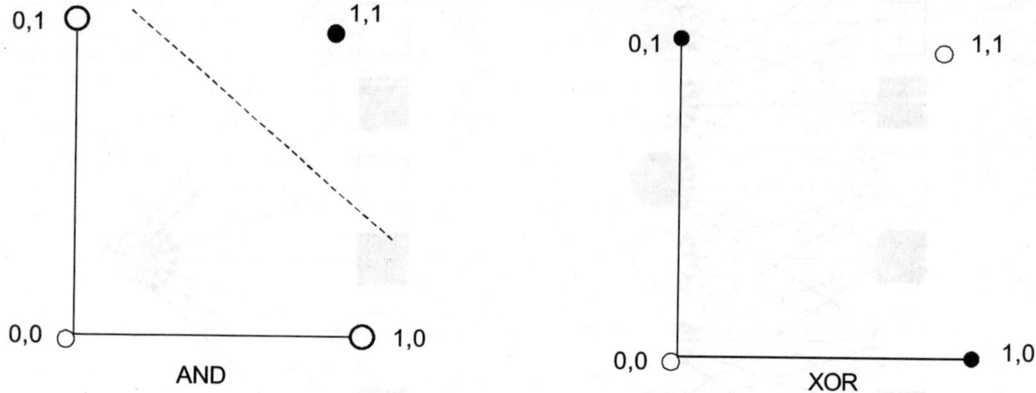

Figure 9.12 Dimensional view of the linear separability.

If you look at the AND graph you will see that we can divide the ones from the zeros with a line. This is not possible with XOR. Functions such as AND are called *linearly separable*.

It was the proof by Minsky and Papert in 1969 that perceptrons could only learn linearly separable functions that led to decline in neural network research until the mid-1980s when it was proved that other network architectures could learn these type of functions.

Although, only being able to learn linearly separable functions is a major disadvantage of the perceptron it is still worth studying as it is relatively simple and can help to provide a framework for other architectures. It should however, be realized that perceptrons are not only limited to two inputs (e.g. the AND function). We can have n inputs which gives us an n-dimension problem.

When $n = 3$ we can still visualize the linear separability of the problem as shown in Figure 9.13.

But once n is greater than three we find it difficult to visualize the problem.

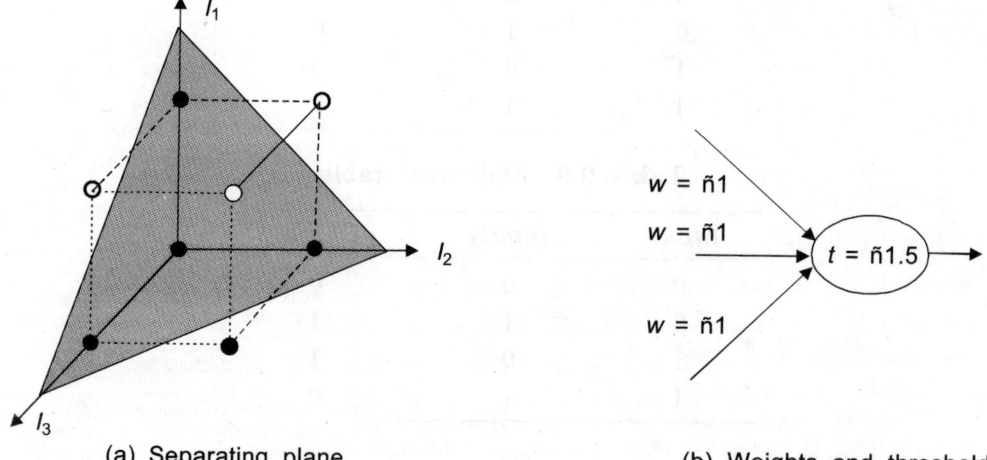

(a) Separating plane

(b) Weights and threshold

Figure 9.13 Dimensional view of the linear separability.

9.9.2 Learning Linearly Separable Functions

With a function such as AND (with only two inputs) we can easily decide what weights to use to give us the required output from the neuron. But with more complex functions (i.e. those with more than two inputs, it may not be so easy to decide on the correct weights). Therefore, we would like our neural network to learn so that it can come up with its own set of weights.

We will consider this aspect of neural networks for a simple function (i.e. one with two inputs). We could obviously scale up the problem to accommodate more complex problems, providing the problems are linearly separable.

Consider the truth table in Table 9.7 and the AND network with input neuron shown in Figure 9.14.

Table 9.7 AND truth table

$Input_1$	$Input_2$	*Output*
0	0	0
0	1	0
1	0	0
1	1	1

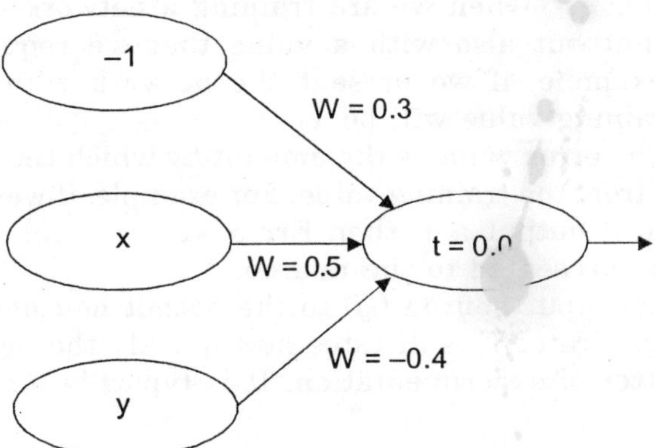

Figure 9.14 AND network with input neuron.

In fact, all we have done is set the weights to random values between –0.5 and 0.5. By applying the activation function for each of the four possible inputs to this neuron gives us the following truth table (Table 9.8).

Table 9.8 ANDX truth table

$Input_1$	$Input_2$	*Output*
0	0	0
0	1	0
1	0	1
1	1	0

The truth table can be graphically represented as shown in Figure 9.15.

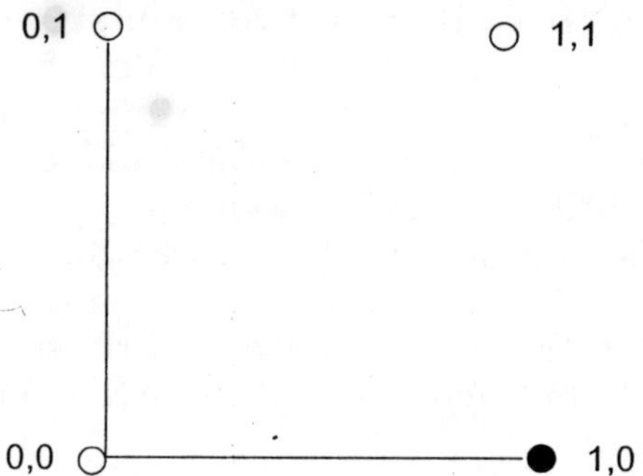

Figure 9.15 Graphical representation of Table 9.8.

The network, obviously, does not represent the AND function so we need to adjust the weights so that it "learns" the function correctly.

Before solving the algorithm. Let us define some terminologies:

- ***Epoch.*** An *epoch* is the presentation of the entire training set to the neural network. In the case of the AND function an epoch consists of four sets of inputs being presented to the network (i.e. [0,0], [0,1], [1,0], [1,1]).
- ***Training value, T.*** When we are training a network we not only present it with the input but also with a value that we require the network to produce. For example, if we present the network with [1,1] for the AND function the training value will be 1.
- ***Error, Err.*** The error value is the amount by which the value output by the network differs from the training value. For example, if we require the network to output 0 and it output a 1, then Err = –1.
- I_j. Inputs being presented to the neuron.
- W_j. Weight from input neuron (Ij) to the output neurons.
- ***LR.*** The learning rate. This dictates how quickly the network converges. It is set by a matter of experimentation. It is typically 0.1.

9.9.3 The Perceptron Training Algorithm

While
    epoch produces an error
    Present network with next inputs from epoch

    $Err = T - O$
    If
      $Err <> 0$ then

Note: If the error is positive we need to increase O. If the error is negative we need to decrease O. Each input contributes W_jI_j to the total input so if I_j is positive, an increase in W_j will increase O. If I_j is negative an increase in W_j will decrease O).This can be achieved with the following:

$$W_j = W_j + LR * I_j * Err$$

This is often called the delta learning rule.

End If
End While

9.9.4 Perceptron Learning—An Example

Let us take a look at an example. The initial weight values are 0.3, 0.5, and –0.4 and we are trying to learn the AND function.

If we present the network with the first training pair ([0,0]), from the first epoch, nothing will happen to the weights (due to multiplying by zero). The next training pair ([0,1]) will result in the network producing zero (by virtue of the $step_0$ function). As zero is the required output there is no error, thereby training continues.

The next training pair ([1,0]) produces an output of 1. The required output is 0. Therefore, the error is –1. This means we have to adjust the weights.

This is done as follows (assuming LR = 0.1):

$W_0 = 0.3 + 0.1 * -1 * -1 = 0.4$
$W_1 = 0.5 + 0.1 * 1 * -1 = 0.4$
$W_2 = -0.4 + 0.1 * 0 * -1 = -.04$

Therefore, the new weights are 0.4, 0.4, –0.4.

Finally we apply the input [1,1] to the network. This also produces an error and the new weight values will be 0.3, 0.5, and –0.3.

As this presentation of the epoch produced an error (two in fact) we need to continue the training and present the network with another epoch. Training continues until an epoch is presented that does not produce an error.

If we consider the state of the network at the end of the first epoch (weights = 0.3, 0.5, –0.3) we know the weights are wrong as the epoch produced an error (in fact, the weights may be correct at the end of the epoch but we need to present another epoch to show this). We can also produce a graph that shows the current state of the network.

We are trying to achieve the AND function which can be represented as in Figure 9.16.

The current linear separability line can be drawn by using the weights to draw a line on the graph. Two points on the I_1 and I_2 axis can be found as:

I_1 point = W_0/W_1
I_2 point = W_0/W_2

W_0 actually represents the threshold. Therefore, we are dividing the threshold by the weights. That is, $I_1 = 0.6$ and $I_2 = -1$.

This line is shown (roughly in the right position) in Figure 9.16. It is clearly not in the correct place for the AND function as the line does not divide the ones and the zeros correctly. If we continue with the training until we get no errors from an entire epoch the weights would be 0.4, 0.4, 0.1. If we plot these weights on the graph

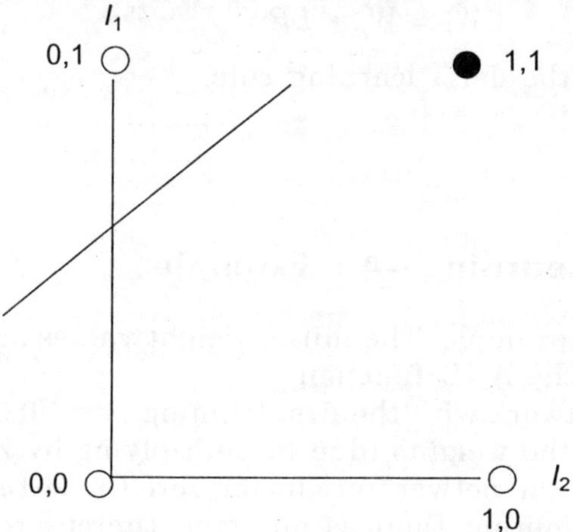

Figure 9.16 AND function representation.

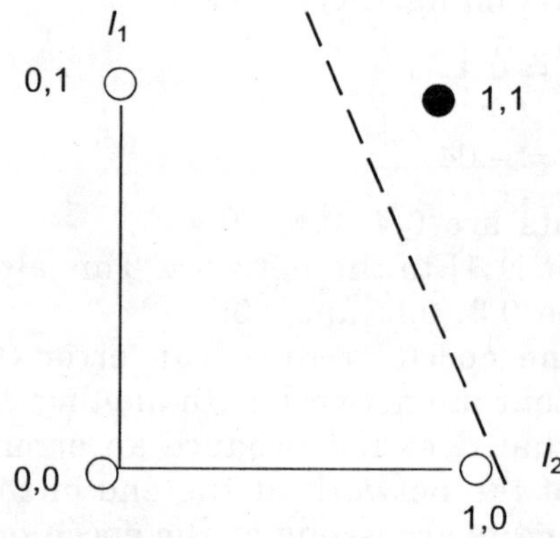

Figure 9.17 The graph of AND function.

we get the graph of AND function (again the line is approximately in the correct position) as in Figure 9.17.

And we can see that the linearly separability lies in a valid position and this can be confirmed by checking that the neural network is producing the correct outputs.

9.10 COMPARISON OF NEURAL NETWORKS AND RULE-BASED METHODS

Neural networks are flexible tools in a dynamic environment. Neural networks have the capacity to learn rapidly and change quickly. As circumstances, data values, and outcomes change, the model quickly learns and adapts. Rule-based systems are limited to the specific situation for which they were designed whereas, neural networks are excellent at adapting to constantly changing information.

9.11 COMPARISON OF NEURAL NETWORKS AND EXPERT SYSTEM

Expert systems are rule-based computer programs. They make decisions by applying a set of rules which reflect the knowledge of people (or experts) that would otherwise make the decision. Expert systems are good for applications with logical separators between decision-influencing factors. Since they have explicit rules, it is easy to understand how their decisions are made. But expert systems are difficult to build because the rules don't always exist and the 'expert' information is difficult to acquire. Often the experts don't exist or they cannot communicate accurately how they weight various factors to reach a conclusion. And once an expert system has been programmed, it cannot be adapted easily to changing conditions—the rules are the rules until a new system is built.

9.12 BENEFITS OF NEURAL COMPUTING

There are a variety of benefits that an analyst realizes from using neural networks in his work.

Pattern recognition is a powerful technique for harnessing the information in the data and generalizing about it. Neural networks learn to recognize the patterns which exist in the data set. The system is developed through learning rather than programming. Programming is much more time consuming for the analyst and requires the analyst to specify the exact behaviour of the model. Neural networks teach themselves the patterns in the data freeing the analyst for interesting work.

Neural networks are flexible in a changing environment. Rule-based systems or programmed systems are limited to the situation for which they were designed—when conditions change, they are no longer valid. Although neural networks may take some time to learn a sudden drastic change, they are excellent at adapting to constantly changing information.

Neural networks can build informative models where more conventional approaches fail. Because neural networks can handle very complex interactions they can easily model data which is too difficult to model with traditional approaches such as inferential statistics or programming logic.

Performance of neural networks is at least as good as classical statistical modelling, and better for most problems. The neural networks build models that are more reflective of the structure of the data in significantly less time.

Neural networks now operate well with modest computer hardware. Although neural networks are computationally intensive, the routines have been optimized to the point that they can now run in reasonable time on personal computers. They do not require super computers as they did in the early days of neural network research.

9.13 LIMITATIONS OF NEURAL COMPUTING

There are some limitations to neural computing. The key limitation is the neural network's inability to explain the model it has built in a useful way. Analysts often want to know why the model is behaving as it is. Neural networks get better answers but they have a hard time explaining how they got there. This is the reason *neural connection* provides so many tools for exploring output and so many operational choices on the tools which build the model. By experimenting with different parameters, and fully exploring the results both in text and graphics, neural connection users can gain more understanding of the model's behaviour and more confidence in the results.

There are a few other limitations that should be understood. First, it is difficult to extract rules from neural networks. This is sometimes important to the people who have to explain their answer to others and to those who have been involved with artificial intelligence, particularly expert systems which are rule based.

In most analytical methods, you cannot just throw data at a neural network and get a good answer, but you have to spend time understanding the problem or the outcome you are trying to predict. And, you must be sure that the data used to train the system are appropriate (i.e. reflects factors involved) and are measured in a way that reflects the behaviour of the factors. If the data are not representative of the problem, neural computing will not produce good results. This is a classic situation where 'garbage in' will certainly produce 'garbage out'.

Finally, it can take time to train a model from a very complex data set. Neural techniques are computer intensive and will be slow on low end PCs or machines without math coprocessors. It is important to remember though that the overall time to result can still be faster than other data analysis approaches, even when the system takes longer to train. Processing speed alone is not the only factor in performance, and neural networks do not require the time programming and debugging or testing assumptions that other analytical approaches do.

EXERCISES

1. For each of the truth tables below say whether it is possible for a perceptron to learn the required output. In each case, explain the reason behind your decision.

(a)

Input	0	0	1	1
Input	0	1	0	1
Required Output	1	0	0	1

(b)

Input	0	0	1	1
Input	0	1	0	1
Required Output	1	1	0	0

(c)

Input	0	0	1	1
Input	0	1	0	1
Required Output	1	1	1	1

2. A perceptron with two inputs has a threshold level set at the point at which it will fire (i.e. output a one). It is sometimes convenient to always set the threshold level to zero. Show how this can be achieved by describing two perceptrons which act in the same way but one has its threshold set to a non-zero figure and the other perceptron has a zero threshold. Why might it be a good idea to build a perceptron with a zero threshold figure?
3. Compare artificial and biological neural networks.
4. Discuss major advantages of artificial neural networks.
5. Why are learning algorithms important to artificial neural networks?
6. Briefly describe backpropagation.
7. Explain how neural network can improve natural language processing.
8. For the following applications, which would be better—neural network or expert systems? Justify your answer.
   (a) Price look-up subsystem for high-volume merchandize sales.
   (b) Automated voice-inquiry processing system.
   (c) Diagnosis of a well-established, but complex disease.
9. Give possible applications of neural networks for the following:
   (a) Decision support
   (b) Transaction processing
   (c) Character recognition.

CHAPTER 10

Case-based Reasoning

10.1 INTRODUCTION

A case-based reasoning system (CBR System) can be seen as a special type of knowledge-based system. The roots of case-based reasoning in AI is found in the works of Roger Schank on dynamic memory and the central role that a reminding of earlier situations (episodes, cases) and situation patterns (scripts, MOPs) has in problem solving and learning. Case-based systems deal with cases or episodes which represent instances of concepts or their generic form. They are special in the sense of different knowledge they use and consequently different representation and management requirements they have. The performance of case-based reasoning system directly depends on the quality and quantity of its encoded knowledge. On the one hand if there is not enough knowledge the problem solving capabilities are limited, on the other hand the system can become useless because of unmanageable amounts of knowledge.

Case-based reasoning systems can also be viewed as a continuous knowledge acquisition and learning systems. Knowledge acquisition together with other types of learning are essential characteristics of an intelligent system. The representation and management of large case knowledge bases are not trivial tasks and have not been sufficiently elaborated so far. These tasks can be characterized as a process of representation, visualization, and application of episodic knowledge specifying the content of the case episode describing a retrieval algorithm and precisely defining matching criteria characterizing strategies to make past cases.

The representation and management issues for case-based reasoning are challenging because many applications require large case bases with space and time efficient processing. Even though the representation and management of cases can be handled similarly as in knowledge-based systems there are particular differences which need to be considered, mainly cases that are suitable for capturing problem-solving processes by representing episodes of these processes and thus are suitable not only in easily formalizable areas as are traditional knowledge-based systems but in less formalizable areas as well. Because knowledge acquisition is supported by learning from past experience CBRSs are able to supplement weak domain models.

A case can represent a complete solution plan design which can be retrieved, adapted and reused later eliminating the need for decomposition and recomposition. In contrast to earlier AI systems, case-based systems use specific past experience in solving problems.

In fact, case-based reasoning is just one of a set of terms used to refer to systems of this type. This has led to some confusions, particularly since case-based reasoning is a term used both as a generic term for several types of more specific approaches, as well as for one such approach. To some extent, this can also be said for analogy reasoning. An attempt of a clarification, although not resolving the confusions, of the terms related to case-based reasoning are given below:

Exemplar-based reasoning. The term is derived from the classification of different views to concept definition into *the classical view*, *the probabilistic view*, and *the exemplar view*. In the exemplar view, a concept is defined extensionally, as the set of its exemplars. CBR methods that address the learning of concept definitions (i.e. the problem addressed by most of the research in machine learning), are sometimes referred to as exemplar based.

Instance-based reasoning. This is a specialization of exemplar-based reasoning into a highly syntactic CBR-approach. To compensate for lack of guidance from general background knowledge, a relatively large number of instances are needed in order to close in on a concept definition. The representation of the instances are usually simple (e.g. feature vectors), since a major focus is to study *automated learning* with no user in the loop. Basically, this is a non-generalization approach to the concept learning problem addressed by classical, inductive machine learning methods.

Memory-based reasoning. This approach emphasizes a collection of cases as a large memory, and reasoning as a process of accessing and searching in this memory. Memory organization and access is a focus of the case-based methods. The utilization of *parallel processing* techniques is a characteristic of these methods, and distinguishes this approach from others.

Case-based reasoning. Although case-based reasoning is used as a generic term in this chapter, the typical case-based reasoning methods have some characteristics that distinguish them from the other approaches listed here. First, a typical case is usually assumed to have a certain degree of richness of information contained in it, and a certain complexity with respect to its internal organization. That is, a feature vector holding some values and a corresponding class is not what we would call a typical case description. What we refer to as typical case-based methods also have another characteristic property: They are able to *modify*, or adapt, a retrieved solution when applied in a different problem solving context. Paradigmatic case-based methods also utilize *general background knowledge*, although its richness, degree of explicit representation, and role within the CBR processes varies. Core methods of typical CBR systems borrow a lot from cognitive psychology theories.

Analogy-based reasoning. This term is sometimes used, as a synonym to case-based reasoning, to describe the typical case-based approach. However, it is also often used to characterize methods that solve new problems based on past cases from a different domain, while typical case-based methods focus on indexing and matching strategies for single-domain cases.

10.2 THE CBR PROCESS

In CBR terminology, a *case* usually denotes a *problem situation*. A previously experienced situation, which has been captured and learned in a way that it can be reused in the solving of future problems, is referred to as a *past case, previous case, stored case*, or *retained case*. Correspondingly, a *new case* or *unsolved case* is the description of a new problem to be solved. Case-based reasoning is, in effect, a cyclic and integrated process of solving a problem, learning from this experience, solving a new problem, etc.

In general, CBR cycle can be described by the following four processes:

(a) RETRIEVE the most similar case or cases.
(b) REUSE the information and knowledge in that case to solve the problem.
(c) REVISE the proposed solution.
(d) RETAIN the parts of this experience likely to be useful for future problem solving.

Thus, the CBR cycle is diagramatically illustrated in Figure 10.1.

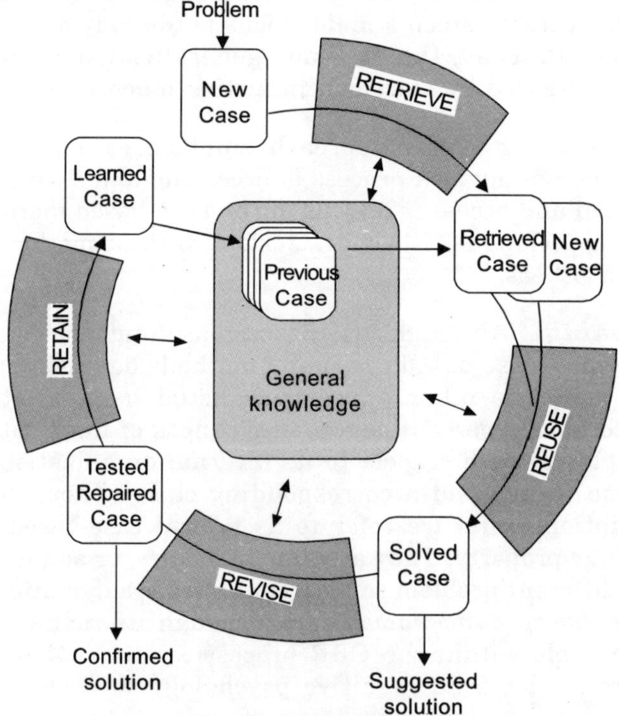

Figure 10.1 The CBR cycle.

Initial description of a problem defines a new case. This new case is used to RETRIEVE a case from the collection of previous cases. The retrieved case is combined with the new case through REVISE into a solved case, i.e. proposed solution. Through, REVISE process this solution is tested for success and repaired if failed. During RETAIN, useful experience is retained for future reuse, and the case base is updated by a new learned case or by modification of some existing cases. General knowledge, i.e. main dependent knowledge supports the CBR process.

10.2.1 Case Base

Case base in the CBR systems is a representative set of cases. A set covers the goals and subgoals that arise in reasoning and both successful and failed attempts aim at achieving those goals. A case is a piece of knowledge representing an experience in a particular context. Typically a case comprises of: 1. the *problem statement* including contextual information (e.g. invariant and pre-conditions); 2. the *solution* to the problem; 3. the *outcome* of applying the solution (e.g. post-conditions); and 4. any underlying *facts and supporting reasoning* that the system knows how to make use of.

1. *Problem statement* in case is problem or situation description, majorly consisting of goals of system (solving type, viz. diagnose, create, plan or interpretive type, viz. understand, explain, evaluate), constraints to situation and features of the problem. CHEF a CBR system for planning Chinese recipe uses only constraints as problem description, whereas PROTOS a CBR for hearing disorder diagnosis, CASEY a CBR for heart failure diagnosis, and HYPO which creates arguments in legal domain, maintain only situation description as problem description.
2. *Solution* to the problem in case may consist of other exponents that aid adaptation and critiquing are as follows:
   (a) Solution, i.e. diagnosis, plan, explanation.
   (b) Set of reasoning steps used to solve the problem.
   (c) Set of justifications for decisions that were made in solving problem.
   (d) Acceptable solutions that were not chosen.
   (e) Unacceptable solutions that were ruled out.
   (f) Expectations of what will result upon deployment of the solution.
3. *Outcome* includes feedback from the world and interpretations of that feedback. If expectations are violated or if the solution failed, outcome might also include the explanation for the problem and repair method. There are several parts of outcome as follows:
   (a) The outcome itself.
   (b) Whether or not the outcome fulfilled or violated expectations.
   (c) Whether the outcome was a success or a failure.
   (d) Explanation of the expectation violation and/or failure.
   (e) Repair strategy.
   (f) What could have been done to avoid the problem.
   (g) Pointer to next attempt at solution.

Cases can be represented in variety of forms like frames, semantic networks, predicate notation rules or mixed format. Cases should be organized in memory for effective retrieval and reuse. There may be different case organization methods. Two influential case memory models are: dynamic memory model and category exemplar model.

10.2.2. Case Retrieval (Retrieve)

The Retrieve process gives the best matching previous (old) case from the case base. Its subtasks are referred to as identify features, initially match, search, and select which are to be executed in order. Identification task basically comes up with a set of relevant problem descriptors, the goal of the matching task is to return a set of cases that are sufficiently similar to the new case (using a similarity threshold of some kind), and the selection task works on this set of cases and chooses the best match.

Some case-based approaches retrieve a previous case largely based on superficial, syntactical similarities among problem descriptors which is referred to as *Knowledge-point* approach, this is applicable in domains where general knowledge is very difficult or impossible to acquire. Some approaches attempt to retrieve cases based on features that have deeper, semantical similarities which is referred to as a *Knowledge-intensive* approach where contextual meaning of the problem description is being used for domains where general domain knowledge is available.

Identify Feature

This task involves simply noticing its input descriptors, but more elaborate approach is to understand the problem within its context. Unknown descriptors may be disregarded or requested to be explained by the user, filter out noisy problem descriptors, to infer other relevant problem features, to check whether the feature values make sense within the context, to generate expectations of other features. Other descriptors than those given as input, may be inferred by using a general knowledge model, or by retrieving a similar problem description from the case base and use features of that case as expected features.

Initially Match

This task involves finding a good matching previous case. This task is split into subtasks, viz. (a) initial matching process, which retrieves a set of plausible candidates, (b) a more elaborate process of selecting the best one among the subsets.

Finding a set of matching cases is done by using the problem descriptors as indexes to the case library in direct or indirect way. There are three ways of retrieving a case or a set of cases, viz. by following direct index pointers from problem features, by searching an index structure, or by searching in a model of general domain knowledge. Cases may be retrieved solely from the input features or also from features inferred from the input. Cases that match all input features are, of course, good candidates for matching, but depending on the strategy cases that match a given fraction of the problem features (input or inferred) may also be retrieved. Some tests for relevance of a retrieved case are often executed, particularly if cases are retrieved on the basis of a subset of features. Matching process will be easy if representation of case is properly designed. This is a problem of indexing vocabulary. A way to assess the degree of similarity is needed and several *similarity metrics* have been proposed based on surface similarities of problem and case features.

Similarity assessment may also be more knowledge-intensive by trying to understand the problem more deeply, and using the goals, constraints, etc. Another option is to weigh the problem descriptors according to their importance for characterizing the problem. In the process of comparison, sometimes additional features of the situation need to be derived from it. This is situation assessment problem. To search massive case library in an efficient way to find appropriate cases a retrieval algorithm will work. Here one need to give proper search algorithm as well as matching algorithm. This also can be referred to as *indexing problem.*

Select

This task is related to find best match from set of similar cases. The best matching case is usually determined by evaluating the degree of initial match more closely. If a match turns out not to be strong enough, an attempt to find a better match by following difference links to closely related cases is made. The selection process typically generates consequences and expectations from each retrieved case, and attempts to evaluate consequences and justify expectations. This can be done by using the system's own model of general domain knowledge, or by asking the user for confirmation and additional information. The cases are eventually ranked according to some metric or ranking criteria. Knowledge-intensive selection methods typically generate explanations that support this ranking process, and the case that has the strongest explanation for being similar to the new problem is chosen.

10.2.3 Reuse

Using the past case retrieved through RETRIEVE step, propose solution to current problem. This considers two aspects:

- The differences among the past and the current case and
- What part of a retrieved case can be transferred to new case.

Past case may be reused either by applying some solution to new case as its solution or by considering differences in both cases, adapt the required part of past case and apply to new case.

Considering goal of system there are the following two main ways to adapt past cases:

- Transformational reuse—reuse the past case solution
- Derivational reuse—reuse the past method that constructs the solution.

In transformational reuse, the past solution is not directly used as a solution for the new case. But new knowledge in the form of transformational operators {T} is applied to the past solution. This gives us a desired solution for the new case. This operator can be organized with the help of indexing the cases around the differences detected among the retrieved and current case. Transformational reuse focuses on the equivalence of solutions, so this requires a strong domain dependent model in the form of transformation operators {T} plus a control regime to organize the operators application.

Derivational reuse focuses on solution method. The retrieved case holds information about method used for solving the problem including justification of the operators used, subgoals considered, alternatives generated, failed search paths, etc. Derivational reuse then reinstantiates the retrieved method to the new case and replays the old plan into the new context.

During the reuse successful alternatives, operators and paths will be explored first while failed paths will be avoided, new subgoals are pursued based on the old ones and old subplans can be recursively retrieved for them.

10.2.4 Revise

When solution generated by the reuse phase is not correct one need to revise the retrieved case. This consist of two tasks (a) evaluate the case solution. If successful, learning from the success, (b) otherwise repair the case solution using domain specific knowledge.

Solution evaluation task considers feedback of real world by applying the solution in the real environment. This involves the application of a suggested solution to the real problem. The result from applying the solution may take some time to appear, depending on the type of application. The case may still be learned, and be available in the case base in the intermediate period, but it has to be marked as a non-evaluated case.

The solution may also be applied to a simulation program that is able to generate a correct solution. With the evaluation process compare the reused case with expected/proposed solution. The feedback of evaluation process either incorporates explanation about differences between expected solution and actual happing, justification difference, projecting outcome and comparing and ranking alternative possibilities. This feedback suggests additional adaptation or repairs requirement of proposed solution.

The second task of revision phase is the solution repair task. This task uses feedback of evaluation phase to modify the solution in such way that failure does not occur.

The repair module of CBR system possesses general causal knowledge and domain knowledge about how to disable or compensate causes of errors in the domain. The revised plan can then be retained directly if it is correct, otherwise it can be evaluated and repaired again. The evaluation and repair is recursive process, till correct solution not achieved.

10.2.5 Retain

The outcome of evaluation and possible repair helps learning from success or failure of the proposed solution. This involves selecting desired part of the case to retain, in what form to retain it, how to index the case for later retrieval and how to integrate the new case in the memory structure.

Extract

If case was solved by using a previous case, a new case may be built or the old case may be generalized to subsume the present case as well. If the problem was sólved by other methods, including asking the user, an entirely new case will have to be constructed. Now question comes, which part of the case is to be retained? Problem descriptors, problem solutions, explanation or justification of the solution to the problem solving method are the structures those may be extracted for learning. Information about repair may also be extracted and retained, either as separate failure cases or within total problem cases. Which will help to improve the understanding or correct the present failure case.

Index

Here the type of indexes and structure of indexes is decided. This is actually a knowledge acquisition problem, and should be analyzed as a part of the domain knowledge analysis and modelling step. A trivial solution to the problem is to use all input features as indices this is syntax-based method. In memory-based method relevant features are determined by matching in parallel all the cases in the case base and filtering out features that belong to cases with few features in common with the problem case.

Integrate

Here the knowledge base gets updated with a new case. This is done by modifying the indexing of existing cases. Index importance for a particular case or solution and adjusted due to the success or failure of using the case to solve the input problem. The features relevant for retrieving successful cases strengthen the case. While it is weakened for features that lead to unsuccessful cases being retrieved. Thus index structure helps tuning and adapting the case memory to its use.

In knowledge-intensive approach to CBR, learning may also take place through interaction with the user or other machine learning methods, e.g. rule-based approach. CBR provides tools and methods for continuous enhancement of the knowledge base. Knowledge integrity is assured through expert review and classification of all completed sessions (Figure 10.2).

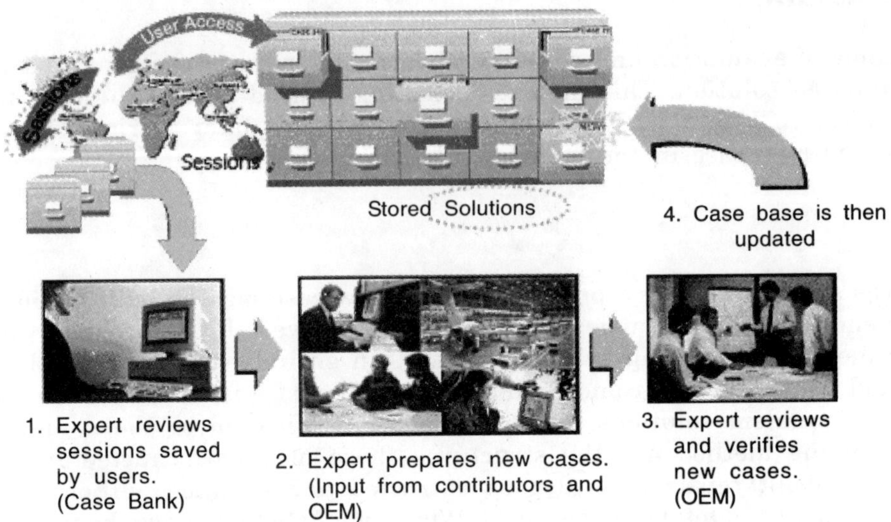

Figure 10.2 Continuous enhancement of knowledge base.

10.3 APPLICATIONS

In this section, we shall describe some successful real-world applications of the use of CBR.

10.3.1 Clavier

One of the first CBR applications was developed by the US aerospace company Lockheed. It was concerned with determining an efficient method for curing (heating) aircraft components during their manufacture. Several components at a time are cured in an autoclave (type of large pressurized oven). The heating characteristics of the autoclave are not fully understood and there is no definite model of its behaviour.

Operators relied on drawings of previously successful parts layouts to guide them in the layout of a new set of parts by looking for similar cases. This clearly fits into the CBR paradigm and so a solution was sought using this technology.

A CBR system, CLAVIER, was developed with the following objectives:

- Reuse previously successful configurations.
- Reduce the work load of the experts.
- Secure the expertise for the future.
- Train new personnel.

The cases of the successful layouts contain the following information:

- Parts and their relative positions in a table.
- Tables and their relative positions in the autoclave.
- Parameters such as start and finish times, pressure, and temperature.

From the case base CLAVIER will find the nearest match and recommend new layouts to the operators. The adaptation involves:

- Creating new layouts from the pieces of previous layouts.
- Minimizing the number of required parts not in the layout.
- Maximizing the number of high–priority parts in the layout.
- Maximizing total number of parts in layout.

CLAVIER provides a useful way of transferring expertise between operators.

Producing a model-based system would have been difficult as often operators could not say why a particular layout was successful. The system also shows the ability to learn new layouts; for once it has suggested a new successful layout which can be stored in the case base. CLAVIER has grown from 20 to over 150 cases in its database and produces a successful layout 90% of the time.

10.3.2 CHEF—A Meal Planner

CHEF is a case-based planner (Hommand, 1990). It accepts goals that recipes can achieve and produce recipe plan that can achieve given goals in the domain Szechwan cooking. CHEF views the planning as a memory task doing in the loop of reasoning, execution, and learning. CHEF's planning procedure is dependency—directed transformation.

Algorithm

Step 1: Retrieve an old recipe that fulfills as many of its new goals as possible using case library.

Step 2: Adapt the old plan, to fit the new situation. This does in two steps:

(a) Reinstantiates the old plan. It creates an instance of plan that substitutes new objects for the ones used previously. Here it uses similarity metrics to substitute objects considering role of object in old plan.

(b) Applies special-purpose object critics to modify the old plan for the new situation.

Step 3: Use the plan and collect feedback about working of the plan. If it worked properly then store for reuse in memory, otherwise creates a causal explanation of why the plan have not work and index into its general knowledge, which it uses to repair the faulty plan.

Step 4: CHEF has simulator module to predict the feedback of proposed plan. It tests a plan by acting as if the plan is executed in world. Compare feedback with expected results/goals.

Step 5: If plan is going to fail then

(a) The reason of failure is explained in terms of causal relationship between goals, plans, and steps in plans that provide general vocabulary for describing general planning situation.

(b) Using classification provided by CHEF assigns proper class from explanation to new plan.

(c) Chooses repair strategy by searching similar cases stored in TOP that suggest a repair and select most appropriate repair plan.
(d) Applies appropriate plan and fixes its faulty plan.

To avoid repetition of same mistake, CHEF updates its understanding of world. To do this, it finds out predictors of failure and uses those as indexes to a warning that a failure might happen. If chooses its indexes by examining the previously derived explanation of this failure, extract environmental features responsible for the failure. It uses this index to organize both the cases with the failed plan as a working case and with the repaired plan as a solution plan to the problem.

Knowledge Sources

CHEF uses the following knowledge sources

1. Case library consists of cases organized through indexes
   Case structure. In case, terms are represented in frames structure and those are organized with respect to each other in semantic network.
   Index method Cases are indexed according to goals they achieve.
2. *TOPs (Thematic Organization Packets).* This is dynamic memory for having learning effect in system. It maintains strategies those help in repairing of failed plans.
3. *Object critics.* This helps to adapt old plans to fit new circumstances.
4. *Semantic memory.* This holds definitions of the terms CHEF uses. It is used for partial matching and finding the correspondences between cases.

Features of CHEF

It has new approach to planning that avoids many of the problems of more traditional planning system. It reuses plans, repairs its plans, and learns from experiences.

As a result of learning and the anticipation step performed before attempting to device a solution, CHEF can predict problems before they happen. CHEF also views planning as a memory task rather than as a construction task.

10.3.3 Selector—A Case-Based Scheduler

Selector is a manpower planning with CBR (Chaudhury, Bhattacharya and Gupta, 1998). This system accepts a job specification and find a complete, comprehensive (minimal) and consistent requirement list for the job, based on experiences of similar type of jobs that were handled in the organization in the past, e.g. user can issue a general type of query like, 'I want a manager' or 'Give me the requirement list of a small group manager who also has network programming experience and knows Japanese language'. The system has to answer all such types of general as well as specialized queries with a good amount of clarity.

The Process of Working

Input: The user query as a form
Output: The requirement list generated by the system.

Step 1: Retrieve all cases under the taxonomy or subtaxonomy that the user has mentioned.
Step 2: Use the selection module to give merits to all those cases.
Step 3: Merge all the cases that pass the threshold of merit and call the resultant case as the core case.
Step 4: For each requirement missing in the core case, use the search module to get possible cases, find out a set of requirements need to be added to satisfy this requirement and add them to the core case.
Step 5: Give the requirement list built so far, to the acceptor module to find out if there is any more unsatisfied requirement. If there is one, repeat step 4.
Step 6: When all the requirements are present in the requirement list, check the consistency. This step deletes requirements.
Step 7: After the final requirement is built, store the new case back under the same taxonomy and subtaxonomy from where the search started.

Case Structure

Case is designed in such a way that it will be efficiently reused to built new cases. It consists of case number and name and a table containing rows. Each row includes:

- Requirement in the form of attribute value pair.
- Tags (optional field) which gives reference (or binding) with other requirement.
- Forbidden occurrence list (this is opposite to tags) of requirement which should not be appeared in the current case.
- Foreign flag—associated with a requirement indicates that it is not generic requirement of the class to which the case belongs, but is imported from another taxonomy.

Index Structure

The cases are organized according to requirement breadthwise and widthwise at two levels as

(a) Taxonomy
(b) Subtaxonomy.

Repair Module

The working of repair module is as follows:

1. Start with an empty case.
2. Get the taxonomy and subtaxonomy specified in the query.

3. Pick up all the cases under that taxonomy and subtaxonomy.
4. Give merit to each case using selection module.
5. Merge all the cases that pass a merit threshold.
6. Give the case built so far to the accepter module to find out all the desired requirements missing in the case.
7. For each requirement if it is taxonomy or subtaxonomy then merge all the cases under it and add to new case.
8. For other than taxonomy and subtaxonomy requirement find a case which contains that requirement and add that requirement with requirements tagged with it to the new case.
9. Repeat step 6 until all the requirements are present in the answer case.
10. Check consistency, using the forbidden lists in the answer case.

For working, repair module uses the following parameters:

Tolerance. This decides how strict the match between the query and the base case should be.

Fraction. Fraction of cases in which a particular requirement should be present for that requirement to be selected.

Bonus and penalty. If a case matches the given requirement and has its foreign flag set then it gains a merit equal to the bonus otherwise if requirement doesn't match and foreign flag is set then it gets a penalty.

Positive point. How much point a case will gain for one ordinary match while giving merit to the case.

Acceptor Module

This module checks the acceptability of a candidate case built through repair module in terms of completeness and consistency. The defects in the cases are categorized in the following errors:

(a) Empty case
(b) Necessary requirement missing
(c) Necessary tagged requirement missing
(d) Unnecessary foreign requirement present
(e) Requirement in a forbidden list present.

Integrator Module

After repairing, the case is stored back in the case base to enrich it. The integrator module sets foreign flags and places the case under the same taxonomy and subtaxonomy, from which the base cases were taken.

10.3.4 PROTOS an Exemplar-based Classification Model for Hearing Disorder Diagnosis

An exemplar-based approach is used for learning heuristic classification. An exemplar-based approach is suitable for domains with inadequate theories, but it has problems in determining similarity and indexing exemplars. PROTOS, an application to the domain of clinical audiology, overcomes the problems and effectively implements the exemplar-based approach to classification. The approach of PROTOS is different from usual concept learning task in the ways as classification is explained, incomplete case descriptions also accommodate in this task and learn domain-specific knowledge for inferring case features needed for classification (Porter, 1990).

Classification

A case is described by a collection of features. Case description may have problem in two ways, viz. (a) A case description may be incomplete, in the sense that it does not include some of the features present in other case descriptions. (b) The features with which cases are described may not directly indicate category membership.

Here classification is done by determining category using knowledge-based inference. In addition to classification, PROTOS gives explanation to classification. This explanation is used to justify classifying a case in a particular way and to establish the degree of similarity of two cases. It is also used to relate domain-specific terms with domain-independent terms.

The explanation can be constructed by rephrasing or reorganizing some details of the inferential path that leads to a classification. Knowledge acquisition in PROTOS is done by maintaining an exemplar base of training cases which are classified and explained by the expert.

Exemplar-based Concept Learning

Concepts are represented with a collection of exemplars described with features in the case language. Classify a new case by searching for an exemplar that strongly matches the case (the direct match method). Explain the classification showing the line of reasoning used during match (the list of common features of the case and the exemplar). Learn by adjusting the categories, so that the case will be properly classified and explained.

The problems in this method are matching cases. Explanation to classification and adjusting the categories to learn are solved in PROTOS.

To solve matching problem PROTOS uses matching knowledge, a form of domain theory. The matching knowledge has two types: one is relation among concepts and another is featural importance.

Given matching knowledge, PROTOS can match dissimilar features by finding a path of relations connecting them. PROTOS acquires matching knowledge from explained cases, or from explanation provided by experts (in case of failure). PROTOS requires feature-to-category explanation relating each case feature to the case classification. To explain the relationship, the expert typically introduces new concepts and relations. Experts provide feature-to-feature explanations and PROTOS completes the explanation of the classification.

The relations are classified into three classes:

- Definitional relations denote invariant facts
- Causal/functional relations denote known mechanisms
- Correlational relations denote experimental knowledge.

Each relation can be strengthened with qualifiers, such as always, usually, sometimes, occasionally.

PROTOS heuristically estimates the importance of a feature to a category by analyzing a feature-to-category explanation. Internally featural importance is represented as numbers between ϕ (spurious) and 1 (essential). PROTOS estimation of featural importances may be revised by the expert if they result in a misclassification or an unacceptable explanation.

PROTOS applies knowledge-based matching technique to explain similarity of new case with an exemplar. During this process it determines which features are important for a successful match. The missing important feature in case description is inferred from case features using matching knowledge. This search begins from each unmatched exemplar feature and chains through the network of matching knowledge until reaching either a case feature or the depth bond relation. A path connecting an exemplar feature with a case feature is an explanation of how the features are equivalent in the sense that the features suggest the same classification.

Here heuristics are used to find the strongest explanation by evaluating the potential contribution of each relation, which makes path and develop explanation. This function considers the individual relation and qualifiers and also the overall explanation constructed so far.

PROTOS retains a case as an exemplar if the case differs from existing exemplars in significant ways that cannot be explained using existing matching knowledge.

Indexing

To select and order the exemplars to match with a given case, protos uses three types of indexing—knowledge remindings, prototypicality and exemplar differences. Remindings index categories and exemplars by new cases features. PROTOS uses reminding as cues to the case's classification. Each reminding has an associated strength, which is used to order the list of candidate exemplars.

When searching for an exemplar that matches a new case, PROTOS first collects *reminding* to categories, related categories are combined by summing the strengths of duplicate reminding and by inserting reminding from general categories to subcategories. Only the N strongest combined reminding are returned. PROTOS then selects several of the most prototypical exemplars to represent each category. Finally, PROTOS collects reminding from case features to particular exemplars. The result is an ordered list of exemplars to try matching with the new case. PROTOS learns a reminding by compiling an expert-supplied explanation of a case feature.

Some remindings called *censors* are negative associations between case features and categories or exemplars. These suggest that case described with the feature should be classified into the categories. These are useful to remove entries from the set of candidate classifications. These are derived from mutual exclusion relations used in explanation.

Second type of indexing knowledge is *prototypicality*, which orders the exemplars within a category according to their record of success in previous classifications. When a new case reminds PROTOS of a category, the exemplars of that category are matched with the case in order of decreasing prototypicality. Prototypicality is a heuristic estimate of degree to which an exemplar is similar to other category members. Prototypicality is incrementally learned, if a match between a case and an exemplar is accepted by the expert then the exemplars prototypicality is increased by an amount proportional to the strength of the match.

The third type of indexing knowledge is *exemplar differences*, which index exemplars by the features that distinguish them from exemplars with similar descriptions. After finding an exemplar that matches a new case, PROTOS climbs to the best matching exemplar. PROTOS learns an exemplar difference by matching a new case to a 'near miss' before matching the case to an exemplar preferred by the expert. The near miss and the preferred exemplar may be the members of the same category or different categories. PROTOS relates them by their differences to improve classification accuracy on subsequent cases.

Algorithm of Classification and Learning Process in PROTOS

Given: a case (New case) to classify

Collect and combine remindings from New Case's features. Retain only the N strongest combined remindings.

Create a list of exemplars ordered by reminding strength.
REPEAT
  REPEAT (consider the exemplars in decreasing order)
    Let Exemplars be the exemplar with the next higher reminding strength
    Determine the similarity of New Case and Exemplar's
  UNTIL a sufficiently strong match is found.
Use exemplar differences from Exemplar1 to locate better match (Exemplar2)
Use Exemplar2's category to classify NewCase and use the match between Exemplar2 and NewCase to explain this classification. Discuss this classification and explanation with the expert.
If the expert rejects the classification or explanation.
THEN reassess the remindings from NewCase's features.
  Request new matching knowledge from the expert.
ELSE (the expert approves the classification and explanation)
Increase prototypicality of Exemplar2.
  If sure features of Exemplar2 are unmatched.
  THEN Request feature-to-feature explanation from export.
  IF the match is very strong.
    THEN Discard NewCase.
  ELSE Retain NewCase as an exemplar.
Construct feature-to-category explanations.
Estimate featural importances.
Learn remindings for NewCase.
IF NewCase was initially classified or explained incorrectly.
THEN Record exemplar differences.
UNTIL the expert approves the classification and explanation.

10.3.5 CAROL (Case-Assisted Reuse of Object Library)

CAROL represents object-oriented classes as cases in a case base, computer similarities between class descriptions and returns list of given class descriptions which are most similar to a given target class specification (Shankaraman, 1989).

Case base is a collection of cases. Cases are LOOM (Language for Object-Oriented Modelling developed at Napier University) scripts stored as PROLOG database facts representing classes, attributes and relationships.

Components of CAROL

1. *Case base creation:* LOOM scripts (library files) processed through modules for syntax analysis, semantic analysis, classify and extract necessary features of classes to build case. The class features like class name, super class name(s), class type, instance variables, and others are assigned to corresponding attributes of the case.
2. *Specification:* Input template is provided by user for specifying a new case as target class. Specification provides values for some or all attributes, which will proceed to retrieve modules.
3. *Retrieval:* Retrieval matches a user specification either against all or user specified parts of the case base and returns a list of matched cases names, with their similarity score and goodness which matches default goodness criterion. Settings are available like retrieval settings and attribute weightings which allow user to select search technique.

This system is lacks to provide support for reuse of classes at a high level of abstraction. It also cannot facilitate explaining to justify the retrieved class and to adapt a retrieved class to fit the current user requirement.

To overcome these limitations, new version of CAROL is developed.

Additional Features in CAROL–II

1. ***Reuse at a higher level of abstraction.*** Here, design analysis and specification are considered as higher level of abstractions. ROME, a tool developed at Napier University, is used as a teaching tool. This is interactive object at modelling environment which supports design documentation and C++ code generation. LOOM defines an abstraction at design level.

As input and output class of retrieval process is a LOOM script, it supports reuse at a higher level of abstraction.

2. ***Explanation of the retrieval process.*** In CBR, matching score for different attributes of the case is useful for explanation. In CAROL-II, the list of matched attributes is used to provide an explanation. The explanation is provided in terms of overall score and weighted score for each matched attribute, score attained for the instance-variable and link attributes, any unweighted scores attained for the method identifiers and method labels.

3. ***Adaptation of the retrieved class.*** Here retrieved class is adapted to suit the user requirement. CBR systems suggest method like substitution, transformation, heuristic based and derivational replay for adaptation. CAROL-II uses substitution method called local search for adaptation. Local search provides a way of searching an auxiliary knowledge structure, or part of the case base which is close relative to a substitute for some old structure, attribute or value that is inappropriate for the new situation CAROL-II considers that if a retrieval class is very similar to the target class then it is probable that the underlying data structures are correct, but some operations on them are missing.

Adaptation in CAROL-II

(a) Load the primary candidate LOOM script into an editor window. For each case retrieved, maintain lists of matched and unmatched attributes.
(b) User-selected categories of the case base are searched (local search) using the same predicates used in the initial search but with the lists of OPERATIONS, PROPERTIES and LINKS attributes, initially derived from target class, replaced by the corresponding lists of unmatched attributes of the candidate case. The retrieved second candidate LOOM script is loaded into secondary candidate editor window.
(c) Search secondary editor window for relevant keywords and identifiers derived from the matched attribute lists of the secondary candidate class, then using dialogue boxes, query user to copy each relevant section into an appropriate point in the primary editor window.
(d) The user is then allowed to manually edit the composite as required and save to file.

With the explanation and adaptation facilities CAROL-II provides better support for reuse.

10.4 CASE-BASED DIAGNOSIS

Diagnosis is performed in a rule-based system by backward chaining followed by forward chaining to eliminate many of the logical possibilities that are inconsistent. They imply deductions that are known to be *false*. In case-based reasoning, we rely on the cases built up over time to provide the expertise, but diagnosis is very different from other types of CBR. A synopsis of diagnosis via CBR is given below:

(a) Present a tree of questions to the user where later questions depend upon previous answers.
(b) Compare the tree of answers to the trees of case answers, select similar cases.
(c) Select solutions of most similar cases, check solutions with rules or tables.

The first few questions are usually the same, but after that, the questions asked depend upon the previous answers and thus form a tree. It is possible to use just the resulting branch of the tree of questions and answers for the retrieval. After one or more solutions have been checked with rules or tables, etc., there is a feedback part where the solutions are tried. If the solution is successful, then it is put with the answer tree and stored as a case, else the process above is repeated with at least some minor variation. In the CBR approach it is the patterns of answers that are important because these determine the symptoms. A determined branch is used to retrieve similar branches from the case base. If a retrieved branch is the same then its diagnosis is used as a solution. How close must a retrieved branch be to be applicable? This depends upon the types of diagnosis and the judgement that must be made from some type of knowledge built into the system. But CBR diagnosis can be used as an aid to humans to guide them and make sure that they do not overlook important possibilities. Diagnosis CBR can be used, for example, in medicine, automotive repair, computer repair, system control, etc.

10.5 SOME ADVANTAGES

In contrast to rule-based systems (expert systems), CBR does not require an explicit model, as cases are gathered and added to the case base during development and after deployment that identify the significant features. This is easier than creating an explicit model, as it is possible to develop case bases without passing through the knowledge acquisition bottleneck.

Experts may find it hard to express their knowledge as rules, but they usually have little difficulty in recalling concrete cases which they have encountered in their practice. Thus, their mental set appears to be oriented towards a case-based approach, at least for shallow knowledge decisions. Model based systems may be used for shallow or deep levels of knowledge. Indeed, for deep knowledge a model-based approach is the only feasible solution.

However, for representing shallow knowledge, which is all that is required for many practical diagnostic systems, CBR has obvious advantages. In an investigation, undertaken by Cognitive Systems, it is stated that a system based on rules was developed which took four months to be built, whereas its equivalent CBR system required only two weeks. Similar impressive claims also exist that suggest developing a CBR system is much faster and easier than constructing a rule-based equivalent. Case bases do not have to be complete when they are deployed for use, as cases can be added to the existing structure at any site and by non-computer experts. Maintenance with case bases is extremely straightforward, especially when compared with a rule-based system, which is more of a debugging task.

This is due to the interdependencies of attributes that have to be considered. Cases are typically stored as records in a database, which can manage and store large volumes of data satisfactorily. Maintenance is made easier as these systems are capable of learning or reporting cases that need to be revised. These CBR systems also provide highly contextualized explanations as help can be attached to individual or generalized cases.

EXERCISES

1. Define case-based reasoning.
2. List five advantages of case-based reasoning.
3. Discuss each step in the case-based reasoning processing.
4. Explain relationship between case-based reasoning and scripts.
5. Compare and contrast rule-based versus case based reasoning.
6. Discuss some potential problems with case based reasoning.
7. Compare and contrast case-based reasoning and learning by analogy. How may transformational and derivational analogies can be applied in case-based reasoning systems.
8. Forgetting is one aspect of human memory. How could this be modelled in a case-based reasoning system? Under what circumstances might this be beneficial?
9. Develop a case-based reasoning system for converting grayscale images to line drawings. The neighbourhoods of a pixel are the problems and the solution is the new value of the centre pixel.
10. Build a CBR scheduler system that assigns a set of classes that may be small, medium, or large to classes that may be small, medium or large, respectively. Assume that there are many more classes than rooms and so the classes must be scheduled on the hour from 8 am to 4 pm and that the classes meet 5 days per week (no classes are scheduled for the weekend).
11. Develop a CBR system that diagnoses the problems with a computer network. Obtain whatever knowledge or make the assumptions necessary to get a working system.
12. Develop a theory of rule-based reasoning using CBR to deduce the final truths from a given set of initial truths and falsities of atomic propositions. Assume each proposition is known to be true or false. The case base is to associate a problem (given initial truth states) with the deduced truths (solution). The system learns by running the rule-based system and obtaining the deduced results and then saving the case as a problem and a solution. Make a small working model using C or C++ to demonstrate that rule-based reasoning can be done by CBR based on the experience of executing the rule-based system.
13. Develop a CBR system that diagnoses the problems with a PC (computer) for a user who connects in on the Web and answers a series of questions. Assume that you are the expert and provide the knowledge for the system by making any necessary assumptions about what causes computer problems.
14. Find a new application of CBR based on some process or problem that exists. Write software to implement it, generate some data and show it working.

CHAPTER 11

Constraint Programming

11.1 INTRODUCTION

Constraint programming (CP) is the study of computational models and systems based on constraints. The idea is to model and solve a problem by exploring the constraints that can fully characterize the problem, hence any solution of the problem must satisfy all of the stated constraints. Constraint programming is one of the most exciting developments in programming languages in the last decade. Languages such as PROLOG based on predicate calculus and LISP based on functional programming were closer to realize the goal of "programmer states the problem, the computer solves it".

CP is a comparatively recent trend in this line. However, like its predecessors, of which PROLOG and LISP are perhaps classic examples, constraint programming is also yet to find large base in the software industry. The presence of such an event itself is an indication that CP is yet to be a commonly accepted development language.

However, the lack of widespread acceptance should not be interpreted due to some inherent weaknesses in the language or paradigm. Much of the weakness is due to lack of understanding among the industry and academia about the possibilities and a realistic estimate of the risks involved. Compared to the early days of logic programming, the advent of WAM-like abstract machines made compilation of logic programs possible resulting in significant improvements in execution speeds of programs written in PROLOG-like languages. Similarly for complex problems, many constraint programming languages can, today, work at speeds comparable to languages such as Java, and offer tremendous advantages in terms of expressive power, compactness, higher level of abstraction, etc. During the last few years, there has been tremendous growth in the field with a number of practical applications.

One of the interesting aspects of the field of constraint programming is its inter-disciplinary nature with a number of other fields, including numerical analysis, operations research, programming languages, artificial intelligence, logic, mathematics, etc. Ideas and techniques are being borrowed from all these to solve specific problems. Such an integration is difficult in almost any other paradigm of programming. Since much of the solution strategy and details are left out of the problem specification, the system can formulate suitable linkages to apply appropriate algorithms from any of these fields.

The origins of constraint programming can be traced back to Sutherland's pioneering work in Computer Graphics (Sketchpad) where the various shapes were specified in terms of constraints imposed on each other, e.g. David Waltz's work in edge labelling for computer vision, and Alan Borning's work on Thinglab. Since then, constraint programming has indeed come quite far. A number of languages and frameworks are available, including a number of commercial ones. These include ILOG Solver, PROLOG III, etc. But then, the way remaining to go is perhaps much more than what has been covered so far. Lack of powerful development environments including debugging support is one strong weakness. Available constraint languages differ substantially in their approach to constraint programming, making choice of a framework difficult. The field is also rich for further research work. More visibility among the academics and industry, particularly for solving complex problems would be a welcome boost to further work in the field.

11.2 CONSTRAINT SATISFACTION PROBLEMS (CSPs)

The CSP has been a subject of research in artificial intelligence for many years. The pioneering works on networks of constraints were motivated mainly by problems arising in the field of picture processing. AI research, concentrated on difficult combinatorial problems, is dated back to 60s and 70s and it has contributed to considerable progress in constraint-based reasoning. Many powerful algorithms were designed that became a basis of current constraint satisfaction algorithms.

A Constraint Satisfaction Problem (CSP) consists of:

- a set of variables $X = \{x_1, ..., x_n\}$,
- for each variable x_i, a finite set D_i of possible values (its domain),
- and a set of constraints restricting the values that the variables can simultaneously take.

Note that values need not be a set of consecutive integers (although often they are), they need not even be numeric.

A solution to a CSP is an assignment of a value from its domain to every variable, in such a way that every constraint is satisfied. Thus, we may want to find:

- just one solution, with no preference as to which one,
- all solutions,
- an optimal, or at least a good solution, given some objective functions defined in terms of some or all of the variables.

Solutions to CSPs can be found by searching systematically through the possible assignments of values to variables. Search methods divide into two broad classes, those that traverse the space of partial solutions (or partial value assignments), and those that explore the space of complete value assignments (to all variables) stochastically.

EXAMPLE 1. Suppose we have variables X, Y, Z, and their domains are:

$$D\_X = D\_Y = \{1, 2, 3\},\ D\_Z = \{2, 3, 4\}$$

and the constraints are

$$X < Y \text{ and } Y < Z$$

Its clear that this CSP is satisfiable. For example, the assignment

$$X = 1,\ Y = 2,\ Z = 3$$

is a solution.

EXAMPLE 2. Using the 4-queen problem as an example, we can use a variable to represent each queen, thus we have 4 variables, say,

$$x1,\ x2,\ x3,\ x4$$

Assume $x1$ is placed in the first row, $x2$ in the second row, and so on. The domain for each queen then consists of 4 columns. Thus, we have domains for the variables as

$$\begin{aligned} D\_x1 &= \{1, 2, 3, 4\}, \\ D\_x2 &= \{1, 2, 3, 4\}, \\ D\_x3 &= \{1, 2, 3, 4\}, \\ D\_x4 &= \{1, 2, 3, 4\}, \end{aligned}$$

The constraints that must be satisfied can be stated as relations, e.g. the constraint that says $x1$ and $x2$ cannot be on the same column can be expressed by the set of tuples satisfying it:

$$\begin{aligned} r1(x1, x2) = \{&(1, 2), (1, 3), (1, 4), \\ &(2, 1), (2, 3), (2, 4), \\ &(3, 1), (3, 2), (3, 4), \\ &(4, 1), (4, 2), (4, 3)\} \end{aligned}$$

Defining a relation by stating satisfied tuples is tedious. In a suitable language, one may express this by

$r1(x1, x2)$ if $x1$ is not equal to $x2$,. and

$x1$ takes a value from D_x1 and $x2$ takes a value from D_x2

It is obvious that we need a language to state all three parts of a CSP.

11.3 WHY CONSTRAINT PROGRAMMING?

Programming is essentially a process of communicating our requirements to the computer for obtaining a solution. What kind of information does our "requirements" normally consist of? Most of the time, our solution to this is biased by the framework we are using—the programming language being used. However, we can list out a number of types of information—the entities relevant to the problem at hand, their properties and behaviour, relationships among the various entities, constraints on the behaviour of the various entities, constraints on the properties, the various tasks that need to be performed and the entities involved in them, and so on. Procedural programming languages provide a good base for describing how to perform certain tasks. Object-oriented languages provide a mechanism for describing the entities and their properties and behaviours.

Another fundamental type of information is *constraints*. They are applicable to a variety of contexts and almost all entities.

Constraints are a common kind of information in our day-to-day communication and they do arise in many programming specifications. For example:

- The width of the north side should not exceed 55 metres.
- The circle is inscribed inside the triangle (in other words, if the triangle is enlarged, the circle also must grow and so on).
- Number of child objects of A should be between 3 and 14.
- Salary is an integer between 4,000 and 40,000.

However, the currently popular languages do not allow us to encode these kinds of information explicitly. Often these are converted into a set of different partial representations which are scattered throughout the program. For example, restricting the number of child objects would be done by an explicit check in the constructor of an object and in the method which adds children to another object, and any other method which may add/delete children to an object. This is a cumbersome process.

Equally important is the fact that such constraints provide additional information in many cases. If we know that X and Y are less than 10, and $X + Y > 20$, then there is no solution for the specification. For this, we don't need to test out all values of X and Y. A collection of constraints on X, each individually incapable of deciding a value for X, may together help to fix its value. This is a significantly powerful reasoning and problem solving model useful in many problems. Conventional programming frameworks do not support this.

Constraints have something more, compared to other types of information:

- They can represent partial information $X > 4$ is a valid constraint, which does not assign a unique value to X.
- They can deal with and relate different types of information.

$$\text{length}(S) > \text{cardinality}(Y)$$

- They are additive and hence independent of the order of specifying them. $X > 4$ and $X < 6$ is the same as $X < 6$ and $X > 4$. This is a powerful degree of freedom where conventional languages impose a fixed order to be selected and enforced.
- They are non-directional $X + Y = Z$ does not impose a direction really, if you read it as "Z is equal to the sum of X and Y". If X and Z are known, we can deduce Y from the same equation.

  In conventional languages such statements are directional and can be used strictly in one direction. Semantically, they overwrite the previous value of the left-hand side (LHS) variable. If any of the right hand side (RHS) variables are unbound, an error results. However, as a constraint, the equality can even be used simply for validation, if all three variables are bound.

5. They are more declarative than most other types of information and normally do not include any procedural component.

11.3.1 Basic Issues

How does constraint programming differ from the other models? Is it comparable to other models?

We will take a look at the basic ideas and related issues to answer these questions. We can view our programming problems as being defined by a set of variables—for the time being, we don't care if the set is finite or infinite. And the task is to assign values to these variables, satisfying all the specifications. This is an adequately powerful view of programming for our requirements. Traditionally, we start with a set of variables, some initialized automatically, some initialized using user input and the rest are computed during the problem solving process. This is normally an iterative process, where based on values of other variables, the value of another variable is computed. These dependencies can be captured as constraints in a compact form, e.g. $x2 + y2 = Z$ is not a recipe to compute Z. It also embodies a procedure to compute X or Y from the other two variables. In traditional models, we are forced to represent these cases as separate procedures.

How does constraint programming work around such problems? In constraint programming models, we represent the constraints as it is. As mentioned earlier, the order of specifying the constraints is immaterial. So $X = 2$; $Y = X + 1$; is equivalent to $Y = X + 1$; $X = 2$. Therefore, unlike in the traditional languages, we cannot discard a statement after it is processed. When you encounter $Y = X + 1$, all you know is that the value of Y is one more than that of X; we know neither X nor Y. Therefore, we need to store these constraints and periodically check if something more about X or Y is known. Thus an essential component of any constraint programming system is a constraint store, which represents the constraints currently in force. When a new constraint is encountered, it is added to the store.

How do we use a constraint? Essentially, we need an agent to ensure that a given constraint is never violated, as the variables involved keep changing. In the above example, initially X and Y is unbound, so there was nothing to do. Then we may be told that $X > 10$. Though, there is no danger of constraint violation, now looking at the constraint constructively, we see that we can restrict the possibilities of Y, to be greater than 11. Before we explore this 'agent' let us look at constraints in more detail.

We can broadly classify constraints in the following categories:

1. ***Domain constraints:*** These specify the range of valid values that a variable can take as a subset of the domain of the variable. For example "integer age; age 1#100" means that age is an integer valued variable with possible values in the range 1 to 100.

2. ***Basic constraints:*** These depict simple constraints on a variable, not involving other variables, e.g. $X < 10$.
3. ***Other constraints:*** These include all other types and presumably is a large class covering items such as $X*X + Y*Y < 200$, $X - Y < Z$, $X > 2*Y$, etc.

How do we represent a constraint internally? In traditional computational models, either a variable is bound or unbound to a known value. We have predefined data types which encode the different values. How about when you are told that X is 10#100? There are two ways in which such information is normally captured.

In *interval representation*, the allowed sets of values are represented by an interval. For example, age, [10#50] indicates that age is between 10 and 50. In *domain representation*, a list of available values is stored. This is obviously feasible only for small domain sizes. Of the two, interval representation is more efficient to represent, since just a pair of values are used. But it is also less effective. For example, if it is known that age is an even number, in the domain representation, we can chop off all the odd numbers; but in the interval representation, the representation is unaffected. Most commercial systems use the interval representation largely for reasons of efficiency.

Now let us consider what happens when a constraint is given to the system. If it is a domain constraint, the processing is easy. We capture an interval corresponding to the domain and store that. We can then discard the constraint—as we have captured the entire information from the constraints in the representation. For basic constraint also, we can do a similar process. If the constraint is $X < a$, we can revise the upper bound of the interval corresponding to X to a, if it is higher than a. The constraint cannot provide any more information, and hence we can discard it from the store. For other constraints such as $X + Y < Z$, this is not possible. We may be able to eliminate some values from the domains of all the three variables, but we cannot absorb all the information provided by the constraint. For example, if $X > 5$, $Y > 3$ and $Z > 2$, then from this constraint we can revise Z's lower bound to 8. But till at least two variables are bound to a single value, we cannot ensure this constraint by changing the domain representation.

Thus we see that we can process certain constraints completely, whereas for other constraints we need to keep monitoring the values of the variables involved to ensure that the constraint is satisfied.

For example, if later we know that $Z < 15$, we can reduce X's upperbound to 11 (10 for integers). This in turn may trigger other constraints involving X, which may affect the domains of other variables. This process is called *constraint propagation* and is a critical part of constraint programming.

In some cases, where there are adequate constraints, it may be possible for the system to come up with unique values for all variables at the end of this repeated propagation process. However, this is normally not the case, for two reasons. At first, as we saw earlier, our representation is not normally adequate to capture the implications of a constraint completely and therefore, the propagation may stop earlier. Secondly, the constraints alone may not determine a unique solution. Therefore, all constraint programming systems incorporate a search module. When constraint propagation stabilizes, there are three possibilities:

1. One or more variable has their domain becoming empty. This implies an inconsistent set of constraints and therefore, there is no valid solution.

2. All variables are bound to unique values. In other words, all domains are singleton sets. A proper solution has been arrived at.
3 Neither of the above. At least one variable has a non-singleton domain and no domain is empty. We need to search for a solution further, in this case.

The search process works as follows. An unbound variable V is picked up which has a value range $a\#b$, say. We can say that in the solution either $V = a$, or $V <> a$. Thus we have two possibilities.

We explore both in the search. In one branch, we have $V = a$ and in the other we have $V <> a$.

These act as new constraints, from which further propagation is possible. The two branches are independently explored as if they were two different problems. Solutions from both the branches are merged and returned as solutions to the given problem.

This process may repeat further in the two branches. If case 3 persists even after assuming $V = a$, we may take another variable and bind it similarly. This process is repeated till no further variable is remaining to be bound, or a failure is noticed.

Thus, in general, a constraint programming system contains a constraint store to keep track of non-basic constraints, a constraint propagation module, and a search module. The more effective the propagator, the less the cost of the search. But, in general, to ensure that the solution process is complete, a search module is essential.

11.3.2 Consistency Models

In general, the job of the propagator is to reduce the possible values of another variable given additional information on one variable. This, in general, requires one to check and process every constraint in the system for every change in the domain of every variable. And potentially a change in the domain of one variable can lead to changes in every other variable's domain. We remove those values from a variable's domain which are not consistent with any value of another variable. Thus, we get a very expensive propagation model. More work may be done in checking for possibilities of propagation compared to actual work required to solve the problem by other means.

For constraint propagation to be effective in practice, we must have an efficient way to do this.

There are obvious improvements such as keeping a list of affected variables and picking only those constraints which refers to one of the affected variables. Based on analysis, other variables in those constraints which are affected are identified and added to the pool. This avoids an exhaustive examination of every constraint till the propagation stops. Even then the cost is prohibitive in general.

As we have seen earlier, generally, we are unable to exploit the full power of most constraints. And the cost of this inability is higher search cost (less constraint propagation). Using this "fact", a compromise is often used in the amount of propagation and the amount of search cost. There are many such consistency models.

The simplest consistency model is *node consistency*, which restricts attention to unary constraints. Values are removed from a variable's domain which is inconsistent with unary constraints on the variable. For example, remove even values if the variable is defined as odd. This is easy to enforce and is not expensive computationally, being restricted to a single scan of the variables.

The next level is *arc-consistency*, where we consider a pair of variables, $v1$ and $v2$, and remove all values from the domain of $v1$ (or $v2$) which is inconsistent with all values of $v2$ (or $v1$). This is more expensive due to propagation. When subsequently considering the pair $v2$–$v3$, further values may get removed from $v2$'s domain. In the light of this reduced set, the $v1$–$v2$ may be able to shed more values from $v1$'s domain. So the pairwise combinations have to be examined repeatedly till no further change is applicable.

There are higher level models such as k-consistency, where k-tuples of variables are considered, where $k > 2$. These are computationally much more expensive and rarely used.

However, if a system with N variables can be made to be N-consistent, maximum propagation is possible.

As mentioned, even arc-consistency is expensive to implement. Here the entire process has to be repeated every time a change is observed in one variable's domain. Therefore, most practical implementations use restricted forms of arc-consistency. A number of algorithms are known in the literature including AC1, AC2, etc. An example of the restriction would be to check arc-consistency of only the variable under consideration against all variables which have been processed (and ignore the ones yet to be processed). For example, in the n-queens problem, when placing the ith queen, we check for violations against all queens from 1 to $i - 1$ only, and not the queens $i + 1$ to n. A variety of strategies have been implemented based on these algorithms and other optimizations. *Forward checking* incorporates the restricted arc-consistency model, where future variables are checked against the current variable for consistency. This helps early detection of future failures and helps contributing to efficiency. *Backjumping* tries to improve the backtracking behaviour beyond the simple chronological backtracking commonly employed. *Backmarking* is an attempt to reduce repeated consistency computations.

11.4 SOLVING REAL-LIFE PROBLEMS

A significant element of solving real-life problems using constraints is modelling the problem in terms of constraints, i.e. transforming the problem description from the natural language to the language of constraints. We will consider two examples here. At first we will see the problem of assigning labels of symbolic microcode to binary addresses and then problem of DNA sequence alignment.

11.4.1 Microcode Label Assignment Problem

The problem is to assign labels of symbolic microcode to binary addresses in a 256-address page of microcode memory. A typical microcode instruction has the following form:

L0: opcode L1,...,Ln.

where L0 is the origin label and L1, ..., Ln are the target labels. To improve efficiency and decrease memory usage, the labels share certain bits and contain the branch condition as a part of the address. Therefore, the labels cannot be assigned to consecutive addresses as in assembly language, but must be distributed over the address space to satisfy all constraints. For example, a 4-way branch instruction is:

L0: branch4 L1, L2, L3, L4

Look at the following binary representation of each label that consists of eight bits (remember, 256-address page).

```
L0: X7 X6 Y5 Y4 Y3 Y2 Y1 Y0
L1: X7 X6 X5  0  0 X2 X1 X0
L2: X7 X6 X5  0  1 X2 X1 X0
L3: X7 X6 X5  1  0 X2 X1 X0
L4: X7 X6 X5  1  1 X2 X1 X0
              ↑  ↑
            ——— condition bits
```

Note that some (most) bits are common for some labels.

Naturally, each label can be represented by a variable with a domain between 0 and 255 and to express the following constraints one needs bitwise & operation with a mask:

- **Equal bits**. Some bits are shared among the labels (L0&11000000=L1&11000000).
- **Condition bits**. Condition bits are fixed (L2&00011000=00001000.
- **Increments**. Some labels directly follows other labels (L1=L0+1)
- **All different**. All labels must be assigned to different addresses.

Source: Hentenrysk, P.V., *Constraint Satisfaction in Logic Programming*, MIT Press, 1989.

11.4.2 Multiple Protein/DNA Sequence Alignment

Multiple alignment of a family of protein/DNA sequences is a fundamental step in the study of similarity in their shape and function. The goal of multiple alignment is to insert symbols "–" representing gap into k sequences in such a way that the resulting k sequences have the same length and if the resulting sequences are treated as a matrix then every column contain at least one character different from "–". For example,

```
LIMITED-      LIMIT-ED--      LIMIT--ED
LITTLE--      LIT-TLE---      LIT-TL-E-
LISTENER      LIS-T-ENER      LIS-TENER
```

The key point is that we do not simply want an arbitrary alignment, we want to find a good alignment which can indicate the similarity of a group of sequences as accurately as possible (the definition of "good" is based on biological knowledge).

Suppose that the input data is k sequences of length n and a maximum number of inserts (to each sequence) is m. We can use two arrays of finite domain variables to represent the data:

- **Position array S** with size $k \times n$; each element $S_{i,j}$ corresponds to the shift of jth letter in the ith sequence, i.e. the domain of each $S_{i,j}$ is $\{0, ..., m\}$.
- **Letter array P** with size $k \times (n + m)$; each element corresponds to the letter in final alignment, i.e. the domain of $P_{i,j}$ is $\{-, s_{ij}, s_{i\,j-1}, ..., s_{ij-m}\}$ where s_{ij} is jth letter in the original ith sequence. (Note that the two occurrences of the same letter should be distinguished by assigning an offset to each letter).

Now, two sets of constraints can be defined:

- **Non-overlap constraints**: $S_{ij} <= S_{ij+1}$
- **Link constraints** (bind the above tables):
  - for each $z = 0, ..., m$: if $P_{ij} = s_{ij-z}$ then $S_{ij-z} = z$
  - for each $z = 0, ..., m$: if $S_{ij} = z$ then $P_{i\,j+z} = s_{ij}$ and remove s_{ij} from P_{ij+z+1}, ..., P_{ij+m}
  - for each $z = 0,..., m-1$: if $S_{ij} > z$ then remove s_{ij} from P_{ij}, ..., P_{ij+z}

11.5 LANGUAGES AND TOOLS

As mentioned earlier, the basic elements of a constraint programming system are a constraint propagation mechanism and a search mechanism. A number of models for representing constraints and reasoning with them have been proposed over the years. We look at two models: constraint logic programming and concurrent constraint programming.

Constraint logic programming language is a class of languages based on a common semantic model. The fundamental notion here is to incorporate constraint handling into a logic programming (LP) framework. LP has a rich and sound semantic base in first-order logic, with resolution refutation forming the basis of its execution model.

A logic program consists of a set of rules and facts (facts are rules with no conditions). Its execution proceeds starting with a query which is a conjunction of goals. The execution model is to pick an item from the current goal list, identify a rule or fact which can unify with that specific goal, and replace that goal in the list by the conditions of the matched fact/rule. The process of unification introduces additional binding constraints on the variables existing in the goal list which is propagated to all the goals in the resulting goal list.

Obviously there are many open issues here. What happens if there are multiple rules/facts that unifies with a goal? And what happens if there are none? In most sequential languages one of the options is chosen to proceed, and later, if that option is found not to lead to a solution, the control backtracks to this point and chooses another option. Parallel languages may try the different options in parallel, but without the bindings interfering with each other. If the goal list contains a goal which has no fact/rule which can unify with it, the goal list is unsatisfiable and a failure is reported.

The expressiveness of such a framework for logic programming can be enhanced significantly by incorporating constraint handling in them. And CLP shows a natural way to do so. The state of a PROLOG computation is represented by the current goal list and the current set of bindings. With CLP, this is expanded to include current set of constraints as well, on the variables. If a unification process invalidates a constraint, that is considered as a failure as in the case of unification failure.

Similarly, the rules and facts are extended to include zero or more constraints in addition to predicates. For example,

```
fib(N, M) : N > 2, % constraint
fib(N–1, M1), fib(N–2, M2), M is M1+M2.
```

When a matching takes place, as additional bindings are added to the binding list and bindings are checked for consistency, additional constraints are added to the constraint store and existing constraints are checked for consistency.

A set of languages have been developed essentially based on this concept. Some of the prominent ones are PROLOG-III, CLP(R), CHIP and CHR. The kind of constraints supported and the kind of inference performed from them vary from language to language. CHR, for instance, allows the programmer to specify how constraints are to be handled using constraint handling rules. These rules monitor the constraint store for constraints matching their LHS and either replaces the matching constraints with a simpler form or derives additional constraints to be added to the constraint store. For example, here is a simple program in CHR to determine the prime numbers from 1 to *N*.

```
primes(1) <=> true
primes(N) <=> N > 1 | M is N–1, prime(N), primes(N)
prime(I), prime(J) <=> 0 is J mod I | prime(I)
```

Here the primes predicate acts as a generator, producing a prime predicate for each value in the range 1 to N. The third rule is a simplication rule, which filters out the "prime" predicate for numbers which are not actually primes.

Another category of prominent languages is represented by the popular public-domain language Oz. Oz is a multi-paradigm language supporting concurrency, constraints, functional, logical, and object-oriented methodologies. With respect to constraint programming, Oz builds in both the propagation and search explicitly. It uses interval representation for most constraint variables and absorbs basic constraints by modifying the intervals. For non-basic constraints, propagators are created which monitor changes in any of the variables within the constraint and propagates the change to other variables. Explicit, user programmable search interface allows the user to specify how search of a solution is to be carried out. Various types of search strategies lead to different pay-offs in terms of efficiency, etc. Examples of commonly used search strategies are fail-first, and naive.

Here is a sample Oz program for solving the famous *cryptarithmetic* problem,

SEND + MORE = MONEY:

```
proc {Money root}
S E N D M O N E Y in // defining variables
root = sol(s:S e:E .... y:Y)
```

```
// structure of solution
root:::0#9 // domain for the variables
{FD.distinct root} // constraints
s \=: 0 m \=: 0
... expression ...
{FD.distribute ff root}
end
```

Oz restricts constraint handling to finite domain variables. FD is a library of constructs for finite domain constraints. FD distribute specifies the search strategy—note the ff indicating a choice of fail-first strategy, so that variables which are most restricted (smallest domain) are taken first. A variety of constraints are built-in for finite domain variables in FD.

Based on this, we can find the solution using built-in calls such as SearchAll and SearchOne. Oz also provides a Branch and Bound optimizer which, given a function comparing two solutions, returns the optimal solution which is best as per the comparison function provided.

There are also other attempts and models for languages, particularly to extend traditional languages with the power of constraints. The CLP family member, CHR has a Java-based implementation which can be incorporated into Java applications. However, the Java and CHR variables are entirely disjoint and hence is not really an extension for CP. Kaleidoscope is an attempt to bring CP into procedural framework. However, these attempts have not been as popular as the CLP or complete languages, for their inability to integrate well into the basic paradigm.

The source code given below solves arbitrary cryptarithmetic problem. The code is written by Matthew Hammond in 2000.

```
% This Eclipse program solves arbitrary cryptarithmetic problems.
%:It works by setting up a single constraint for the summation.
% Thus it does not use any "carry" variable.
%

:–lib(fd).

solve(First,Second,Result) :-
    reverse(First,F),
    reverse(Second,S),
    reverse(Result,R),
    uniques(First,[],U1), % The calls to the 'uniques/3' predicate
    % could be replaced with the merge/predicate.
    uniques(Second,U1,U2),
    uniques(Result,U2,VarList),
    constrain(VarList,F,S,R),
    labeling(VarList).

uniques([],L,L).
uniques([H | T],InList,List) :-
    uniquein(H,InList),
    !,
    uniques(T,[H | InList],List).
```

```
uniques([_|T],InList,List) :-
    uniques(T,InList,List).

uniquein(_,[]).
uniquein(X,[H|T]) :-
    X \== H,
    uniquein(X,T).

constrain(Vars,F,S,R) :-
    alldistinct(Vars),
    Vars :: 0..9,
    sumterm(F,FSum),
    sumterm(S,SSum),
    sumterm(R,RSum),
    FSum + SSum #= RSum.

sumterm([],0).
sumterm([H|[]],H) :-
    H #\= 0.
sumterm([H|T],Result) :-
    T \= [],
    Result #= H + 10*R2, %% can use '=' here instead of '#='
    sumterm(T,R2).

labeling([]) :- !.
labeling(List) :-
    deleteff(H,List,Rest),
    indomain(H),
    labeling(Rest).
```

11.6 SCOPE FOR FUTURE DEVELOPMENT

Though much work has been done, and useful languages and frameworks for practical usage are available, the field of CP provides plenty openings for advance research.

Partial Constraint Satisfaction. There are other directions prompted particularly by the use of CP in AI problems. It is often observed that the problem domain contains conflicting constraints among which a compromise has to be arrived at before finding a solution. There are also many cases, where the full set of constraints pose an over constrained problem and hence no solution. In such cases, the strategy would be to isolate some less important constraints and relax them to find a solution which violates minimal constraints or incurs least cost. These issues form the focus of partial constraint satisfaction.

Backtrack-Free Search. As we stated before, search is an essential component of constraint programming systems. Selection of variables to be bound at each stage of the search tree, and the value to which it is to be bound, affects the search-tree complexity in general. Bad choices lead to failure at the end, and have to backtrack to earlier branches. One area of work is to explore the relation between variable-value selection and search complexity to reduce the amount of backtracking required. There are results ensuring backtrack-free search for certain ordering for some restricted tree structures.

Development Environments. Development environments are still to reach maturity though there are GUI based interfaces available for most commercial products as well as Oz. Therefore, there is scope for identifying subclasses which are tractable and therefore amenable to efficient implementations.

EXERCISES

1. What is constraint programming?
2. Explain in brief constraint satisfaction problem.
3. Identify the constraints in four queen problem.
4. A ball is pushed at some start point with the initial speed V_b and rolls on the ground with deceleration 0:5 m/sec^2 until it stops. After 1 sec another ball is thrown in the air from the same start point with the intention to hit the first ball while it is still rolling. Write a PROLOG program that describes this problem. Use it to compute the initial speed vector of the second ball provided that V_b = 5 m/sec and the second ball hits the first one at 10 m from the start point. Discuss what other possible uses of your program are.
5. Write a program that can solve following cryptarithmetic (secret arithmetic) puzzle,

```
  DONALD
+ GERALD
  ------
  ROBERT
```

where it is known that $D = 5$. The goal is to figure out the arithmetic values of the other letters in the range 0 to 9.

Applications of Artifical Intelligence

12.1 INTRODUCTION

In this chapter, we will consider some of the current applications of artificial intelligence in fields like e-commerce, tourism, medicine and industry.

On the practical applications side, there are an enormous number of them waiting to be exploited in the Indian domestic scene itself. Expert systems, Indian language processing including translation support, scheduling and planning systems, information retrieval systems, and so on have a lot of potential.

12.2 AI IN E-COMMERCE

AI approaches are useful in the development of both B2C and B2B e-commerce systems. Much of the attention in AI for e-commerce has focussed on B2C transactions. In B2C e-commerce, AI is used mainly for product selection and recommendations, negotiations, auctions, solving real-world scheduling problems and enhancing scalability, generating automated responses, and bundling and pricing goods. In B2B e-commerce, AI is used mainly for supply chain management (SCM). Some AI technologies, such as ontologies, are used in both the types. The details are explained in the following sections.

12.2.1 AI in B2C E-Commerce

In this section we present different AI approaches that are useful in B2C e-commerce.

AI in Product Selection and Recommendation

AI is used in advising the users on the items they want to examine or buy through Internet. This advice is helpful in navigating a large range of product descriptions.

There are a number of different types of product selection and recommendation approaches, such as automated collaborative filtering (ACF) approaches, knowledge-based (KB) approaches, and hybrid approaches, etc.

- ***ACF approaches.*** These approaches aggregate data regarding previous consumers' preferences or purchase patterns, and provide recommendations to prospective buyers based on similarity in overall patterns. For example, *GroupLens* system recommends news articles based on similarities between users' reading behaviour. This approach has been used in many other areas such as consumers' products and web pages, etc. and has become a standard marketing technique in e-commerce. Some ACF systems can even provide the reason and data behind a recommendation. A main drawback with ACF is that it is not effective until a large number of users enter their profiles, and a sufficient number of rating items are available in the database.
- ***KB approaches.*** These approaches are based on the product knowledge base. Some of them are explained below:
  - *Case-based reasoning (CBR) approaches:* CBR systems basically accept user preferences, retrieve similar product offered from case base and offer it to the user. The user may modify his preferences if there is no exact match. The above steps are repeated until the user selects a product or quits. The most common technique in e-commerce applications of CBR is *nearest neighbour retrieval*.
  - *Content-based recommendor approaches:* These approaches depend on machine learning-based classification. For example, the news filtering system *NewsDude* suggests news stories that a user might like to read. These systems primarily use *supervised machine learning* to induce a classifier and the classifier is used to discriminate between items likely to be of interest to the user and items that are likely to be uninteresting.
- ***Hybrid approaches.*** Hybrid approaches are primarily a combination of ACF and KB approaches. In some systems, the ACF is used in the post-processing stage and the systems are predominantly knowledge based. Other systems check whether there are a sufficient number of feedbacks from previous users. This number is used as a threshold value to decide on what approach is to be used. If the value is less then a proper KB approach is used, otherwise ACF approaches are used. The threshold value can be determined interactively based on the products and business. Some systems attempted to utilize CBR approaches for ACF
- Apart from the above, there are other approaches such as interviewing the user to determine pairwise relative feature importance, forming user models depending on observations of user decisions, either in response to system suggestions (candidate/revision or learn-on-failure) or through passive observations, and learning customer preferences by observing customers' selections from return sets.

AI in Online Negotiation

In e-commerce, negotiation is a process where the buyer and the seller bargain resources, using tools and techniques of e-commerce, for an intended benefit. Negotiation can be categorized as either *adaptive* or *non-adaptive*. It can also be categorized as *cooperative* or *competitive*. Negotiation techniques in e-commerce are primarily of the competitive type. CBR approaches are extensively used for negotiation. Some important characteristics/methods to represent a CBR-based negotiation process are: active or passive agent method, modifications of demands or modifications to demands and the item, and single or multiple dimension modification method. Other CBR based approaches utilize *agent technologies*. In these approaches, negotiation agents use *episode strategies* to incrementally modify offer or counter-offer parts toward an agreement. There are other approaches for negotiation and are based on *Bayesian learning*. Bayesian learning is used to learn negotiation strategy. All the above approaches are of the adaptive type.

AI in Online Auctions

Today, there are around 200 online auction sites on the Internet. Most of the online auctions are *common-value auctions*. For example, auctions for cars or computers. Configurable agent techniques are used to represent users in online auctions, specifically in the *Michigan AuctionBot*. The agents can be configured, initiated, and monitored from an online interface.

It is a difficult task for users to work with multiple auction sites simultaneously, and one can bid for an optimal price if he can predicts the market value of the product. AI approaches are used for this prediction purposes. These approaches are based on agent technologies. They incorporate a number of bidder agents and a master agent to coordinate them. Different bidder agents are assigned to different auction sites. The agents simultaneously monitor prices of an item in several auction sites and cooperate among themselves, with the help of the master agent, to arrive at an estimated value of the required item.

AI in Solving Real-world Problems and in Enhancing Scalability

E-commerce systems should be able to solve realistic problems. For example, in a travel domain, searching the flights with restrictions such as fare, schedule, safety, and break-journeys, etc. is important in selecting the most convenient flight(s). Planning, scheduling, and optimization approaches are generally used for solving these kinds of problems.

E-commerce servers should also be scalable, so that they can be accessed by a large number of customers simultaneously. *Smart client* techniques are used for this purpose. Smart clients are based on constraint satisfaction methods and provide solutions for catalogue-type e-commerce systems. They are efficient autonomous problem solvers, and are small enough to be sent over the Internet in a short time. These techniques are also widely used for solving the real-world problems mentioned above.

AI in Generating Automated Responses

Providing automated response to most of the customer queries eliminates the need of skilled persons to answer the queries in organizations. *Classification techniques* are used in developing this type of system.

AI in Automated Bundling and Pricing Goods

If a producer has different goods (either *tangible* or *intangible*) then he can bundle and price them in different ways, such as per article pricing, pure bundling, and mixed bundling, etc. Different satellite television packages with different price listings, available to us in the present day market, are an example of this. Proper pricing and bundling decisions are vital to expand the customer base and also to increase profits. *Decision theoretic* approaches are helpful to the producers in making the bundling decisions. The producer has to introduce a series of bundles over time to maximize his profit and satisfactory performance while modifying the existing bundles. *Product classification hierarchies* are also helpful in arriving at a proper decision.

Apart from all the above, AI techniques are also useful for a number of other B2C e-commerce purposes. Some of them are mentioned here.

- AI is useful in the development of domain independent database browsing tools. The tools are designed for on line information access, particularly for electronic product catalogues. They are based on *preference-based navigation* methods, rather than using traditional *text-based* or *query-based* search techniques.
- AI techniques are also useful for development of *buyer agents*. Most of the e-commerce services are viewed as "sellers" agents because their goal is to push services and/or merchandize onto the users. Buyer agents work for the buyers rather than the sellers. Some key responsibilities of such agents are: informing customers of complex interactions between specified preferences and prevailing market conditions, providing differential analysis for decision support, and use of ontology to help the user formulate queries.

12.2.2 AI in B2B E-commerce

AI techniques are extensively used in supply chain management. An integrated supply chain makes businesses to share real-time information and significantly reduce the inventory carrying costs. This is very important for B2B e-commerce. A number of AI-based SCM problem solving approaches are available. Most of them are agent-based and each agent is responsible for one or more activities of the SCM. Majority of the agent-based approaches treat the problem as a centralized constraint-satisfaction problem. Some of the agent-based approaches model human beings or organizations and are used for simulation purposes. Other systems even utilize agents for sub-contracting. In sub-contracting systems, the supply chain coordination is transformed to virtual supply chain in a multi-agent system through the negotiation process among software agents.

12.2.3 Ontologies in E-commerce

A number of e-commerce systems are developed, configured, and used by different organizations for a variety of business purposes. Standardization of business models, processes, and knowledge structures are vital in achieving the promised *return on investment*. The main obstacle to successful e-commerce is the need of systems that can meaningfully share information. Ontologies are vital in achieving this goal. They fundamentally stand for vocabulary for basic terms and their meanings. The purpose of an ontology is to enable communication between computer systems and/or persons in a way that is independent of the individual system technologies, information architectures and application domain. Ontologies are very important for collaboration, agent-to-agent communication, knowledge management, and for different database systems to interoperate.

12.3 AI IN E-TOURISM

The exponential development of the World Wide Web has changed traditional concepts in many human concepts like business, commerce or tourism. These changes are mainly due to different reasons; the number of users connected to Internet, the vast amount of information stored in it, and especially the easiness that this information is available to the user. Characteristics like electronic-mail and secure information transmission (https, ssl) have opened news research and application fields. Currently it is possible to do (secure) commercial transactions using the web. This section explains how these new technologies should applied to the tourism field.

Nowadays it is possible to find an enormous number of companies that are using the web to exhibit and sell products. In the tourism field, it is possible to find travel agencies (Amadeus, FourAirlines, Halcón Viajes...), transportation, hotel, or car companies that offer different products in the web. In fact, it is possible to find bargain prices only for users that buy through the web. It is possible to consult prices, time tables, buy tickets (flight tickets, train tickets, car and/or hotel reservations, lodging a room, etc...) by the user. Therefore the tourism field has been modified by the electronic transactions that are being made possible through Internet.

However there are serious problems to retrieve, manage, and reuse the information stored in the web. These problems could be summarised as:

- Number of "sites" (web addresses) which offers potential useful information.
- The information served by companies could change along the time.
- Access to the information sources is not always possible.
- Heterogeneous representation for the information (it may be difficult to manage or understood for a user).
- The bargains offered by the companies can be modified over time.

Actually, to solve these problems there are many systems that extract, filter, and represent efficiently the information obtained from the Web. However, most of those systems (Search engines, MetaSearch engines, WebBots, Spiders, etc.) are focussed mainly on the amount of the information to be retrieved on the information representation (Mediators), etc. Unfortunately these systems are not able to solve all afore mentioned problems.

To develop the potential capabilities of the web, it is necessary to find new approaches to allow design and build systems that automatically:

- Search and retrieve useful information.
- Manage and reason with different solutions.
- Adapt to the profile user, to customize the answers.
- Gain efficiency using the learned knowledge by other agents (human or software). It will be necessary for the interaction among these agents.

12.3.1 The Electronic-tourism Domain

It is possible to define the electronic-tourism domain (*E-tourism*) as:

> "Those different electronic resources available for a travel agent (human or software) tha could be used to plan a travel."

An electronic-travel agent must have the ability to manage all the necessary information to schedule the travel user requirements. In this kind of domain, the planning agent needs to represent several towns, transports, lodging places, etc. And the agent needs to know how the user could travel between towns, airports, train stations, rent a car, or book a room in a hotel. Figure 12.1 shows the graphical representation of an example in this domain, where a user might take different transports and hotels to reach his/her desired goal.

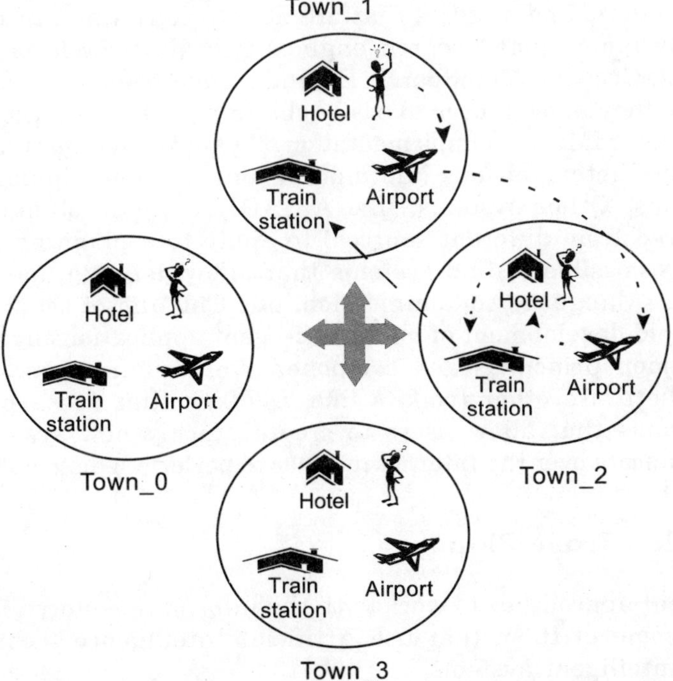

Figure 12.1 Graphical description of the electronic-domain.

The most important points in the management of a travel are:

(a) Moving from the origin to the destination town.
(b) Lodging at destination.
(c) Transport possibility at target town.
(d) Returning to initial (or other) town.

To handle item 1, so far we have considered the airplane, train, or bus as travel transport. Also, the user may need to take a local train, bus, or taxi to move to the airport, train station, or bus station. This means that the agent needs also to decide which local transport to use. This is an important and complex part of the problem because the number of possible solutions grows exponentially. The moving possibility around the target town refers to the possibility of renting a car, or to provide to the user information about public transport (bus, subway).

Another important issue is that there are many different solutions to a given problem and all of them should be ordered according to several parameters. For example, the solutions could be ordered according to cost, amount of time to complete the travel, or user preferences (for example, if a customer decides not to travel by plane).

The travel agent should also be able to reason without all the information, because many times not all the information is accessible, or part of this necessary information fails. That situation should not stop the problem solving task and should try to look for alternative solutions. In the e-tourism domain, the main electronic information sources will be accessible by the web. Therefore, the travel agent needs to manage with the information stored in it.

Some popular approaches used in the web have been the *Web Agents*, especially the *softbots and spiders*, and systems that are able to collect and filter the data that the web offers. Systems named search engines (Google Search Engine) or search meta-engines (MetaCrawler MetaSearch Engine), have been very successful in the last years, because they allow a user to easily obtain useful information from the web.

Another approach, SIMS is an implementation of a kind of systems (named Mediators) that try to integrate heterogeneous information sources to manipulate those data to reach new solutions. Other systems, like ARIADNE, try to obtain heterogeneous knowledge (acquired from different sources) to apply to a planning process.

Nowadays it is possible to find systems that allow defining and proving agents with different skills, language communication, etc. The aim of the *Zeus* project was to facilitate the rapid development of new multi-agent applications by abstracting into a toolkit the common principles and components underlying some existing multi-agent systems. There are other toolkits like *JATLite,* that are a package of Java classes and programs that allow users to create quickly new systems of software agents that communicate over the Internet in order to perform a distributed computation.

12.3.2 Example: TravelPlan

There exist different approaches to work with the information stored in the web. This section analyzes some of them that use Artificial Intelligence techniques to build autonomous and intelligent systems.

Intelligent agents are a new paradigm for developing software applications. Currently, agents are the focus of intense interest on the part of many subfields of computer science and artificial intelligence. The key abstraction used in these systems is the *agent* concept. It is difficult to summarize the main characteristics for an agent because there is no real agreement of exactly what an agent is. However most researchers are in broad agreement with:

- Each agent has an incomplete amount of information or does not have the accurate abilities to solve the whole problem.
- It does not exist a system global control.
- Data are not centralized, so all agents must share data.
- System execution is asynchronous; any agent can be working while it receives queries anytime.
- It is possible to define and use characteristics like agency, autonomy, social behaviour, mobility, adaptability, etc.

An agent-based system may contain any non-zero number of agents. A multi-agent system must contain several agents that could interact among them, and therefore is both more general and significantly more complex than a single-agent system.

Multi-agent Systems (MAS) are a subfield of distributed artificial intelligence that deals with the interaction of groups of intelligent agents attempting to cooperate to solve problems. MAS are successful due to several causes (we only mention more relevant causes):

- They are able to solve big-size problems, especially those where classical systems are not successful.
- They allow different systems to work interconnected and cooperate.
- They provide efficient solutions where information is distributed among different places.
- They allow software reusability, therefore there is more flexibility to adopt different agent capabilities to solve problems.

In Figure 12.2, a graphic representation of a generic MAS is shown. In this representation, there is a set of agents that can communicate and cooperate among them to reach the problem solution.

During the last years, people have developed a set of systems with several agents that try to solve a particular problem. To reach the goal efficiently, they use different techniques such as competition (where the agents fight for the system resources) or cooperation (where the agents cooperate to reach the solution).

TravelPlan is a distributed and cooperative multi-agent approach to problem solving in dynamic environments (for instance, the web), applied to the e-tourism domain. We have decided to use MAS techniques because this type of systems is very flexible and highly adaptive. We use wrapping techniques to add classical planning systems like Prodigy4.0 into a multi-agent system.

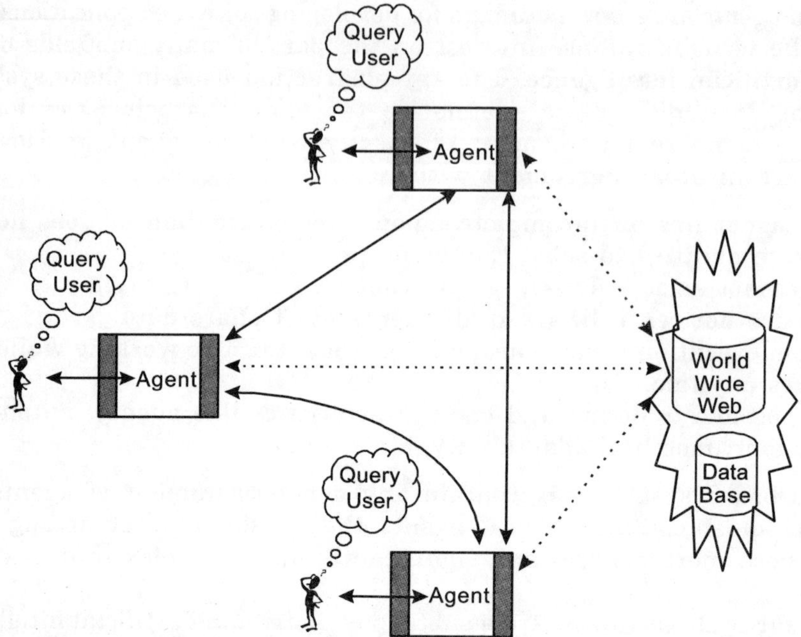

Figure 12.2 General MAS structure.

12.3.3 TravelPlan Architecture

TravelPlan is a MAS approach that integrates different types of agents. It could be summarized as:

- ***UserAgent.*** This agent pays attention to the user's queries and shows the solution. It analyzes the problem and obtains an abstract representation. Subsequently it requests to a PlannerAgent for a solution to that problem. The UserAgent has different skills like communication with PlannerAgents and users, or learning the users profiles necessary to customize the system answer.
- ***PlannerAgent.*** The main goal of Planner Agent is reasoning about UserAgents and other PlannerAgents problems, and find out a set of possible solutions. PlannerAgents have different skills like communication (with different agents in the system), planning (its main reasoning module) and learning (using CBR techniques to index and to categorize each stored plan).
- ***WebBot.*** This agent fills in the details (requested by PlannerAgents) obtaining the required information from Internet. Different partial solutions given by the web agents are combined by the PlannerAgents to obtain a detailed solution (or solutions) to the UserAgent queries.

In Figure 12.3, a graphic representation of TravelPlan is shown. The system is made by a set of agents that can communicate and cooperate among them to reach the problem solution.

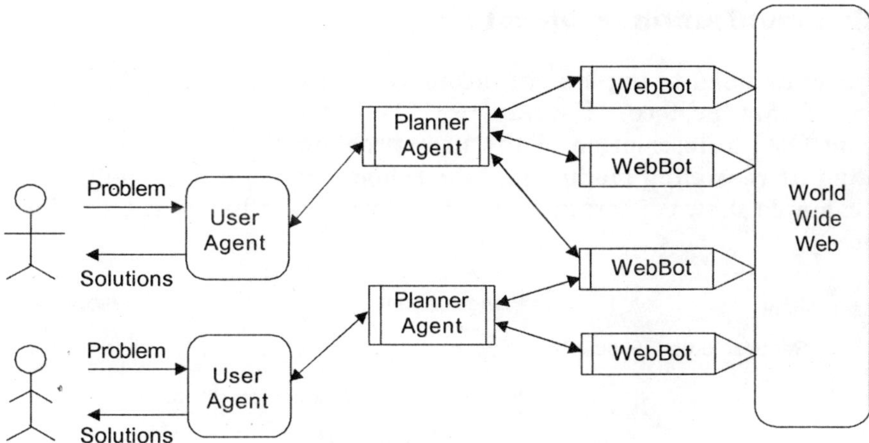

Figure 12.3 TravelPlan general architecture.

TravelPlan has a cooperative architecture where different agents need to cooperate to reach solutions. Different agents need sharing knowledge and skills to complete the abstract solutions obtained by the PlannerAgent. It is possible to obtain a complete solution from other agent system too. TravelPlan success needs both characteristics, sharing knowledge to obtain new solutions (or retrieve old stored solutions) and learning users preferences to find and sort the most useful solutions for him/her. In the next section, a format to sharing knowledge is analyzed.

12.3.4 Shared Information among Agents

Agents in TravelPlan use a common representation for the knowledge. This characteristic allows simplifying the processes of sharing and reasoning with the knowledge. The communication among agents uses *performatives*. Any performative stores an implicit order to other agent. To communicate two system agents a subset of the KQML format is being used. In Figure 12.4 shows the representation for some performatives: request, inform, accept, and reject.

The first performative *request* is sent by a PlannerAgent to a WebBot asking for a travel airplane between (Madrid, Spain) and (Zaragoza, Spain). The second performative *inform* is the request from the WebBot to the PlannerAgent. The performatives *accept* and *reject* are used to make the cooperation and negotiation among agents possible.

Using the communication protocol, the PlannerAgent completes the semi-complete solutions obtained from the user definition problem and from the abstract solutions given by the planner. Next section shows how this protocol works between two system agents.

12.3.5 Communication Protocol

TravelPlan agents need to implement a communication language. Figure 12.4 shows an example of that protocol. UserAgent (UA) initiates the process, sending to a PlannerAgent (PA) a description of the user problem. The PlannerAgent solves the problem using its reasoning module and the cooperation of other agents like WebBots (WB). The example shows different types of performatives like request, inform, accept, and inform.

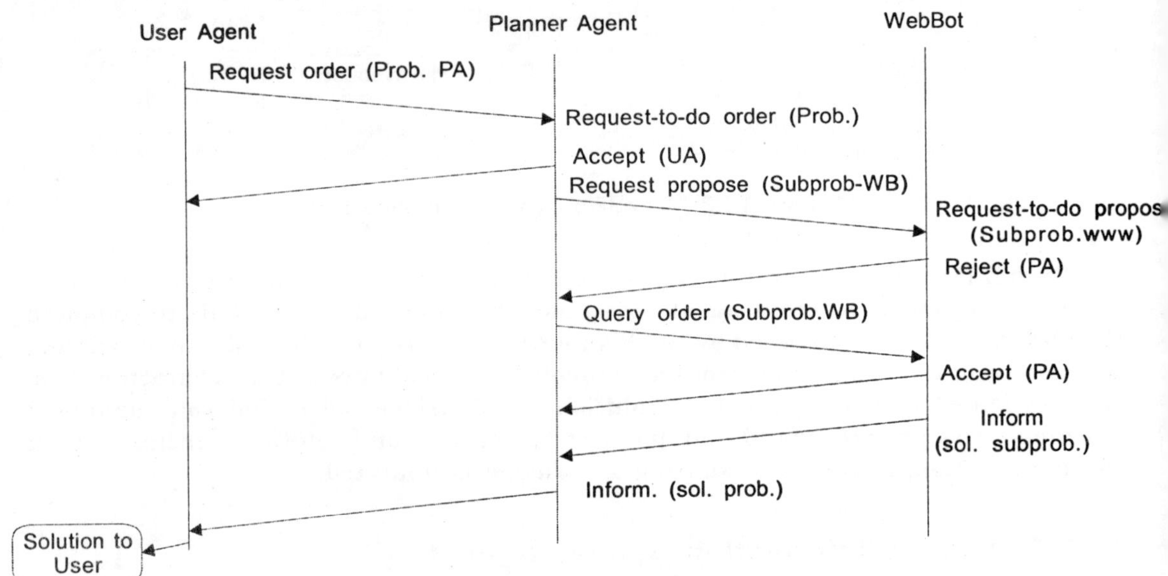

Figure 12.4 Example of communication protocol in TravelPlan.

In the communication process each agent acknowledges the messages (sent by any other agent) generating the performative accept(agent). When processed, they send an answer message to the sender agent, and the task starts. If the agent is not ready to perform the task, it generates the performative reject (agent). When processed, it sends a message to the agent. When a request performative is sent it may generate different types of *act* (actions performed by the agent). Using request.order(prob, agent) the sender *orders* the execution of a task (without negotiation). However if an agent sends a request.propose(prob, agent) it is possible to have the negotiation by the receiver agent.

In Figure 12.4, the PlannerAgent sends a proposal for cooperation to the WebBot, and this agent rejects the request. When the PlannerAgent really needs the information sends a new request.order to finally obtain the desired information. When the WebBot information has been processed, the PlannerAgent can complete the solution and send to the UserAgent that will finally show it to the user.

TravelPlan like other MAS uses a set of graphical user interfaces (GUI) to communicate with the users.

The UserAgent has different user interfaces to communicate with the user. The first interface is used to input the problem from the user, and the second one is optional and it is used to define the user preferences. The user profile is stored by the UserAgent, analyzes the problem and connects to a PlannerAgent to ask for a solution (or solutions). When the system solves the problem example, the PlannerAgent returns sample solutions to the user, from maximum possible solutions, and the UserAgent shows these solutions to the user. The system rejects a set of possible solutions in order to gain in efficiency, and only a subset of solutions is shown to the user. TravelPlan recommends a particular solution if this solution matches with the learned preference from the user (if any learned profile exists). To do this, the UserAgent that pays attention to the users, extracts the main characteristics from the old stored solutions by the user, and uses them to classify all the possible solutions. Using the user profile and the different solutions found by the systems, a subset of solutions is shown to the user.

12.4 AI IN INDUSTRY

Apart from neural networks, there are several other AI techniques that have gained popularity not only in research but also in industrial applications. Fuzzy logic is one technique that can be considered as successful in terms of industrial applications.

Zadeh proposed a methodology to deal with imprecision which he called fuzzy sets. Fuzzy sets overcome the problems of crisp sets, where instead of only "true" or "false", "yes" or "no", "1" or "0", a membership of degree from "0 to 1" can be assigned to a set. Fuzzy logic has been successfully applied in pattern recognition, decision-support systems and control. The choice of using fuzzy logic in control is the possibility of developing a controller along linguistic lines. In fuzzy logic applications, linguistic rules are developed such that based on current conditions the next set of actions can be formulated.

One of the most recent developments in AI is genetic algorithms (GA). GA is a form of search and optimization technique. GA has been developed by Prof. J. Holland and his colleagues at the University of Michigan in the mid-60s. The basic inspiration in the formulation of GAs is the observation of the evolution mechanisms of natural system which have worked so well. The important features of self-repair, self-guidance and reproduction which exist in biological systems have been adopted in the formulation of GAs. Figure 12.5 shows the basic GA operators and cycle. With these criteria plus a unique set of search techniques make GAs a robust search and optimization technique.

The set of search techniques which GAs adopted differs from other optimization techniques such as hill climbing, calculus-based, enumerative or random in the following category:

- GAs work with a coding of parameters.
- GAs search from a population of points and not from a single point.
- GAs use objective function information and not the derivative or other auxiliary knowledge.
- GAs use probabilistic transition rules and not deterministic rules.

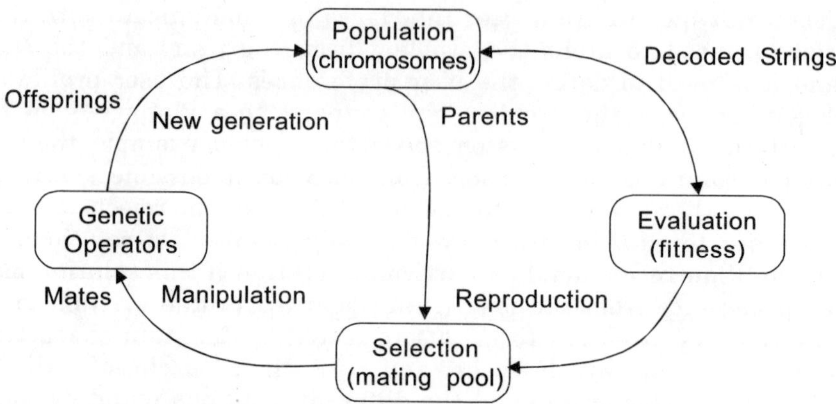

Figure 12.5 The GA operators and cycle.

There have been many successful applications of GAs such as in wire-routing, VLSI design, game playing, face recognition, etc.

There has been a growing trend of combining several AI techniques to develop a more powerful tool. One example is the fusion of the fuzzy logic technique and neural networks which leads to the popular label of *neuro-fuzzy systems*. This is due to the fact that the fuzzy technique is structured in nature which is an advantage for humans to develop rules along linguistic lines, however, it has no learning capability. Neural networks, on the other hand, has got an inherent learning capability but not structured. The fusion of these two techniques have created a new area of research in AI. Several combinations of different neural network paradigms with fuzzy logic have been proposed. For example, the radial basis function (RBF) neural network is implemented as a neuro-fuzzy controller (NFC) and the general regression neural network (GRNN) is used as a predictor in an adaptive neuro-fuzzy control system configuration as shown in figure 12.6. The technique can provide automatic tuning of the NFC based on an online prediction model of the plant realized by the GRNN.

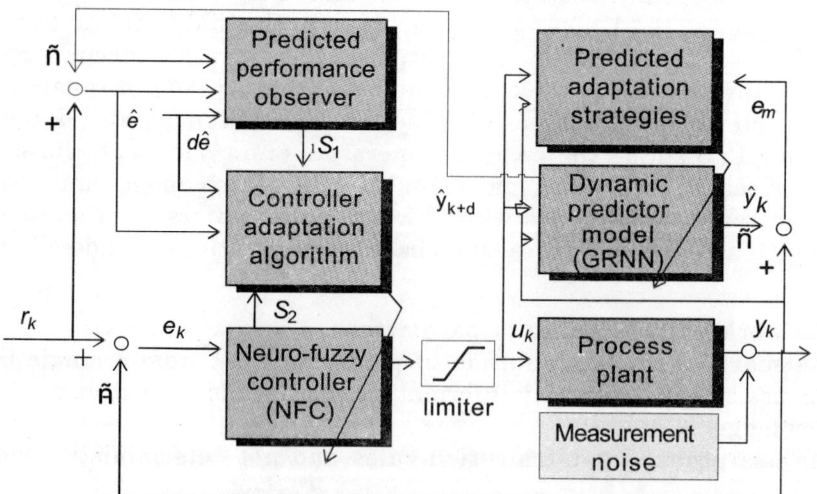

Figure 12.6 A block diagram of the adaptive neuro-fuzzy control system.

Using this architecture, the adaptive system is able to respond quickly to changes in the set-points. This proposed integrated adaptive system is robust even when there is an occurrence of a significant change in the plant dynamics when compared to a generalized predictive controller.

Taking both the qualitative and quantitative advantages of the NFC which can be related to the availability of human domain knowledge as discussed, only the consequent of the control rules are adapted in this approach. Still more, if a rough set of control actions is initially available, it can also be incorporated into the control system which is then further fine-tuned automatically. Besides continuous adaptation, the methodology can also be viewed as a self-organizing algorithm, due to the fact that the system is able to learn the necessary control knowledge without any readily defined control actions during the initial stage.

In general, the methodology is inspired by the basic idea of how a technician or an operator with minimum control knowledge will tune the control actions of the controller, which is mainly based on his or her observation of the system response. The adaptation of the system involves three procedures as follows: (1) tuning of the control actions or rules (2) trimming of the control actions, and (3) adjustment of the controller output gain. The tuning method is a non-gradient descent method based on the predicted system response, which is able to self-organize the control actions from initial stage. The trimming scheme can help to reduce the aggressiveness of the particular control rules in order to stabilize the response to the set-point more effectively. The controller gain adjustment scheme can be applied if the appropriate controller output gain is difficult to be determined heuristically.

There have also been efforts in the fusion of fuzzy technique and expert systems which lead to the paradigm referred to as fuzzy-expert systems. However, fuzzy-expert systems have not been as successful as neuro-fuzzy systems. There have also been some developments in the fusion of the fuzzy technique and GA, however, this has not been popular.

Due to the combination of several AI techniques to form a hybrid system, there are bound to be some advantages and disadvantages.

12.4.1 Industrial Applications of AI

Among the first successful applications of AI in industry were in the areas of symbolic machine learning or expert systems applications which started in the late 60s and early 70s. Though research in neural networks has started much earlier, real-world application of such techniques are rather stifled due to their iterative nature that needs powerful hardware which were non-existence at that time. Two examples of early applications of expert systems are MYCIN for the diagnosis of infectious blood diseases developed by Stanford University in 1972 and CADACEUS for the diagnosis of human internal diseases by University of Pittsburgh in 1970. The first commercial application of expert system is XCON which was used for the configuration of VAX Computer Systems by DEC in 1980.

The advent of microprocessors spurred the interest of many industries in Japan to apply the fuzzy logic technology into many consumer products. Coupled with their

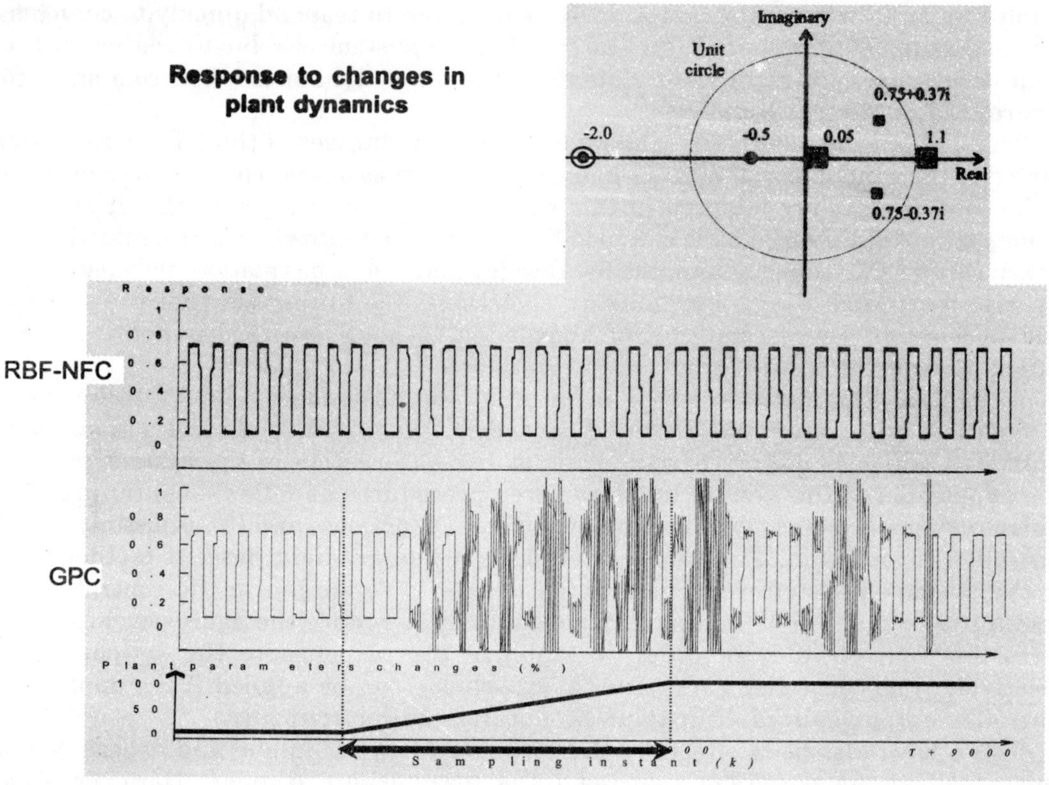

Figure 12.7 Comparison of the adaptive neuro-fuzzy (RBF-NFC) controller based on the RBF neural networks to a generalized predictive controller with respect to changes in plant dynamics.

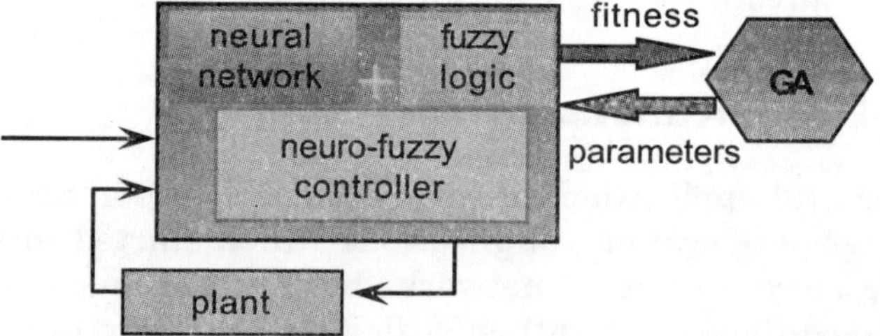

Figure 12.8 A block diagram of a neuro-fuzzy-GA technique. GA is used to optimize the parameters of the RBF-based neuro-fuzzy controller.

strong capability of developing sensor technologies and electronics, the Japanese manufacturers have a distinct advantage over other manufacturers around the world. When Matsushita first developed the fuzzy logic washing machine referred to as "Aisai Go (Beloved Wife) Day Fuzzy" in 1989, sales were so successful that this prompted many other Japanese industries to apply the fuzzy logic technology into their products. Today, it would be difficult to find a consumer product that does not employ the fuzzy logic technology.

In the mid-90s, the neural network technology was also used in the many consumer products together with the already successful fuzzy technology. Much of the applications of these neuro-fuzzy technologies in consumer products are at the design stage where the controllers are designed and embedded into the systems. Figure 12.9 shows a block diagram of an intelligent system design which consists of four main components: intelligent man-machine interface, perception, cognition, and execution.

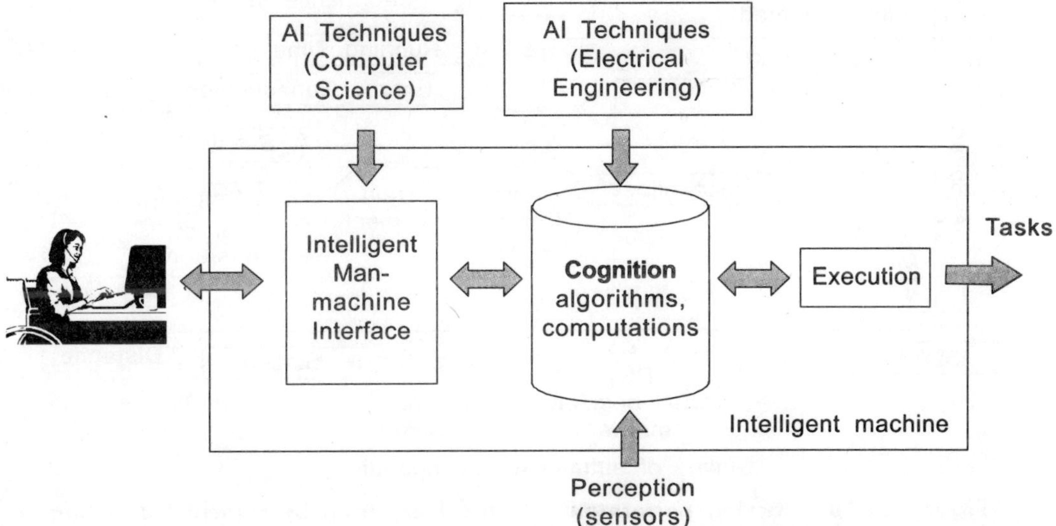

Figure 12.9 A block diagram showing the main components of an intelligent system which are intelligent man-machine interface, perception, cognition and execution.

Research in AI involves a number of disciplines such as neuro science, biological science, psychology, philosophy, physics, mathematics, and computer science, however, its applications largely fall into two major disciplines: computer science and electrical engineering. In intelligent system or machine design, it can be observed that in the realm of computer science, a large part of the research and developments (R&D) are focussed in the intelligent man-machine interface component. Some examples of R&D in this area are natural language processing, expert systems, man-machine interface, data mining, text mining, etc. In the realm of electrical engineering, efforts in R&D are mainly concentrated in designing the cognition component of the intelligent machine. For example in the design of consumer products, a variety of AI techniques have been used in designing the embedded controller, such as those of washing machines, rice cookers, refrigerators, camcorders, etc.

Other than consumer products, AI technology has also been applied into many industrial systems. At Hitachi Ltd. Japan, fuzzy logic train control was first started as early as 1978. After 3,00,000 simulations and 3,000 empty runs, they were granted permission to operate in 1986.

Figure 12.10 shows the tracking profile of the fuzzy train with 6 performance indices that are considered by the fuzzy controller to improve model performance which are: running time, energy consumption, traceability, safety and comfort. Hitachi shows that the fuzzy train can improve stop permission by 3 times, reduced power setting by 2 times and reduced power consumption by 10% compared to the PID controller. The success of the fuzzy train spurs more applications of AI in industry.

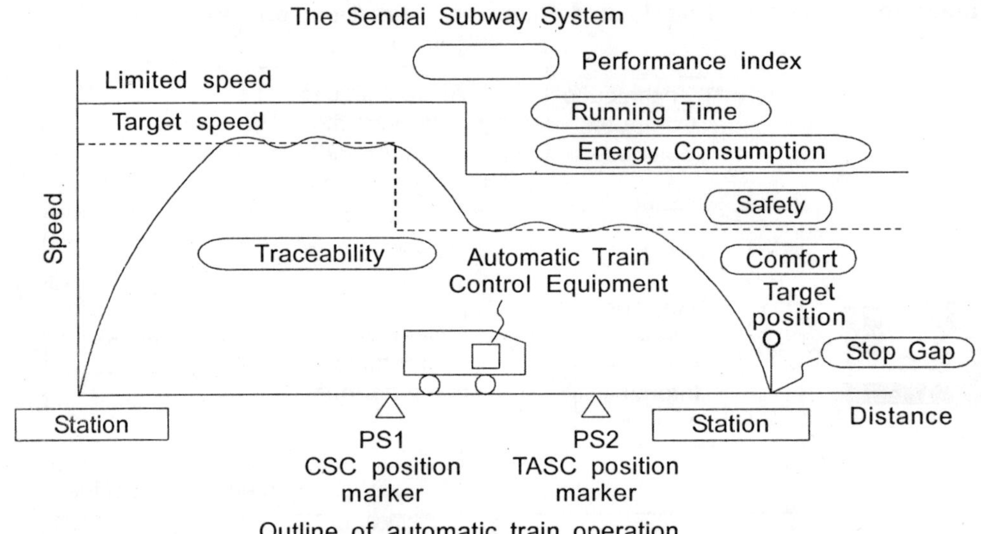

Figure 12.10 Tracking performance of the fuzzy train by Hitachi Ltd. Japan.

Based on the error backpropagation neural network algorithm and fuzzy logic, Pavilion Technologies Inc., an American company, developed a software for process modelling and optimization called *Process Insights*. The software can be used to read large amount of steady-state process data from the historian and neural network is used to model the plant which is done offline. Fuzzy logic is used to handle fuzzy constraints during the online stage for control purposes. Savings of more than one million US dollars annually by many industries through optimization have been reported by Pavillion Inc. using the Process Insights software. Figure 12.11 shows the diagrammatic view of the process insight software.

Recently, many industries in Japan have been concentrating on research in humanoids or humanlike robots. Industries like Honda, Mitsubishi, Sony, Fujitsu, NEC, NTT, Panasonic, etc. have begun developments of humanoids with the intention to use them as domestic helpers as well as entertainment. The main technological breakthroughs in these humanoids are their enhanced walking ability, improved speech and image recognition, and improvement in motors and actuators. ASIMO (Advanced Step in Innovative Mobility) which was developed by Honda (see Figure 12.12) shows significant walking ability that allows the humanoid to even walking up and down stairs. However, their physical ability is still no match compared to a 5-year-old human. The Japanese government has pledged 50 billion yen ($400 million)

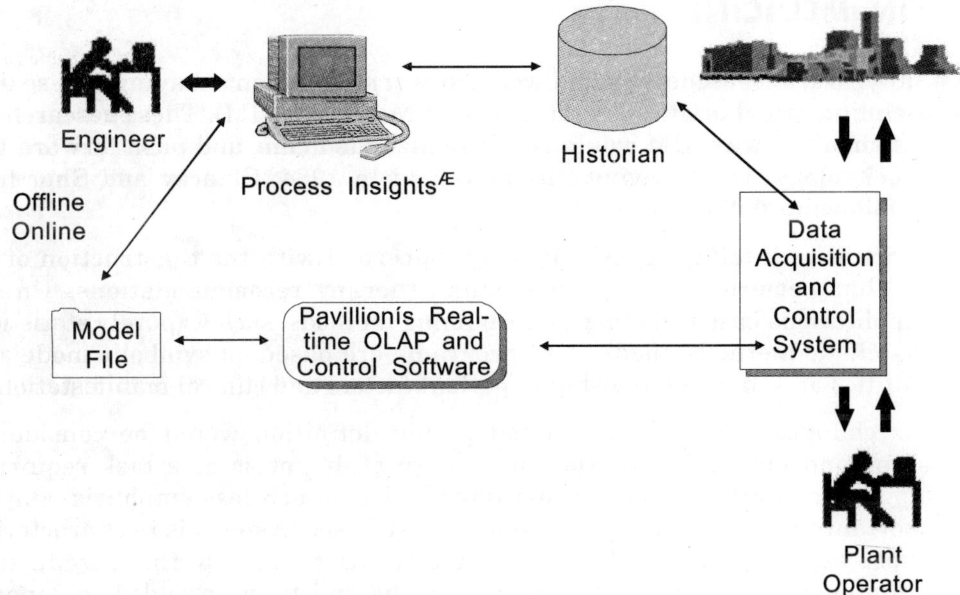

Figure 12.11 Pavilion Technologies Inc. software Process Insights which first modelled a process offline and then used for control purposes online.

Figure 12.12 The new ASIMO moves in respond to a human gesture.

a year over three decades to develop a humanoid robot with the mental, physical and emotional capacity of a 5-year old human which is known as the "Atom" project. Researchers believe the Atom Project, inspired by the popular robot animation series "Tetsuwan Atom" by the late cartoonist Osamu Tezuka, would help promote scientific and technological advances in Japan, just like the US Apollo Project, which not only succeeded in landing men on the moon but contributed to a broad range of technological breakthroughs.

12.5 AI IN MEDICINE

In the last 30 years, researchers of the western world set about shaping a research for a new discipline called artificial intelligence in Medicine (AIM). These researchers had a bold vision of the way AIM would revolutionize medicine, and push forward the frontiers of technology. In reviewing this new field in 1984, Clancey and Shortliffe provided the following definition:

> "Medical artificial intelligence is primarily concerned with the construction of AI programs that perform diagnosis and make therapy recommendations. Unlike medical applications based on other programming methods, such as purely statistical and probabilistic methods, medical AI programs are based on symbolic models of disease entities and their relationship to patient factors and clinical manifestations."

Much has changed since then, and today this definition would be considered narrow in scope and vision. Today, the importance of diagnosis as a task requiring computer support in routine clinical situations receives much less emphasis. One of the most important tasks now facing developers of AI-based systems is to characterize accurately those aspects of medical practice that are best suited to the introduction of artificial intelligence systems. AIM systems are by and large intended to support healthcare workers in the normal course of their duties, assisting with tasks that rely on the manipulation of data and knowledge. An AI system could be running within an electronic medical record system, for example, and alert a clinician when it detects a contraindication to a planned treatment. It could also alert the clinician when it detected patterns in clinical data that suggested significant changes in a patient's condition.

Expert or knowledge-based systems are the commonest type of AIM system in routine clinical use. They contain medical knowledge, usually about a very specifically defined task, and are able to reason with data from individual patients to come up with reasoned conclusions. Although there are many variations, the knowledge within an expert system is typically represented in the form of a set of rules.

There are many different types of clinical task to which expert systems can be applied.

- ***Generating alerts and reminders.*** In so-called real-time situations, an expert system attached to a monitor can warn of changes in a patient's condition. In less acute circumstances, it might scan laboratory test results or drug orders and send reminders or warnings through an e-mail system.
- ***Diagnostic assistance.*** When a patient's case is complex, rare or the person making the diagnosis is simply inexperienced, an expert system can help come up with likely diagnoses based on patient data.
- ***Therapy critiquing and planning.*** Systems can either look for inconsistencies, errors and omissions in an existing treatment plan, or can be used to formulate a treatment based upon a patient's specific condition and accepted treatment guidelines.
- ***Agents for information retrieval.*** Software agents can be sent to search for and retrieve information, for example on the Internet that is considered

relevant to a particular problem. The agent contains knowledge about its user's preferences and needs, and may also need to have medical knowledge to be able to assess the importance and utility of what it finds.

- ***Image recognition and interpretation.*** Many medical images can now be automatically interpreted, from plane X-rays through to more complex images like angiograms, CT and MRI scans. This is of value in mass-screenings, for example, when the system can flag potentially abnormal images for detailed human attention.

Machine learning has a potential role to play in the development of clinical guidelines. It is often the case that there are several alternate treatments for a given condition, with slightly different outcomes. Machine learning systems can be used to develop the knowledge bases used by expert systems. Given a set of clinical cases that act as examples, a machine learning system can produce a systematic description of those clinical features that uniquely characterize the clinical conditions. This knowledge can be expressed in the form of simple rules, or often as a decision tree. A classic example of this type of system is KARDIO, which was developed to interpret ECGs.

12.5.1 Example: HELP System

HELP is a complete knowledge-based hospital information system. It was developed by Department of Medical Informatics at University of Utah, USA. It supports not only the routine applications of an HIS including ADT, order entry/charge capture, pharmacy, radiology, nursing documentation, ICU monitoring, but also supports a robust decision support function. The decision support system has been actively incorporated into the functions of the routine HIS applications. Decision support has been used to provide alerts/reminders, data interpretation, patient diagnosis, patient management suggestions and clinical protocols. Activation of the decision support is provided interactively within the applications and asynchronously through data and time drive mechanisms. The data driven activations are instantiated as clinical data are stored in the patient's computerized medical record. Time driven activation of medical logic is triggered at defined time periods. The HELP system supports an integrated database structure which facilitates the decision support functions of HELP. The database structure also lends itself to design of application independent patient reports.

EXERCISES

1. Describe what artificial intelligence means.
2. Explain the two fundamental approaches to artificial intelligence.
3. Illustrate several hard problems that artificial intelligene research has not yet been able to solve.
4. Describe several practical applications of artificial intelligence.

5. The modern economy includes a variety of markets, and the Internet has opened opportunities for efficient online trading. Researchers have developed algorithms for various auctions, which have become a popular means of online sales. They have also designed algorithms for exchange markets, which support fast-paced trading of standardized goods. On the other hand, there is a little work done on exchanges for complex non-standard goods, such as used cars. Can you suggest a proper model for trading complex goods? Further can you present an exchange system that allows traders to describe desirable purchases and sales by multiple attributes? For example, a car buyer can specify a model, options, colour, and other properties of a desirable vehicle. Furthermore, a trader can enter complex constraints on the acceptable items; for instance, a buyer can specify a set of desirable vehicles and their features. Your system should support markets with up to 1,00,000 orders, and generates hundreds of trades per second.
6. The goal of a clinical trial is to evaluate a new treatment procedure. When medical researchers conduct a trial, they recruit participants with appropriate medical histories. To select participants, the researchers analyze medical records of the available patients, which has traditionally been a manual procedure. Can you develop an intelligent agent that helps to select patients for clinical trials? If the available data are insufficient for choosing patients, the agent should propose additional medical tests and suggest an ordering of the tests that reduces their total cost.
7. Forgetting is one aspect of human memory. How could this be modelled in a case-based reasoning system? Under what circumstances might this be beneficial?
8. Scan through some recent AI journal articles and select a survey of a given topic (e.g. some expert system, NLP, vision, planning, robotic etc.). Then
   (a) analyze what basic AI processes are involved.
   (b) determine to which application domains they can be employed in.
   (c) determine the current state of understanding of the topic.
   (d) compare the current state of understanding to normal human abilities.
9. Symbolic differentiation: AI application area is symbolic mathematics, especially calculus. Here, you have to create a function derive which differentiates simple, single-variable mathematical expressions. The function takes two arguments. The first is a mathematical expression in standard LISP syntax, containing numbers, atoms (representing constants and variables) and the binary functions +, –, f, *, /, expt. The second is the name of the variable with respect to which to differentiate. Other symbols in the expression are treated as constants. The rules of differentiation are as follows (where u and v are arbitrary expressions):

   u = constant implies $du/dx = 0$
   $dx/dx = 1$
   $d(u+v)/dx = du/dx + dv/dx$; $d(u-v)/dx = du/dx - dv/dx$
   $d(uv)/dx = udv/dx + vdu/dx - udv/dx)/v^2$

$d(u/v)/dx = (vdu/dx - udv/dx)/v^2$

v = constant implies $d(u^V)/dx = (du/dx)vu^{(v-1)}$

$d(e^u)/dx = (du/dx)e^u$

(Test your function on some interesting inputs. Add more rules (e.g. for trig functions) if you wish. Further, you can write a simplifier to reduce the resulting expressions to their simplest form. For example, $0 * u$ simplifies to 0 and so on.

10. Computer systems are rapidly becoming complex that maintaining them with human support personnel will be extremely expensive and inefficient. Nowadays, researchers have begun proposing that computer systems be imbued with the ability to configure themselves, diagnose failures, and ultimately repair themselves in response to these failures. However, despite convincing arguments that such a shift would be desirable, as of yet there has been little concrete progress made towards this goal. Let us consider these problems as fundamentally machine learning challenges. Can you explore these problems and come up with a network simulator design to study the application of machine learning methods from a system-wide perspective. You may consider learning-based methods for addressing the problems of job routing and scheduling in the networks you simulate.

APPENDIX A

Projects

PROJECT 1—A RULE INTERPRETER

Write a program that will take a set of Situation-Action rules and execute them. This is a simple, general-purpose (inference-making) problem-solving system. The actions in the rules can include frame manipulations for project 4, but do not need to do so for project 1. Each rule should be of the form *Situation recognized leads to Action executed causing change in situation* or Situation-Action for short. A rule executor, or inference engine, (IE) acting on a set of rules, will incrementally transform a description of some initial situation into a description of some terminal situation, by using one rule at a time. Each rule makes a small change in the situation.

For the demonstration of the system, use a simple working memory consisting of a list, or record, of attributes and values.

PROJECT 2—A FRAME SYSTEM

Write a set of routines that will build and access frame representations of knowledge. The if-needed and if-added triggers can start up a set of rules. This is a simple, general-purpose way of representing knowledge, with the addition of a limited inference capability. You should demonstrate that your frame functions work by using some appropriate example or examples.

PROJECT 3—AN ATN INTERPRETER

Write a program that will accept restricted natural language input and parse it according to a grammar expressed as a augmented recursive transition network. Actions embedded in the network can include actions on frames. This can act as a simple natural language interface. The interpreter must be independent of the actual grammar and dictionary used. It would be ideal if both of those can be input from files. Sentences are input from the user directly or via a file.

PROJECT 4—AN INTELLIGENT SYSTEM

Use the tools you have developed in projects 1–3 to build a system that does some intelligent task. The task and the domain is up to the developer. You may consult your instructor and prepare project proposal. The input must include natural language facts, commands or questions. The rules could use the frames as the working memory. The frames could use the rules as attached actions. Tasks might include diagnosis, design, advice, interpretation, planning, etc.

PROJECT 5—THE COMMUNICATING BLOCKS WORLD AGENT

The goal of this project is to develop a knowledge-based planning system which is acting in a world consisting of several objects ("Blocks") with certain known descriptive features (shape, size, colour). The agent is supposed to perform actions in this world like moving objects or give information about the state of the world, e.g. "The big blue block is on top of the large red block."—triggered by a Natural Language input of the user ("Put the blue block on top of the red block!" or "Where is the blue block?"). The system could be based upon a visual representation of the scene, to recognize objects and their positions (in space and relative to each other).

An extended scenario would involve more objects in the agent's world and also include tasks the agent is doing on its own, e.g. getting energy supply, pre-scheduled or after a certain time has elapsed.

The agent performs actions in a kind of blocks world upon user's request. But it could also have its own desires. So, agent might hold up user's requests till it complete its own needs. For example, The user asks the system to move certain blocks (complex task like building a pyramid). The system estimates that this task takes half an hour. But it is hungry. So, it says "I have to eat first. I'm hungry". Thus, it goes to the food supply first, and eats. Then, it picks up the user's request and performs the task.

PROJECT 6—IMPLEMENT A PLAYER AGENT FOR AN EMPIRE BUILDER GAME

A rail-building board game that can be played by 2–6 players (ages 12 to adult). Players take turns paying money to "build track" (draw edges connecting nodes on a map of India) Moving along this track. Each player starts with a certain amount of money. Spends money to build track. Receives money for delivering goods from cities that produce them to cities that want them. First player reaches the specific money limit is winner.

PROJECT 7—IMPLEMENT A GENERIC UNINFORMED SEARCH FUNCTION TO SOLVE THE RUSH HOUR PUZZLE

Rush Hour is a game that consists of a 6×6 grid and a set of 1×2 and 1×3 vehicles positioned on the grid. The goal is to move a designated vehicle out of traffic and off the board. The goal vehicle always starts somewhere in the 3rd row (i.e. $x = 2$ in a 0-based array), and must move off the board to the right. A vehicle can only move along its axis of orientation (i.e. the goal vehicle and other horizontally aligned vehicles can only move left or right, and vertically aligned vehicles can only move up or down). In order to move a vehicle, the position it is moving into must be empty.

PROJECT 8—TEXT CATEGORIZATION

We have been hired to create a program to scan headlines and first paragraphs of online news articles and pick out those that fit a particular topic. Our client runs a web page for a preschool, and wants to post links to articles relevant to parents of preschoolers.

We will use a Naive Bayes model, where individual words or phrases are evidence of category. In a naive model, the different words or phrases are assumed to be independent of each other. Your model will have 20 evidence nodes (for 20 different words or phrases), and two category nodes: relevant and not relevant. You might be able to get away with only one category node, though.

(a) Design a set of 20 words or phrases that will be used as evidence. Relevant articles will be about parenting, child-rearing, preschooling, and so forth. Bear in mind that some words or phrases might be negative evidence: the word "gourmet" may reduce the likelihood of the article being relevant.
(b) For each word, determine a value for the *P(word | category)* term needed to compute the ultimate probability. How you do this is up to you, either make up reasonable numbers, or get a better system (and a better grade) by sampling from articles somehow.
(c) Implement a program that reads in headlines and first paragraphs from news stories and reports on the probability that the article is relevant, using the naive Bayes model designed in the previous steps. Any word not in the set of 20 should be ignored. Repetitions of a word from the set of 20 may be taken into account.

Write a report that gives your design of the naive Bayes model, how you developed your probability values, how your program works, and how well it works on some sample data.

PROJECT 9—IMPLEMENT A TIC-TAC-TOE PLAYING AGENT

It uses the minimax algorithm to decide what move to make at each point in the game. Your program should cut off the search in such a way that it never takes more than 3–4 seconds to finish its search, using a reasonable heuristic for states that do not represent the end of a game. Your program should never lose. It should take a win when one is available.

PROJECT 10—ATTRIBUTION OF INTELLIGENCE

The aim of this project would be to explore some of the factors that affect our attribution of intelligence to programs. Clearly humans have a sophisticated ability to talk about their own mental states, and to understand the perspectives of other people. The idea of this project is to see whether an ELIZA like program that is able to discuss and answer questions about its own mental states, will be more likely to be rated as exhibiting intelligence than one which does not have such an ability. The aim here is not to create intelligence, but to identify and make use of some of the things that predispose humans to think that something is intelligent. As stated earlier the details of the project are open-ended, and could be altered depending on your contribution and interests.

PROJECT 11—NEURAL NETWORKS

Instead of training a single neural net on a task, it is often found that better results can be obtained when the task is solved by means of a combination of nets, or a multinet system. A task can be simplified by splitting it up into a number of smaller problems. After subdividing the task, neural nets can be trained on each subtask, and then their outputs recombined to form a solution to the entire task. The performance on such subtasks is likely to be better, since they are now each required to solve a simpler task. However, in order to provide a solution to the entire task, the outputs from these modular components need to be put back together in some way. Although there is a growing literature that shows the benefits of such modularization of neural nets, there has not been much research on the relative advantages and disadvantages of different methods of recombining or controlling the operation of such modular components. The starting point for the proposed research is the idea of identifying different methods of combining modular components, and of comparing their effectiveness for different datasets, and different decompositions.

PROJECT 12—WEB DESIGN

The aim would be to conduct experimental investigations to explore an aspect of web design. Having identified some feature of good web design, a student would conduct experimental studies with human users with the aim of establishing whether or not that feature did make a web site better (e.g. that users could find information more quickly, that they remembered the contents of the web site better, that they preferred web sites constructed with that feature etc). Although the project could be modified in the light of a reader's own interests, a starting suggestion would be to investigate the extent to which mode of presentation interacts with the material being presented. Given texts of varying length and detail, what are the effects (in terms of ease and speed of reading and recall) of different methods of presenting those texts, and how do these effects interact with the task given to the readers of the text. An underlying idea here is an exploration of the differences between reading a regular newspaper, and skimming the same articles in an online version: is it demonstrably easier to skim a text and identify its main points when it is presented on a web page than when it is presented in hardcopy form? The project could be directed towards distance learning: given specific material that students need to learn, are there some demonstrable advantages to presenting it on the web, where scrolling and skimming are perhaps easier?

APPENDIX B

PROLOG

Logic programming is characterized by programming with relations and inference. A logic program consists of a set of axioms and a goal statement. The rules of inference are applied to determine whether the axioms are sufficient to ensure the truth of the goal statement. The execution of a logic program corresponds to the construction of a proof of the goal statement from the axioms.

In the logic programming model the programmer is responsible for specifying the basic logical relationships and does not specify the manner in which the inference rules are applied. Thus

$$\text{Logic} + \text{Control} = \text{Algorithms}$$

Logic programming is based on tuples. Predicates are abstractions and generalization of the data type of tuples. Recall, a tuple is an element of

$$S0 \times S1 \times ... \times Sn$$

The squaring function for natural numbers may be written as a set of tuples as follows:

$$\{(0,0), (1, 1), (2, 4), ...\}$$

Such a set of tuples is called a *relation* and in this case the tuples define the squaring relation.

$$sqr = \{(0, 0), (1, 1), (2, 4), ...\}$$

Abstracting to the name sqr and generalizing an individual tuple we can define the squaring relation as:

$$sqr = (x, x2)$$

In the logic programming language PROLOG this would be written as:

sqr(X, Y) ← Y is } X*X.

Note that the set of tuples is named sqr and the parameters are X and Y. PROLOG does note valuate its arguments unless required, so the expression Y is X*X forces the evaluation of X*X and unifies the answer with Y. The PROLOG code

$$P \leftarrow Q$$

may be read in a number of ways; it could be read P where Q or P if Q. In this latter form it is a variant of the first-order predicate calculus known as *Horn clause logic*. A complete reading of the sqr predicates the point of view of logic is: for every X and Y, Y is the sqr of X if Y is X*X. From the point of view of logic, we say that the variables are universally quantified. Horn clause logic has a particularly simple inference rule which permits its use as a model of computation. This computational paradigm is called logic programming and deals with relations rather than functions or assignments. It uses facts and rules to represent information and deduction to answer queries. PROLOG is the most widely available programming language to implement this computational paradigm.

The basic constructs of logic programming terms and statements are inherited from logic. There are three basic statements: facts, rules, and queries. There is a single data structure: the logical term.

One of the features introduced by logic programming is to attempt automatic programming: given that a programmer can give a precise description of what is to be computed, the programming language should provide the how. PROLOG is a partial implementation of the ideas behind logic programming.

Lists

PROLOG has a list construct denoted [...]. Elements are separated by commas, e.g. [0, 2, 4, 9] is a list.

The notation [a|L] adds the element a at the beginning of the list L, e.g. [3|[1, 2, 5]] = [3, 1, 2, 5]. There does exist a rarely used alternative notation, (a, L). If we write [X|Y], it is understood that the X is the first element of the list [X|Y] and Y consists of all the other elements, e.g. if [X|Y] is [3, 1, 2, 5], then X = 3 and Y = [1, 2, 5]. The notation generalizes,

e.g., [X, Y, Z|R] is a list with X, Y, and Z as the first 3 elements and R as the rest of the list: [3, 4, 5|[1, 2, 5]] = [3, 4, 5, 1, 2, 5]. Thus, if [X, Y, Z|R] is [3, 1, 2, 5], then X = 3, Y = 1, Z = 2, and R = [5].

EXAMPLES. The length of a list (NOTE that [ ] is an empty list) mylength([ ], 0). /* the prefix "my" is to avoid redefining built-in relations in some PROLOG versions*/

```
mylength([X|Y], N):- mylength(Y, N1), N is N1+1.
? – mylength([1, 7, 9], X).
X = 3
? – mylength(jim, X).
no
mymember(X, [X|_ ]).
mymember(X, [ _|Z]) :- mymember(X, Z).
```

Note that the underscore '_' is a "don't-care" variable name. The above is equivalent to:

```
mymember(X, [X|Y]).
mymember(X, [W|Z]) :- mymember(X, Z).
```

If the underscore occurs twice in the same rule, PROLOG interprets it differently each time, e.g.

```
? – [1, 3, 4, 6] = [ _, _, _, _ ].
_1 = 1,
_2 = 3,
_3 = 4,
_4 = 6.
```

The query above could have been written:

```
? – [1, 3, 4, 6] = [X, Y, Z, W].
```

The following query fails to succeed.

```
? – mymember(a, [b, c, 6]).
no
whereas,
? – mymember(a, [b, a, 6]).
yes
```

We even have the possibility of putting variables where we would normally have constants. The semicolon (';') in this example has been typed by the user, followed by a <return>. The 'no' at the end means "no more answers."

```
? – mymember(X, [b, c, 6]).
X = b;
X = c;
X = 6;
no
```

NOTE: If you use PROLOG2, the system will ask if you want more solutions and you respond 'y' or 'n'. Typing 'y' corresponds to typing in the ';<return>' above. Typing 'n' corresponds to typing simply <return>.

The first example illustrates PROLOG's interpretation of negation as a failure in a search. The PROLOG version simply gives up without finding a way to solve the relation 'member (a, [b, c, 6])' and that is interpreted as negation (i.e. something being false). The following function 'add_to_set' only inserts an element in a list if it is not already there.

```
add_to_set(X, [ ], [X]).
add_to_set(X, Y, Y) :- mymember(X, Y).
add_to_set(X, Y, [X|Y]).
```

The most significant internal operation, which is a part of the PROLOG implementation, is unification which is a general purpose pattern matching. Examples of unification (see book and then consider the following):

? – f(a) = f(X, a). /* fails because f/1 cannot unify with f/2 */

NOTE: 'f/i' means "the version of the relation f that takes i parameters." The number of parameters (i) is usually called the *arity* of the relation (f).

? – f(X) = f(g(X)). /* fails because the constant x cannot unify with g/1*/

? – X = f(X).

may succeed but will fail if the PROLOG implementation has included the "occurs check"; if unification does succeed it is unusable because there is a match of X with f(f(f(...)))

? – [A, B | X] = [2, 1]. /* succeeds with A = 2, B = 1, X = [ ] */

? – p(X, X) = p(Y, f(Y)). /* fails if "occurs check" implemented, else succeeds with the unusable binding X = Y, Y = f(f(f(...))) */

? – f(X, g(X)) = f(a, Y). /* succeeds with X = a and Y = g(a) */

? – f(X, b, g(X)) = f(A, A, g(a)). /* fails, first X = A = b and then X = would have to be a */

The rules for unification are the following:

1. Constants only unify if they are the same (floating point number may allow some rounding when testing for equality)
2. Structures (e.g. f(g(X), h(y))) unify only if their functors and arities agree and their corresponding arguments unify recursively.
3. A variable X can unify with any PROLOG term. In subsequent unifications, X will be replaced by that term automatically

Any PROLOG rule for a relation has the general form:

rel(<parameters>) :- subgoal_1(...), subgoal_2(...), ..., subgoal_n(...).

The query ? – rel(<actual parameters>) is a "goal" which PROLOG tries to solve. Whenever it comes to use the above rule to try to satisfy the goal it has to try to solve, in turn, each of the "subgoals" subgoal_1(...) through subgoal_n(...). Any unification which result from calling the rule for rel(...) and from solving subgoal_1(...) through subgoal_j(...) will be used when solving subgoal_j+1(...) through subgoal_n(...). At any point a failure may occur and then PROLOG attempts a new solution at the most recent point where an alternative exists. The easiest way to understand the process is to see and then program lots of examples.

MORE EXAMPLES

1. Define "parent(X, Y)" where X is a parent of Y, if X is either the mother or the father of Y.

Similar definitions can be made for grandparent, sibling, and both-parent sibling:

```
parent(X, Y) :- mother(X, Y).
parent(X, Y) :- father(X, Y).
```

```
grandparent(X, Z):- parent(X, Y), parent(Y, Z).
sibling(X, Y) :- parent(P, X), parent(P, Y), X \= Y.
both-parent-sibling(X, Y) :- mother(M, X), mother(M, Y), father(F, X), father(F, Y),
X \= Y.
```

These statements give rules of implication among the variables X, Y, Z, M, F. The following facts can then be added, and questions can be asked regarding those facts and the above rules.

```
mother(mary, ann).
mother(mary, joe).
mother(sue, mary).
father(mike, ann).
father(mike, joe).
grandparent(sue, ann). /* redundant */
```

Questions such as the following can then be asked:

```
?- parent(X, ann), parent(X, joe).
X = mary;
X = mike

?- grandparent(sue, Y).
Y = ann;
Y = joe

?- both-parent-sibling(X, ann).
X = joe
```

2. Write a PROLOG relation that accepts a list of integers, and counts the number of zeros in the list, e.g.

```
?- zeros([1, 0, 0, 5], X).
X = 2

?- zeros([ ], X).
X = 0
```

Relation definition:

```
zeros([ ], 0).
zeros([0|T], Z):- zeros(T, Z1), !, Z is Z1 + 1.
zeros([ _|T], Z):- zeros(T, Z).
```

Note that the cut, written '!,' is very significant. If you type ';' after the answers above you do not get any more solutions. Without the 'cut' you get the following:

```
fragile-zeros([ ], 0).
fragile-zeros([0|T], Z):- fragile-zeros(T, Z1), Z is Z1 + 1.
fragile-zeros([ _|T], Z):- fragile-zeros(T, Z).
```

```
?- fragile-zeros([1, 0, 0, 5], X).
X = 2;
X = 1;
X = 1;
X = 0;
no
```

The cut ensures that if you get a match on a list with 0 at the head, you count the 0 once and only consider the tail T of that list. You do not try to pass the whole [0|T] list to the third rule.

3. Write a PROLOG relation which accepts two lists of integers L and M, and succeeds if M is a list of the squared numbers in L, e.g.

```
?- squares([0, 2, 3, 1], X).
X = [0, 4, 9, 1]

?- squares([ ], X).
X = [ ]

?- squares([2, 4, 6], [4, 16, 36]).
```

Relation definition:

```
squares([ ], [ ]).
squares([N|T], [S|ST]):- S is N*N, squares(T, ST).
```

4. Write a PROLOG relation "intersect(L1, L2, R)" that succeeds if R is the intersection of L1 and L2. (Assume no duplicates), e.g.

```
?- intersect([0, 1, 6, 3], [5, 1, 8, 2, 3, 9], X).
X = [1, 3]

?- intersect([1], [4], X).
X = [ ]
```

Relation definition:

```
intersect([ ], X, [ ]).
intersect([X|R], Y, [X|Z]) :- mymember(X, Y), !, intersect(R, Y, Z).
intersect([X|R], Y, Z) :- intersect(R, Y, Z).
```

Again, the cut is necessary to avoid spurious answers. You should test the code without the cut.

5. Write a PROLOG relation union(L1, L2, R) that succeeds if R is the union of L1 and L2, e.g.

```
?- union([3, 7, 1, 6], [5, 7, 2, 4, 1], X).
X = [3, 6, 5, 7, 2, 4, 1] /* or some other order of elements */

?- union([4], [1, 6, 8], X).
X = [4, 1, 6, 8] /* or some other order of elements */
```

Relation definition:

```
union([ ], X, X).
union([X|R], Y, Z):- member(X, Y), !, union(R, Y, Z).
union([X|R], Y, [X|Z]):- union(R, Y, Z).
```

6. Write a PROLOG relation which accepts a list of integers and counts the number of positive entries in an arbitrary list of integers, e.g.

```
?- positive([0, –1, –5, 5], X).
X = 1

?- positive([1, -2, 4, 2, 3], X).
X = 4

?- positive([ ], X).
X = 0
```

Relation definition:

```
positive([ ], 0).
positive([H|T], Z):- H > 0, !, positive(T, Z1), Z is 1 + Z1.
positive([ _ |T], Z) :- positive(T, Z).
```

7. Write a PROLOG relation which separates all (strictly) positive and negative entries from an arbitrary list of integers, e.g.

```
?- selectpn([0, –1, –5, 5], X, Y).
X = [5]
Y = [–1, –5]

?- selectpn([1, –2, 4, 2, 3], X, Y).
X = [1, 4, 2, 3]
Y = [–2]
```

Relation definition:

```
selectpn([ ], [ ], [ ]).
selectpn([0 | T], X, Y) :- selectpn(T, X, Y), !.

selectpn([H | T], [H|Z], X):- H > 0, !, selectpn(T, Z, X).
selectpn([H | T], X, [H|Z]):- selectpn(T, X, Z).
```

8. Write a relation to compute Fibonacci numbers:
Double recursion to compute Fibonacci numbers (exponential growth of recursive calls):

```
fibonacci_1(X, 1):- X < 2.
fibonacci_1(X, Y):- X > 1, X1 is X – 1, X2 is X – 2,
fibonacci_1(X1, Y1), fibonacci_1(X2, Y2), Y is Y1 + Y2.
```

Storing Fibonacci numbers, once computed:

```
fibonacci_2(0, 1).
fibonacci_2(1, 1).
fibonacci_2(X, Y):- X > 1, X1 is X – 1, X2 is X – 2, fibonacci_2(X1, Y1), fibonacci_2(X2,
Y2), Y is Y1 + Y2, asserta(fibonacci_2(X,Y)).
```

Run a few queries of fibonacci_2 and use listing(fibonacci_2) to see how the database grows.

A more efficient recursive program using accumulating parameter:

```
fibonacci3(X, N) :- fib_aux(X, 2, 1, 1, N).
fib_aux(M, Count, Last_fib, Second_last_fib, Last_fib) :- Count >= M.
fib_aux(M, Count, Last_fib, Second_last_fib, N) :- Count < M, Next_count is Count
+ 1,
New_fib is Last_fib + Second_last_fib,
fib_aux(M, Next_count, New_fib, Last_fib, N).
```

9. Write a PROLOG relation which produces the permutations of a list, one at a time (after the first one, the program must be prompted by the user typing ';'), e.g.

```
?- perm([1, 4, 7], X).
X = [1, 4, 7];
X = [1, 7, 4];
X = [4, 1, 7];
X = [4, 7, 1];
X = [7, 1, 4];
X = [7, 4, 1];
no
```

Relation definition:

```
perm([ ], [ ]).
perm(L, [X | Y]):- sel(L, X, T), perm(T, Y).
sel([X | Y], X, Y).
sel([X | Y], Z, [X | T]):- sel(Y, Z, T).
```

Let us consider

```
callperm(X):- perm(X,Y), write(Y), nl, fail.
```

The query

```
?- callperm([1, 4, 7]).
```

gives all permutations.

A simple term is a number, a variable or a constant atom. A compound term is an atom (also called a functor) followed by a parenthesized sequence of terms separated by commas. The grammar of PROLOG is exceedingly simple:

<term > <number > | <atom > | <variable > | <atom > (<terms >)
<terms > <term > | <term >, <terms >
<fact > <term >.
<rule > <term >:- <terms >.
<query > <terms >.

There are a number of special notations added for convenience: = is a predefined functor which represents the relation "can be unified with". It can be written using infix or prefix notation: =(X, Y) or X = Y and similarly for several other operators. The list notation [X | Y] is used instead of (X, Y) There is an operation "or" which is written ';' and is sometimes useful:

```
parent(X, Y) :- mother(X, Y); father(X, Y).
```

It can be used with parentheses to form an "or" of sequences of subgoals.

Data structures can be represented using functors, e.g. a binary tree can be written

```
node(Self, Leftsubtree, Rightsubtree):
```

This representation of a tree needs the existence of a constant empty. The following PROLOG relation would check whether something is a binary tree (not a search tree):

```
binarytree(empty).
binarytree(node(X, Y, Z)):- binarytree(Y), binarytree(Z).
```

Suppose we are able to construct a binary search tree T using the above representation, which has a number stored at each node. To test whether the number E occurs in T, we can use the following recursive tree search:

```
tree-member(E, node(E, _ , _ )):- !. /* cut off search after first time the element
is found */
tree-member(E, node( N , L, _ )):- E < N, !, tree-member (E, L).
/* cut if E < N to avoid searching the right subtree */
tree-member(E, node( _ , _ , R )):- tree-member(E, R).
```

The guess and verify technique, which is available in PROLOG, is illustrated by:

```
have-elements-in-common-ver1(X,Y):- mymember(E,X), mymember(E,Y).
have-elements-in-common-ver2(X,Y):- mymember(E,X), mymember(E,Y), !.
```

The first call to member will give values to E which run through the list X in sequence, each such E will be checked to see if it belongs to Y. The cut in the second version will stop the search after the first success (if any) and disallow additional solutions. Notice the following behaviour:

```
? - have-elements-in-common-ver1(X, [1, 2, 3]).
X = [1| _14];
X = [2| _14];
X = [3| _14];
```

```
X = [ _16, 1|_18];
X = [ _16, 2|_18];
X = [ _16, 3|_18];
...
? - have-elements-in-common-ver1([1, 2, 3], Y).
Y = [1| _33];
Y = [_35, 1|_36];
Y = [_35, _39, 1|_40];
...
```

Order of evaluation problems:

```
? - X = [1, 2, 3], write(X), nl, mymember(a, X).
X = [1, 2, 3]
no
?- mymember(a, X), write(X), nl, X = [1, 2, 3].
X = [a| _3];
X = [_5, a|_7];
X = [_5, _8, a|_9];
X = [_5, _8, _11, a|_12];
X = [_5, _8, _11, _14, a|_15];
...
```

Accessing the end of a list using variables as place holders:

```
? - L = [a, b|X], X = [c, Y].
L = [a, b, c|_2]
X = [c|_2]
Y = _2
```

Note that _1 was the first value of X. The unification inserts a c at the end of L.

A queue implementation, q(X, Y) is a queue with X representing the whole queue and Y representing a place holder at the end of the queue:

```
create-queue(q(X, X)).
```

Hence, create-queue(Q) unifies Q with q(_n, _n).

Consider:

```
add-queue(E, q(X, Last), q(X, NewLast)):- Last = [E|NewLast].
(alternatively: add-queue(E, q(X, [E|Y]), q(X, Y)).)
```

Here, add-queue(a, Q, R) first unifies Last with _n and then with [a|_n+1]. That makes Q unify with q([a|_n+1], [a|_n+1]), NewLast with _n+1 and R with q([a|_n+1], _n+1):

Similarly add-queue(b, R, S) make the unifications:

```
Q = q([a, b|_n+2], [a, b|_n+2])
R = q([a, b|_n+2], [b|_n+2])
S = q([a, b|_n+2], _n+2)
```

Next we have:

del-queue(E, q(X, Last), q(NewX, Last)):- X = [E|NewX].

del-queue(A, S, T) unifies q(X, Last) with S, i.e. X **unifies with [a, b|_n+2]** and Last with_n+2.

Therefore, A unifies with a and NewX with [b|_n+2]. Finally, T unifies with q([b|_n+2], _n+2).

The relation force-empty-queue (q([ ], [ ])) would appear to be a reasonable characterization of an empty queue but it is too restrictive: it checks that the terms inside q are really empty, not just identical. For example, while Q is bound to q(_1, _1), emptyQ(Q) will succeed by unifying _1 and [ ]. However, as soon as Q unifies with q([a|_2], [a|_2]) or q([a, b|_2], [a, b|_2]), the match with [ ] is no longer possible and force-empty-queue(Q) will fail. In fact, we need to check whether the pointers are identical:

empty-queue(q(X,Y)):- X = = Y.

Thus:

```
? - create-queue(Q), add-queue(a, Q, R), empty-queue(Q).
Q = q([a|_n ], [a|_n ])
R = q([a|_n ], _n)
yes
? - create-queue(Q), add-queue(a, Q, R), empty-queue(R).
no
but:
? - create-queue(Q), add-queue(a, Q, R), force-empty-queue(Q).
no
also:
```

? - create-queue(Q), add-queue(a, Q, R), add-queue(b, R, S), del-queue(A, S, T), write(A), n1, del-queue(B, T, U), write(B), n1, force-empty-queue(U).

```
a
b
Q = q([a, b], [a, b])
R = q([a, b], [b])
S = q([a, b], [ ])
A = a
T = q([b], [ ])
B = b
U = q([ ], [ ])
```

Note the rather unexpected behaviour:

? - create-queue(Q), del-queue(X, Q, R), write(X), nl, add-queue(a, R, S), write(X), n1.

```
_m
a
Q = q([a|_n ], [a|_n ])
```

X = a
R = q(_n, [a|_n])
S = q(_n, _n)

If force-empty-queue(S) is added as the last subgoal, then _n unifies with [ ]:
? - create-queue(Q), del-queue(X, Q, R), write(X), nl, add-queue(a, R, S), write(X), nl, force-empty-queue(S).

_m
a
Q = q([a], [a])
X = a
R = q([ ], [a])
S = q([ ], [ ])

Difference lists are an important PROLOG technique. Some relation diff_list (L, E) is used, with no special meaning in PROLOG, but the user thinks of the relation as representing the list that remains when E is removed from L, where E is some tail part of L. PROLOG allows some of the predefined symbols: +, –, etc. to be used in the representation of difference lists. Since we are working with difference lists, the symbol – is the most frequently used:

The following queue is: (just replace q(X, Y), above, by X – Y).
First we need to introduce "not":

```
not(P) :- call(P), !, fail.
not(P).
alternatively not(P):- P, !, fail; true.
```

If the call to P fails, then the second rule makes not(P) succeed for any P. If the call to P succeeds, then the first rule fails but the cut prevents any other solutions, so the whole of not(P) fails.

Next the difference-list queue:

```
create-queue(L – L).
add-queue(E, L – [E | R], L – R)).
```

Now, the naive definition like the one used before:

```
del-queue(E, [E | Rest] – Last, Rest – Last)).
```

is unsatisfactory because, when a queue is empty (i.e. Rest is the same as Last), this del-queue produces "negative difference lists" del-queue(_n – [E | _n])

Correct version:

```
del-queue(E, L – Last, NewL – Last):- not (L = = Last), L = [E | NewQ].
empty-queue(L – M):- L = = M.
```

The graphic for this queue is essentially same as before with q(X, Y) replaced by X–Y.

Difference lists can eliminate recursion and thus improve efficiency:

```
append (L – X, X – Y, L – Y).
compared to:
append([ ], X, X).
append([X|Y], Z, [X|T]):- append(Y, Z, T).
? - append([1, 2, 3|X] – X, [4, 5] – [ ], Y – Z).
X = [4, 5]
Y = [1, 2, 3, 4, 5]
Z = [ ]
? - append([1, 2, 3|X] – X, [4, 5|Y] – Y, W – Z).
X = [4, 5|_n]
Y = _n
W = [1, 2, 3, 4, 5|_n]
Z = _n
```

The following simple code extracts the list corresponding to the difference list:

```
simplify(X – Y, [ ]) :- X == Y.
simplify([X|Y] – Z, [X | W]):- simplify (Y – Z, W).
```

The "occurs-check" problem: for efficiency reasons, the check may not be made in PROLOG, hence:

```
? - append ([ ], E, [a, b|E]).
E = [a, b, a, b, a, b, a, b, a, b, a, b, a, b, a, b, a, b, a, b, a, b, a, b, a, b, a, b, a, b, a, b, ...
```

Some PROLOGs may construct a cyclic data structure for terms derived in the above way.

The following is meant to illustrate the elegance and clarity of PROLOG:

```
qsort([X|L], Outlist) :- partition (X, L, Small, Large), qsort(Small, Localsmall),
qsort(Large, Locallarge),
append (Localsmall, [X|Locallarge], Outlist).
qsort([ ], [ ]).
```

where partition separates the elements of L into those X and those > X:

```
partition (X, [ ], [ ], [ ]).
partition (X, [Y|Tail], [Y|Small], Large) :- X > Y, !, partition (X, Tail, Small, Large).
partition (X, [Y|Tail], Small, [Y|Large]) :- partition (X, Tail, Small, Large).
? - qsort(<some input list>, X).
```

Alternative using an auxiliary parameter to avoid append:

```
quicksort([X|L], Aux, Outlist):- partition (X, L, Small, Large), quicksort(Large, Aux, Local),
quicksort(Small, [X|Local], Outlist).
quicksort([ ], Any, Any).
? - quicksort(<some input list>, [ ], X).
```

Alternative using difference lists, also avoiding the expensive form of append:

```
qsort1(Inlist, Outlist):- qsort2(Inlist, Outlist - [ ]).
qsort2([X|Tail], A1 – Z2):- partition (X, Tail, Small, Large), qsort2(Small, A1 –
[X|A2]),
qsort2(Large, A2 – Z2).
qsort2([ ], Z – Z).
```

EXAMPLE. Solving the Towers of Hanoi puzzle: (Refer to Appendix B on LISP)

```
hanoi(N) :- move(N, left, center, right).
move(0, _ , _ , _ ) :- !.
move(N, A, B, C) :- M is N–1, move(M, A, C, B), inform(A, B), move(M, C, B, A).
inform(X, Y) :- write([move, a, disc, X, to, Y]), nl.
```

User-defined Operations

PROLOG allows the user to introduce new operations. The precedence of the operator can be specified in relation to the other operators and it can be specified as left- or right-associative.

Definite Clause Grammars (DCGs)

A standard library that can be found with many PROLOG systems provides the translation from grammar-rule notation into normal PROLOG syntax automatically. The grammar below can then be typed into PROLOG directly. It becomes easier to work with grammars and typing errors are avoided:

```
move step.
step [up].
move step, move.
step [down].
```

LISP

The LISP was the work of John McCarthy in the late 1950s. It has existed in many forms and dialects since. The most widely used dialects today are Common LISP and Scheme. LISP as it was originally conceived of was a pure functional language, but that is not necessarily the case any more. Common LISP offers a variety of programming styles. Programs written in Common LISP consequently tend to be a pragmatic combination of a variety of programming styles. These tutorials begin with an emphasis on functional programming, and slowly introduce examples of mixing in some imperative programming.

Programs written in Common LISP do not require the programmer to declare the type of data ahead of time. A function written in C is often restricted in the type of argument it can take. A function written in LISP is not restricted in this way. The data objects themselves however are typed. So the burden of type checking falls on the Common LISP environment, not on the programmer. The symbol is perhaps one of the first data types that students learning Common LISP are taught. The ease and flexibility with which Common LISP can manipulate symbols is one of the primary reasons why the language is a mainstay of AI research.

Some modern Common LISP environments have a fancier graphical interface available. The listener is however still the primary means for interacting with the environment. The remaining components often include editors, inspectors, debuggers, profilers, and a host of other tools.

LISP Expression

s-expressions are the primary constituent of LISP programs. Their syntax tends to be very simple. s-expressions are composed entirely of atoms and lists, where an atom is (approximately) anything but a list. Atoms may be directly evaluated, while lists involve function calls.

```
s-exp ::= atom | (symbol s-exp*)
atom ::= symbol | number | string | <other things>
```

In other words, an s-expression is an atom or a list expression. Each s-expression returns a value. The definition of an s-expression is recursive. Arbitrarily complex expressions can be created by composing s-expressions in this manner. This can however lead to programs that are hard to read, and is not advisable.

If the s-expression is a single atom, then the action the LISP environment takes depends on the type of atom. If it is a symbol, then the value of the symbol is accessed. Otherwise, atoms usually evaluate to themselves. (5, for example, returns 5 as its value.)

List s-expressions are quite straightforward too. The first component of these s-expressions is always a symbol. Evaluating the s-expression corresponds to executing the function associated with this symbol. The s-expressions following the symbol are also evaluated, and their values are used as arguments to the function. In the example below, the function associated with the symbol + is accessed. The atoms 2 and 3 are evaluated, and their return values (themselves) are used as arguments to the function +. The value of the s-expression is returned as the atom 5.

```
> (+ 2 3)
5
```

LISP, as we can see, uses prefix syntax.

Factorial

We shall first go over a simple example to demonstrate LISP syntax before examining more details of the language. Factorial has a simple recursive mathematical definition:

```
fact(0) = 1
fact(n) = n*fact(n–1)
```

Below are two methods for implementing factorial. In general, you will find that there are any number of ways of expressing an idea in LISP, and some of them turn out to be better than others.

Method 1:

```
(defun factorial (n)
  (if (= n 0)
  1
  (* n (factorial (1 – n)))))
```

This is the literal interpretation of the definition of factorial. Remember that each expression in LISP returns a value, which allows for a simple translation of a variety of mathematical and logical constructs into equivalent programs.

The entire form is a single s-expression that constructs a function definition. The return value of this s-expression is the name of the function. Defun is a symbol in the function slot of the s-expression. It is not a function, but a special form. Unlike a function invocation, it does not necessarily evaluate all its arguments.

Like defun, if is a special form. It takes a variable number of s-expressions (two or three) in its argument slots. The first argument is necessarily evaluated. It is usually a predicate (a function that returns a boolean value). If the predicate returns *true*, then the second argument is evaluated. If false, the third argument is evaluated. The value of the entire if s-expression is either the value of the second argument or the third, depending on which one is evaluated. If the third argument is absent, then NIL is returned.

The remaining s-expressions are mathematical functions that evaluate as you would expect them to. Let us run a few tests:

```
> (factorial 4)
24
> (factorial 30)
265252859812191058636308480000000
```

Note on the last one that the result value was an exact integer. Common LISP is limited only by memory in the size of the integers it can work with. You need not to worry about overflows and such.

Method 2:

```
(defun factorial-1 (n product)
  (if (= n 0)
      product
      (factorial-1 (1 – n) (* n product))))

(defun factorial (n)
  (factorial-1 n 1))
```

At first glance, this method of factorial seems to be inferior to the first. It uses two functions, while the first uses only one. Method 2 is thus more verbose, and potentially more confusing. But this version has a very important advantage, for it allows a type of optimization called *tail call elimination.* Consider the stack usage of Method 1:

```
(factorial 3)
  (* 3 (factorial 2))
  (* 3 (* 2 (factorial 1)))
  (* 3 (* 2 (* 1 (factorial 0))))
  (* 3 (* 2 (* 1 1)))
  (* 3 (* 2 1))
  (* 3 2)
  6
```

Now let's look at Method 2:

```
(factorial 3)
  (factorial-1 3 1)
  (factorial-1 2 3)
  (factorial-1 1 6)
  (factorial-1 0 6)
  6
```

Method 1 requires the LISP environment to keep track of the partial results of the recursive calls, while Method 2 keeps track of the partial result as an explicit argument. This allows the LISP environment to optimize Method 2, by reusing the stack space of the previous call. Thus, Method 2 can be easily reduced to a simple loop.

LISP Commands

Lists

Lists, like symbols, have a special place in the LISP type hierarchy. They are a very convenient default representation when exploring various aspects of a program or problem. A list in turn is composed of a series of cons cells. A cons cell is abstractly an object made of two slots.

Lists have a recursive definition.

1. ( ) is the empty list.
2. A cons cell with its second component ( ) is a list of length 1.
3. The length of a list is one more than the length of the list in its second component.

Note:

```
> ( )
NIL
```

Thus, NIL is also the empty list.

cons
Allocates a cons cell.

```
> (cons 1 2)
(1.2)
```

The result of the above expression is called the dotted pair representation of a cons cell.

consp
Tests if the argument is a cons cell.

```
> (consp (cons 1 3))
T
```

list
This function is the primary list constructor.

```
> (list 1 2 3)
(1 2 3)
```

It automatially allocates and strings together all the necessary cons cells. The above expression is equivalent to

```
> (cons 1 (cons 2 (cons 3 ())))
(1 2 3)
```

car
This accesses the first component of a cons cell.

```
> (car (cons 1 2))
1
```

cdr
This accesses the second component of a cons cell.

```
> (cdr (cons 1 2))
2

> (cdr (list 1))
NIL
```

caar, cadr, cdar, cddr...
These functions are abbreviations for a series of applications of CAR and CDR. Thus,

```
(caar x) ↔ (car (car x))
(cadr x) ↔ (car (cdr x))
```

Though convenient, excessive reliance on CAR and CDR can quickly make a program unreadable.

first, second... tenth
These access the first, second... up to the tenth element of a list.

```
> (first (list 1 2 3))
1

> (second (list 1 2 3))
2
```

nth
This retrieves the nth element of a list. Note that the elements of a list are zero based, rather than one based.

```
(nth 0 x) ↔ (first x)
```

nthcdr
This function retrieves the nth cons cell of a list. The elements are again zero based.

```
(car (nthcdr 0 x)) ↔ (nth 0 x)
> (nthcdr 1 (list 1 2 3))
(2 3)
```

last
This function returns the last cons cell of a list.

```
> (last (list 1 2 3))
(3)
```

length
This function returns the length of a list (and other objects that have a length).

listp
This function tests if the object is a list. It returns true if the object is either a cons cell or the empty list. CONSP on the other hand tests only if the object is a cons cell.

```
> (listp ())
T

> (consp ())
NIL
```

endp
This function tests if we are at the end of a list. In other words, it tests if the object is ().

```
> (endp ())
T

> (endp nil)
T
```

Symbols
Symbols are special objects in Common LISP. They are used for naming a variety of objects, including variables and functions.

symbolp
This predicate tests if an object is a symbol. It returns T if the object is a symbol, and NIL otherwise. Look below for more information about T and NIL.

```
> (symbolp nil)
T

> (symbolp 4)
NIL
```

Atoms
Atoms are anything that are not cons cells. The rest of the types listed below (including strings) are thus classified as atoms.

atom
This predicate tests if an object is an atom. It can quite literally be defined in terms of consp.

(atom x) $\leftrightarrow$ (not (consp x))

```
> (atom 1)
T

> (atom (list 1))
NIL

> (atom nil)
T
```

Arithmetic operators (+, –, *, /, 1+, 1–)

The function + without any arguments returns 0. With one argument it returns the number it was given. With more than one argument it returns the sum of all of its arguments.

The function – requires at least one argument. If given only one argument, the return value is the argument's negation. If given more than one argument, the return value is the first argument minus the sum of the remaining arguments.

The function * without any arguments returns 1. With one argument the result is the argument itself. With more than one argument the product of all the arguments is returned.

The function / requires at least one argument. With one argument it returns the inverse of the argument. When more than one argument is supplied, the result is the first argument divided by the product of the remaining arguments.

1+ and 1– add 1 and subtract 1 from their arguments, respectively.

integerp

Tests if the argument is an integer.

oddp/evenp

Tests if the argument is odd or even, respectively.

Functions

Functions, as has been noted, are first class objects in Common LISP.

function

This is a special form, not a function. It returns the function value of the symbol supplied, and an error if none exists.

```
> (function +)
#<Function +>
```

The special form function is hardly ever used. Special syntax provided in Common LISP gives us a handy short cut.

```
> #'+
#<Function +>
```

functionp

This predicate tests if the supplied argument is a function.

```
> (functionp #'+)
T
```

funcall
This function invokes the function supplied as its first argument on the arguments supplied.

```
> (funcall #'+ 1 2 3)
6
```

Thus, the above function call is equivalent to (+ 1 2 3).

apply
Apply, like funcall, executes a function. However, it takes arguments in a different format. The last argument to apply is interpreted as a list of arguments to be given to the function in the first argument's place.

```
> (apply #'+ (list 1 2 3))
6

> (apply #'+ 4 (list 1 2 3))
10
```

All arguments other than the last are interpreted as individual arguments for the indicated function.

Strings
Strings are vectors of characters. Literal strings are indicated by double quotes surrounding a series of characters, and evaluate to themselves.

```
> "foo"
"foo"
```

stringp
This function returns T if its argument is a string.

length
This function returns the length of the string.

Booleans and Predicates

eql
EQL tests if two objects are the same. Integers are usually eql if they are the same number. Symbols are always eql to each other.

equal
Equal, unlike eql, ignores the issue of cons cell identity.

```
> (equal (cons 1 2) (cons 1 2))
T
```

typep
As has been stated earlier, data rather than variables in Common LISP are typed. TYPEP is a predicate intended to check the type of the data.

```
> (typep 5 'number)
T

> (typep nil 'list)
T

> (typep nil 'cons)
NIL
```

Control Structures

In addition to functions, Common LISP has a variety of special forms.

defun
This form is responsible for constructing globally accessible functions. It returns the name of the function as its value. The full syntax is:

```
(defun <function-name> <argument-list>
  <form1>
  <form2>
  ...
  <formN>)
```

<function-name> has to be a valid symbol.

lambda
Defun is limited such that it can only construct globally accessible functions that are named. For taking advantage of functional programming paradigms, it is necessary to be able to create functions at run-time. The lambda form provides this functionality. It creates an anonymous (unnamed) function that is otherwise identical to regular functions. The syntax of the lambda expression is also identical to the syntax of a regular function definition. For example,

```
> (funcall #'(lambda (x) (if (oddp x) (1+ x) x)) 5)
6
```

quote
The QUOTE special form instructs LISP to take the argument literally. That is,

```
> (quote x)
X
```

if
If is one of the many conditional evaluation forms in Common LISP. Its syntax is:

```
(if <test>
    <then-form>
    <else-form>)
```

cond
COND can be thought of as a series of IF expressions. The full syntax is:

```
(cond (<test1> <form11> <form12> ... <form1K>)
  (<test2> form21> ... <form2L>)
  ...
  (<testN> <formN1> <formN2> ... <formNM>))
```

A cond expression may have its last test (<testN> above) be T. This, then is the default clause, whose forms are evaluated if all the other tests fail.

```
> (let ((x 50))
  (cond ((oddp x) (1+ x))
  ((> x 10) (/ x 2))
  (t x)))
25
```

when/unless
When and Unless share a common syntax:

```
(when/unless <test>
<form1> ... <formN>)

> (when t 5)
5

> (when nil 5)
NIL
```

or
It takes multiple arguments. It evaluates its arguments until it finds one that is non-NIL. This value is its return value.

```
> (or nil 5 t)
5
```

and
and, like or, takes multiple arguments. It evalutes its arguments until it finds one that is NIL. If one is found, the return value of the and expression is NIL, otherwise it is the value of the last argument evaluated.

```
> (and nil 5 t)
NIL

> (and 5 t 'x)
X
```

not

It takes a single argument. If the argument is NIL, it returns T, otherwise it returns NIL.

```
> (not 'x)
NIL

> (not nil)
T
```

defvar

defvar defines a global variable. It returns the name of the variable as its value.

```
> (defvar *foo* 5)
*foo*
```

The circumstances in which global variables are used are few, and excessive use can make programs difficult to read and debug. Use them sparingly.

setq

It destructively modifies the variable value of a symbol. Its full syntax is:

```
(setq <symbol1> <value1>
   <symbol2> <value2>
   ...
   <symbolN> <valueN>)
```

It does not establish a new lexical scope, but simply modifies the value of a variable within the current scope. It should be used as sparingly as possible. The return value of SETQ is the result of evaluating <valueN>.

```
> (let ((x 5))
   (setq x (1+ x))
   x)
6
```

setf

It destructively modifies the value in a place. A place is an abstract concept. A symbol's variable value is an example of a place, so setf is more general than setq in its scope.

```
> (let ((x (cons 1 2)))
   (setf (car x) 4)
   x)
(4 . 2)
```

EXAMPLE. *Towers of Hanoi*

The Towers of Hanoi is a relatively simple problem that turns out to be very difficult to solve. The problem involves moving rings from a start peg to a destination peg, using a third peg as spare space. The only constraints are that only one peg at a time may be moved, and a larger peg may never be on top of a smaller peg.

To move n rings from the start to the destination, move n – 1 from the start to the spare, then move the nth ring from the start to the destination. Finally, move the n – 1 rings on the spare to the destination, using the start peg as the spare. Our task is to write a function that tells us what moves to make to get all n rings from the start peg to the destination peg.

In typical LISP style, we want to write a function "Towers-of-Hanoi" which takes one argument, the number of rings on the start peg. Our return value should be a list of moves. Given the nature of the problem, a very simple system suffices for describing the move. We can only move one ring, the top one, at a time, so it is sufficient to state the source peg and the destination peg to fully describe a move. A cons cell is ideally suited for storing such a pair. We thus have a data input and output specification in LISP terms, and a conceptually straightforward algorithm. This yields the following implementation:

```
(defun toh (height start-peg-name extra-peg-name end-peg-name)
  (cond ((= height 0) nil)
    ((= height 1) (list (cons start-peg-name end-peg-name)))
    (t (append (toh (1 – height) start-peg-name end-peg-name extra-peg-name)
      (toh 1 start-peg-name extra-peg-name end-peg-name)
      (toh (1 – height) extra-peg-name start-peg-name
        end-peg-name)))))

(defun towers-of-hanoi (height)
  (toh height 'start-peg 'extra-peg 'end-peg))
```

Glossary

Abduction: A form of reasoning by which, given a fact or state, we can hypothesize some prior fact or state which might have given rise to it. For example, if we know that the streets are always wet after it has been raining, and that the streets are wet now, we can guess that it has recently been raining. The streets could be wet, of course, for some other reason entirely, so abduction is not always a reliable form of reasoning.

Agenda: A list of possible tasks for a system to perform, ordered according to usefulness. Agenda may be used, for example, in a search program to determine the next path to investigate.

Algorithm: A fixed set of operations on numbers or symbols - of a sort that can be automated on a digital computer. See also Heuristic.

Analogue computer: See Digital/Analogue Computer.

Analogical: In an analogical representation there is a direct correspondence between the important properties of the representation and the properties of the domain; for example, by using a two-dimensional array to represent a two-dimensional picture.

Ancestor: An ancestor of a goal is the goal's parent or its parent's parent, etc. For example, if we have the following database:

```
a :- b.
b :- c.
c :- d.
```

then a, b, and c are ancestors of d.

Anonymous variable: An anonymous variable is a variable that is written in a special way to show that it is different from every other variable in the clause. Another way of regarding the anonymous variable is as a variable whose value we are not interested in. It is written '_'. If we consider the following clause

```
a(_, _).
```

there are two variables whose values we are not interested in (the two variables can be equal), whereas in

    a(X, _).

there is only one variable.

Arc/Link/Pointer: Nodes in a semantic network are connected by labelled directed arcs (also sometimes called links or pointers), which indicate the nature of the connection between adjacent nodes. In is-a hierarchies, the most basic links are taxonomic (is-a) and partonomic (is-part) relations; other name features or attributes; their values are given by the node pointed to by the link.

Architecture: As applied to computers, the structured organization of elements in a computational mechanism, for example, the difference between sequential processing and parallel distributed processing machines is said to be a difference in architecture. See also Computation, (non-) von Neumann Architecture.

Argument/Result: A procedure may take input values and produce output values. The former are called the procedure's arguments; the latter its results. Thus the POP-11 procedure call length([1 2 3]) has one argument (the list [1 2 3]) and produces one result (the number 3). In logic, an argument represents individual entities, such as "John", or "apple". A predicate is applied to one or more arguments to produce a formula. See also Axiom/Theorem.

arity: The arity of a goal or query is the number of arguments it has. The arity of a predicate is the number of arguments that the head of the clause has. The arity of:

    a(1, two, Three).

is 3.

Array: A data object consisting of an ordered series of elements that can be accessed by number index.

ASCII Code: The widely used American Standard Code for Information Interchange (ASCII Code) assigns a number to each character that can be typed on a **computer** keyboard. The code aids programming and communication between computers.

Assignment: The operation in computer programming of giving a value to a variable.

Attribute/Feature/Property: An attribute (or feature, or property) is a distinguishing aspect, quality, or characteristic of an object. An attribute of a canary, for example, is yellowness.

atom: An atom is an object referred to by name. Anything that begins with a lower case letter and consists entirely of letters, numbers, and the underscore character is an atom.

    two is an atom
    1 is not

Three is not
this_is is an atom
_var is not an atom but a variable

Axiom/Theorem: Most logical systems contain fundamental propositions or axioms, which cannot themselves be justified from within the system itself. Any conclusions derived from these axioms by the system's rules of inference are called theorems. See also Logic, Predicate Calculus/Predicate Logic, Propositional Calculus.

Backtracking: Returning to a previous state in a computation in order to try an alternative strategy. In terms of a *search tree*, backtracking occurs when the end of a branch is reached without a solution being found, and a different branch is chosen.

backtrack (in PROLOG): When PROLOG answers no to a goal, it returns to the previous goal and tries to find another solution to it. This is called *backtracking*. If we have the following database:

```
a(1).
a(2).
b(2).
```

and ask:

```
?- a(X), b(X).
```

then a(X) succeeds with X equal to 1, b(1) fails and so PROLOG backtracks to find another solution for a, finding X = 2.

Backup Memory: See Main Memory/Backup Memory.

Behaviourism/Behavioural Psycholog: An influential twentieth-century school of thought in psychology and in the philosophy of mind that claimed that only the outwardly observable aspects of human behaviour produced scientific data for the study of the mind. Behaviourists thus rejected introspectionism.

Binary Digit (Bit): Most modern computers use the binary counting system, employing only 1's and 0's, to represent any number or other character. Binary numbers can be easily stored in electronic form. See also Central Processor.

Boolean: A data object which represents whether some condition is *true* or not. There are only two such objects: <true> and <false>.

Branch and Bound: A search strategy in which the lowest cost node in the agenda is always considered first. This strategy is guaranteed to find the lowest cost solution if more than one solution to a problem exists.

Branching: See Conditional.

Breadth-First: A search strategy in which each level of the search tree is considered in turn. All the nodes at any given level of the search tree are considered before any nodes at a deeper level.

Built-in/User-defined: Most programming languages have a variety of terms which are primitive to the language; these are the built-in terms. Many languages, such as POP-11, allow you to define your own terms or procedures. These are known as user-defined terms.

Built-In Predicate: A built-in predicate is a predicate about which PROLOG can answer queries without any information being supplied by the user. The user cannot define clauses for a built-in predicate, even if the predicate has a different arity.

Calling a Procedure: Instructing a computer to interpret the series of instruction defined in a procedure. See also Argument/Result.

Case/Case Relationship/Case Slot: The case is the functional relationship of noun-phrases to the main action of sentences as expressed in the verb. Every verb has a certain number of case slots. For example, the verb "cut" presupposes someone cutting (the "agent" case slot), something cut (the "object"), and something with which the act of cutting is performed (the 'instrument').

Central Processor: That part of a conventional digital computer which performs the direct operations upon sequences of sysmbols stored as sets of binary digits (bits). See also Architecture, Compilation/Interpretation, Computation, Hardware, Main Memory/Backup Memory, Parallel Distributed Processing, Sequential Processing, Software.

Children: The relation of nodes to the node that immediately dominates them in an isa hierarchy is that of children to a parent node. See also Taxonomic Tree.

Clause: A clause is a piece of information PROLOG uses to establish whether a goal is *true*. It will either say that a certain query is *true*, or that it is *true* under certain conditions, e.g.

```
a(1).
a(X) :- b(X).
```

are both clauses.

Cognitivism: In contrast to behaviourism this school of thought claims that psychology should be concerned with a person's internal representations of the world and with the internal or functional organization of the mind. See also Computationalism, functionalism.

Command: Procedural programming languages such as POP-11 are composed of statements that can be interpreted as commands to the computer to perform various operations, for instance, adding two numbers and assigning the result to a variable.

Commutative: A *commutative* relation in a semantic network is one which is symmetric. That is, for any relation R, if xRy is *true*, then yRx is also *true*. For example, if Frank is married to Hilda, then Hilda is also married to Frank.

Competence Knowledge: An abstract description of the knowledge characterizing a particular domain. See also Performance Knowledge.

Competence/Performance: A person's linguistic competence is the ability to produce and understand an indefinite number of novel sentences, to detect ambiguities, and to recognize grammatical errors. Performance refers to a person's use of language in particular situations. The distinction is mirrored in natural language processing by grammars, which are usually stored declarative representations of the rules governing the well-formedness of sentences, and parsers, which are programs that process utterances by reference to such rules.

Compilation/Interpretation: Two widely adopted methods for converting the instructions of a program into binary machine code instructions specifying basic operations on the machine's central processor. Compilation involves converting a program as a whole, whereas interpretation involves translating each instruction singly.

Compiled Representation: A representation of human knowledge in the form of an automatic process that runs without calling on declarative knowledge nor making demands on working memory.

Compositionality: The principle that the meaning (or semantic value) of a sentence is a function of the meanings of its constituents together with their mode of combination (just as the meaning of a complex expression in propositional calculus is a function of the truth-value of the atomic propositions together with the truth-functional connectives by which they are combined together).

Computation: The manipulation of numbers or symbols according to fixed rules. Usually applied to the operations of an automatic electronic computer, but by extension to some processes performed by minds or brains. See also Cognitivism.

Computationalism: The notion that the operation of the mind can be explained entirely in terms of the formal, or functional, properties of a computational system. See also Cognitivism, Eliminativism, Functionalism, Materialism, Turing Test.

Computer: A machine for performing operations on numeric or symbolic data. Nowdays the term usually refers to digital computers capable of being instructed by stored programs. See also Algorithm, Hardware, Software.

Concept: A *concept* is a stable mental representation of objects, classes, properties, and relations. When we encounter a new object or event for the first time, we draw upon our mental store of concepts in order to identify it. One of the most important parts of the human learning process is concept-formation, where after a number of distinct experiences of the same object or event, we acquire by a process of induction, a concept for it.

Conceptual Dependency Representation: A formalism for representing the meanings of sentences, in a manner similar to that of a semantic network, as structured configurations of basic language-independent conceptual elements, or conceptual primitives. See also Knowledge Representation, Semantics.

Conceptual Primitive: One of a small number of fundamental sorts of action or event, such as the physical movement of an object (*ptrans*) or the transfer of some mental content (*mtrans*). Used in conjunction with scripts as a method of knowledge representation.

Conditional: Used to describe an instruction, or a sequence of instructions, that is only to be executed when certain specified conditions are met. For instance, the Automated Tourist Guide should only print information about the river when the user has asked a question about the river. Programming languages often introduce a conditional instruction by means of the word if. The possibility that a program can carry out different actions under different circumstances is called branching.

Conflict Resolution Strategy: A strategy used by a production system interpreter for deciding which production rule is to be fired if the heads of more than one rule match the contents of working memory.

Connectionist Model/Neural Network: A system consisting of a network of processing units each of which carries out a simple computation. The units are all interconnected and knowledge is represented as patterns of connection. See also Parallel Distributed Processing.

Constant: See Variable/Constant.

Consult: To *consult* a collection of clauses means to record them in PROLOG's database so that they can be used for answering questions.

Data Object: Computer programs involve operations on different kinds of symbolic entities, known as *data objects* or *types*.

Data Structure: A specific data object used as an object of computation.

Database: A means of recording and accessing large amounts of relatively simple items of data, such as bibliographical information.

Declarative/Procedural Representation: A *declarative representation* contains knowledge in the form of facts or images. In a procedural representation, knowledge is stored as processes or procedures. Different programming languages can be characterized as having a declarative or procedural style.

Declare: When a variable name is *declared* by means of the vars instruction, POP-11 enters the word in its list of variable names and allocates memory for the variable.

Deduction: A form of logical reasoning by which, from a given set of facts (premises), certain consequences (conclusions) can be inferred. For example, if I know that on every occasion on which it rains the streets get wet, and that it is raining now, then I can deduce that the streets are now wet.

Define: To specify the set of instructions associated with a procedure, as used in computer programming.

Deictic Expression: An expression which picks out some individual, time, or place relative to the context of utterance. For example, 'I', 'you', 'here', 'these', 'yesterday' have no intrinsic semantic value; the reference of each on an occasion of speech is determined by the appropriate component of the speech situation.

Demon: A type of procedure associated with a frame. The two main types are if-needed and if-added demons.

Depth-First: A search strategy in which all the nodes on one branch of the search tree are considered before backtracking to try nodes on other branches. All the successors of a given node are considered before any other nodes at the same level as the given node.

Digital/Analog Computer: An analog computer uses continuously variable quantities, such as voltages, to represent similarly varying enities in the domain. Digital computers operate upon discrete, coded symbols.

Distinguished Symbol: In a generative grammar, the distinguished symbol is the only non-terminal symbol which can appear at the root of a parse-tree. It is conventionally 'S' for 'sentence'.

Distributed Processors: See Parallel Distributed Processing.

Distribution: Two syntactic items have the same distribution if they can be substituted for each other in the same context within a sentence.

Domain: The area of enquiry and associated tasks to which an artificial intelligence system is applied. (For instance, MYCIN has as its problem domain the diagnosis of blood disorders.) See also Domain-Independent/Domain-Specific Knowledge, Heuristic, Knowledge-Based System.

Domain-Independent/Domain-Specific Knowledge: Many artificial intelligence systems operate within a specific domain, i.e. their knowledge is mainly *domain-specific*. However, they may also contain *domain-independent* knowledge, in the form of principles of common sense, or general scientific laws common to many areas of expertise.

Dualism: A philosophical theory of mind associated with the philosopher Descartes according to which human beings are constituted by two distinct metaphysical substances or realms: Thought and Extension. See also Functionalism, Materialism.

Dynamic Value: In game playing, the estimated value of a state is arrived at by considering the results of a static evaluation function applied to possible future states. These static values are propagated back in time using, for instance, a minimax strategy.

Edge: An image contour along which intensity changes abruptly.

Edge Element: The smallest piece of edge detectable by examining neighbouring pixels in an image.

Edge Map: A 2-D array, recording the position of edge elements derived from an image. Typically there is a one-to-one correspondence between array cells and image pixels at the centre of edge elements.

Eliminativism: An approach to understand the mind in which it is claimed that terms like 'beliefs' and 'intentions' belong to an outmoded 'folk-psychology' and are not capable of scientific justification. See also Functionalism, Intentional System/ Intentional Stance, Materialism.

ELIZA: A program which can be taught to respond to sentences typed by a user in a way that can give the illusion of understanding them, but which in fact relies on pattern matching and substitution to produce answers based on a predetermined set of stock phrases. ELIZA was originally developed by Joseph Weizenbaum in the mid-1960s, and now serves as a demonstration of the technique and as a warning against taking the responses of a computer at face value.

Embed: When a syntactic constituent has another of the same category nested within it as one of its constituents, the nested constituent is said to be embedded within the larger one.

Evaluate: To perform an operation on given arguments producing a canonical (or simplified) result. For example, given an appropriate definition for the procedure maximum, the expression maximum(5,7) will evaluate to 7.

Expert System: A computer program that incorporates the rule-governed expertise of human experts such as doctors, engineers, or economists within a restricted problem domain. See also Heuristic, Knowledge-Based System.

Expression: In a computer program, a combination of data objects linked by operators.

Fact: A *fact* is a clause which is unconditionally *true*, that is once the clause has been matched the goal is proven, e.g.

```
a(1)
```

is a fact, but

```
a(X) :- b(X)
```

is not.

Feature: See Attribute/Feature/Property.

Fire: (Pertaining to production rules.) See Trigger.

Flow of Control: The sequential behaviour of a program, as it carries out the processing of input.

Formal Semantics: A theory of meaning based on the analysis of a natural language as though it were a formal language, such as the propositional and predicate calculi. Typically, it is truth-conditional and compositional.

Formalism: A set of symbols and a collection of systematic rules governing their uses and interrelations. See also Knowledge Representation, Logic.

Formula: In predicate logic a *formula* consists either of a predicate applied to one or more aguments, or a combination of such atomic formulae linked by the connectives 'not', 'or', and 'and'. See also Axiom/Theorem.

Frame: Frame systems are a particular kind of knowledge representation formalism, consisting of structured descriptions of stereotyped objects or situations, with slots filled in with particular values. See also Demon, Script.

Functionalism: A philosphical view of mind according to which mental processes are characterized in terms of their abstract functional (or computational) relationships to one another, and to sensory inputs and motor outputs. See also Cognitivsm, Computationalism, Eliminativism, Turing Test.

Functor: A *functor* is the part of a goal or query that comes before the "(". Functors must obey exactly the same naming rules as atoms.

Generate: A formal set of rules which explicitly defines the grammatical sentences of a language is said to *generate* that language. Such a set of rules constitutes a generative grammar.

Generic: A *generic* term is one which picks out a class of individuals, or the prototype of the individual, rather than the individual itself. For example, in the sentence "The wolf has disappeared from northern Europe", we are referring to the genus rather than to a particular wolf.

Goal: A *goal* is something that PROLOG is trying to prove (i.e. is searching for), either because the user typed it in, or because it needs to prove something else. A goal can be an atom or a functor followed by some arguments separated by commas, enclosed in parentheses.

```
a(X, Y)
```

is an example of a goal.

Grammar: A *grammar* may be informally thought of the set of words and category symbols in a language, together with the rules governing their combination into sentences. It is, in human terms, what speakers know of their language independent of their ability to use that knowledge. See also Competence Knowledge, Competence/Performance, Syntax.

Grammatical: A *grammatical* sentence is one which is well-formed with respect to the rules (grammar) for generating the sentences of the language. See also Syntax.

Grey-Level: A numerical measure of the intensity of a single pixel. The number is typically an integer between 0 and 63 or 0 and 255, where 0 signifies minimum intensity and 63 or 255 signifies maximum intensity.

Hardware: The physical machinery of a computer and its associated devices. See also Algorithm, Central Processor, Computer, Program, Software, Visual Display Unit (VDU).

Heuristic: A rule of thumb which may help in solving a problem, but is not guaranteed to find a solution. A method for cutting down useless searching amongst possibilities. *Heuristics* provide much of the knowledge contained in expert systems. Contrasts with algorithmic procedures. See also Knowledge-based Systems.

Heuristic Search: Any search strategy which makes use of heuristics to suggest the best nodes to consider at each stage of the search.

Induction: A form of reasoning by which we derive general principles from particular facts or instances sharing common properties. For example, if all ravens of which we have had experience are black, then we might inductively reason that all ravens are black.

Information Processing System: Generally speaking, any system which operates on symbolic data given as its input so as to generate an appropriate output. See also Computer, Program.

Inherit: See Property Inheritance.

Input/Output: (a) The values that are passed into a procedure, and which are returned as the results of the operation of a procedure. (b) In general, those aspects of a computer system which involve the transmission of data into the system, and the communication of results back to the outside world. See also Argument/Result, Calling a Procedure.

Intentional System/Intentional Stance: Some philosophers claim that intentionality should be understood instrumentally as a feature of certain kinds of systems; these would include intelligent computers as well as people. It is necessary to use terms such as 'intending', 'believing', 'wanting' in order to explain the behaviour of such systems. Adopting this 'intentional stance' does not commit one to believe that there really are intentional states as such. See also Cognitivsm, Computationalism, Eliminativism, Functionalism, Turing Test.

Intentionality: The quality of 'aboutness', or 'world-directedness', that has been claimed to be a distinguished feature of mental processes as opposed to physical ones. It has been proposed that 'intelligent' computer performances possess only a secondary or derivative, intentionality; this has been used as an attack on the pretensions of artificial intelligence to explain the human mind. See also Computationalism, Functionalism, Intentional System/Intentional Stance, Turing test.

Internal Representation: A symbolic representation in a computer of the states and processes of problem solving, search, etc. See also Cognitivsm, Knowledge Representation.

Interpretation: See Compilation/Interpretation.

Introspection: A process of inward attention or reflection, so as to examine the contents of the mind. *Introspectionism*, as a method in psychology, is contrasted with, and was supplanted by, behaviourism.

Is-a Hierarchy: A series of nodes joined by links of the form 'X is a Y' in semantic networks, which allow efficient forms of inference. See also Knowledge Representation, Property Inheritance, Structural Description.

Keyword: In a program based on pattern matching, a *keyword* is a word in the input sentence which determines the actions to be taken. In a simple program such as ELIZA, recognition of a keyword may completely determine the response of the program; in more sophisticated programs the keyword may determine the context in which further analysis is undertaken.

Knowledge Representation: The term used in artificial intelligence to cover the study of formalisms which model human forms of knowledge. See also Frames, Predicate Calculus/Predicate Logic, Production Systems, Scripts, Semantic Networks.

Knowledge-based System: A computer program which represents relatively complex kinds of information, often as rules governing judgements in particular problem domains. See also Database, Expert System, Knowledge Representation.

Lexical Category: Every word in the language belongs to some lexical category, that is, instances some part of speech. Thus, 'dog', 'brain', and 'syllogism', for example, all belong to the lexical category 'noun'.

Lexicon: The lexicon of a language is dictionary of all the words in the language, and may contain many types of information about each word, for example, what part of speech it is (its lexical category), and what its distributional properties are.

Link: See Arc/Link/Pointer.

LISP: A programming language that uses the list as its primary data object. The most widely used language for artificial intelligence.

List: A special kind of data object, found in artificial intelligence languages. A *list* consists of a sequence of zero or more elements, each of which may be any kind of data object (including another list).

Logic: The study of formal principles of reasoning. The two fundamental systems of *logic* are propositional calculus and predicate calculus, although many extensions to these systems exist. Logic is used extensively in computer science and artificial intelligence. See also Axiom/Theorem, Rules of Inference.

Main Memory/Backup Memory: The part of the computer's circuitry which provides instructions and data to be fed into the central processor, and which stores the output of the latter's operation, is known as the *main memory*. By contrast, the backup memory, such as disc or tape, contains information in a form which can be transported from one machine to another.

Materialism: A general philosophical view that only physical processes exist. The term is also applied to philosophical theories of mind which claim that mental states are identical with brain states. See also Dualism, Eliminativism, Functionalism.

Microworld: A representation of some well-defined domain, such as Newtonian physics, such that there is a simple mapping between the rules and structures of the *microworld* and those of the domain.

Minimax: A strategy to determine good moves in computer game playing by choosing the move that minimizes the loss, the player can expect to incur, under the assumption that the player's opponent is adopting the same strategy (and hence trying to cause the maximum loss). The possible gain or loss for a sequence of moves is usually assessed using a static evaluation function applied to the state of play at the end of the sequence. See also Dynamic Value.

Model: In vision, an internal description of the structure of an object, whether in terms of the structure of image features in a two-dimensional image or solids in three-dimensional space.

Neural Network: See Connectionist Model.

Node: A single state in a state-space representation. In search, a junction point in the search tree, representing a state which may need to be considered either as a possible solution to a problem or enroute to reaching such a solution.

Non-terminal Symbol: In a generative grammar, a *non-terminal symbol* labels a syntactic or lexical category, and is used in the formulation of the rules of the grammar. Examples of non-terminals are Prep, VP, Det, Pronoun, NP.

Operator: (a) A symbol to denote an operation, such as multiplication or comparison, which is applied to numbers or other data objects in a computer program. (b) A discrete atomic mental operation that transforms one knowledge state, or state of working memory, into another. See also Problem Behaviour Graph.

Operator Schema: A knowledge representation formalism similar to a frame, representing the type, preconditions, and actions of an operation. Used in artificial intelligence planning and problem solving systems.

Parallel Distributed Processing: Computing by means of a network of simple computational elements, working in parallel, each of which influences the other elements and is influenced by them. See also Connectionist Model, Sequential Processing.

Parent: When PROLOG tries to establish a goal, it sometimes uses a rule that causes it to try other goals in the tail. The former goal is called the parent of the latter.

Parser: A program which, given as input a grammar, a lexicon, and a word-string, will output, if the string is a well-formed sentence, a structural description of the sentence. Otherwise, the parser will reject the string. The structural description is often represented as a parse-tree, also called a phrase-marker, a diagrammatic representation of the sentence's constituent structure.

Parse-Tree: See Parser.

Pattern Matching: A programming method for matching a list of words (or other symbols) against a template, to discover whether particular words or combinations of words occur in the list. *Pattern matching* is built into POP-11. See also Wild Card.

Performance: See Competence/Performance.

Performance Knowledge: The knowledge posessed by a particular person which determines what or how they will perform on a given task See also Competence Knowledge.

Phrase-Marker: A diagrammatic representation, in the form of an inverted schematic tree, of a sentence's constituent structure. See also Parser.

Phrase-Structure Rule: A rule which specifies the internal structure of a syntactic category. Rules are generally written in the following manner: X :- Y Z, where X, Y, and Z are syntactic category symbols, and Y and Z can replace X in its context within a sentence. A set of such phrase-structure rules, where at least one of the rules has the distinguished symbol on the left-hand side of the arrow, constitutes a phrase-structure grammar.

Pixel: A tiny patch of an image. Images are normally broken down into a rectangular lattice of square pixels like tiles on a wall, although hexagonal tessellations have also been used.

Plan: A routinized program for behaviour that is triggered when certain specific environmenal conditions are satisfied.

Planning: The selection of a sequence of operations in order to bring about one or more goals. An important area of enquiry of artificial intelligence. See also Problem Behaviour Graph, Problem Reduction.

Pointer: See Arc/Link/Pointer.

POP-11: A programming language for artificial intelligence teaching and research.

Pragmatics: Those aspects of the study of language that pertain to the identity and intentions of the speaker and hearer, and the context in which speech takes place. The context is sometimes most narrowly regarded as the body of world knowledge to which speakers and hearers have access in generating and interpreting speech. Pragmatics belongs to the study of linguistic performance. See also semantics, speech act, syntax.

Predicate: In logic, a function whose value is is either *true*, or *false*. It specifies a relationship between arguments. See also Axiom/Theorem, Formula.

Predicate Calculus/Predicate Logic: A system of logic in which one can formalize inferences by representing relationships between predicates such as '...is happy' and '...is wise'. *Predicate calculus* incorporates, but extends, propositional calculus. See also Axiom/Theorem, Logic, Quantifier/Quantification.

Problem Behaviour Graph: A schematic representation of a subject's problem space, in the form of labelled boxes denoting knowledge states, and directed links representing the mental operations that transform each such state into a new state. See also Knowledge Representation, Planning.

Problem Reduction: A method of solving problems by splitting them into more manageable parts.

Problem Space: A set of knowledge states, including a start-state and a goal-state, and a set of admissible problem-specific operations which can be performed on these states. The *problem space* can be represented schematically by a problem behaviour graph.

Procedural: See Declarative/Procedural.

Procedural Programming Language: A programming language consisting procedure definitions together with sequences of commands for invoking them.

Procedure: A sequence of instructions in a programming language designed to carry out a coherent operation or set of operations. *Procedures* often operate on data, passed to them through arguments, and return results, which may be used by other parts of the program. Procedures are first defined, to establish the actions they take, then called to carry out those actions.

Production System: A knowledge representation formalism consisting of collections of condition-action rules (called production rules), a database which is modified in accordance with the rules, and a production system interpreter which controls the operation of the rules. See also Conflict Resolution Strategy.

Production System Interpreter: The 'control mechanism' of a production system, determining the order in which production rules are fired.

Program: A set of abstract instructions or procedures for a computer to perform. When the instuctions are written in a high-level language like POP-11, they have to be converted, either by compilation or interpretation, into basic operations that the computer can perform. See also Algorithm, Hardware, Software.

PROLOG: A programming language with a strongly declarative style, which is based on predicate calculus. See also Resolution.

prompt: The prompt is the symbol, usually ?- used to indicate that PROLOG is waiting for the user to type in a query.

Property: See Attribute/Feature/Property.

Property Inheritance: A process by which features attached to parent nodes (more general concepts or inclusive classes) in an is-a hierarchy are passed down to (inherited by) their children (more specific concepts or subclasses) in such cases where no properties or attributes of the same type are associated explicitly with the children nodes. For example, if we know that birds can fly and that canaries are birds, then we can infer that canaries too can fly.

Propositional Calculus: A simple but powerful system of logic for representing implications between logically compound sentences, such as "either A or not B", "if B then A", etc. The system will prove, for example, that each of these two sentences implies the other. See also Predicate Calculus/Predicate Logic, Rules of Inference.

Protocol Analysis: A method of studying subjects' mental processes in the performance of tasks by recording their spontaneous 'thinking aloud' and subsequently segmenting the running commentary into the discrete atomic mental operations that the subjects have used in the accomplishment of the tasks. See also Operator, Problem Space.

Quantifier/Quantification: *Quantifiers* play an important role in predicate calculus logic. There are two kinds of quantifier: the universal quantifier (as in "all dogs are mammals") and the singular or existential quantifier (as in "some mammals are dogs").

Query: A *query* is the same as a goal but the term is more often used for a goal entered by the user.

Recursion: Self-reference, particularly in the form of a procedure containing, within its body, a call to iteslf. A recursive phrase-structure rule is one in which the symbol on the left-hand side of the arrow also appears on the right-hand side.

Region: An area of an image which is homogeneous in intensity or texture.

Region Map: A 2-D array representing a segmentation of an input image into regions. The array is typically the same size as the input image, so that there is a one-to-one correspondence between array cells and image pixels. Array cells belonging to the same region contain a label which is unique to that region.

Relation: A *relation* is a predicate with arity greater than 1. For instance:

christian(carlton).

christian is a property here, but in

likes(masoud, books).

likes is a relation.

Repair Heuristic: A general-purpose heuristic used to effect a repair.

Repair Theory: An analysis of errors, based on the assumption that a learner who reaches as impasse as a result of following a wrong method, will devise a *repair* to be able to continue solving the problem.

Repeat Loop: A structure in a program which allows an instruction, or a sequence of instructions, to be carried out repeatedly. The repetition may continue indefinitely, or for a fixed number of times, or may end when some condition specified in the program becomes *true*. See also Until Loop, While Loop.

Resolution: A popular technique used in automated theorem proving systems. A version of *resolution* underlies the logic programming language PROLOG.

Restriction Procedure: Matching of variables in lists can be constrained, in POP-11, by a restriction procedure, which specifies some property or feature a variable must have.

Result: See Argument/Result, Input/Output.

Root: The node of a search tree from which all other nodes can be reached by moving down the branches. Often represents the starting state of a problem or game.

Rule Body: The 'action' part of a production rule, which specifies what actions are to be performed if the rule is fired (i.e. there is a successful match of the rule head against the contents of the working memory). Most typically, these are actions which change the contents of the working memory by *adding* and *removing* facts. See also Conflict Resolution Strategy, Production System.

Rule Head: The 'condition' part of a production rule consisting of one or more facts which the production system interpreter attempts to match against the contents of the working memory. See also Conflict Resolution Strategy, Rule Body.

Rule-by-Rule Principle: Maintains that the meaning of a sentence can be compositionally built up by semantic rules in tandem with the syntactic parse. See also Formal Semantics.

Rulebase: The set of rules in a production system. See also Rule Body, Rule Head.

Rules of Inference: Any system of logical deduction uses general rules of inference to allow logical formulae to be derived from others. For instance, a rule of inference in many systems of propositional calculus is *modus ponens*, which, given the propositions "if P then Q" and "P", allows one to infer "Q".

Script: A structure rather like a frame which represents situations or events, and which is used as a knowledge representation formalism. It is particularly suited to natural language understanding systems. See also Conceptual Primitive.

Search: A technique of problem solving in which possible solutions are explored in a systematic way, in effect by asking a series of "What if ...?" questions. Asking each a question corresponds to trying out a possible state of the domain in which the program operates to see if it leads to a solution of the problem.

Search Strategy: Any way of organizing the questions asked in problem solving by search, so as either to find a solution as rapidly as possible or to find a particularly good solution when more than one solution is possible.

Search Tree: The exploration of possibilities in problem solving by search generally leads to a branching structure, in which each state may give rise to a new set of states (sometimes called successor states) and each of these may give rise to successor states of its own, and so on. This structure is not usually represented in full in computer memory, but is implicit in the problem itself. Finding a solution involves systematically traversing this tree.

Semantic Network: A knowledge representation formalism which describes objects and their relationships in terms of a network consisting of labelled arcs and nodes.

Semantic Value: In formal semantics, the semantic value of an expression is the individual(s) or state(s) in the world to which the expression refers, or which make that expression true.

Semantics: The study of meaning in language. See also formal semantics, pragmatics, syntax.

Sequential Processing: A computer architecture in which a central processor carries out a series of operations in sequence. See also Computation, Parallel Distributed Processing.

Slot: An element in a frame, which can be filled with a value. For instance a 'chair' frame may have a 'number of legs' slot, perhaps filled with the default value of 4.

Software: A program for a computer, together with the data upon which the program operates. See also Algorithm, Hardware.

Speech Act: The theory of *speech acts* views natural language utterances as actions—for example, questions, orders, statements on the part of speakers. Speech act theory belongs to the field of pragmatics.

State: A description of a possible arrangement of a domain. For instance, in game playing, a state may correspond to a position of pieces on the board; in route finding, a state may correspond to arrival at a specified place at a specified time; in planning, a state may correspond to an arrangement in space of some objects to be manipulated.

State-Space: The set of all the states which could possibly need to be considered in the course of solving a particular problem.

Static Evaluation Function: In computer game playing, any method of determining the advantage to the player of a given state of play, without looking ahead at possible future moves.

Structural Description: A description of the formal constituents, features, and relationships that exhaustively account for the structural integrity and cohesion of an object. A *structural description* of, for example, an arch will include such terms as 'block', 'supported by', and 'abutting'. See also Knowledge Representation, Semantic Network.

Structure: A *structure* is something that can be decomposed into simple elements. Atoms, integers, reals, and strings are simple elements whereas lists and trees, for example, are structures.

Substitution: In a program such as ELIZA, using part of the user's input sentence to produce response. In general, replacing part of a string of words or other symbols by different symbols, depending on context.

Successive Refinement: A method of software design characteristic of artificial intelligence program development, which involves starting with a relatively crude working program and gradually increasing its complexity and sophistication.

Syntactic Category: A grammatical class determined on the basis of the syntactic role it fills in the construction of sentences, used in the formal description of language. It is labelled by a category symbol, such as NP, VP, PrepP. See also Phrase-Structure Rule, Syntax.

Syntactically Well-formed: See Grammatical.

Syntax: (a) In programming, the rules by which the words in a program are combined to form commands to a computer. (b) For natural languages, the study of the rules governing the way in which words and phrases are combined to form sentences in a language. The word is also sometimes used to refer to the rules themselves; thus one may speak of "English syntax", "the syntax of German", and so on, to mean much the same thing as 'English grammar', "the grammar of German", and so forth. See also Grammar.

Tail: The *tail* of a rule is the part after the ':-'. Thus the tail of

```
a :- b, c, d.
```

is b, c, d. b, c, and d are called *tail goals*.

Taxonomic Tree: See is-a Hierarchy.

Template: In vision, a stored subimage with which to compare incoming images.

Terminal Symbol: *Terminal symbols* are the output of the syntactic component of a grammar, and are usually identified with the words and grammatically meaningful subparts ('morphemes') of words. In a phrase-structure grammar, they will only appear on the right-hand side of lexical rules. See Lexical Category, Lexicon, Phrase-Structure Rule, Syntax.

Theorem: See Axiom/Theorem.

Top-level Interpreter: The *top-level interpreter* is the part of the PROLOG system that accepts queries from the user and prints the answers.

Transitive: A relationship which, for any relation R, if xRy and yRz, then xRz. For example, if a canary is a bird and a bird is an animal, then a canary is an animal.

Trigger: A production rule is said to be triggered if there is a successful match of the rule head against the facts in working memory. See also Conflict Resolution Strategy, Production System.

Truth-conditionality: The assumption that meaning can be defined in terms of the conditions in the real world under which a sentence may be used to make a true statement. See also Formal Semantics.

Turing Test: A hypothetical test for computer intelligence, proposed by Alan Turing in 1950, involving a computer program generating a conversation which could not be distinguished from that of a real human.

Until Loop: A structure in a computer program which allows a sequence of instructions to be repeated until some condition becomes *true*. See also Repeat Loop, While Loop.

Use-value Variable: In POP-11 when a use-value variable occurs in a list, the value of the variable is inserted at that place in the list. See also Set-Value Variable, Wild Card.

User-Defined: See Built-In/User-Defined.

Value: The actual data which have been stored in a section of computer memory and which are associated with a variable. The value can change as new assignments to the variable are made.

Variable/Constant: In many programming languages, there is a class of terms which do not have a fixed value, but to which values can be assigned. These are called *variables*. Constants, on the other hand, are terms whose values are fixed. See also Local/Global.

Visual Display Unit (VDU): A screen, usually like a TV set, that displays text or pictures representing the output of a program while it is running on a computer. See also Hardware, Input/Output.

von Neumann Architecture: The 'classic' design for computer hardware, named afer the mathematician John von Neumann, who formulated the main elements of the standard, sequential, stored program, computer architecture in the late 1940s. Non-von Neumann architectures are now being developed that exploit various forms of parallel or distributed processing. See also central processor, computation, connectionist model, parallel distributed processing.

While Loop: A structure in a computer program that allows a sequence of instructions to be repeated while some condition remains true. See also Repeat Loop, Until Loop.

Word: A particular kind of data object.

Word Concept: The stored mental representation of a word.

Working Memory: Sometimes also called *short term memory* by psychologists, it is a mental workspace consisting of a small set of data items representing the current state of knowledge of a system at any stage in the performance of a task, and which is transformed into a new set, in humans by the application of a discrete mental operation (operator), and in production systems on the firing of a new production rule. See also Production System.

Bibliography

1. Akerkar, R. (Ed.), "Artificial Intelligence and its Applications", *Proceedings of ICAAI 2003*, Technomathematics Research Foundation, Kolhapur, 2003.
2. Akerkar, R. (Ed.), "Future Trends in Artificial Intelligence", *Proceedings of ISAI 2001*, (Ed.) Allied Publishers, New Delhi, 2002.
3. Aleksander, I. and P. Burnett, *Thinking Machines: The Search for Artificial Intelligence.* Oxford University Press, 1987.
4. Allen, J., *Natural Language Understanding.* Benjamin/Cummings, 1995.
5. Anderson, J.R. and G.H. Bower, *Human Associative Memory,* John Wiley and Sons, New York, 1973.
6. Ballard, D.H. and M.B. Brown, *Computer Vision,* Prentice Hall, Englewood Cliffs, 1982.
7. Bobrow, D.G. and A. Collins (Eds.), *Representation and Understanding,* Academic Press, New York, 1975.
8. Boden, M.A., "What is Computational Psychology?" *Proceedings of the Aristotelian Society*, Supplementary Volume, 17–35, 1984.
9. Boden, M.A., *Artificial Intelligence and Natural Man,* 2nd ed., Harvester Press and Basic Books, Brighton, 1986.
10. Brachman, R.J., "On the Epistemological Status of Semantic Networks" in N.V. Findler, (Ed.), *Associative Networks: Representations and Use of Knowledge by Computers,* Academic Press, New York, 1979.
11. Brachman, R.J., "What IS-A Is and Isn't: An Analysis of Taxonomic Links in Semantic Networks", *Computer*, 16, 30–36, 1983.
12. Bundy, A., "The Limitations of Artificial Intelligence and the Distinction between Special-Purpose and General-Purpose Systems." Report prepared by the Edinburgh Computing and Social Responsibility Group, 1987.
13. Chappell, V.C. (Ed.), *The Philosophy of Mind,* Prentice Hall, Englewood Cliffs, 1962.

14. Charniak, E. and D. McDermott, *Introduction to Artificial Intelligence,* Reading, Addison-Wesley, Massachusetts, 1985.

15. Chomsky, A.N., "A Review of Verbal Behavior," *Language*, 35, 26–58, 1959.

16. ________, *Cartesian Linguistics,* Harper and Row, New York, 1966.

17. ________, *Reflections on Language,* Fontana/Collins, Glasgow, 1975.

18. ________, *Rules and Representations,* Basil Blackwell, Oxford, 1980.

19. Clocksin, W.S. and C.S. Mellish, *Programming in Prolog,* Springer-Verlag, Heidelberg, 1994.

20. Collins, A. and R. Quillian, "Retrieval Time from Semantic Memory." *Journal of Verbal Learning and Verbal Behavior*, 8, 240–247, 1969.

21. Feigenbaum, E.A. and P. McCorduck. *The Fifth Generation,* Pan Books, and Reading, Addison-Wesley, Massachusetts, 1984.

22. Findler, N.V. (Ed.), *Associative Networks: Representation and Use of Knowledge by Computers.* Academic Press, New York, 1979.

23. Forsyth, R., "AI: East/West Conference Report," in *AISB Quarterly,* 66, Autumn, 1988.

24. Kolodner, J.L., *Case-based Reasoning*, Morgan Kaufmann, 1993.

25. Luger, G. and W. Stubblefield, *Artificial Intelligence and the Design of Expert Systems*, Benjamin/Cummings, 1989.

26. Minsky, M. (Ed.), *Semantic Information Processing,* MIT Press, Cambridge, Massachusetts, 1968.

27. Minsky, M., "A Framework for Representing Knowledge", in Winston, P. (Ed.), *The Psychology of Computer Vision*, McGraw-Hill, New York, 1975.

28. Minsky, M. and S. Papert, *Perceptrons,* Cambridge, MIT Press, Massachusetts, 1969.

29. Newell, A. and H.A. Simon, *Human Problem Solving,* Prentice Hall, Englewood Cliffs, N.J., 1972.

30. Newell, A., J.C. Shaw, and H.A. Simon, "Elements of a Theory of Human Problem-Solving", *Psychological Review*, 65, 151–166, 1958.

31. Newell, A., J.C. Shaw, and H.A. Simon, "Chess-Playing Programs and the Problem of Complexity", in E.A. Feigenbaum, and J. Feldman (Eds.), *Computers and Thought,* McGraw-Hill, New York, 1963.

32. O'Shea, T. and M. Eisenstadt, *Artificial Intelligence: Tools Techniques and Applications,* Harper and Row, New York, 1984.

33. Patterson, D.W., *Introduction to Artficial Intelligence and Expert systems*, Prentice-Hall of India, New Delhi, 1998.

34. Quillian, M.R., "Semantic Memory", *Semantic Information Processing,* in M. Minsky (Ed.), MIT Press, Cambridge, Massachusetts, 1968.

35. Rich, E., *Artificial Intelligence,* McGraw-Hill, New York, 1983.

36. Robinson, J.A., "A Machine Oriented Logic Based on the Resolution Principle," *Journal Assn of Computing Machinery*, January 1965, 23–41, 1965.

37. Russell and Norvig, *Artificial Intelligence: A Modern Approach*, Prentice Hall, 1995.

38. Sloman, A., "Towards a Computational Theory of Mind", in *Artificial Intelligence: Human Effects,* M. Yazdani and A. Narayan, (Eds.) Ellis Horwood, Chichester, 1984.

39. Shapiro, S. (Ed.) *Encyclopidia of AI*, Vols. I&II, New York: John Wiley & Sons, New York, 1987.

40. Sloman, A., "Why We Need Many Knowledge Representation Formalisms", in *Research and Development in Expert Systems,* M. Bramer, (Ed.), Cambridge University Press, Cambridge, 1985.

41. ________, "Real-Time Multiple-Motive Expert Systems", in *Expert Systems 85,* M. Merry, (Ed.) Cambridge University Press, Cambridge, 1985.

42. ________, "Did Searle Refute Strong Strong or Weak Strong AI?", in *Artificial Intelligence and Its Applications,* A.G. Cohn and J.R. Thomas (Eds.) John Wiley, Chichester, 1986.

43. Tsang, E., *Foundations of Constraint Satisfaction*, Academic Press, 1993.

44. Turban, E., *Expert Systems and Applied Artificial Intelligence*, Macmillan, New York, 1992.

45. Van Hentenryck, P., *Constraint Satisfaction in Logic Programming*, MIT Press, 1989.

46. Winograd, T., *Understanding Natural Language,* Academic Press, New York, 1972.

47. Winograd, T., *Language as a Cognitive Process,* Addison-Wesley, Reading, Massachusetts, 1983.

48. Winston, P.H., *Artificial Intelligence,* Addison-Wesley, Reading, Massachusetts 1984.

Journals

1. *CONSTRAINTS*, an International Journal
The journal covers all aspects of computing with constraints: theory and practice, algorithms and systems, reasoning and programming, logics and languages. Published by Kluwer Academic Publishers.

2. *International Journal of Computer Science and Applications*
The online journal covers all aspects of computer science and its applications. Published by Technomathematics Research Foundation.

3. *Journal of Logic Programming*
The journal covers topics from logic programming in general and it also contains some papers on constraints and constraint Logic Programming (CLP), in particular.

4. *Journal of Artificial Intelligence*
The journal covers all topics from artificial intelligence (AI).

Index